THE CITY IN SOUTH ASIA

CENTRE OF SOUTH ASIAN STUDIES
SCHOOL OF ORIENTAL AND AFRICAN STUDIES
UNIVERSITY OF LONDON

COLLECTED PAPERS ON SOUTH ASIA

1. RULE, PROTEST, IDENTITY: Aspects of Modern South Asia
Edited by Peter Robb and David Taylor

2. POLITICAL IDENTITY IN SOUTH ASIA
Edited by David Taylor and Malcolm Yapp

3. THE CITY IN SOUTH ASIA
Edited by Kenneth Ballhatchet and John Harrison

COLLECTED PAPERS ON SOUTH ASIA NO. 3

THE CITY IN SOUTH ASIA
PRE-MODERN AND MODERN

Edited by
KENNETH BALLHATCHET and JOHN HARRISON

CURZON PRESS
HUMANITIES PRESS

First published 1980

Curzon Press Ltd : London and Dublin
and
Humanities Press Inc : Atlantic Highlands, NJ : USA

ISBN
UK 0 7007 0133 8
US 0 391 01129 4

ISSN
0141 0156

Printed in Great Britain by
Biddles Ltd, Guildford, Surrey

CONTENTS

LIST OF ILLUSTRATIONS

CONTRIBUTORS

S.U. Ahmed, formerly research student, SOAS.

K.A. Ballhatchet, Professor of the History of South Asia, SOAS.

C.A. Bayly, Fellow of St. Catherine's College, University of Cambridge.

Christine Cottam, formerly Research Fellow in Anthropology, SOAS.

Sarojini Ganju, Indian Administrative Service, formerly research student, SOAS.

J.B. Harrison, Reader in Indian History, SOAS.

Raffat Khan Haward, formerly research student, SOAS.

Elaine Holley, Cartographer, SOAS.

Nazia Hussain, research student, SOAS.

M.S. Islam, Associate Professor of History, University of Dacca, formerly Commonwealth Academic Staff Fellow, SOAS.

Rosie Llewellyn-Jones, Administrative Assistant at the Architectural Association, London, formerly research student, SOAS.

Anthony D. King, Associate Senior Lecturer, Sociology and Environmental Studies, Brunel University.

John McGuire, Senior Lecturer in Research Methods, Department of Social Sciences, Western Australian Institute of Technology, formerly research student, SOAS.

K.M. Mohsin, Associate Professor of History, University of Dacca, formerly Commonwealth Academic Staff Fellow, SOAS.

Percival Spear, formerly Fellow of Selwyn College, University of Cambridge.

PREFACE

This volume contains a selection of papers presented to an inter-disciplinary seminar which has been meeting at SOAS, under the auspices of the Centre of South Asian Studies, since 1975. The seminar's concern is the city in South Asia, in pre-modern and modern forms, and some of the main questions discussed are outlined in Anthony King's paper, which was presented at an early stage in the seminar's proceedings: in particular, the distinctive characteristics of South Asian cities, the differences between pre-modern and modern, whether pre-modern can be equated with pre-industrial, and whether distinctions should be made between modern, western and colonial forms.

We include towns as well as cities, and the importance of small towns, in both quantitative and qualitative terms, is analysed in Christopher Bayly's paper. After identifying different types of small town he considers the case of Kara - under Akbar an important city, subsequently a mere district headquarters and finally a market town still dominated by 'service gentry' educated in the Indo-Persian tradition. Its decline must be attributed in large measure to political change. But not wholly. There were also the shifts in commercial geography that tormented the area. The names of the scattered hamlets which form the ghost town of Kara today recall the manufacturing and commercial quarters of the old city as well as its political past. The curve of the river under the fort-crowned bluff once carried a rich commerce to the town. But eventually it was taken elsewhere - first by the clanking trucks of the East Indian Railway and later by the pounding lorry traffic of the Grand Trunk Road. Kara now stands off both the political and the commercial map.

There is also ample evidence in other papers of the importance of political change in the history of the pre-modern city in South Asia.[1] Percival Spear argues that the intermittent growth of Delhi must be explained by political factors. Rulers early valued its strategic advantages, and in time its traditions conferred prestige. But he questions whether it can long remain a capital city since the partition of the sub-continent has left it so much closer to the Indian frontier.

K.M. Mohsin admits both geographical and climatic

reasons for the instability of the pre-modern city in
Bengal. The straggling city along a river bank, most
of it single-storey, much of it built of bamboo,
unfired brick and thatch, interspersed with gardens,
tanks and cultivation, was, thanks to the materials of
its construction and the looseness of its organization,
easily moved, expanded or abandoned. But the urban
transience that Mohsin demonstrates in Bengal was
perhaps only an extreme form of a fluidity more
generally observable in India - geography and climate
there dramatically exaggerating the play of other
persistent forces. Above all there was the influence
of political change, and Mohsin illustrates this with
reference to Murshidabad, which rose and fell in
company with the Nawabs of Bengal.

Lucknow, as Rosie Llewellyn-Jones shows, was a
trading and manufacturing centre long before the
Nawab of Oudh made it his capital. South Asian cities
indeed served a variety of economic functions, whether
as units in a vertical chain of markets or elements in
a horizontal pattern of entrepots. Kara, and neighbouring Manikpur and Sahzadpur, were towns of a
significant type - transhipment or exchange centres
where two regions meet, whether geographical, at the
junction of hill and plain, or political, on a frontier.
Kara lost its function as an exchange point, or
frontier town, when Oudh was absorbed into the British
system. Murshidabad and Dacca were both manufacturing
centres as well as capitals, and their importance was
increased by acting as major customs stations through
which government for fiscal reasons sought to funnel
trade. And in a negative way, as Bayly shows, towns
might grow upon the need to avoid customs dues in
established cities - Shahzada, outside Delhi, or
Barragaon, outside Benares.

But given its commercial and industrial importance,
Lucknow received a cultural dimension from the Nawabs,
and Rosie Llewellyn-Jones shows how they used architecture to reflect their authority. As in other Indian
cities, a succession of architectural styles reflects
both political change and economic function - the
crowded manufacturing and commercial quarters, the
majestic mosques and palace complex, and finally the
civil lines and cantonments with which the British
made their mark. There were also shops in the European
style, and a hunting-lodge for the Nawab. Another sign
of change - and of new technology - was an iron bridge

over the Gumti.

Dacca, in the days of the East India Company, also
boasted an iron bridge, though built by public subscription rather than by a benevolent Nawab. In an age of
laisser-faire, the British government was loath to play
a positive role in municipal development, and officials
with improving ideas took the initiative with some
effect, as S.U. Ahmad shows. But their nostrums were
those of an alien people - the creation of a riverside
walk, where one could take the evening air, the
straightening and paving of the two main streets, the
ventilation of the more crowded areas, the draining of
swamps to stop the poisonous exhalations which were
thought to cause malaria - all this with the aim of
promoting salubrity, that word so characteristic of
the improving era. They cleared yet more ground for a
racecourse. But their activities were checked by a
government bent on economies.

Later in the century such efforts were resumed.
Concern for public health, and especially for the
health of British troops, encouraged further attempts
to refashion Asian cities as Chadwick had refashioned
British ones. John Harrison examines the programme
pursued in Allahabad to impose upon the city the
sanitary system approved by western medical science -
to provide pure drinking water, to prevent overcrowding, to build and even rebuild in accordance with
western notions of regularity and fresh air. Some
of these changes were popular - piped water, electric
light and paved roads. Others, in particular western-
style latrines, were openly or covertly opposed.

All classes did not benefit equally from public
utilities, however, and Nazia Husain shows, in her
paper on Dacca between 1920 and 1947, that the
colonial part of the city was better equipped with
water and electric street lighting than the Asian part.
She also reveals the importance of caste and community
in urban settlement patterns, and subsequent papers,
which are concerned with urban life, provide further
evidence of persistence of traditional attitudes and
practices in urban settings. M.S. Islam, in his survey of the country towns of nineteenth-century Bengal,
describes an admixture to which the term 'rurban' might
well be applied.[2]

Similarly, John McGuire shows how, even in nineteenth-century Calcutta, caste and kinship ties were
used by leading Hindu families as means of influence,

but also how traditional techniques of dominance were
modified to accord with the wide range of social
interactions necessitated by life in this great city.

Sarojini Ganju also demonstrates the strength of
traditional ties among Muslims in twentieth-century
Lucknow, and explains the existence of Shia-Sunni
rather than Hindu-Muslim conflict by reference to
recent history, in that the dominant problem was the
decline of the Shia elite as a long-term consequence
of the fall of the Nawabi regime.

Raffat Khan Haward, on the other hand, shows how
religious institutions provided security for the Goan
Christian community in Karachi and facilitated the
transition from rural to urban life. Marginality and
a sense of communal identity were a source of strength
to Goan Christians in an urban setting, but whether
they will continue to be so if the government pursues
consciously Islamic policies remains to be seen.

Finally, in her study of a small market town in
Rajasthan, Christine Cottam shows how open to outside
influence even so religiously and socially conservative
a group as the Marwari traders and bankers who dominate
the town have proved to be, and how widely even such an
oasis town is linked with the wider world outside it.
Merchants who were wholesale or retail traders of the
traditional type have seized upon the opportunity to
become commission agents and factory owners, and in
the new political world of post-independence India to
make use of their extended kinship links to establish
contacts in distant centres of administrative power.
Change as well as tradition can be seen in 'Mandi' as
well as in Calcutta.

Our seminar continues to meet, and we hope, on
another occasion, to present work on cities of an
earlier date as well as on more contemporary forms.
Meanwhile, our particular thanks are due to Elaine
Holley, whose maps illustrate this volume, to Elizabeth
Robb for typing the final manuscript, to Anne
Mackintosh and Marion Sweny for secretarial support,
and to the research projects committee of SOAS for
financial support to the seminar. We are indebted to
the India Office Library and Records for permission
to reproduce the photographs of Lucknow to illustrate
the paper by Rosie Llewellyn-Jones. Peter Robb's
services as editor of this series have been both
unobtrusive and indispensable.

K.A.B. and J.B.H.

1. Cf. Gideon Sjoberg, *The Pre-Industrial City: Past and Present* (New York 1960), passim.

2. Richard G. Fox, 'Rajput "Clans" and Rurban Settlements in Northern India', in Fox (ed.), *Urban India: Society, Space and Image* (Duke University Press 1970), pp.167-185.

COLONIALISM AND THE DEVELOPMENT OF THE MODERN SOUTH ASIAN CITY: SOME THEORETICAL CONSIDERATIONS[1]

A.D. King

With the creation of a global commercial network, the spread of industrialisation and the techno- logical revolution in transport and transferability, cities everywhere are becoming more like one another ... confronting the same kind of problems.

> Rhoades Murphy, 'Historical and Comparative Urban Studies' in R.G. Putnam et al (ed.) *A Geography of Urban Places: Selected Readings* (Toronto 1970), pp.25-32.

The controversial issue, one that intrigues geographer, sociologist, and historian alike, turns to a considerable degree on the relationships between value systems and social organisation, on the one hand, and the development of city systems and various types of urban morphological patterns, on the other ....
    Studies ... suggest major differences between Indian cities and models of spatial arrangements hypothesized for Western cities. The nature, causes, and longevity of these differences provide an admirable field for both theoretical and applied research. One can speculate that technology, levels of living, capital available for urban improvement, caste and ethnolinguistic and religious diversity, and other cultural concomitants are involved, but to what extent and for how long?
    Clearly, here is support for raising once again the most important question in cross-cultural urban research. To what extent are basic differences in culture, even given the spread of 'modern Western' technology and values, likely to give rise to different urbanisation processes and the creation of cities as artifacts that differ from culture to culture? ... What kinds of cities can be expected to evolve in different societies as these societies make their decisions to select, adopt, and modify

1

those elements that characterise Western city-
building functions and structure?

> Norton Ginsburg, 'Urban
> Geography and "Non-Western"
> Areas' in P.M. Hauser and
> L. Schnore, *The Study of
> Urbanisation* (London 1965),
> pp.311-346.

1. *The meanings of 'modern'*

Any investigation of the modern and pre-modern
South Asian city pre-supposes at least two levels of
comparison. The first, cultural or geographical, is
relatively easy to conceptualise. In what way or ways
is the city in South Asia different from the city in
Latin America, Africa or Europe? What, if anything,
distinguishes it from these and other cities?

The second level of comparison is less easy to
define. In what ways does the modern city (in South
Asia or elsewhere) differ from its pre-modern
predecessor? At first sight, such a comparison would
appear to be based on the dimension of *time* just as the
first level is based on the dimension of *space*: how
does the city of the nineteenth or twentieth century
differ from its seventh or seventeenth century
predecessor? Yet it is clear that it is not the
temporal dimension alone which we are interested in
but rather the form of social, economic, political,
technological or spatial organisation which
characterises the city in any one place or time. The
conventional distinction, for example, is between
'industrial' and 'pre-industrial' cities where urban
types are characterised according to such criteria as
the energy system on which they are based (whether
animate, in the form of man and beast, or inanimate, in
the form of fossil fuels, electricity or atomic power);
the technology related to these energy systems (e.g.
steam-powered machinery or locomotion); the spatial
morphology developing from this technology; and the
types of social, political and economic organisation
which they would appear to generate.[2]

Such distinctions between 'pre-industrial' and
'industrial' cities are clearly not related to *time* per
se, for it is evident that 'pre-industrial',

2

'industrialising', 'industrial', and 'post-industrial'[3]
cities exist simultaneously even today.

The crucial factor, therefore, is how we define
'modern' and what criteria of 'modernity' we use to
classify cities (whether Asian or otherwise) as 'pre-
modern' or 'modern'.

Ignoring for the moment the large and increasingly
sceptical literature on the concept of 'modern' and
'modernisation' as applied to societies and nations,[4]
it is as well to start with the lay definition of
modern as 'of the present and recent times'.[5] By doing
this, we are immediately aware of the cultural,
political and economic assumptions we make when we
refer, in general, to the 'modern city'. What is
usually meant, in contemporary European and North
American, usually capitalist circles, is not *any* city
'of the present and recent times' but one based on
specific energy sources, an advanced transport and
communications technology, a complex system of urban
government and administration, a 'high technology'
built environment, the whole supported by an advanced
form of capitalist industrial society and generally
found - with the occasional Asian exception - in the
specific cultural context of Europe and North America.
In this obviously ethnocentric framework, 'modern' is
understood as that which most closely approximates to
the Western model.

If, on the other hand, we use the phrase the
'modern South Asian city' simply to mean the city 'as
of the present and recent times' then we may assume
there is no intention to refer to 'levels' of social,
economic or technological organisation. By definition,
any extant Asian city 'as of present times' is 'modern':
in this sense, Katmandu can be compared with Karachi;
Delhi, with Durgapur. Such an approach would also
eliminate the notion of one city being more 'modern'
than others. Consequently, two methods of measuring
'modernity' arise: the first, to compare the particular
city with the model of the 'modern' Western city,
simultaneously ignoring the culture - and economy -
specific basis of the latter. The second, to compare
the particular city with its own immediate past,
measuring the amount of 'development' according to
changes in, for example, its social, economic,
political or physical-spatial organisation. Or more
productively, perhaps to construct, on the basis of a
number of South Asian cities, an 'ideal type'

traditional or 'pre-modern' city and use this as a
model to chart the nature of changes in the 'modern'
South Asian cities.

In either case, specific criteria or dimensions of
the city will be needed to be stated with which to
distinguish the 'pre-modern' from the 'modern' phases.
These might be provided by one or more of the following:
(1) Spatial morphology, built environment, location.
(2) Economic structure (measured in terms of energy and
industrial base, occupational structure, size of hinterland, etc.).
(3) Demographic and social structure (measured in terms
of population size, sex ratio, vital statistics, family
structure, literacy, etc.).
(4) Socio-spatial structure (degree and nature of
residential differentiation, relationship between
social and spatial characteristics, etc.).
(5) Technological structure (energy base, levels of
technology).

If we apply these criteria, comparing, on one hand,
the 'modern' and 'pre-modern' South Asian city and, on
the other, the 'modern' South Asian city and its
counterpart in the West, certain propositions can be
suggested. The following, made at a very broad level
of generalisation, are illustrative rather than comprehensive.

1. *Spatial morphology and location.* The four
largest cities in India, from the late nineteenth
century to the present day[6] have either been on coastal
sites 'founded by foreign colonialists or owing the
bulk of their growth to foreign enterprises'[7] or, like
Delhi, developed for political-administrative purposes
by the colonial power. Morphologically, like many
colonial cities in other non-Western societies many
South Asian cities have developed historically as
'dual cities', comprising a 'modern' or 'Western'
section and the 'traditional' indigenous town.[8] The
pattern of 'civil lines' plus 'cantonment' and indigenous 'city', is particularly common in northern India
and New Delhi is a classical model of the dual city.

2. *Economic structure.* The traditional South Asian
city was primarily concerned with religious, ceremonial,
political or administrative functions. Its contemporary
counterpart, however, is 'essentially Western in nature
and function, dominated by trade and manufacture.[9]
However, like the majority of so-called 'Third World'
cities, it is also, in comparison to Western industrial

cities, characterised by an overly-large tertiary
(service) sector. Assuming such comparison is valid
(which is questionable) it has also relatively little
industrialisation in terms of its population size.[10]

3. *Demographic and sociological structure.* In
comparison with its pre-modern predecessor and its
counterpart in the West, the 'modern' South Asian city
has not been affected by the so-called 'demographic
transition'. Whilst urban death rates have fallen
dramatically, birth rates have continued as before, or
even risen, and, with relatively large falls in the
infant mortality rate, natural population increase in
large cities (irrespective of any increase due to in-
migration) has been far grater than in the 'pre-modern'
Asian city or the Western city in the early phase of
industrialisation-urbanisation.

Moreover, other social and demographic trends
supposedly characteristic of 'modernisation' (such as
changes in family structure, literacy, sex ratio etc.)
have not been monitored by demographic indices in the
Indian city.[11] In the less tangible and more arguable
sphere of changes in values, attitudes and forms of
social relations, theoretically supposed to be inherent
in the notion of 'urbanism' it is now commonplace that
'rural' and 'non-urban' forms of social organisation
values, attitudes and social organisation persist in
the city, both in Asia and other non-Western
societies.[12]

4. *Social and spatial structure.* In many South
Asian cities, forms of residential segregation are
characterised not simply by indigenous criteria of
stratification (such as caste, religion, language) but
by additional criteria derived from a relatively large
bureaucracy. Additionally, in some cities at least,
ethnic and racial distinctions add further dimensions
to residential differentiation and occasionally provide
the basis for communal conflict.

5. *Technological structure.* In comparison to the
'pre-modern' (and pre-industrial) indigenous city, many
parts of the South Asian city (and the whole of New
Delhi, for example) are based on the *assumptions* of
Western technology (for example, road networks,
distances and widths as well as urban forms such as
individual dwelling types and suburbs, are based on
the assumption of motorised transport).

2. The 'contribution' of colonialism to the development of the South Asian city

By positing two phases of the South Asian city as 'pre-modern', and 'modern' a process is implied by which the first is transformed into the second, a process of 'becoming modern' or 'modernisation'. Such a phrase, when applied to the Western City is probably rightly conceived as 'industrialisation', provided that this is understood, firstly, as an inter-related process of economic, social, cultural, political, technological and psychological transformation, secondly, as taking place within a particular cultural context and, thirdly, as taking place within the particular inter-national power relationship of colonialism. This last context is important in the formative stages of industrialis-ation, for the 'modern' Western city relies heavily on the economic and political relations of colonialism for the supply of materials, manpower and markets.

However, whilst 'modernisation-as-industrialisation' in the West was largely an autonomous, 'internal' process, in South Asia it was largely induced from 'outside'. It is therefore difficult (and possibly misdirected effort) to attempt to distinguish between 'internal' modernisation (the multi-dimensional trans-formation of Indian society from within) and 'Western-isation', understood as the transfer of values, attitudes, forms of knowledge, technology and a whole range of institutions and 'cultural models' as a product of colonialism. In some aspects of the city, however, this problem is possibly easier to analyse than in other spheres for particular urban models and residential practices in India can be identified which owe their origin much more to the particular cultural context of 'Westernisation' (even Anglicisation) than to the more economic process of 'modernisation-as-industrialisation'.

Thus, whilst distinguishing between the 'pre-modern' and 'modern' in the Western city is a relatively straightforward task of deciding between the 'pre-industrial' and 'industrial', the same task in the South Asian city also requires that we distinguish between the 'modern' (industrial) and the 'Western' (cultural).[13] For it is evident that the major difference (other than the cultural) which distinguishes the historical development of the 'modern' South Asian city from its European counterpart over the last four

centuries is the phenomenon of colonialism. It is with
a more precise understanding of the conditions comprised in the concept of colonialism that some of the
problems raised above can be understood. In particular,
a method is needed by which the variable of 'Westernization', understood as a form of cultural diffusion or
acculturation, can be isolated and examined.

3. *Colonialism*

Colonialism has been defined as 'the establishment and
maintenance, for an extended time, of rule over an
alien people that is separate and subordinate to the
ruling power'.[14] The particular variety of colonialism
understood in this context is that associated with
modern industrial capitalism.

The main conditions comprised in this form of
colonialism are threefold:

(1) It implies a *contact situation between two cultures*
and the value-systems on which they are based.

(2) The contact takes place between two cultures which
represent *different forms or 'levels' of economic,
social, technological and political organisation and
development*. Such differences result partly from the
differences in value-systems indicated above and
partly from the power structure of the colonial
situation itself.

(3) The relationship in which this contact takes place
is one of *dominance-dependence* where the ultimate source
of social, economic and political power resides in the
metropolitan society.

It is evident that, initially, the first and over-
riding variable is that of *culture*, out of which the
other two components or conditions of colonialism, the
economic-technological order and the *power structure of
colonialism* arise. Technology is a cultural product
and political systems depend, among other things, on
the values and beliefs of a culture and the relationships they foster with other societies. Once the
political system of colonialism is effective however,
it is convenient, for heuristic reasons, to treat these
three 'components' as independent though interrelated
variables. The justification for this will, it is
hoped, become apparent in the following discussion.
For convenience, these three variables may be briefly,
if somewhat inaccurately, summarised as *culture,
technology* and the *power structure of colonialism*.

Thus, the impact of colonialism on the city in South Asia is to be understood as the impact of a *'modern'* (i.e. industrial), *Western* (i.e. British) and *colonial* (i.e. politically and socially dominant) power. In this sense, 'modern' (industrial) is manifest in the form of technology and its related socioeconomic dimensions; 'Western' (British) as a type of culture, and 'colonial' as a form of power relationship.

As an illustration, we may take the study of the impact of colonialism on the indigenous, pre-industrial city of Delhi between 1803 and 1947 undertaken as a case study in colonial urban development.[15] In this study it proved to be both necessary and appropriate to distinguish between the three overlapping roles played by representatives of the immigrant Western culture, i.e. their roles as 'British', that is, as members of a *particular European culture* with a distinctive set of values governing, for example, the development of social institutions or modifications to the physical and spatial environment.

Secondly, their role as members of a *'modern' industrial society* with characteristics typical of such societies such as, for example, highly differentiated economic and social structures or the separation of place of work from place of residence.

Thirdly, their role as members of a *colonial society*, exercising a monopoly of power over members of the indigenous community. This relationship, for example, gave them power to control the development of the indigenous city, access to manpower resources and power to modify the environment according to their own cultural preferences.

A second illustration is provided by another type of urban environment, unique to colonial urban development in Asia, the so-called 'hill station'.[16] The variable of culture is crucial in three respects. It accounts for the particular set of environmental preferences explaining settlement in 'the hills'; it explains the distinctive 'residential models' available for the colonial community in the earlier decades of the nineteenth century when the hill stations were established, such models being based on the state of urban development in the metropolitan society; and thirdly, it explains the particular ethnomedical theories supporting the view that 'hill stations' were 'healthier' than residence on 'the plains'. The variable of technology is important in that levels of

economic, scientific and technological development
attained in the metropolitan society were utilised so
that substantial urban settlement could be located on
previously uninhabited mountain areas at heights
between 6000 and 8000 feet. And perhaps of most
importance, the power-relationship of colonialism both
enabled the settlements to take place and the resources
to be organised to maintain the hill stations once they
were established.

Whilst the breakdown of the concept of colonialism
into these three components and the use of these
components as variables to explain aspects of the
colonial city in South Asia can be applied to all of
the five 'dimensions' of modernity suggested above, in
the following analysis, particular attention is paid to
explaining the spatial morphology and built environment
of the city and, to a lesser extent, aspects of its
socio-spatial structure prior to the end of colonial
rule.[17]

These variables are discussed in more detail below.

4. *The component parts of the colonial city*

Culture. The first characteristic of the colonial
city is that it is the product of a contact situation
between at least two different cultures. The impli-
cation of this is that there exists, in the indigenous
and colonial sectors of the city hereafter referred to
as 'the colonial urban settlement', areas of urban
space which are perceived, structured and utilized
according to value-systems unique to the culture in
question.

In each cultural section of the city (i.e. that of
the indigenous and that of the immigrant culture), the
form of that section is governed by the *institutional
system* of each culture.[18] Whilst the institutional
system of each culture includes kinship, education,
religion, law, economic institutions and recreation,
the values, beliefs and forms of activity related to
these institutions are different.

For example, caste is a form of social organisation
which can only be explained in cultural terms. It
comprehends, with its notions of purity, pollution and
hierarchy, a system of 'social space' which partially
accounts for the physical-spatial form of the city.
The insitution of religion is characterised by a set of
values, beliefs and practices and these regulate

attitudes to the environment, location of settlement
and the physical-spatial provision required for worship.
For example, the belief-system of Hinduism requires
that the dead be cremated; those of Islam or Christianity, that they be buried. In one area of the city there
are no burial grounds, in others, there are. Likewise,
the institution of kinship and the family takes
different forms in Indian and European society and such
differences explain the model dwelling type in each
cultural section.

Similarly, in the 'European' sector, though certain
social and spatial patterns can be explained in terms
of technology and the prevailing power structure,
certain kinds of culturally-preferred visual experience,
unique to members of the metropolitan society, account
for particular physical-spatial characteristics in that
sector.

In this way, the built forms and spatial morphology
of each cultural section can be partly explained in
terms of the institutions of each culture, understood
as systems of value, ideas, activity and behaviour.

Accordingly, with the variable of *culture* are
explained those characteristics of the indigenous or
colonial areas which can be put down to culture-
specific values, and which cannot be explained in terms
of the two other variables.

Technology is an inadequate abbreviation to indicate that the colonial settlement is not only a product
of cultural interaction but also, of cultures with
different forms or 'levels' of technological, social,
economic and political development. In a grossly over-
simplified way, it can be said that the colonial urban
settlement expresses the physical, spatial and social
forms of the industrial city which, in turn, result
from the use of inanimate sources of energy - steam-
power, electricity, and in the twentieth century, the
internal combustion engine, rather than man and animal
power. By the same logic, the indigenous settlement
area is the product largely of an agrarian and craft-
based economy, based on animate sources of energy.

In the colonial urban settlement or 'European'
sector of the city, two physical-spatial characteristics have to be explained. The first is the overall
spatial character of the settlement itself. The
second, its location with respect to the indigenous
settlement area.

The socio-spatial structure of the colonial urban

settlement can be understood in terms of two reference
models. The first of these is to be found in earlier
patterns of colonial settlement in the indigenous
society; the second, in the urban forms of the
metropolitan society already determined by an advanced
stage of industrial urbanisation. The more important
spatial, temporal and social consequences of this
process can be briefly summarized as follows:

Spatially, it meant that functional specialization
of land use had taken place, resulting in the separation of place of work from place of residence.
Temporally, it meant a division of time in which human
and social activities were clearly organized into two
distinct categories, work and non-work. This in turn
meant, for the industrial urban population, that not
only were work and residence separate but also, place
of residence was separate from place of recreation.
Socially, the elite-mass dichotomy characteristic of
pre-industrial society had been replaced by a social
structure which was increasingly differentiated in
terms of occupation, income, life-style and, of
particular importance for our analysis, location, style
and scale of residential expectation.

There was, therefore, in the metropolitan society,
as part of this process of social differentiation, an
emerging middle and upper-middle class elite from
whose ranks the residents of the colonial urban
settlement were drawn.

It is in terms of these processes that the
characteristics of the colonial urban settlement can
be at least partially explained. With regard to
residential provision, norms of accommodation and
'residential style' are those of the metropolitan
middle-class elite, though with two important qualifi-
cations. The first results from the existence of
another reference model, namely, earlier patterns of
colonial settlement in the indigenous society. The
second is explained by the third variable, the power-
structure of colonialism, to be discussed subsequently.

With regard to institutional provision on the
colonial settlement, these are the institutions
required by the state of urban development and accepted
cultural norms prevailing in the metropolitan society;
the 'church', 'club', 'library', 'theatre', 'racecourse' and occasionally, the 'museum'. Apart from
the European barracks on the cantonment, there is
nothing on the colonial urban settlement which can be

said to represent 'working class housing' as there is
no 'working class', in its modern, urban-industrial
sense, their function being performed, albeit in a
totally different capacity, by the inhabitants of the
indigenous town or those in the rural villages. The
only other metropolitan 'working class' institutions
existing in the colonial city are the 'canteen',
'Temperance Rooms', 'Presbyterian' or 'Wesleyan Chapel'
which, like the 'barracks', are confined to the
cantonment.

For an explanation of this complex social, technical and organizational process which we term
'industrialization' we must go back to the 'scientific
revolution' of the seventeenth century, whose occurence
in turn, can only be explained with reference to the
value-system of the culture and the social and ideological structure which it supported.

A further outcome of this process, was the increasing competence of the society, both in terms of
knowledge as well as organization, to deal with the
kind of social disorganization which it generated. As
far as *organization* is concerned, this meant new
institutions (local government), new methods of social
control (police), new technologies (transport,
communications, energy systems), new occupational roles
(civil engineers, sanitary inspectors) and new systems
for promoting and organizing knowledge (institutionalised research, professional associations, scientific
journals). Of the new *knowledge* that was promoted, the
most important was the scientific and medical theory
which explained - or purported to explain - the breakdown in the man-environment relationship which
industrial-urbanisation brought about and which manifested itself in rates of mortality and morbidity which
exceeded previous levels of tolerance.

These developments, both in organization and knowledge, are reflected in the institutions and socio-
spatial structure of the colonial city. Thus, in the
indigenous city in India are to be found the 'town-
hall', 'police station', 'public works offices',
'water works' and 'library', to mention only the most
common.

Of more significance, physical space in the
colonial settlement and between it and the indigenous
city, is organised according to mid- and late nineteenth
century scientific and especially medical theories
which, in brief, assume a causal connection between

aerial distance and bacterial infection. Such theories were a direct outcome of industrial urbanization in the metropolitan society.

To summarize: one has in the metropolitan society an urban system which, in its socio-spatial dimension, is the outcome of a two-century-long process of social and technical transformation. Fundamentally, it arises from a value system which generates the 'scientific revolution'; this, in its turn, produces the new energy systems which lead to industrialization. Industrialization, embracing a whole series of social, economic, technological and organizational processes, produces a unique pattern of urbanization and urban development, with an equally unique social structure.

The importance of these processes is that the social structure and physical-spatial forms of the metropolitan city which they produced, provide an important reference model for the colonial urban settlement. It is these which partly explain the characteristic lay-out, the 'sanitary space' dividing individual units within the system as well as the system as a whole from the indigenous settlement area, typical of such cities as Delhi, Allahabad, Rangoon or Lusaka. It is these processes which also produce a particular social structure which has its origin, as well as its main reference group, in the metropolitan society.

However, to understand why such spatial and social forms in the colonial settlement, whilst being comparable to those in the European metropolitan society, are nonetheless quite different from them, we must consider the last and most important variable, the power structure of colonialism.

Power structure of colonialism. The third element inherent in the concept of colonialism is the dominance-dependence relationship. This is a crucial explanatory variable, for it is clear that urban forms can result from processes of culture contact, even where such cultures manifest different forms and 'levels' of organisation and development, without resulting in the particular patterns which characterize the colonial city. These patterns may be described as those of social, ethnic and spatial segregation and, in comparison with the 'organic' growth of cities in politically autonomous societies, of spatial distortion.

The dominance-dependence relationship intercedes at two levels. Firstly, the colonised society is

dependent on the metropolitan. One consequence of
this is that the colonial settlement is primarily
devoted to political, military and administrative
functions. Their inhabitants keep order, administer
justice, control aspects of the economy but not, as is
the case in the industrial city, generate production.
It is this kind of phenomenon which Castells has in
mind in his concept of 'dependent urbanization':
urbanization takes place in the colonial society but
industrialization, which historically has generated
urbanization in modern, politically autonomous
societies, takes place in the metropolitan society.[19]
Significantly, the colonial urban settlement in the
Indian colonial city consisted of the 'cantonment' and
the 'civil station'. In the civil station of a typical,
small town lived those members of the colonial bureaucracy whose political, administrative and cultural
function is manifest in their designations, the
'collector', 'judge', 'district superintendent of
police', 'civil surgeon', 'missionary' and 'teacher'.
In addition, there were representatives of European
business interests as well as, in the later stages,
those members of the indigenous society who either
belonged to the colonial bureaucracy or who subscribed,
economically and culturally, to the values of the
colonial system. In the 'cantonment' lived the army,
the ultimate means of social control. The colonial
urban settlement then, contained the 'managers' of
the colonial system.

Secondly, the dominance-dependence relationship
can be seen at the city level. Here, for a variety of
reasons other than those already discussed, the
indigenous and colonial parts of the city were kept
apart. Such reasons were economic, social, political
and racial. Elsewhere, Banton has shown why ethnic
segregation characterized the colonial city in Africa[20]
This was either explicit and legally enforced through
the creation of distinct areas (or 'reserves') for
different racial groups with separate (and unequal)
facilities, or it was implicit (as in twentieth century
'imperial' India), with residential areas so characterized by cultural characteristics or economic
deterrents (for example, the cost of land and housing)
as to effectively prevent residential infiltration
except by those willing and able to adopt the attributes and life-style of the colonial inhabitants.
Movement into such areas, as a mark of social mobility,

meant that 'modernization' was necessarily 'westernization'. These were the 'culturally constituted
behavioural environments' of the colonial community.

The segration of areas performed numerous functions.
For the colonial community they acted as instruments of
control, both of those outside as well as those within
their boundaries. They helped the group to maintain
its own self identity, essential in the performance of
its role within the colonial social and political
system. They provided a culturally familiar and
recognizable environment which - like dressing for
dinner - was a formal, visible symbol providing
psychological and emotional security in a world of
uncertain events.

Segregation of the indigenous population provided
ease of control in the supervision of 'native' affairs.
It was economically useful in cutting down the total
area subject to maintenance and development. Segregation was also an essential element in preserving the
existing social structure where residential separation
in environments differing widely in levels of amenity
and quality, simply reflected existing social relationships. Segregation had many other functions and
Wirth's essay on 'The Ghetto' provides a useful insight
into many of them.[21]

It would, however, be misleading if no reference
were made to the contribution of the indigenous culture
to the maintenance of this system. Though the overall
distribution of power was fundamentally important in
maintaining this system of social and spatial segregation, indigenous socio-spatial categories, inherent in
the system of caste, are not to be ignored. It is
clear that traditional values were important in preserving the structure of the indigenous city, as well
as the distribution of power.

The physical segregation of the urban population
in the colonial city on the basis, ostensibly, of
political and socio-economic criteria, but effectively,
on ethnic and cultural criteria as well, has numerous
implications, not least of which is the tendency for
the behaviour of all ethnic groups to be explained in
what Mitchell calls 'categorical' terms. 'Thus, any
person recognised as a member of a particular race is
expected to behave in a standardised way.'[22] It is
clear that this process of classification is greatly
assisted by the fact of physical segregation.

The colonial city was a 'container' of cultural

pluralism but one where one particular cultural section
had the monopoly of political power.[23] The extensive
spatial provision within the colonial settlement area,
as well as the spatial division between it and the
indigenous settlement, are to be accounted for not
simply in terms of cultural differences but in terms of
the distribution of power.

Conclusion

> The word 'theory' is like a blank cheque; its
> potential value depends on the user and his use
> of it.
>
> > Percy S. Cohen, *Modern
> > Social Theory* (London 1973),
> > p.1.

In all historical investigations, indeed, any
studies of human and social phenomena, theories of
human behaviour are used, even though they are not
always explicit. Our assessment of the relative
importance of phenomena (such as, for example, the
South Asian city in relation to cities in other
geographical areas) governs the data we gather and the
framework in which it is presented; as urban historians,
the temporal boundaries we impose on our study, the
number of cities examined at any one time, the scope of
the enquiry are all a function of the theoretical
assumptions made.
It has been suggested that 'there is nothing so
practical as a good theory'. To the extent that a
theory helps us to collect and organise our data and
provides hypotheses which can be tested by that data,
the proposition must surely be true. Any investigation
of 'the South Asian city: pre-modern and modern',
comprising as it does the study of a large number of
presumably comparable phenomena along a dimension of
social change and development over time, must require
some kind of conceptual framework within which the
historical experience of any one city may be compared
to that of another.
In the first instance, therefore, the theoretical
formulations outlined above, whilst developing out of
a detailed study of Delhi and, to a lesser extent,
studies of other 'colonial cities' in India and elsewhere, are suggested here for criticism and comment.

As Ginsburg suggests, the non-Western city provides immense opportunity for both applied and theoretical studies. At the theoretical level, the colonial city provides an ideal laboratory situation for examining two fundamental issues: how does the distribution of social and political power affect the form and function of the city? By comparing the structure of pre-colonial, colonial and post-colonial city some insight might be gained into this problem. Secondly, in an urban situation where two totally different cultures operate in exactly the same environment, we can examine how the values, beliefs and institutions of each govern the provision which each culture makes for its human and social needs.

Finally, as others have surmised, we can ask whether there is a distinctive urban type which we can classify as 'the colonial city', in the same way that the 'pre-industrial' or 'industrial' city has been suggested as a particular urban category.

For policy-makers, such theoretical issues would appear to have equal relevance. In the modification and renewal of ex-colonial cities in South Asia and elsewhere, the ability to identify and isolate the 'imported' cultural models from those of the indigenous society would seem to be of considerable importance in arriving at culturally-relevant solutions to problems of housing and urban design.[24] An understanding of the economic process by which colonialism transformed the South Asian city (of which little or no mention has been made in this paper) is clearly relevant to the process of economic development in the city of today.

One might conclude, however, by returning to the somewhat contradictory propositions suggested by the opening quotations of Murphy and Ginsburg. These suggest, on one hand, that a global technology and its ramifications will reduce all cities to a similar pattern, and, on the other, that cultural values will continue to distinguish one city from another. Henry Ford was once reported as saying that he knew that half the money he spent on advertising was wasted but he could never discover which half. If half of the 'modern' city in South Asia or elsewhere results from the application of 'culturally-neutral' technology and half from the cultural values of the society in which it exists, we would go a long way to understanding both the city, as well as its problems, if we knew 'which half was which'.

King, 'Colonialism and the Development of the Modern
South Asian City: Some Theoretical Considerations'

1. This paper is adapted from a chapter in *Colonial
Urban Development: Culture, Social Power and Environ-
ment* (London 1976). An abridged version of the main
issues is included in 'Towards a Theory of Colonial
Urban Development', Open University, *Urban Development:
The City in the Developing World* (Milton Keynes, Open
University 1973).
2. Cp. G. Sjoberg, *The Pre-Industrial City* (New
York 1960).
3. The phrase is from D. Bell, *The Coming of Post-
Industrial Society* (London 1974).
4. For a recent review and criticism of such
theories see D.C. Tipps, 'Modernisation Theory and the
Comparative Study of Societies: A Critical Perspective',
Comparative Studies in Society and History, 15, 2,
(1973), pp.199-226.
5. *Concise Oxford Dictionary* (Oxford 1965).
6. S. Saxena, *Trends of Urbanisation in Uttar
Pradesh* (Agra 1970), p.226. Also J.E. Brush, 'The
Growth of the Presidency Towns' in R.G. Fox (ed.),
Urban India: Society, Space and Image (Duke University
Press, North Carolina 1970), pp.91-114.
7. R. Murphy, 'City and Countryside as Ideological
Issues: India and China', *Comparative Studies in
Society and History*, 12, 1 (1972), pp.250-267, p.254.
8. Cp. 'The major metropolis in almost every newly-
industrialising country is not a single unified city,
but, in fact, two quite different cities, physically
justaposed but architecturally and socially distinct....
These dual cities have usually been a legacy from the
colonial past.' Janet Abu-Lughod, 'Tale of two cities:
the origins of modern Cairo', *Comparative Studies in
Society and History*, 7 (1965), p.429. J.E. Brush goes
so far to construct a typology based on this phenomenon, 'Spatial patterns of population in Indian cities',
Geographical Review, 58 (1965), pp.362-391.
9. Murphy, op.cit.
10. See Sovani's argument against the assumption
that India suffers from 'over-urbanisation'. N.V.
Sovani, *Urbanization and Urban India*, (New Delhi 1966),
pp.1-13.
11. M.A. Qadeer, 'Do Cities "modernize" the

developing countries? An examination of the South
Asian experience', *Comparative Studies in Society and
History*, 16, 3 (1974), pp.266-283.

12. See for example, A. Southall (ed.), *Urban
Anthropology* (London 1973), especially W.R. Rowe,
'Caste, kinship and association in urban India', pp.
211-250.

13. Whilst the term 'Westernisation' is commonly
used to express, among other things, the transformation
of the indigenous culture by contact with a 'Western'
culture and the introduction of 'Western' institutions
and values, it is clear - particularly in India - that
one particular society and culture, that of Britain,
was the principal agent of this transformation. Hence,
the obvious need to recognise the 'Englishness' of many
so-called 'Western' institutions.

14. *International Encyclopaedia of Social Sciences*
(New York 1968).

15. A.D. King, *Colonial Urban Development*, part 3.

16. Ibid., chapter 7.

17. Support for the use of these variables in
explaining colonial urban development, derived independently in the manner outlined above, is to be found
in G. Sjoberg, 'The modern city', *International Encyclopaedia of Social Sciences* (New York 1968), vol.ii,
p.456. '[T]echnology, cultural values and social power
appear to be the most useful variables for predicting
the changing patterns within the modern city, that is,
one built upon the industrial and scientific revolution.'

18. M.G. Smith, *The Plural Society in the British
West Indies* (London 1965), p.81.

19. M. Castells, *La Question urbaine* (Paris 1973).

20. M. Banton, 'Urbanisation and the Colour Line',
in V. Turner (ed.), *Colonialism in Africa, 1870-1960*
(Cambridge 1971).

21. L. Wirth, 'The Ghetto', in A.J. Reiss (ed.),
Louis Wirth on Cities and Social Life (Chicago 1964).

22. C.J. Mitchell, 'Theoretical Orientations in
African Urban Studies' in M. Banton (ed.), *Social
Anthropology of Complex Societies* (London 1966), p.53.

23. J. Rex, *Race Relations and Sociological Theory*
(London 1970), p.20.

24. For example, in A. Cain, et al, 'Indigenous
building and the third world', *Architectural Design*,
45 (April 1975), pp.207-224.

THE SMALL TOWN AND ISLAMIC GENTRY IN NORTH INDIA: THE CASE OF KARA

C.A. Bayly

In its early stages the growing interest in Indian towns has been almost exclusively concentrated on the larger centres of population. The port cities and ancient inland centres - Lahore, Lucknow, Allahabad, Benares, Hyderabad - have largely claimed our attention. Despite the relatively small percentage of India's population which lived in cities of over 50,000 people, it can reasonably be argued that the importance of these cities was much greater than their small share of the total population would suggest. Still, this should not be allowed to obscure the fact that seven out of every ten 'urban' people in nineteenth century north India by census definition were inhabitants of small towns and this proportion was even higher in Bengal and south India. If we move beyond the rough quantitative definitions to definitions in terms of 'quality', then the small town would seem to be even more significant. The U.P. Census Commissioners of 1911 suggested that many places with a population of less than 5,000 had the distinctive characteristics of towns, and that measured by this somewhat subjective index, between 12 and 15% of the population may have been urban rather than the 9% usually recognised.[1] A similar point has been made by Richard Fox:

> Rather than indices of mere size, heterogeneity and density, (aspects of urban functions more significant in industrial than in preindustrial centres) greater attention should be given to qualitative measurements of urban style which may be duplicated at a local, small-scale level in the absence of a quantitive base.[2]

In terms of the major themes of Indian history, too, the small town has been unduly neglected. Much of the late nineteenth century Muslim elite of upper India, for instance, came not from the great cities but from small market towns, each dignified with its own Persian histories, shrines and strong cultural traditions. For Bengal, Pradip Sinha has demonstrated the importance of the small town to the Bengali *bhadralok*.[3] Places like Bikrampur of the 'Bikrampuri' babus retained their

social and cultural importance for men whose normal
abode had been the city of Calcutta for more than a
generation.[4] In political history too, there is good
reason to think that the small town provided the crucial
meeting point for the town intelligentsia of the Congress movement and the substantial rural people who
were to become its most important supporters in the
1920s and '30s. This paper focuses on the particular
historical experience of one small town which is taken
to be characteristic of a wide range of small urban
places in north India, and I have tried to set this
type - the Islamic service *qasbah* - against the background of other types of small towns.
    Preliminary studies of village notes and maps
suggest that the requirements of easy communication
spread periodic standard markets (*haths*) across the
map with the same regularity that characterised market
systems elsewhere.[5] The emergence of some centres as
lineage headquarters (Fox's 'urban centres') was
probably internal to the process of growth in the marketing system. This was because Rajput, Bhumihar or
Jat lineage elites and rajas founded markets where
there was already a good degree of peasant interaction
and where merchants would be expected to gather. While
most central places combined several functions, political circumstances or temporary economic situations
related to non-local trade might determine that some
were overwhelmingly more important in one function
than others. The residual functions of earlier
political, trading or 'manufacturing' complexes, and
the 'quality' to which they gave rise persisted in townships even when their rule as higher-level centres in
the market system had declined along with changes in
communications or demography. In early nineteenth
century north India there were several types of intermediate townships whose historical experience determined their later 'quality'. They included:
(a) Entrepot markets. These differed from standard
market centres because they owed their importance as
population centres to the conditions of through trade
rather than local trade. They were not, like *haths*,
locations through which goods from larger centres
passed downwards in any bulk and were not by origin
places where farmers marketed produce in quantity.
Though local merchants might come to assume an important role in storage or brokerage facilities, these
places were concerned in the non-local trade and their

rapid growth was determined by administrative boundaries
or by the growing conditions of particular long-distance
trades (e.g. as points suitable for cotton-bulking)
rather than by regular local demand. One sub-type was
the *dispersed market* which reflected the impact of
state and regional power and the incidence of dues
such as *sayer*, 'town duties' and *octroi*, taken from
merchants by eighteenth century and colonial authorities.[6] Rather than have their profits reduced by 10%
or more, agents and brokers would locate themselves in
these places and deal with merchants in towns of larger
population. Consumers would travel from the major
centres to buy goods there. Items of through-trade
would be stored there temporarily to avoid the cumber-
some and costly process of first paying dues and then
taking rebates on the export of goods not designed for
local consumption. In some cases merchants employed
large bands of carriers, to break up their goods into
units of under Rs.10 which were not subject to levies,
and dispose of bulk in this manner. Such centres as
Barragaon,[7] within two miles of Benares, Shahzada,[8]
near Delhi, and Salem[9] near Allahabad were examples of
dispersed marts of this sort. The fact that most
large towns in the early nineteenth century were ringed
with such places severely reduces the value of early
British figures as gauges of population.
(b) Another sub-type might be called the regional
entrepot. These marts or 'mundovies' (the origin of
this Anglicised corruption is not clear) were established at nodes of communication, at points where
geographical regions met or near political borders.
Here the characteristic products of the one area were
exchanged for those of another. For instance, markets
at the foot of the Himalayas where 'hill people'
exchanged borax, shawls, etc., for plains products were
of this sort.[10] Again, the location of the Oudh border
determined the rapid growth of the market of Phulpur in
north Allahabad.[11] Here the products of Oudh, printed
cloths and tobacco, were exchanged for iron and other
central Indian goods which had crossed the Ganges. By
the 1840s the redirection of the trade by political
authorities had reduced Phulpur to the status of a mere
hath, but several of its merchant families remained
significant in inter-district trading.
    The typical inhabitants of such entrepots were
brokers (*arethias* and *dalals*) who were either appointed
by councils of the local merchants on an ad hoc basis

or by some local magnate who had been accepted as protector of the bazaar. These places were also serviced by large numbers of inn keepers (*bhatiyaras*) or experts in transport such as headmen of mule and camel drivers. They were extremely tenuous social units which could break up and reconverge in response to commercial or political conditions.

In a sense some of the rural market fairs were examples of this type on a larger scale. By 1800 the great fair of Hardwar for instance had acquired the status of a kind of 'counter-city'.[12] Like cities, it attracted and distributed in bulk a massive variety of articles of long-distance trade. At Hardwar as in major broker cities such as Mirzapur, merchants (in this case Gosains), controlled the mart, arbitrated between merchants and dealt with 'outside powers' such as the Sikh or Maratha bands.[13] But in another sense fairs like this were not cities, as they performed no state administrative functions, were not 'hinges' in the land revenue system, and did not become the residence of rural lineages or land-controlling elites. Despite the congregation for nearly half the year of up to 3,000 people no features of urban life-style developed and no permanent buildings were constructed beyond the temple complex.

(c) A further distinct type of settlement is what might be called the suburban *artisan village*. These paralleled almost exactly the artisan muhallas of large towns, but were located outside city limits, sometimes up to a day's bullock journey away. They were residences of large numbers of Hindu and Muslim weavers or brass-making artisans. Some merchants with correspondents in the towns lived there, but in many cases the artisans would themselves market their goods piece by piece in the towns, thereby avoiding the payment of town duties.[14] These places were by origin products of the 'putting-out' system of late Mughal rule. When the early European sources refer to the location of large numbers of 'looms' at certain towns, they are often aggregating the production of many small centres such as these.[15] Their location may of course have reflected the protection or patronage of particular magnates, but their production was largely directed to consumers outside the neighbourhood. A rural location was advantageous because of a) the relative cheapness of materials such as thread, copper, dye, which were not subject to import or town duties, giving artisans

a price advantage over their urban fellows, b) availability of untaxed space, and running water, c) a
guaranteed food-supply and chance for some family
members to participate in agriculture. The cohesive-
ness of such communities, reinforced in the case of
Muslim weavers by a strong sense of religious community,
made them less liable to collapse in the adverse
conditions of the later nineteenth century.

(d) The 'quality' of places of this sort was determined
by the historical features of certain trades and types
of non-local demand. In the case of what we shall call
the service *qasbah*, however, it was the conditions of
state and regional level clerical and military service
which determined their emergence, location and subsequent decline. Places such as this are found throughout north India near all the historic centres of
political power of the Muslim period. Examples are
Kakori near Lucknow, Koil near Aligarh, Macchlishahr
near Jaunpur and Bhagbanpura near Lahore. A famous
nineteenth century legal judgement summarised the
features of this category of small towns

> A Mussulman settlement in a defensible military
> position, generally on the site of an ancient Hindu
> headquarters, town or fort, where, for mutual pro-
> tection, the Musalmans who had overrun and seized
> the proprietary of the surrounding villages
> resided; where the faujdar and his troops, the
> pargana qanungo and chaudhri, the mufti, qazi and
> other high dignitaries lived; and, as must be the
> case where the wealth and power of the Moslem sect
> was collected in one spot, a large settlement of
> Sayyads' mosques, dargahs, etc sprang up ....[16]

In this paper, the characteristics and historical
experience of Kara near Allahabad, will be taken to
apply to the whole category. The choice of Kara is
more than usually appropriate. For here stands the
tomb of the celebrated saint, Maulana Khwajagi. The
tradition is that any scholar, however dull, who
studies at the tomb forty days, will become a learned
man.

Kara, 1583-1830

The three centres of Kara, Shahzadpur and Manikpur
formed a complex of townships associated with Khilji
and early Mughal government in the lower Doab. All

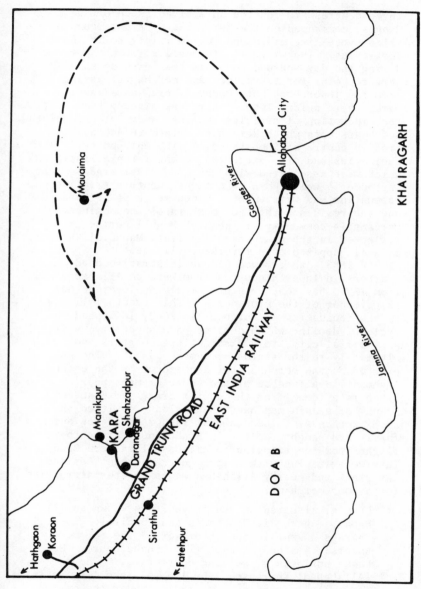

PARTABGARH DISTRICT

three centres are located on a broad sweep of the
Ganges, commanded on the Kara side by high ground on
which successive Hindu and Muslim rulers built their
fortresses. The river was fordable at Shahzadpur
during the dry season, and this town grew up as a
service point for travellers and merchants passing
from the lower Doab into Oudh. There was a large
sarai there before 1600.[17] Kara was already known for
the production of articles such as paper, printed cloth
and brass pots which were appropriate to an administrative centre of importance.[18] The entrepot
facilities had also attracted merchant banker families
which were associated with the down-river trades. For
instance, a well-known seventeenth century treatise on
accounting was written by a Hindu merchant of Kara,[19]
and the residence there of members of the dominant
mercantile community of the high Mughal period is
reflected in the place-name 'Gujarati Mohulla' which
is still applied to a riverside village.[20]

In 1583, Akbar moved his administrative headquarters in lower Hindustan from Kara to Allahabad and
from 1597, his son, Prince Daniyal was located there
as governor of the Province.[21] This event, followed
by the foundation of Fatehpur in 1602, initiated the
cycle of decline which demoted Kara successively from
an imperial city, to a district headquarters and
ultimately to the status of a mere *qasbah*. The pull
exerted on the merchants of Shahzadpur by the establishment in Allahabad of the court of mansabdar of
7,000 is evident from the contemporary verse autobio-
graphy of a Jain merchant, Banarsidas, entitled the
Ardha Kathanak.[22] Banarsidas' father Kharagsen and his
family had sought shelter in Shahzadpur during their
flight from the troubled conditions of eastern Oudh.
They were staying with a local merchant, but business
was slack and nearby Allahabad was a greater attraction
for a poor merchant.

> Prayag, situated on the Triveni was known as Illa-
> habas. There lived Akbar's son, Daniyal.
> Kharagsen went in search of work. The boy
> Banarsi remained at home [i.e. Shahzadpur]. He
> began business by selling cowries .... There
> [Allahabad] Kharagsen, the liberal jeweller, dealt
> in jewels in cash and on credit, under the patron-
> age of Prince Daniyal.

As a provincial quadquarters under the Mughals,

however, the Kara area remained sufficiently important to continue to attract major families of service people and merchants. The main local Srivastava Kayasth families date from this period. According to H.M. Elliot, 'they seem to have been the marked recipients of favour from the Mahomedan Emperors. The Kanungoships of several parganahs and other possessions were given to several families of Delhi Kayasths.'[23] While some of the Kara and Karari Shaikh families date land grants to the days of the Khilji monarchs, the assumption of other revenue rights by Muslim families seems to have occurred between the date of the *Ain-i-Akbari* and cession to the British in 1802.[24] The weakening of state authority after 1715 and the tendency of the Oudh rulers to grant *talukas* which became hereditary made it easier for local service groups to establish areas of land-control in which they enjoyed rental income. Crucial to the survival of these families, however, was the continued participation of some members in the military or clerical service of regional rulers. Throughout the Doab and the Delhi catchment area seasonal military service remained the norm. The Shaikhs of Mau Aima in Allahabad appear to have secured revenue free villages through service in the Oudh army under Shuja-ud Daula.[25] Pathan families in the trans-Jamna tract of Arail pargana date their appearance in the Allahabad locality to periods of military service with Shaista Khan, Nazim of Allahabad in the 1630s.[26] Their extensive holdings in the area were built up during the eighteenth century. These families typically established themselves in a rural *qasbah* while at the same time retaining property in and links of kinship with a major city adjacent to the provincial headquarters. As with the connection of the Kara Kayasths and the predominantly clerical quarter of Yahiyapur in Allahabad city, so the Khairagarh Pathans maintained residences in and followers in the suburban village of Dariabad. These links remained significant in the passage of information and personnel between city and countryside in the nineteenth century. For instance, the major Kayasth *biradari* of Allahabad city remained located in Kara and caste disputes were referred back to the *qasbah*.[27]

If this dual status of *rentier* and courtly service could not be maintained, the families, and often the *qasbah* as a whole, would decline. An example of such deterioration faced by service gentry in a time of rapid political change is that of Namdar Khan, resident of Dariabad.[28] In 1802, nearly 90 years of age, he petitions for the return of lands near Dariabad. He had, he says, been in the military service of the East India Company as early as the battle of Buxar and had relatives who were revenue officials in the trans-Jamna areas. But he had grown too old for military service and had suffered from the high land-revenue assessments levied by the later *amils* of Oudh and by the first British settlement. Ultimately, the seizure of his garden lands had denied him the last honourable income left to a Muhammadan gentleman, an income of Rs.7-800 per annum derived from 'mangos, jacks, guavas and roses' which he sold in the nearby city. He and his many dependents had been reduced to a state of indigence, 'and without your support I cannot maintain my respectability and rank'. The fragility of service *qasbahs* and their related craft industries reflected the fact that the loss of rental income for service gentry could mean total collapse. Families like these, gathered around the catchment towns of the Doab and western U.P., were in a wholly different position to the 'dispossessed' among cohesive Rajput or Bhumihar groups in the east of the area who might retain considerable control over land and followers at village-level even after the loss of revenue rights. The service gentry did not always have personal cultivation, or lineage or caste links in their erstwhile villages to fall back on. Their status demanded patterns of high consumption which were difficult to restrict as they determined access to the officials who controlled patronage.

Other service families, however, maintained their position by moving rapidly into the employment of the East India Company. Such were the Kayasths of Hathgaon in Fatehpur, who had first risen to prominence in the service of Almas Ali Khan, one of the last of the Oudh '*amils*' in the area and a eunuch who controlled a hugh fiscal lordship in the lower Doab. Members of the family began as tahsildars on a 10% commission basis, and in the course of the century the family provided lawyers, government servants and educationists who worked in Fatehpur, Allahabad and Lahore.[29] The technique for guaranteeing family continuity remained the same. Members retained a strong presence in state and district service appointments, but each generation invested in the purchase of small parcels of land-rights throughout the Fatehpur District. By the 1880s, the Hathgaon family was one of the largest Kayasth *rentier* groups in Hindustan, and Hathgaon itself had grown from a small weekly market to a flourishing *qasbah*.

In the case of Kara-Shahzadpur too local conditions tended initially to preserve the position of its service gentry. Ironically, it was the commercial requirements of the up-country agents of the East India Company which allowed a temporary lease of life to the area after its superior political importance finally evaporated with the departure of the staff of the exiled Delhi Emperor in 1773. Shahzadpur and Phulpur, it was said, were 'much resorted to' by Oudh merchants until 1794, when

> the cloths manufactured in the lower part of the Dooab, were much in demand for the European market. Many mercantile houses were enabled to invest with great facility from 15 to 20,000 Rupees monthly in the article of cloth alone. At present cloths called sullum, the bafta, the Shahzadpore chintz, the red khurwa appear to be most in demand, and since the Company's authority has been established in the Ceded provinces, I understand that sums to a very large amount have been advanced on the part of agents in Calcutta as well as by other European merchants whose native agents are now employed in collecting cloths in almost every pergunneh of Allahabad and Currah [Kara].[30]

At the same time the Kara-Shahzadpur families had secured some new openings in Lucknow, the only remaining arena of advancement in north India for traditional service people. For instance, the grandfather of Lalji, author of the administrative treatise *Mirat-ul-Auza*, had achieved a position as writer in the Lucknow Residency in the 1770s or '80s. The Kara-based family continued to hold this position and participated in the literary life of Lucknow until the 1860s.[31]

Yet the first signs of decline were already evident. Augusta Deare on her travels in 1815 noted that the earlier luxury trades had 'fallen off'.[32] By 1816 the decline of the local chintz dyers and merchants had been exacerbated by the inflexible duties levied by the British authorities on imported cloth and dyes for printing, so that

> The mahajuns and chintz printers of Shahjadpore are
> now migrating and establishing themselves in the
> Gun [market] of Zalim Singh, near Shahjadpore on
> the opposite bank of the Ganges in Pergunna
> Manickpore in the Domains of the Nawab Vizier.[33]

The proximity of Manikpur to Kara had given it a
similar mix of service gentry, and this area of the
Partabgarh District remained one of the few parts of
southern Oudh where there was a substantial population
of landholding and cultivating Muslims and Kayasths.[34]
However, in 1880, cloth production in the area was
negligible, suggesting that the Shahzadpur artisan
families had either been reduced to the status of
cultivators or had moved on again from Manikpur. In
the case of the merchant families who had financed them,
we can be more definite. The histories of several
Benares Agarwal families, notably that of 'Bulaki Das
Devi Prasad' record Kara or Shahzadpur as their native
villages and say that they migrated to Benares between
1820 and 1840.[35] These families had re-established
themselves within a generation and had moved into the
Benares trade in silk *saris*. By 1836 chintz printing
was declining in the Kara region, its demise had been
hastened, according to contemporary accounts, by the
importation of English cloth into its traditional Doab
home markets, but also by the rise in grain prices in
the 1830s which had put considerable pressure on the
'manufacturers'.[36]

A service catchment area in the late nineteenth century

Kara stands as a paradigm for service *qasbahs* in the
late nineteenth century; places such as Koil (Aligarh),
Macchlishahr (Jaunpur) and Kakori (Lucknow) all displayed such typical features as
1. Population decline or stagnation. In the case of
Kara the process almost amounted to de-urbanisation.
The population in 1820 was about 18,000 which was more
than half that of Allahabad itself. In 1870 it was
6,000 and in 1890, 3,000.[37] Shahzadpur suffered a
similar decline, though its annual fairs on the banks
of the Ganges continued to attract large numbers.
Before the settlement surveys of the 1870s the *muhallas*
of Kara had shrunk to a series of villages dominated by
zamindari *kothis*. As a reminder of Kara's urban past,
however, these were, and are still called 'Muhallas'.

Thus Kagaziana Muhallas, now a cluster of huts, was once the scene of paper-making for which the town was famous, as the name implies. 'Gujarati Muhalla' on the river has seen few Gujarati mercantile people since 1750. Nearby 'Muhalla Bazaar' (in fact a few straggling *kothis*) is centred on a pre-Mughal mosque, and most of the lineaments and characteristic features of a typical Islamic city can still be made out. Moreover, the whole area of four or five square miles is scattered with the remains of tombs, *mazhars*, and the shrines of Sufi holy men, still venerated, which are situated on religious charitable land. The scene is reminiscent of the outskirts of Delhi, Jaunpur or Faizabad.

As the centre of a moderately rich, grain-growing terrain, Kara might have maintained itself as a flourishing intermediate market centre for the bulking of cash crops as some similar service *qasbahs* did in other districts. But the river trade, through which such goods had continued to pass in smaller quantities, dwindled rapidly after 1860 and the coming of the railway to Allahabad. The result was the stagnation of the riverine marts and the drift of many remaining labourers and merchants to new centres along the railway line which ran five or six miles to the south along the line of the old Grand Trunk Road. In particular, two nearby grain trading marts and thrice-weekly haths, Daranagar and Koraon, increased rapidly in importance as Kara and Shahzadpur declined. After the 1830s the Kara-Shahzadpur service gentry had begun rapidly to lose their land rights throughout the pargana and along with them their rights to exact customal dues and levies on local trade which they had previously engrossed. The Kayasth *kanungo* families for instance, lost approximately 25% of their land rights between 1830 and 1870.[38] It must be stressed again that these families were overwhelmingly in a *rentier* status and that such a decline did reflect a substantive change in local economic power.[39] Assessment reports on villages for the late 1870s, give many examples of 'old proprietors' of Kara, predominantly Kayasths or Muslim *ashraf* families who had mortgaged and sold their shares in villages. The new proprietors were often city men connected with law and government service, though among local groups who gained were three families of grain traders of Koraon and Daranagar.[40]
2. A second distinctive feature of late nineteenth

century service *qasbahs* and their localities,
reflected in the 1891 village census data,[41] was the
persistence of exceptionally high rates of literacy
both in Kara-Shahzadpur and in neighbouring villages.
Since the rates were high both for males under 15 years
of age and also in the adult category,[42] this concentration of literates probably reflects both the
persistence of private Islamic primary education and
the return to the area of men who had been in service
outside the locality. The area also had the highest
concentration of flourishing state schools (*tahsili*
and *halkabandi* schools) throughout Fatehpur and Allahabad Districts.[43] The high attendance of Muslim boys in
these schools reflects other recent findings concerning
the alleged Muslim backwardness in education in the
U.P. In general, central place studies have emphasised
the tendency of all facilities and functions, commercial, service and educational, to build up into
hierarchies centred on places at the same 'level'. For
historical reasons, however, there appear to be cases
in north India where hierarchies of service and
educational facilities did not remain congruent with
economic and marketing networks of equal importance.
Evidently the family 'ethos' of government service and
the ideal of the literate Indo-Persian gentleman
persisted in the *qasbahs*, which were much less
important economically than nearby market towns. By
comparison with the Kara region, for instance, the
inhabitants of Karma, a flourishing oil seed trade
mart, also within Allahabad District, were said to be
'far too busy with their large market pursuits' to be
concerned with the business of education.[44] Such
divergencies in networks may have had important consequences for social and political movements. In the
lower Doab, in fact, a sharp difference in social and
political styles (to some extent reinforcing Hindu-
Muslim distinctions) emerged between the Kara-
Shahzadpur area and the Koraon-Daranagar railway tract.
Rural Hindu populists and Congress activits were
centred on Daranagar enlisting the support of petty
local professional men, merchants and high-caste
vernacular literates from Hindu *pattidari* villages.
The first peasants' association in the area was
founded at Daranagar in 1918,[45] and worked among the
Kurmi tenantry. The Kisan workers soon found themselves opposed at local meetings by individuals
specifically noted as 'Mussulman Zamindars of Kara'

who insisted on the continuation of their privileges
of free labour, produce and ejectment in this period
of economic difficulty.[46] Ex-small zamindars of Kara
insist that all had gone well until Congressmen got a
foothold amongst the 'banias and vakils of Daranagar'
and began to incite their Hindu tenantry against them.[47]
Political workers recalled, however, that the Kara
zamindars were among the 'hardest' landholders in the
district, there was a tendency to attribute this to the
zamindars' lack of sympathy with their Hindu tenants;
but the position of the Kara zamindars was economically
fragile so that custumal dues and services were
particularly significant for them.
3. Another distinctive feature of such service *qasbahs*
was the persistence in them of general religious and
literary traditions embracing both Muslim and Hindu. A
number of noted poets were associated with Kara throughout the nineteenth and twentieth centuries. They
included Lala Shital Prasad ('Khurun'), Lala Amer
Singh ('Khush Dil'), Sayyid Shah Kariuddin ('Kabir')
and most notably Sayyid Wahiuddin Wahi, teacher of the
great satirical poet Akbar Illahabadi, who was himself
a product of Kara.[48] The cultural unity of the service
gentry within the Indo-Persian tradition was attested
by the regular participation of Urdu-writing Hindus
within the locality in *mushairas* and similar activities.
Throughout the late nineteenth century Kara had a
printing press and it was from the township that Allahabad District's first rural newspaper, the Urdu *Riyaz-
ul Akhbar* was produced in the early years of the
present century.[49] Even today villagers of the Kara
region, both Hindu and Muslim, display a wide knowledge
of local history and of the cultural traditions of
their respective religions. Kara's local historian (a
typical figure and member of a gentry family) was himself able to outline the decline of Kara in terms of
the progressive removal of political authority. Allahabad, according to local sentiment was on the same
path. It had already been demoted from an Imperial to
a regional capital. In 1923 the government offices
moved to Lucknow; soon Allahabad, like Kara, would be
divested of even the *tahsildari* and it too would become
a *qasbah*. These remarks, as well as the several slim
histories of Kara over the last three generations,
suggest a consciousness of continuity of community and
place not paralleled in the entrepot markets previously
mentioned.

The binding elite ideal of Kara and of other similar centres was that of the Persian gentleman, liberal, beneficent, a worthy servant of the ruler Hindu zamindar families had adopted the same ideal and the Islamic practices that went with it. In the case of the Kayasths of Hathgaon, indeed, they had begun to bury their dead.[50] But in the late nineteenth century these practices were beginning to come under attack. Western educated Kayasth service people in Allahabad involved in social reform movements criticized the extravagant wedding customs of the traditional *biradari* of Kara-Shahzadpur and Yahiyapur Muhalla.[51] Contemporary movements of Hindu revival also placed Kara's Kayasth and other Hindu magnates in an ambiguous position. Their local context still demanded conspicuous display but newly revived Hindu sentiment demanded a more brahminical style. Hindu-Muslim tensions also began to emerge after 1900. In 1909, the first-ever canvassed District Board election was fought in the area between a Hindu and a Muslim zamindar.[52] This was the occasion for some communal bad-feeling. Nevertheless the similar situations of these Hindu and Muslim families remained striking. A more detailed description of some of them will set the scene.

The most prominent of the Kara families was that of Sayyid Farid-ud-din Ahmed[53] which was supposed to have settled in the region during the Khilji period, and lived in Kagziana Muhalla. Sayyid Farid-ud Din's son, Habibullah, and his grandson Nabiullah were both prominent members of the I.C.S.; other relatives were lawyers in Lucknow and members of the Provincial Civil Service. The family played an important part in fostering education locally. In addition to the maintenance of maktabs and madrasahs, Farid-ud-din founded in 1882 the Kara 'Rifah-i-Am' school.[54] This obviated the need for poorer service families in the vicinity to send their children to Allahabad, at considerable expense, to obtain a high school level of education. The school emphasised the reformed syllabuses associated with Aligarh soon became a centre for Persian and Urdu learning in the locality and attracted teachers from the local government schools.[55] The family was also aware of the need to increase their income from purely agricultural sources. Unusually effective estate managers, they also introduced a large number of fine mago groves onto their estates, and other Kara

families followed suit. The cultivation of the mango
with its traditional and aristocratic associations, was
one variety of agricultural improvement and marketing
which would not reflect adversely on their gentry status.
Like many of the north Indian service families, men
from Kara had also established close contacts with the
court of Hyderabad,[56] and drew a steady income from
that source after the 1870s when the durbar began to
introduce larger numbers of north Indians as part of
its efforts at administrative reform. Sayyid Mahomed
Askori, a marriage connection of Jamal Ahmed, the owner
of the whole *mauza* of Kara, became an officer at the
court of the Begum of Bhopal, having begun his career
as an under-tahsildar in Oudh.[57] Shaikh Azhar Faruqi
even became Home Minister of Hyderabad in the present
century; and Sayyid Mahomed Ali was superintendent of
police there. Though the inflow must have been considerable, it is difficult to arrive at an estimate of
the total receipts from outside service flowing back
to Kara at this period. Not only did the service
people remit part of their salaries and help to place
poorer Kara men in inferior employment, but their
contacts in the administration are said to have
secured a better hearing for local public works and
educational projects in the Kara region. Tradition
attributes Kara's *pakka* roads, hospital and inter-
college to the efforts of the Sayyids and other Kara
residents who held appointments in the Board of
Revenue and the Educational Department in Lucknow.[58]
Amongst local Hindu families a similar pattern is
evident. The most prominent were the Kayasths of Shahzadpur and the Khattris of Faridganj. Among the former
were the *kanungo* family of Chaudhri Mahadeo Prasad and
the once poor family of Kali Prasad Kulbhaskar, responsible for the foundation of the Allahabad Pathsala.[59]
This school was seen by local people as a way of maintaining their pre-eminence in district educational and
administrative functions in a period when they, in
common with the Muslim service families, were beginning
to feel increased competition within their 'hereditary
profession' of writing. The Khattris of nearby Faridganj,[60] by contrast, combined successful estate management with a presence in the Allahabad High Court. This
was a Sehgal family of Ludhiana which appears to have
risen in the service of the later Oudh revenue farmers.
In the mid nineteenth century they were reckoned to be
among the most influential residents of Sirathu tahsil.

They lent money to their tenants and used their wealth
to buy up shares in the coparcenary villages in the
interior of the tahsil. In one village it was remarked
that the feud between the Bhumihar coparceners and the
Faridganj dependents was the 'ruin of the village',
suggesting that a determined service gentry unconnected
with the dominant local land-controlling groups could
exert considerable influence if they were skilful
managers. At some time before 1880, the Faridganj
people had also become managers of the local properties
of the big Tandon bankers of Allahabad who had acquired
villages in Kara after 1857.[61] It is interesting that
there is no record in any of the Tandon books of money-
lending or trading connections with any of the Koraon
or Daranagar merchants.[62] Instead, the links between
the major mercantile group in the city and Kara locality were forged through associations relating to the
management of the land. There is very little evidence
for the Allahabad locality to suggest that there were
close connections between Allahabad banker families
and rural merchants. Instead the city merchants dealt
with grain traders in Farrukhabad and Banda, while
local banias acquired credit from their correspondents
in grain trading in Cawnpore or raised it locally.
Socially, however, the Faridganj people utilised the
relations of prestige which the landholding bankers had
established with the authorities in Allahabad. Lala
Kashi Prasad, honorary magistrate, and head of the
family after 1900 made an annual Christmas pilgrimage
to Allahabad. He would stay at the residence of one
of the Tandons, go to the Collectorate and present the
Collector with a Christmas cake, year in year out.
The family will still mention its Tandon connection as
among its major credentials.

Distinctive features of old service *qasbahs* were
not limited to the elites. Despite the collapse of
most of its functions, the Kara-Shahzadpur area still
retained a number of brass workers and weavers at the
end of the nineteenth century. Also, though it was
now some miles away from the major through routes, the
area remained known for its large concentration of
ostlers *bhatiyaras* and horse dealers. The 1891 village
census date records a striking number of 'visitors' in
and around the *qasbah* on the night of the Census,[63]
and this may reflect Kara's continued importance as a
resting and boarding point for travellers. It is also
stated that Kara men went to Allahabad in large

36

numbers at the beginning of the century and it is
known that zamindar families placed their dependents in
positions as orderlies, petty clerks, etc. These
conditions gave rise to close communications between
the city bazaars and Kara. In 1921, the Khilafat
lecturers made Kara one of their bases in rural Allahabad and they were said to have attracted numbers of
artisans and *bhatiyaras*.[64]

The Twentieth Century

The economic condition of the Kara-Shahzadpur and other
lower Doab service gentry appears to have begun to
stabilise the 1920s and '30s, despite the much more
exposed political situation in which they then found
themselves. The mid-nineteenth century had been their
low point. Thereafter they appear to have begun to
respond effectively to the need for new skills.
Several men from the township complex went to Aligarh,
and one at least went to England for education. In
1947, a formidable number of Kara men were employed in
high positions in the civil services of British India
and the Indian states. The successful development of
the mango groves and some other high value vegtable and
fruit crops which could be sold in the expanding
markets of Allahabad and Fatehpur, offset to some
extent the decline of rental income which resulted from
the disappearance of customary cesses and the partition
of holdings. The consequence were to be seen in the
substantial additions made to the old structures of
Muhalla Bazaar and Muhalla Kagaziana during this period.
Partition and Zamindari Abolition, however, changed
all this.[65] A large number of Kara men went to Pakistan, and the effects of the land legislation of the
1950s was to disperse many of the zamindari families
and their dependents to Lucknow, Hyderabad and Allahabad in search of work. The large houses are now
crumbling, and their remaining residents, reduced in
status and wealth, harbour resentment against the
present government and recall the zamindari days with
nostalgia. That the events of Partition would have a
disruptive effect on Kara was to some extent fore-
shadowed by the development of its political and social
traditions after the 1880s. Throughout the late century and the beginning of this, much of the push behind
the demand for separate Muslim institutions, traditions
and electorates had come from the Allahabad region

not from the town itself but from the *qasbah* service
gentry. Men from Kara had been particularly active in
the Urdu Defence Associations of 1873 and 1900.[66] The
early District Muslim League from 1906 to 1913 had
been entirely dominated by them and their connections
in the Allahabad District Court.[67] The push for cooperation between Hindus and Muslims in local politics
had come overwhelmingly from the town Muslim intelligentsia, and particularly from the younger men of the
High Court Bar. Non-elite urban Muslims had also been
particularly prominent. But their gentry status and
attitudes to authority made it particularly difficult
for the *qasbah* elites to work closely with Congress
and rural populists even during periods of rapproch-
ment such as the Khilafat movements. Not only the
demand for the end of cesses and zamindari dues, but
also the Hindu revivalist tone of much early rural
Congress work around Allahabad with its emphasis on
Hindi in panchayats, cattle pounds and Hindi vernacular
schools made them uneasy. Men such as Jamal Ahmed and
Sayyid Mahomed Isa of Niwan were as might be expected
attracted to the Khilafat movement, but otherwise they
took a cautious and generally pro-government line
during the non-cooperation movement[68] and did not
follow the popular, radical Muslim leaders of the town.
Conversely, the need to enlist Muslim support and
retain the small zamindars seriously qualified the
alliance between the Congress and the Daranagar Kisan
Sabha during this period. Latterly, support for the
idea of Pakistan was quite strong in Kara. The
continuities between early expressions of Muslim
cultural separateness and the demand for a separate
state, are of course extremely tenuous. But the strong
local religious traditionalism and the exposed
condition of both service representation in Lucknow and
local gentry status after 1937 appears to have pre-
disposed some Kara men to residence in *Dar-ul-Islam*.[69]

Recently Paul Brass has concluded on the basis of
aggregated figures of Muslim representation in the
provincial civil service and 'urbanisation' that the
Muslim position did not decline between 1860 and 1930
in U.P. and that such a decline was a 'myth' used by a
homogeneous and largely urban Muslim elite to maintain
its position and privileges.[70] Unfortunately, these
aggregated figures conceal shorter term and more local
changes in the status of particular groups of Muslims.
For instance, they take no account of the decline

throughout the region of places such as Kara in the
late nineteenth century and the rise throughout of
other families of Muslims both in town and country.
My view is that continuing detailed studies of Muslim
elites and their dependents are required and that they
would once more enrich the picture. They would in fact
pinpoint areas of substantive economic and social
decline which aggravated tensions locally. At the same
time it is important to take note of the strong local
intellectual and religious traditions among Muslims
which persisted due to the attenuated networks of
communication between the village, the *qasbah* and the
major towns where national and regional political
decisions were made in the 1920s and 1930s.

Conclusion

The paper has addressed itself to the problem of the
'quality' of small towns in post-Mughal north India.
It has suggested several further types of urban place
to be set alongside Fox's Rajput lineage centre,
and especially the service *qasbah*, a seat of an Islamicized
service gentry. The case of Kara near Allahabad has
been taken to illustrate a process of progressive
'de-urbanisation' which may be as helpful in understanding the nature of Indian centres as the more
common studies of urbanisation. Kara felt the effects
of the chronic instability of regional and district
level political power in the period 1750 to 1850, but
it was also damaged by changing patterns of local
transport and marketing related to the coming of the
railways. Town decline was a lagged process. First
Kara lost its superior administrative functions with
the removal of governors and *mansabdars*. Then its
superior commercial and artisan population drifted
away. Only recently has it lost its role as a gentry
seat. The guardians of these traditions and the bene-
ficiaries of the residual connections of state-level
service were what we have called the 'gentry'. Though
they played a comparable 'hinge' function in land-
revenue administration and were often addressed
similarly as the 'Sayyids of Jansath', 'the Shahzadas
of Kakori' or the 'Sheikhs of Kara', they differed in
important respects from the Rajas, chaudhries and
lineage elites of Fox's rurban centres. They were
predominantly Muslims or Islamicized Hindus (Kayasths
or Khattris); they displayed a high level of literacy

2. KARA: a *kothi*

and were not linked by caste or kinship and in the case
of the Muslims even by formal ritualized *jajmani* ties
with the residents of their villages. They supplemented quasi-rental income with service monies and in
this respect were more like the Chinese *shen-shi* than
Rajput or Bhumihar lineage elites. Members of such
families played an important role in linking together
networks of Indo-Persian culture in north India. But
these links were often long distance and did not
necessarily relate to nearby centres. Skinner has
observed in the Chinese case that standard marketing
communities 'nestled' together and were therefore more
important in determining social relations than formal
administrative structures in which a village or market
town was dependent on only one superior centre. In
our case, however, the networks of gentry created
around such administrative centres were extensive and
irregular, though often intangible. They related one
place to many towns, as Kara related to Allahabad,
Lucknow, Hyderabad and Bhopal.

The service gentry, both Hindu and Muslim, played
a significant role in integrating the society of late
nineteenth century towns with certain relatively
leterate and mobile parts of rural society which we
have called 'service catchment areas'. Kara-Shahzadpur
and other such areas were important parts of the social
and political life of Allahabad, in the same way that
Kakori was part of Lucknow, or Bhaghanpura of Lahore.
If we allow to the *qasbahs* the role of urban centres
then late nineteenth century social and political
movements can still be regarded as essentially urban,
but they were never purely 'municipal'. However, there
were strict limits to the degree of political integration which could be achieved by a service gentry.
Those in north India were placed in a similar position
to rural elements of the Bengali *bhadralok*, such as
the Bikrampuri babus, with close links in the society
and politics of Calcutta. Early participation in
social reform, religious and educational movements
linking town to service centre, was not followed by
involvement in the populist movements of the 1920s and
1930s as these were too much of a threat to their
gentry status. Whereas the Doab had been active in the
early Muslim League and the Kayastha Pathshala, it was
exceptionally quiet during the Civil Disobedience
movement. This was said to be in part a reflection of
the fear which their tenants held toward the small

41

3. KARA: a *kothi*

resident gentry of the area.

After more than a generation of 'urban studies',
historians and sociologists are coming more and more
to abandon the idea of 'the city' as an entity in
itself which can be isolated, measured and classified
between different cultures and historical periods.[71]
The new, more satisfactory approach will be to concentrate on cities as creations of the elites and classes
of different societies, rather than as 'givens'. What,
then, does the Islamic *qasbah* tell us more generally
about Indian society? First, the emergence of the
qasbah was a continuous process which stretched from
the high Mughal period into the twentieth century. It
represented above all the emergence of an Indian
'gentry' with a definite stake and interest in local
societies. The *qasbah* elites were not of course European gentlemen farmers; but nor were they simply
'parasites' or the rootless creations of an oriental
despotism taking a temporary lien on tribute rent.
While not direct agriculturalists, they were certainly
managers who invested effort and money in the fruit
and garden crop farming of their localities and built
wells, roads and schools. In the environs of the
qasbahs the picture of Indian agriculture as the preserve of peasant family farms unaffected by the
management of external elites does not hold true.
Moreover, we see here the emergence of the town as a
definite corporate entity with traditions and history
of its own which long survives the vicissitudes of
violent political change at the centre. Pride of
birthplace became as significant as pride in Arabian
origin, or direct descent from Abraham, for the *qasbah*
gentry. Thus the view from Kara or Bilgram, or Kakori
is likely to dissolve some of the stereotypes about
Indian towns, Indian agriculture and the origins of
Hindu-Muslim conflict. But who can afford forty days
at the tomb of Maulana Khwajagi?

Bayly, 'The Small Town and Islamic Gentry in North
India: The Case of Kara'

1. *Census of India, 1911, XV.   United Provinces of
Agra and Oudh*, Pt.I. *Report* pp.23-32.
2. R. Fox, 'Rajput 'Clans' and Rurban Centres in
Northern India', in R. Fox (ed.), *Urban India, Society,
Space and Image* (Duke University, North Carolina 1969),
pp.167-185.
3. Pradip Sinha, *Nineteenth Century Bengal*
(Calcutta 1965).
4. For the role of the 'Bikrampuri Babus', see,
Rajat Ray, 'Politics and Social Conflict in Bengal,
1850-1905', (unpublished Ph.D. thesis, Cambridge
University, 1973), Chapters 2, 5, passim.
5. Preliminary work on this subject has been done
by A. Yang and J. Hagen, formerly of the University of
Virgina, Charlottesville, to whom I am grateful for
comments; see also Carol A. Smith (ed.), *Regional
Analysis*   (2 vols., New York 1976).
6. C. Trevelyan, *Report on the Town and Transit
Duties of Upper India* (Calcutta 1834), passim.
7. Collector Government Customs, Meerut, to
Commissioner, Saharanpur, 14 February 1823, Conquered
and Ceded Provinces Revenue (Customs), hereafter CPC,
22 February 1823, India Office Records, Range 95/10;
District Gazeteers of the United Provinces (Allahabad
1906-11) hereafter *DGUP*, lV, *Meerut*, 61.
8. Deputy Collr. Govt. Customs, Benares, to
Collector Govt. Customs, Mirzapur, 6 July 1815, CPC,
18 July 1815, IOR, 97/56.
9. Throughout the nineteenth century Allahabad was
ringed with suburban marts which reflected minute
changes in *octroi* and other local levies, see, e.g.,
Annual Reports of the Allahabad Municipality, 1885-
1927, preserved in the Allahabad Municipal Archives.
10. E.g. Board of Revenue to President in Council,
22 February 1820, CPC, 94/14.
11. Deputy Collr. Govt. Customs, Allahabad, to
Collr. Govt. Customs, Cawnpore, 29 November 1819, CPC,
5 February 1811, IOR, 97/38.
12. For conditions of trade in North-West Hindustan
at the end of the eighteenth century, see, George
Forster, *Narrative of a Journey from Bengal to England*
(London 1808), I, 214 et seq.

13. T. Hardwick, 'Narrative of a journey to Siri-
nagar', *Asiatick Researches* 6, 1799, 313-15.
14. For the location of Indian weaving, see, K.N.
Chaudhuri, 'The Structure of the Indian Textile
Industry in the Seventeenth and Eighteenth Centuries',
Indian Economic and Social History Review, 11, 2 (1974),
pp.127-183.
15. See, e.g., G. Barlow, 'Report on the Trade of
the Vizier's Country', Foreign Department Secret Consultations, 6 June 1787, 19, National Archives.
16. Judgement in the 'Amethi case' quoted,
Gazetteer of the Province of Oudh, ii (Allahabad 1877),
p.312.
17. See Fida Hussein Obeidi, 'Tarikh-i-Kara'; this
is an MS history in the process of compilation by Kara's
local historian who resides in 'Muhalla Bazaar'. I
must thank John Harrison for accompanying me on the
trip to Kara and asking many of the most pertinent
questions.
18. H.K. Naqvi, *Urban Centres and Industries in
Upper India, 1556-1803* (London 1968), pp.208, 211.
19. This is the 'Intekhab as Saiyaqnamah' of Anand
Ram, IOL Ethe 2125.
20. Gujarati traders were the dominant merchant
group on the Delhi-Murshidabad river route in the
seventeenth century.
21. H.R. Nevill (ed.), *District Gazetteers of the
United Provinces*, xxiii *Allahabad* (Allahabad 1911) art.
'Kara', pp.247-251; N.H. Siddiqui, *The Landlords of
Agra and Avadh* (Lucknow 1950), pp.40-45.
22. M.P. Gupta (ed.), *Arddha Katha (Banarsidas
Jain Krt.)* (Allahabad 1943), trans. abridged R.S.
Sharma, *Indica* (Bombay), 7, 1 (1970), p.60.
23. H.M. Elliot, *Memoirs on the History, Folk-lore
and Distribution of the Races of the North Western
Provinces of India* (ed. J. Beames), (London 1869), i,
p.365.
24. F.W. Porter, *Final Settlement Report of the
Allahabad District* (Allahabad 1878), pp.52-55.
25. *Allahabad Gazetteer*, p.168.
26. H. Conybeare, F. Fisher and J. Hewett (eds.),
*Statistical Descriptive and Historical Account of the
North-Western Provinces of India*, viii (Allahabad 1884)
part 2, p.52.
27. Interview with Justice K.B. Asthana, Allahabad,
November 1968.
28. Petition of Namdar Khan, Conquered and Ceded

Provinces Revenue, 2 September 1800, IOL, 95/11.

29. *DGUP, XX, Fatehpur*, (Allahabad 1911), pp.94, 108-109, 119.

30. H. Wellesley's 'Report on the Commerce of the Ceded Districts', 29 May 1802, Board's Collections 2803, 14-22, 41-43, 81-84, IOL.

31. Communciation from Prof. R. Barnett, University of Virginia, Charlottesville.

32. A. Deare, *A Tour through the Upper Provinces of Hindostan* (London 1823), p.90; in the eighteenth century by contrast, the weavers of Shahzadpur were often in a better position than the Sayyids of Kara, see F. Tieffenthaler in J. Bernouilli (ed.), *Description historique et geographique de l'Inde* (Berlin 1786), I, pp.233-234.

33. Acting Collr. Govt. Customs, Allahabad, to Board, 23 October 1816, Conquered and Ceded Provinces Customs (Revenue) Proceedings, 12 November 1816, IOR, 97/59.

34. *Gazetteer of the Province of Oudh*, II, (Allahabad 1877), pp.458-484.

35. 'Bulaki Das Debi Prasad', *Agrawal Jati ka Itihas* (Indore 1936), II, p.216, family history of Lala Prehlad Das, Chaukambha, Benares.

36. *Reports on the Revenue Settlements of the North Western Provinces of the Bengal Presidency, under Regulation IX, 1833* (Benares 1863), II, 1, p.441.

37. *Allahabad Gazetteer*, p.252.

38. F.W. Porter, *Settlement Report*, p.54.

39. Bernard Cohn's celebrated argument on what happened to the 'dispossessed' does not apply to a group with little *sir* cultivation in relation to the total of its revenue rights; yet there is good reason to feel that it was particularly to groups like the *ashraf* Muslim gentry that Holt Mackenzie's now over-quoted remarks were intended to apply.

40. 'Assessment of certain villages in Kara, Karari and Atharban', North-Western Provinces Revenue and Agriculture Department Proceedings, May 1880, 29-40; this report also exists in the Revenue Department of the Records of the Commissioner of Allahabad, see especially villages 'Lacchipur' and 'Jalalpur Tingain'.

41. Calculated from *Allahabad District Census Statistics, 1891*, (Census of India, North-Western Provinces, 1891), passim (Allahabad 1896).

42. Ibid.

43. The state schools fell off somewhat after the

foundation of the 'Rifah-i-am school' in 1883 (see
below).

44. *Annual Report on Public Instruction for the
NWP and Oudh (1883-4)* (Allahabad 1884), Primary School
reports, p.85.

45. For the background to rural political acitivity
in the area see C.A. Bayly, *The Local Roots of Indian
Politics* (Oxford 1975), pp.217-226.

46. *Leader* (Allahabad), 9 February 1919.

47. Interview with Hamid Sahib of Kara, Allahabad,
February 1974.

48. 'Tarikh-i-Kara', MSS compiled by Shri Fida
Hussein Obeidi, *rais* Kara; and interviews, December
1973.

49. United Provinces Native Newspaper Reports,
monthly 1900-1908, IOL; see, e.g., January 1904,
Hamdard, Kara.

50. Interview with Justice K.B. Asthana.

51. Chaudhri Mahadeo Prasad, *rais* of the Allahabad
Kayastha community, was a major Kara landholder. The
Kayasth *biradari* was closely connected with the Muslim
gentry; indeed several had converted to Islam, 'Tarikh-
i-Kara'.

52. *Indian People* (Allahabad), 11 April 1909.

53. 'Tarikh-i-Kara' passim; the careers of these
officers can be traced in the annual *History of Services of Gazetted Officers Employed under the Government of the North-Western Provinces and Oudh*, IOL; and
in the periodic analyses of the antecedents of district
staff in the establishment departments of Collectors
and Commissioner's offices (Dept.VI) and in e.g. North
Western Provinces General Department Proceedings, 29
June 1861, IOL, 216/6; here the list of Indian
officials in the Ajmere District includes service
people from a number of typical *qasbahs* including Kara,
Bilgram (Oudh) and Kurana, Muzaffarnargar Dist.

54. Letter of Qudrut Ali, Kara, *Tribune* (Lahore),
14 March 1888.

55. *Annual Report on Public Instruction*, NWP, 1884,
p.85.

56. 'Tarikh-i-Kara', passim.

57. Private Secretary, Lieutenant-Governor Bengal,
to Sayyid Mahomed Askari, 3 June 1901, documents in
possession of the Jamal Ahmed family, Kara.

58. Interviews, Muhalla Bazaar, Kara, December 1973.

59. B. Gour, Kali Prasad Kulbhaskar (Kayastha
Pathshala, Allahabad 1940), pp.1-11.

60. Interview with Shri Kampta Prasad Sehgal, Faridganj, December 1973.
61. Tandon Family papers, Ranimandi, Allahabad.
62. Interview with Shri G.P. Tandon, Shri B.P.
Tandon, Allahabad, 1971-4.
63. *District Census Statistics* (op.cit.).
64. *Independent* (Allahabad), 10, 17, 26 March 1920;
the Kara zamindars gave more to the Khilafat and Angora
Funds than any other residents of the city and district,
'Khilafat and Angora Funds', Home Political File 741,
National Archives.
65. Interview with Shri Fida Hussain Obeidi.
66. 'Members of the Central Committee of the Urdu
Defence Association, Allahabad, 9 December 1873'
Aligarh Archives (I am indebted for this reference to
Mrs Z. Jawad); *Hamdard* Kara, January 1904.
67. Bayly, *Local Roots*, pp.221-225.
68. Ibid.
69. In the nineteenth century religious syncretism
had dominated the *qasbah*. Hindus had resorted to the
famous *dargahs* of Muslim saints such as that of Khwaja
Karak at Kara. The double assault on these traditions
by agents of Hindu and Muslim orthodoxy is and the
sublation of religious revivalism into agrarian disputes is clearly a matter of great interest; work being
done by David Gilmartin, University of California,
Berkeley, and F.C.R. Robinson, London University, is
moving in this direction.
70. Paul Brass, *Religion, Language and Politics
in Northern India* (Cambridge 1974).
71. See, e.g. P. Abrams and E.A. Wrigley (eds.),
*Towns in Societies, Essays in Economic History and
Historical Sociology* (Cambridge 1978).

DELHI: INTERRUPTED GROWTH

Percival Spear

In considering Delhi as an Indian city, it may be
thought that it would be proper to begin with a dis-
course on the nature of South Asian cities in general.
But this I will leave to sociological historians or
should they be historical sociologists, or perhaps to
the new race of conurbationalogists, all of whom are
much better equipped for the task.
　　When one thinks of Delhi, I suppose the thought of
it as a capital or metropolis will keep breaking in.
Yet Delhi was probably a provincial and often an
obscure city for longer than it was a capital, and for
long stretches of time hardly breaks the surface of
the historical record. Perhaps it would be well to
begin by asking why this is so.
　　The factors governing the creation and growth of
cities are numerous and of course they have their
special relationships to the condition of South Asia
and, more particularly, of north India. The first of
these may be listed as the climatic. A favourable
climate may encourage development as an agricultural
market or commercial centre; a harsh one could limit
potential to strategic, religious or political compul-
sions. A city could be ruined by a change of climatic
conditions, a fate which overtook the Harappan cities
strung along the Saraswati when that river dried up.
It is thought that climatic conditions connected with a
shift of rain belts drastically affected Mayan cultural
centres and indeed th whole Mayan cultural complex.
The same was true of the rise and fall of Greenland in
the European Middle Ages. But we may accept that such
drastic changes are the exception rather than the rule.
Delhi at any rate escaped them. We have, so far as is
known, a typical north Indian climate with its alter-
nation of rains and dry spells, its sharp cold weather
and burning heat, its sun and its choking dust. Much
was possible on such a site, but what exactly it would
be depended on other factors than climate.
　　The next factor is that of geography, which, given
a reasonable climate can be a vital growth element. A
site in a corner, or at the end of a line, so to speak,
is limited in its possibilities. So is one in mount-
ainous or jungle country. Gorakhpur and Saran district

were examples of out-of-the-way places, while Rajasthan's cities of palaces were so sited that their
growth was limited. In the case of Delhi we have a
site well placed for communications, but not particularly so for defence. From it routes led to the
fertile Gangetic plain, to the Panjab in the north-west
and to central India in the south. The river Jamna was
more important for communication than defence. Until
the canal era of the nineteenth century it was navi-
gable as far as Delhi and was extensively used.[1] The
low stony hills to the west provided possibilities of
refuge (e.g. Suraj Kund) but only at the cost of a
water problem through distance from the Jamna. Geo-
graphically, one might say that the position was in
general favourable with some drawbacks.

   After climate come the human factors, and first of
these is connected with commerce and industry. It is
no use having rivers and roads along which to move
goods if you have no goods to move. A demand for
articles to manufacture with their raw materials, goods
to exchange over long or short distances are needed for
commerce to flow. Some artisans like weavers could
live in the country and dispose of their goods in the
city; agriculturalists growing crops like wheat, sugar
and indigo, need a centre to collect, distribute and
perhaps despatch their goods over long distances.
Salt, extracted from centres like the Sambhar lake near
Ajmir was a perennial bulk article which had to be
collected and distributed. And then there were luxury
articles from the Middle East and Central Asia, and
both early and later from Europe, passing from the
coast inland or from the north-western passes down the
Gangetic plain to the seats of wealth and power. Such
activities required a corps of mercantile managers to
arrange purchase, transfer and sale, and a group of
bankers to provide seasonal advances, loans for long
journeys and insurance. The actual transport was by
boat down the Jamna and Ganges - the cheapest and
quickest - or by bullock cart and pack-animal. The
Brinjaris, a mobile tribe whose profession was the
transport of goods, supplied the needs of armies as
well as of the civil population. Delhi had its share
of these activities, but never a dominant one. Its
accessibility to routes was shared by other sites like
Agra or Mathura or Saharanpur. A place like Mirat in
the Jamna-Ganges *doab* was better situated as a focus
for the production of that fertile region. There was

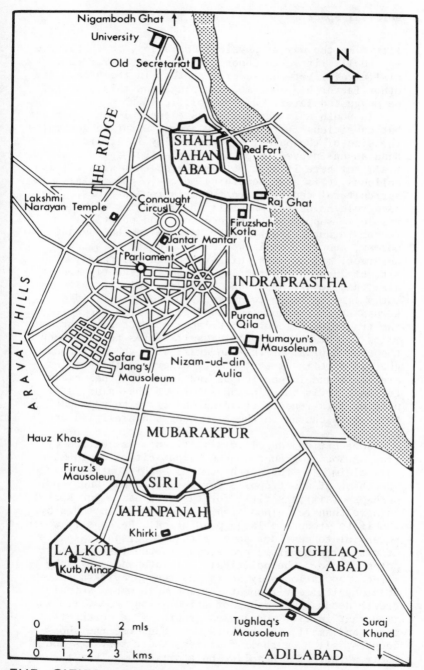

Nigambodh Ghat ↑
University
Old Secretariat

N

THE RIDGE

SHAH JAHAN ABAD
Red Fort

Lakshmi Narayan Temple
Connaught Circus
Raj Ghat
Firuzshah Kotla
Jantar Mantar
Parliament

INDRAPRASTHA

Purana Qila
Humayun's Mausoleum

Safar Jang's Mausoleum
Nizam-ud-din Aulia

ARAVALI HILLS

MUBARAKPUR

Hauz Khas
Firuz's Mausoleum
SIRI
JAHANPANAH
Khirki
LALKOT
Kutb Minar

TUGHLAQ-ABAD

0   1   2 mls
0   1   2   3 kms

Tughlaq's Mausoleum
Suraj Khund ↓
ADILABAD

THE CITIES OF DELHI

little in the way of physical obstacles, so that there
was really little to choose, on the grounds of commercial amenity between several centres in the area. Some
other factor had to come into play, and this, as will
be suggested later, was the political.

In South Asia the religious element is an important
but capricious factor in city growth. But in general
the size of the purely religious city is limited.
Banaras has proved to be both long-lived and substantial; but here it must be remembered that with all its
holiness it is also something more - a commercial and
agricultural centre where two main routes cross. The
same rule holds for Madurai; the magnetism of Minakshi's
temple is supplemented by economic and political
factors. But Brindaban near Mathura on the Jamna is
modest, peopled, as it would seem to the passing
observer, mainly with white-robed widows. Puri, the
site of Jagannath's temple, was until recently modest
also, and so are Nasik and Hardwar. Delhi itself has
but a limited title to holiness. The epic field of
Kurukshetra lies nearly a hundred miles to the north,
the traditional locale of Krishna at Mathura eighty
miles to the south. Delhi itself claims to have been
the epic capital of the Pandavas, with the Nigambodh
ghat as a relic of that time. Otherwise its temples
are small and inconspicuous and its only other claim
to sanctity is the flowing waters of the Jamna, still
used by milk-vendors crossing the river to top up
their milk churns in the twin causes of religion and
profit.

Some cities can claim significance as centres of
clan or social groups. Some Rajput cities could make
this claim. To the north-west of Delhi Rohtak is
something of a metropolis for the Jats; and Pune could
perhaps claim this title for the Marathas. But social
no more than religious significance tends in India by
itself to produce a large population. Perhaps it would
be useful to consider some of the demographic aspects
of city growth before proceeding to the last and most
potent factor, the political. Climate and geography
affect population only so far as they provide a suitable physical environment for a centre whose actual
growth needs other means of stimulation. Commerce is
important in city population growth. The merchants,
large and small, the brokers, the bankers, the shopkeepers, all have their families, their servants and
their workers for handling bulk articles. Then there

was the servicing of the city's needs itself which
might include a periodical religious surge at times of
pilgrimage and the needs of a court and its attendant
followers. The religious factor, as previously
mentioned, does not make for a populous city. *Pujaris*
do not multiply and pilgrims come and go. A social or
clan centre, like Rohtak, is a place to visit rather
than live in; it is not in itself a magnet for numbers
or wealth. Thus one is forced back to the general
rule of religion for producing large numbers periodic-
ally but temporarily, and on trade and commerce to
maintain a stable population and promote steady growth.

This survey brings us to the last factor in the
growth of Indian cities - the political. It is this
factor, which in a number of cases can be checked in
substance though not, except in recent times, in numer-
ical detail, which is mainly responsible for the
mercurial rise and subsidence of many Indian towns.
The reason for this is that a capital was not only the
residence for the raja or shah, but a centre for his
nobles and their followers and for the armed forces and
all their attendants. Every notable had many dependents as a matter of prestige, who in turn had their
servants and so on. Service (*khidmat*) was honourable
with the result that people would accept almost any
terms to have the satisfaction of being 'in service'.
The great man's retinue was the magnet which drew the
surplus manpower from the neighbouring villages to the
city. Then the army, both royal and chiefs's contingents, was prodigal of manpower. It was said that for
every active soldier there were ten dependent on him.
He needed his syce for his horse, his grass-cutter for
fodder, his personal servant for himself and a whole
train of others to provide his military and his
family's personal and physical needs.

This brings us to the question of service in the
modern sense. All these people had to be supplied with
food, clothing, military and civil goods. There was,
therefore, wherever a city became a political centre, a
billowing out of the service side of commerce and
industry. Goods as well as food must be imported to
supply this world of the Court. There must be large
imports paid for by the notables who in turn drew
their supplies from their *jagirs*. There must be
small-scale industries to make locally items in demand.
The size of the service sector naturally depended upon
the size of the court and of the state from which it

drew its sustenance. When the Delhi state was large,
as in the days of the Sultanate and the Mughal empire,
the numbers engaged in 'service' and servicing naturally soared; they fell precipitously if the Court
dwindled in resources or transferred elsewhere.[2] But
it is not to be thought that the 'hangers-on', whether
commercial or personal, sank into indigence in these
circumstances. Power was not so much dissolved as
spread; the returns from service of both kinds not so
much dissipated as redistributed. When Delhi's dimensions shrank after the 1756-61 troubles some of its
power and much of its wealth was transferred to Oudh,
to be eventually focussed again in Asaf-ud-daula's new
capital Lucknow. A little later the Panjab resources
which once flowed to Delhi found a new centre in Ranjit
Sing's Lahore. The cloud of court 'witnesses' was not
only large and sometimes vindictive, but moved like a
swarm of bees to those spots where the nectar of
rewards and influence beckoned.

If it be now agreed that Delhi had no special
endowment as a religious, economic or industrial centre,
but depended for fame and growth on political factors,
we have a clue to its vicissitudes in the long story of
its partly known history. There is no trace as yet, so
far as I know, of a Harappan or Indus valley occupation,
though the hillock of the Purana Qila might have
offered a tempting site. Delhi's metropolitan history,
so far as we know, begins with its identification with
Indraprastha, the capital of the Pandavas. The four
other recorded *pats* or inhabited places along the upper
Jamna all retain their names;[3] it would be difficult to
fit Indraprastha into any other contiguous site in view
of this fact. What were then the motives of the Pandavas in choosing this spot for their capital? One at
once sees the differing viewpoints between the invader
from the north-west and the organiser of an indigenous
power centre. The function of Indraprastha was to look
east, facing the Kuru power at Kanauj. The Jamna ford
at Delhi was more easily defensible than those to the
north because of the hilly country close to the west
bank. Forces could be collected to the south behind
the Jamna screen to fall upon a force crossing upstream
to the flat plains to the north. Perhaps that is why
the decisive battle of the Mahabharata was fought at
Kurukshetra, in the alluvial plain about a hundred
miles to the north of Delhi.

From this time we have a long gap in the Delhi

record both as a country town and as a metropolis.
There is little evidence, literary or archaeological,
for the continuous existence of the city and none for
its eminence. Only remains of the Gupta period in the
Purana Qila have so far been found. It is worth
asking why the one-time capital should have suffered
such prolonged oblivion. The answer, I suggest, is to
be found in the geopolitical facts of ancient Indian
life. The capital of an Indian state needs an agricultural hinterland with some commerce and industry to
sustain it. If it aspires to be an empire it needs
means of communication and trade routes as well, along
which armies and traders can move. Delhi was not well-
favoured in this respect; to the west lay the semi-arid
Mewati country leading on to Rajasthan; to the east it
stood on the edge of the fertile Jamna-Ganges *doab*. It
was a communication centre but no better than other
sites more favoured in other respects. So we find
the centres of Indian power tending to appear elsewhere.
The Mauryan empire, whose base was Bihar and Uttar
Pradesh, had Pataliputra for its capital, situated on
the arterial Ganges and roughly in the middle of its
domain. The Guptas had the same power base and the
same capital. Harsha, whose base was further east, had
Kanauj, which also served for various successor kingdoms down to Jai Chand in the twelfth century. Ujjain
served for Central India.

But what of the invaders? Between 200 B.C. and 200
A.D. there were a series of these. The Greeks from
Bactria only momentarily left the Panjab in their
great raid towards Pataliputra. The Saka and Pallava
invasions, it would seem were more in the nature of
folk migrations, which passed through Sind to Gujarat
and Western India. The Kushans had a large Indian
empire but throughout their rule they retained their
central Asian interests. In consequence Purushapura
(Peshawar) remained its logical centre. Delhi might
have been a subordinate provincial capital, but this
function, guessing from the remains found there, would
seem to have gone to Mathura. The Hun invasions were
destructive and confused and left no lasting state
behind.

It was men of the Turkish race and the Islamic
religion who brough Delhi back into history. Between
1000 and 1200 A.D. we have the rocky site of Suraj
Kund and the fortified city of the Qutab associated
with the Tomara and Chauhan Rajputs. The former,

though it lacked walls so far as one can see, would
seem to have been a hill refuge from marauders like
Mahmud of Ghazni, who in fact sacked the not very
distant Mathura.[4] It was notable for its temple to the
Surya (the sun) with its attached large tank-amphi-
theatre, and for its irrigation works which watered
crops to the west and provided water for the city.
There followed the Chauhan city of the Qutab, presumably built when the insecurity of Mahmud's time had
passed. It was more pretentious than Suraj and was
said to have had twenty-seven temples. But a circumam-
bulation shows it not to have been a great city of the
order of Pataliputra; rather a small state capital
under the Tomaras and a provincial centre under the
Chauhans. The temple remains used in the Quwwat-ul-
Islam do not suggest great size or opulence.

With Qutb-ud-din's Aibak's capture of Delhi begins
its real imperial age. It was not continuous, but
rather an intermittent process. The two hundred years
of the Sultanate left a local and then a medium stage
capital for a hundred and thirty years. Interrupted
growth continued under the Mughals in only whose
declining days was it continuously the capital. If
there was metropolitan instability there was also site
mobility. Both these facts pose questions and we may
consider the second of them first.

We have already noted that 'Hindu' Delhi occupied
three known sites, two several miles away from the
first of them. Under the Muslims the process continued, so that instead of the traditional seven cities
one can distinguish up to twelve sites, a little more
or less according to one's idea of what constitutes a
separate city.[5] One motive for siting was security.
This accounted for Suraj Kund, the Qutab and Tughluqabad. Another was dynastic pride, the desire to leave
a name behind; and this motive could integrate with the
first one. A third motive was that of health. In the
long sultry summer period cooling breezes were the
chief natural means of refreshment. The greatest heat
came from the heat-reflecting stony hills; the chief
relief breezes cooled or at least freshened by the
river Jamna. So the cities moved towards the river as
security increased; they had to stay on the west or
right bank of the river because on the higher ground
there was a safeguard against monsoon flooding. New
sites tended to be north of the older ones as being
more accessible to hill breezes. So we find Siri to

the north of the original Qutab city, then a move to
the river at Firuzabad, with a later move north again
to Shahjahanabad. At Shahjahanabad the nobles' garden
houses extended north again along the river bank. The
British 'civil lines' after 1800 were again to the
north of the Mughal walled city. New Delhi retreated
south and inland but only after an unsuccessful bid to
move north once more.[6] By then water pumped to the
ridge behind the new city could be used to fertilise
and freshen the area more effectively than Jamna water
or breezes.

But why did the new invaders fasten on Delhi as
their Indian capital and in general retain it through
their rule? They looked at India, of course, from a
different angle from that of the Indians themselves.
Coming from the north-west, they needed a bastion from
the east and south. They had a firm base in the Panjab,
which they had ruled for nearly two centuries. Through
it could move reinforcements, tribal, mercenary and
individual, from the hinterland of the Iranian plateau.
Originally, indeed, Delhi was a strong point, or fortified outpost in the expansion of the Ghorid empire.
But when the thrust to the east succeeded Delhi became
the natural centre of the Ghorid successor state of
Aibak and his Slave dynasty successors. There still
remains the question of why Delhi on the Jamna line,
and why not Agra or Mathura or Panipat? The answer
lies in Delhi's strategic advantages from the north-
western invader's point of view. The northern invader
swept across the Indus, along the corridor between the
Salt Range and the west Panjab, and then between the
Himalayas and the Rajasthan desert. The Jamna line
guarded access to this corridor. But it also gave
access to the Gangetic plain to the east, to central
and western India via Agra and Bhopal, to the Rajasthan strongholds via Jaipur and Ajmir. Sites further
north gave less access to the south and south-west;
sites further south were liable to be cut off from the
north. Delhi was both a springboard for further
advance and a link with the power base in the north-
west.

Time and circumstance modified these factors in
certain respects without negating the overall advantage of the site, and experience of a move helped to
confirm the choice. A big change occurred when the
Mongols of Chinghiz Khan and his successors cut off
the Iranian plateau to the north-west in the thirteenth

century from the Delhi Sultanate. It thus became a
self-contained Muslim kingdom dependent largely on its
own resources. It was a minority rule over a hostile
Hindu majority. It had not only to face disaffection
amongst Hindu chiefs down the Gangetic plain and to
the south, but also the hostility of the organised
Hindu bastion of Rajasthan. But for Hindu divisions,
connected not a little with clan jealousies, the
Sultanate's position would have been very precarious.
In this 'tight' situation it was natural for the Delhi
kings to look to the Panjab as their chief source of
strength. With two centuries of Muslim control it
contained a larger and more combative Muslim population than anywhere else within the Sultanate's borders.
Cut off from the central Asian homelands Turkish and
Afghan immigrants equally with Panjabi converts were
committed to the defence of the new realm as a matter
of self-preservation. With the Mongol surge to the
west, the Rajput fortress to the south and Hindu
discontent within, the Sultanate was at first a be-
leaguered armed camp of the Faithful. In this situation Delhi became more than ever a convenient site for
the capital. Its manpower base was within easy reach;
its less stable eastern half was under surveillance;
the marcher regions to the south and towards Rajasthan
could be patrolled and watched.

If it is accepted that there were good reasons why
a north Indian empire, drawing its strength from the
north-west, and exercising minority rule over an ideologically hostile and politically resentful majority,
should choose Delhi as its most convenient centre, it
still has to be explained why the Delhi regimes
suffered from an intermittent process of imperial
expansion and local contraction. The answer, I think,
is to be found partly in personal whims and partly in
changing circumstances. The former did not affect the
principle of power concentration along the line of the
Jamna, but only varied the actual site a few miles to
the south. The one big exception was the transfer of
the capital to Daulatabad by Muhammad Tughluq.[7] But it
was an exception which proved the rule. Muhammad soon
found that he could not control the north from the
Deccan and returned to Delhi wiser if no less wrong-
headed.

The other is more important, for it involved not so
much the transfer of the power centre as a hiatus of
power within the centre itself. It was not any

internal contradiction about the choice of capital as
such; it was rather a breakdown of the cohesive forces
which had concentrated on a political point of power in
the first place. India has notoriously been a place
where centrifugal forces were strong; experience
suggests that they were as strong in Muslim as in Hindu
areas, though of course, for different reasons. In the
Delhi Sultanate the Muslim cause was upheld mainly by
three different races - the Turks, the Afghans and the
Panjabi Muslims - and by two main Muslim religious
sects, the Sunni and the Shia. The empire was a confederation of military chiefs rather than a bureau-
cratically controlled realm. The system, inevitable
though it may have been in the conditions of the times,
encouraged ambition, disaffection and military
emeutes: so much depended on the energy and will-power
of the centre that a failure here risked the break-up
of the whole political edifice. The Sultanate survived
breakdowns at the end of the Slave and Khilji dynasties
by means of what were really military pronunciamentos
by military chiefs. At the end of the Tughluq dynasty
the hiatus was serious, for it was aggravated by the
devasting moral as well as political effect on Taimur's
invasion of 1398. Turkish power was broken up and
Afghan power failed to replace it. Instead three
centres emerged besides that of the Sayyids of Delhi
- the Panjab, the Sharqis of Jaunpur and the kingdom
of Bengal. For half a century Delhi was a local
capital, barely able to hold its own against Jaunpur.
Only when Daulat Khan Lodi of the Panjab seized it
(1451) and later overthrew Jaunpur (1476) could it be
described as an imperial centre again. And then it was
an empire without much power. For it was weakened by
the Afghan love of independence which made it more of
an informal confederation than a closely knit imperial
state. The way in which Babur was able to advance as
far as Panipat in 1525-26, with the aid of disaffected
nobles of the Panjab, is an illustration of this.
     From 1500 to 1750 we have a series of changes of
site partly for personal and partly for political
reasons. The vacuum of power was less than before;
and the movement of the power centre more frequent.
There was always a reason for the changes, but they
do not affect the overiding argument that Delhi was,
on the whole and in the long run, the best centre for
a north Indian empire. Sikandar Lodi moved his seat to
Agra, where it survives as Sikanderabad, better known

as the site of Akbar's tomb. Nevertheless he himself
was buried in Delhi.[8] Babur, after the battle of Panipat in 1526, posted to Agra as the seat of Lodi power.
It was his son Humayun who returned to Delhi, yielding
to a new dynast's urge to found his own imperial city.
Theis was several miles to the north of the old Qutab
complex, but south of Firuzabad, Firuz Shah Tughluq's
fourteenth century city. River breezes were secured,
however, by a curve of the river and the height of the
site. It was centred on the traditional site of Indraprastha which became the place citadel and is now known
as Purana Qila. Humayun's supplanter, Sher Shah in the
Afghan, completed the city so that when Humayun fell to
his death soon after his triumphant return in 1555, it
was Sher Shah's beautiful mosque which was close to him.

Akbar at first resided mostly at Agra; and his preference was confirmed by an unsuccessful attempt on his
life in 1564,[9] when on a visit to Delhi. It is at
least possible that the desire to found his own
imperial city, as well as the neighbourhood of his
preceptor Salim Shah Chishti, had something to do with
this preference. From this time Delhi and Agra were
regarded as twin imperial cities. The site was changed,
or perhaps duplicated, but the strategic axis of the
Jamna remained. There followed the inspired aberration
of Fatehpur Sikri. The later years of Akbar were spent,
partly in Lahore (whose fort he embellished) and partly
in travel. Residence in Lahore was kept up by his son
Jahangir until he moved in a tented city to the Deccan.
Shah Jahan moved back to Agra, where he replaced many
of Akbar's buildings with his own until in the mid-
forties he moved to his own new walled city, palace and
Jama Masjid of Shahjahanabad. Desire for a pro-
cessional way, which was difficult to achieve in Agra,
was said to be one reason for the change, but personal
and dynastic pride was certainly a motive also.[10]
Akbar had built Fatehpur; he would build a better and
grander city.

This first Delhi hiatus lasted for about eighty
years. One reason was the appearance of new strategic
factors. The Mughal Empire, unlike the Sultanate,
included the trans-Indus regions of Afghanistan and
Badakhshan. Threats from this quarter needed supervision nearer than Delhi. The sixteenth century saw
the rise of the Persian Safavid empire, a peer in
power and prestige to the Mughals themselves. Hence
the residence in Lahore of Akbar, Jahangir and

Aurangzeb. From the latter part of Jahangir's reign
Mughal ambitions in the Deccan gave a meaning to the
use of Agra. Shah Jahan was at Agra at the time of
his illness and the war of succession in 1658; Aurang-
zab was there when he received Sivaji in 1666.

A second reason for this gap was the migratory
habits of the Mughals themselves. The Turks of the
Sultanate had enough time in the Panjab during which to
forget their nomadic habits; Babur and his *begs* came
almost straight from the steppes and the wilds. Babur
spent most of his adult life wandering and fighting,
ever on the move, more familiar with tents than palaces.
These habits the Mughals brought with them and
expressed them in stone. Their palaces were petrified
tents; their *khanas* or halls were shamianas anchored
with sandstone and marble. They brought the art of
locomotive life to a perfection never known before.
Their camps were moving cities so organised that they
provided every luxury as well as necessities, could
move complete in a day if required or could stand
stationary for months or even years. Jahangir had one
of these city-camps when supervising his Deccan operations and it was here that Sir Thomas Roe carried on
his negotiations. Later Aurangzeb directed both his
assault on the Deccan kingdoms and his Maratha campaigns from city-camps. In fact the city-camp became
the Mughal solution of the problem of controlling the
Deccan as well as the north from a single centre.
Aurangzeb may have stayed in the Deccan too long; his
son Bahadur Shah spent his five-year reign constantly
on the move trying to settle a series of outstanding
problems in turn. His camp was perpetually mobile;
Bahadur came to rest in Lahore only to die.[11]

Delhi had its next imperial phase from 1712 to
1761. The emperors became static and a consequence
was the virtual succession of the Deccan under the
Nizam Asaf Jah in 1724. Once more Delhi was populous
and prosperous. Monuments were erected, gardens and
garden-houses laid out and built, the streets were
thronged and tensions were rife, as shown by the shoe-
sellers riot in 1738.[12] This imperial Delhi was
engulfed in the Maratha and Afghan marchings and
counter-marchings which culminated in the third battle
of Panipat. Thereafter Delhi was a provincial city
again. For a time under Najib-au-daula and then Shah
Alam it was the centre of a kingdom; for a few years
Mirza Najaf Khan's skill blew it up into a substantial

power. Then came the Maratha occupation (1785),
political extinction with the British in 1803, and
oblivion after the Mutiny and Revolt of 1857. This
hiatus lasted until the proclamation of Delhi as the
capital of British India in 1911.

The last and continuing phase of imperial Delhi
began inauspiciously with a bomb attack on Viceroy
Hardinge as he ceremonially entered the city in 1912;
with the quarrel of the two architects about the siting
of the imperial buildings; with the muddle about the
site of the city itself, which led to the foundation
stone being deposited some miles north of the old city
instead of to the south of it; and with the years of
World War One which reduced construction progress to a
trickle. The twenties were years of building, the
thirties those of first achievement. It was World War
Two which converted a steady flow of development into
a flood. Government buildings and demands escalated,
to be followed in the post-war years by a flow of
commerce, industry and finance. The city which during
most of the nineteenth century had 150,000 to 200,000
inhabitants, and by the outbreak of World War Two not
much more than half a million billowed out to two-and-
a-half millions soon after and to an estimated total
of four millions in 1971.[13]

I should maintain that the forces which have
governed the rise and decline of Delhi in the past
broadly continue to do so. Remove the political
capital from Delhi and it would still suffer a drastic
decline. The multiple economic and social agencies
which today attach themselves to the government would
go with it. Industries would remain, leaving a larger
city than in the nineteenth century, but still a much
reduced one. Such a possibility cannot be permanently
ruled out. The capital which was moved to Delhi to be
closer to the hinterland of India in a historic setting,
is now a near-frontier city whose historic traditions
no longer accord with current aspirations. Cost and
rival claims militate against any early change, but
historic forces have a habit of being persistent as
well as slow-working.

The sociologist can find much of interest in the
recent history of Delhi. Since the British occupation
in 1803 the population has received new elements. The
old service groups, manual and ministerial, the commercial and banking interests, have been reinforced and
variegated. In the nineteenth century before 1857

there was something of a balance between Hindu and
Muslim elements. The Kayasthas, Jains and Marwaris
were balanced by Muslim merchants and courtiers, while
both communities found a cultural focal point in the
Mughal court. Ghalib was flanked by Hindi, Urdu and
Persian poets. The *gardi* of 1857 upset this balance,
driving many *literati* to Lucknow and others to Hyderabad. But other elements came in, tempted by economic
and technical demand. Foremost were the Bengalis who
formed a professional elite until reinforced after
1911 by a wave of secretariat workers. The intellectual and social life of Delhi at this time was one of
tension between Kayastha and immigrant Bengali. After
World War One the Sikhs appeared, most prominently as
contractors but also as merchants and workers. Then
came the flood of post-World War Two migrations which
turned Delhi, according to old Delhiwallahs, into a
Panjabi city. The tome has not yet come to evaluate
the full effect of this drastic change.

Other aspects of modern Delhi accord with the
experience of other Indian cities and do not require
special treatment. The rise in population, the sucking
in of villagers from the surrounding countryside, the
proliferation of shanty-towns, are common to all
Indian urban connurbations. Here children as elsewhere
meet, not as Tagore saw them on the seashore of endless
worlds, but among piles of drain pipes waiting to be
laid and mounds of concrete blocks waiting to be
hoisted. Disease, poverty, squalor, death in the
streets were all part of the common Indian urban
experience, arising from general rather than unique
causes.

It may be thought that this study is lacking in
precise detail and illustrative examples, The answer
must be that over a period of nearly three thousand
years, which is the span of this study, a great deal of
such precise material is necessarily lacking. It is
only when we come to the Muslim period from 1192 A.D.
onwards that figures begin to be quoted and descriptions to be given. For scientific exactitude we have
to wait until well into the British period. However,
there are some illustrative clues, samples of which
may now be quoted. First, here are some figures
concerning the vicissitudes of Delhi's population.
Ibn Batuta,[14] the Moorish traveller, who lived in
Delhi from 1334 to 1342, in the time of Muhammad
Tughluq, described the Delhi of his day as 'vast and

magnificent', the largest city in the entire Muslim
Orient. Thevenot, about 1665, who relied much on the
first hand accounts of Bernier and Tavernier,
reported that Agra was populous when the Court resided;
but 'one will meet with no throng but when the Court
is there'.[15] Bernier from his own experience considered Delhi to be at least as populous as Paris in
the seventeenth century.[16] He and Thevenot both
analyse the city's components to give us an idea of the
population; Thevenot concludes firmly: 'When I say we
consider Delhi void of all those I have mentioned, and
of many more still, it will easily be believed, that
the Town is no great matter when the King is not there
... there hardly remains a sixth part in his absence.'[17]
There were the nobles with their large retinues and
their families, some 45,000 troops with their servants,
their own and the servants' families, the whole mercantile and manual worker establishment. If we allow
for the numerous children with deductions for
unattached men, we might get a total of about a
million. With Thevenot's dividend of six the figure
for Delhi when the Court was absent (c.166,000) would
not vary very much from the known population in the
first half of the nineteenth century.

Francois Bernier's report can be taken as firm
evidence for the size of Delhi in the early years of
Aurangzeb's reign. The city must have dwindled in
size with his departure for the Deccan, but burgeoned
again with the return of the Court after 1712. From
that time there is much literary evidence for its
populousness until about 1760. Though we may discount
Von Orlich's report of two million souls under Aurangzeb,[18] his estimate of half a million in 1740 gets
support from the report of Thomas Fortescue in 1820,
which speaks of 'persons now living who remember the
times when the environs of the city boasted fifty
bazars and thirty-six *mandis* outside the walls'.[19]
After 1760 the decline is testified by a number of
writers including William Francklin,[20] who had personal
knowledge, and Thomas Twining,[21] who visited Delhi in
1794.

It is after the British occupation that we begin to
get estimates based on detailed investigation. The
Court was now too small to attract large retinues; the
throning troops and bustling *mansabdars*' trains had
vanished; only a few visiting local gentry and the
faded pomps of a diminished Court were left. Delhi

was now essentially a provincial town, a medium-sized
commercial centre, and so it remained until 1912. But
unlike previous centuries, we have figures to prove and
measure it. In 1820 an estimate of 150,000 to 200,000,
based upon reports of Malcolm Seton and Charles Metcalfe, is reported by William Hamilton.[22] This was
confirmed by the rough-and-ready estimate of William
Fraser in 1820-23.[23] A.A. Roberts, City magistrate, in
1847 gave a total for the City, the suburbs and the
Palace of about 165,000.[24] There was a decline after
the Mutiny, but the 1881 census figure was 173,000.[25]
Thereafter there was a steady rise to the 1911 census
figure of 232,000.[26] For those who would like to
examine the composition of the provincial city by
community and occupation, there is a detailed description in the *Report on a Census in the Punjab*, published
in Lahore in 1870. Further light on the workings of
a provincial city will be found in Thomas Fortescue's
and others' reports on the administration of Delhi and
its Territory around 1820.[27]

The case set out in this paper is that there is
nothing mystical about Delhi as the capital city of
India. In essence it was a city of moderate dimensions
and pretensions, blown up from time to time by the
descent of the Court with its nobles and its troops,
its merchants and workers. The reasons for these
descents were strategical and political so that
Delhi's fortunes depended on the cogency of these
considerations as applying to the circumstances of the
day. The Pandavas needed a stronghold from which to
face the Kurus; the Turks in the thirteenth century
needed a bastion which the Panjab could sustain and
from which the Gangetic plain could be dominated. The
Mughals needed somewhere about equidistant from Kabul
and Badakhshan in the north and the Bay of Bengal in
the south-east, a convenient watchtower for Rajasthan
and a gateway to the Deccan. As circumstances varied
in one of these regions the capital shuttled between
Agra and Delhi or took wings with its tents to a camp
in the Deccan. At other times Delhi was a provincial
city as the British found it and thereafter maintained
it until 1912. Its last incarnation as a capital city
had political motives behind it which have now (since
1947) ceased to operate. In consequence Delhi is now
an artificial capital in a sense it has never been
before. A near frontier city it continues - and grows
- partly for reasons of prestige, partly for fear of

Percival Spear

the expense of removal, partly for lack of consensus on
an alternative site, and partly by the dead weight of
habit. These considerations are mainly negative; the
city's continuance as a capital therefore depend on the
lack of a strong case and will for another site. Such
cases often arise in times of crisis, after being
perhaps dormant for many years. It is then, with no
positive case for continuance, that we may find that
the glory of Delhi will depart almost as suddenly as it
was thrust upon her in 1912. 'Delhi dur ast', once
from a heavy-handed emperor, but not from the heart of
India itself. Can a political nerve centre, so close
to the political skin of the state and so far from its
sustaining social heart, be considered in the long run
either viable or permanent?

Spear, 'Delhi: Interrupted Growth'

1. *Punjab Govt. Records: Delhi Residency & Agency, 1806-57* (Lahore 1911), p.184-185. T. Fortescue's Report.
2. A good example of the fate of a ci-devant capital not specially endowed for commerce is to be found in Jaunpur (U.P.). As the capital of the Sharqi dynasty in the fifteenth century it was said to be the most populous city in northern India. When I visited it in about 1930 it was just a charming country town, still adorned by surviving stately Sharqi monuments.
3. They are Panipat, Sonepat, Baghpat and Tilpat.
4. 1018-19 A.D.
5. Known sites of Delhi cities are Indraprastha, Suraj Kund, the Qutab, Kilikhri, Siri, Tughluqabad, Jahanpannah, Firozabad, Khizrabad, Mubarakabad, Purana Qila (Humayun's, Sher Shah's cities), Shahjahanabad, New Delhi.
6. The foundation stone was actually laid at the 1911 Durbar ground. See Lord Hardinge of Penshurst, *My Indian Years*, (London 1948).
7. In 1327. *Oxford History of India*, 3rd Edition (London 1958), p.250f.
8. See *List of Muhammadan & Hindu Monuments, Delhi Province* (Calcutta 1919), vol. ii, p.37f.
9. *Cambridge History of India*, vol. v (Cambridge 1937), pp.86-87.
10. See *List of ... Monuments*, 1916, vol. i, p.1f.
11. See W. Irvine, *The Later Mughals* (Calcutta 1922), vol. i, pp.1-157.
12. Ibid., vol. ii, pp.257-263.
13. Census of 1971, *Whitaker's Almanack, 1976*, p.744.
14. H.A.R. Gibb (ed.), *Selections from the Travels of Ibn Batuta* (London 1929), pp.194-196.
15. S.N. Sen (ed.), *Indian Travels of Thevenot & Careri* (New Delhi 1949), p.49.
16. F. Bernier, *Travels in the Mogul Empire, 1656-68* (London 1934), pp.281-283.
17. S.N. Sen, op.cit., p.60f.
18. L. von Orlich, *Travels in India* (2 vols., London 1845), vol. ii, p.4.
19. *Punjab Govt. Records*, p.169, para. 201.
20. W. Francklin, *The Reign of Shah Aulum* (London

1798), pp.199-215.

21. T. Twining, *India a Hundred Years Ago* (London 1894).

22. W. Hamilton, *Description of Hindustan* (2 vols., London 1820), vol. i, p.421f.

23. Judicial Letter from Bengal, 14 February 1832, para. 4.

24. *Selections from Correspondence, North-Western Provinces*, vol. i, p.13.

25. *Delhi Gazetteer*, 1883-4, p.150.

26. Ibid., 1912, p.49.

27. *Punjab Govt. Records,* chapters V, VI, VII.

MURSHIDABAD IN THE EIGHTEENTH CENTURY

K.M. Mohsin

Murshidabad borders on the Cossimbuzar river, and
is famous for nothing more than being at present
the metropolis of the Kingdom of Bengal, and the
usual residence of the Nabob. It is near five
miles in length, and half as many broad; like most
large cities of Indostan, the houses (or with more
propriety the huts) are low and miserable, and the
streets narrow and dirty. The houses of the principal people indeed are made of brick (the common
ones of mud and straw only), but in their structure
is neither consulted design, ornament, nor indeed
convenience, except in one respect, that they are
extremely cool, being open on every side to the
wind ... mosques and pagodas compose the chief
public buildings, but there are none of considerable note, even the palace of the Nabobs has
nothing uncommon in it either of beauty or magnifi-
cence.

> Major Caillaud in 1759.[1]

In speaking of the city of Murshidabad it is not to
be understood that it comprehends a town regularly
planned consisting of good brick houses and over
which a proper and immediate superintending authority can be exercised by the magistrate. On the
contrary Murshidabad is of all places as unlike a
great city as possibly can be. It is composed of
numerous villages crowded together extending nearly
ten miles along the banks of the Bhagirathi and the
greater part of it interspersed by a thick heavy
jungle.

> W. Lock, City judge and
> magistrate, in 1814.[2]

There are no defined limits to it as a city, nor is
there any part known specially by that name; it
appears to be a name given to an indiscriminate
mass of temples, mosques, handsome pucca houses,
gardens, walled enclosures, huts, hovels and
tangled jungle containing the ruins of many

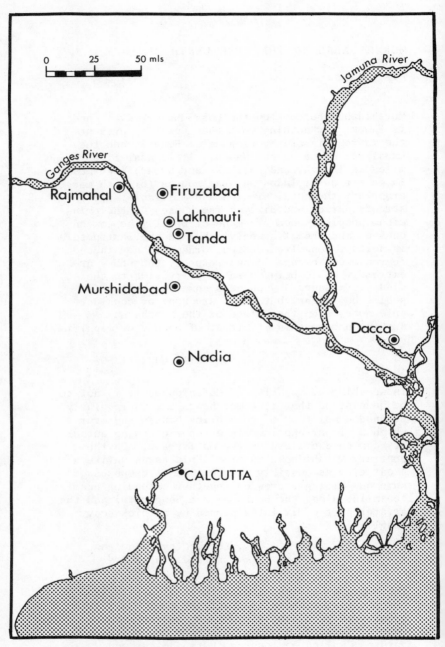

THE CAPITALS OF BENGAL

edifices that have sprung up and decayed, around
the residences of the former and present Nawab of
Murshidabad.

Captain J.E. Gastrell in
1860.[3]

This paper is an attempt to examine the questions
arising from the quotations - what were the functions
of the city of Murshidabad, was it purely an administra
tive city as Caillaud, Lock and Gastrell see it, what
were its spatial characteristics in relation to its
functions and location and finally what were the causes
of its rapid decline?

In order to find an answer to these questions it is
necessary to trace the growth and development of Murshidabad and examine its importance as the capital city
in the eighteenth century.

One of the main characteristics of the pre-modern
Bengal city was its instability. The towns flourished
on the banks of the rivers and owing to the frequent
changes of the courses of rivers - an important geographical feature in Bengal - few towns could take
permanent root. Moreover, owing to the non-availability of lime and stone in the region and also to the
lesser durability of the mud and brick structures
caused by the steady monsoon, permanent buildings of
brick and stone were hardly feasible. The dwellings
were therefore generally made of bamboo, thatch and
mud.[4] The temporary nature of the cities and towns of
Bengal is also reflected in the frequent changes of its
capital. At the time of the Muslim conquest of Bengal
in the early thirteenth century Nadia was the seat of
administration; the Muslim rulers moved it to Gaur
(Lakhnauti). Gaur then developed along the same line
as other cities in the Sultanate, until in the middle
of the fourteenth century Haji Ilyas transferred the
capital to Pandua, renaming it Firuzabad. About a
century later Pandua was abandoned in favour of Gaur.
The Mughals established their capital at Tanda, four
miles west of the older site of Gaur, the situation of
Tanda upon the river Ganges affording her greater
trading facility, from Orissa down to Chittagong.
Apart from this there were also military considerations
for the choice of Tanda, as during the early stages of
Mughal rule in Bengal it was necessary to maintain a
regular flow of supplies and troops from North India in

order to suppress the rebellious Afghan chiefs and
Hindu zamindars.[5] Towards the close of the sixteenth
century Raja Man Singh decided to move to Rajmahal a
few miles up the Ganges from Tanda. The primary reason
for this transfer was that Tanda had become a very
unhealthy place and that Rajmahal had better defences
because of its command of the sea. In 1608
however the new Subahdar decided to move to Jahangir-
nagar (Dacca) as he considered it better situated for
his operations against the Maghs, the Portuguese and
the independent-minded Pathan Chieftains of Eastern
Bengal. Finally in 1704 Murshid Quli Khan, the Diwan
of Bengal, removed the seat of the Diwani administration from Dacca to Murshidabad. Thus in the course of
about five hundred years from 1202 onwards the capital
of Bengal was transferred several times. Hardly any
of the places selected enjoyed the status of a capital
city for more than a century. Murshidabad remained
the capital of the province for about seventy years -
but these years also were not a period of undisturbed
peace and tranquillity for the city to develop and take
root.

The history of Murshidabad city becomes clear from
the early years of the eighteenth century when Murshid
Quli Khan moved from Dacca to Murshidabad; but its
origin is uncertain. According to Ghulam Hussain,
author of the *Riyaz-us-Salatin*, a merchant named Makhsus Khan first improved the present site of Murshidabad.[6] A Makhsus Khan had been mentioned in the *Ain-i-
Akbari* as a nobleman who served in Bengal and Bihar.
during the last decades of the sixteenth century. He
was probably the brother of Said Khan, Governor of
Bengal (1587-95) during the reign of Akbar. He built
a rest house and surrounded it with shops and the place
was called after him Makhsusabad or Makhsudabad.[7]
During the seventeenth century this place became well
known for silk and silk textiles. As early as 1621
English agents reported that huge quantities of silk
could be obtained there. It continued to grow in
importance during the second half of the century and
eventually became a Mughal administrative station.
During the 1660s Murshidabad had become a *Pargana*
headquarters and its officers had jurisdiction over
the European factories at Qasimbazar. The English
agents Streynsham Master and William Hedges mention it
as the seat of a local officer who administered the
area.[8]

Murshidabad

Murshidabad was sitated in the centre of the important places of the *subah*[9] and on the main line of
communication between the upper Ganges valley and the
Bay of Bengal. It also commanded the settlements of
the European companies along the banks of the Bhagirathi
and Hughli rivers.

The decision to move from Dacca was taken after the
governor of Bengal, Prince Azim-ud-din had made an
unsuccessful attempt to kill Murshid Quli Khan, though
apart from personal reasons there were also administrative, political and commercial considerations.
Dacca had lost its strategic importance as a base of
operations against the Maghs and Portuguese, and the
military activities of the European traders may also
have influenced Murshid Quli Khan's decision.[10] He
therefore moved from Dacca with all his revenue
officials and some of the wealthy merchants and
bankers. After his arrival at Makhsudabad he improved
the town, raised public offices and other government
establishments and changed its name to Murshidabad.
The city flourished during his time and became the
centre of political, economic and cultural life under
the Nawabs of Bengal for more than half a century.

In becoming the administrative headquarters of the
province it did not cease to be a commercial centre.
By the beginning of the eighteenth century its importance as the centre of the Bengal silk trade was
already established and the European Companies (the
English, the French and the Dutch) had their factories
at Qasimbazar, Saidabad and Kalkapur respectively - all
within the administrative jurisdiction of the city.
The commercial activities of the various merchants
fostered the steady growth of trade in the city. There
was a large market for foodstuffs and ordinary
consumer goods provided by the Court, the nobles and
the large number of people employed in the administration and by the armed forces maintained at the capital.
There was also a corresponding market for luxury goods.
The demand for ivory work, jewellery and brasswork was
considerable among the nobles and other wealthy people
who crowded the capital city. The establishment of the
Panchotra (Government Custom House) at Murshidabad
greatly added to the importance of the city as a
commercial centre.[11]

The presence of the court, of the army, of artisans
and of merchants, both European and Asian, greatly
increased the wealth of Murshidabad and owing to its

73

administrative and commercial activities financial
houses established their head offices there.

Banking houses, especially the house of Jagatseth
performed the most important transactions for the
government of Bengal. The zamindars paid their
revenue through them and again the Nawab remitted the
annual payment to Delhi through this house. They were
the mint officers and the purchasers of much of the
foreign bullion imported into Bengal.

The Murshidabad mint soon became the largest in
Bengal and the duties collected amounted to three lakhs
of rupees at two percent upon the value of the money
coined.[12]

The administrative requirements and the extension
of government activities and commerce naturally led to
the expansion of the city. The golden period of the
city started, as we have seen from the time of Murshid
Quli Khan and it continued for about three or four
decades. An important feature of this period was the
independence of the administration of Bengal in the
hands of the Nawabs. Murshid Quli Khan not only
secured peace, he also left an efficient administrative
machinery and an established capital for his successor.
He raised the palace of forty pillars (*Chihil Satun*),
built a mosque and *Katra* (a hostel for travelling
merchants) and maintained a large number of readers of
the Quran in the mosque. The Katra has been described
by Hodges as a grand seminary of Muslim learning,[13]
Close to it was the *Top Khana*, the arsenal of the
Nawab, which formed the eastern gateway of the city.
His successor Shuja-ud-din was a great builder. He
considered the buildings constructed by his predecessor
inadequate for state purposes and raised some magnificent buildings at the city - a palace, an arsenal, a
high gateway, a *Diwan Khana* (revenue court), a public
audience hall, a private chamber and a court of
exchequer (Khalsa). He also completed a mosque,
beautifully decorated in an extensive compound with a
large reservoir of water, running canals, artificial
springs, flowerbeds and fruit trees and named it
Farrahbagh (the Garden of Joy).[14]

An idea of the extent of the city may be obtained
from the accounts of the travellers who visited the
city in the eighteenth century from the records of the
East India Company. Most contemporary accounts suggest
that the city extended five miles in length and two and
a half miles in breadth on both sides of the river.

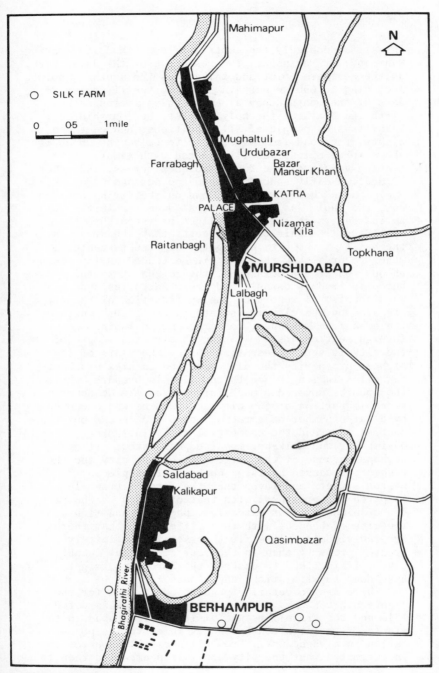

MURSHIDABAD

This is undoubtedly the central area of the city, taking Mahimapur or Mahinagar, the residence of the Jagat Seth, as the northern point and Lalbagh as the southern point. According to Ghulam Hussain, 'during the first twelve days of the month Rubby al Awal, which included the birth and death of the holy Prophet, he [Murshid Quli Khan] feasted people of all conditions: and on those nights, the road from Maheenagar to Lalbough, which is above three miles, was illuminated with lamps, representing verses of the Koran, mosques, trees, and other figures. Nearly a hundred thousand persons were employed on these occasions; and on the firing of a gun, the whole was illuminated at once, exhibiting, in an instant, such a sheet of light as astonished the beholders.'[15] This event suggests that the area was the heart of the city during the eighteenth century. Other records show that the city extended as far south as Qasimbazar and Berhampur, the region where the European traders established their factories and settlements. A report on the jurisdiction of the city prepared by the city magistrate in the 1780s includes the area from Mahinagar to Berhampur including the foreign settlements.[16] Taking this as the length of the city it seems clear that during the years of its highest prosperity the city occupied an area of about ten miles in length and three miles in breadth, while the suburbs covered a much larger area.[17] No doubt a sizeable portion of the city and suburbs was occupied by a large number of gardens, ponds and lakes, but the central part and the commercial sites including Qasimbazar and Kalkapur remained congested. It was perhaps because of the large area of the city and the congestion caused by large numbers of people in narrow streets and lanes that the foreign travellers compared its greatness with that of London. 'The city of Murshidabad is as extensive, populous and rich as the city of London, with this difference, that there are individuals in the first possessing infinitely greater property than in the last city. The inhabitants, if inclined to destroy the Europeans, might have done so with sticks and stones.'[18]

There are no detailed population figures for the eighteenth century. The earliest reference is dated 1815 and the travellers who visited Murshidabad in the middle of the eighteenth century refer to its population in a vague way. From all available sources it is estimated that the city population amounted then to

about two lakhs. (During this time the population of
Dacca was also estimated at two lakhs.) The official
reports of the late eighteenth century suggest that the
population of the city was steadily declining in this
period. There is no doubt that during the 1750s
Murshidabad was the most populous city in Bengal.
According to Karim the Mughal establishment in Bengal
during the seventeenth century would be about one lakh
including soldiers, officers and servants of all ranks.[19]
From the beginning of the eighteenth century the
government establishment must have grown in size and
importance.[20] At that time the city was also encircled
by trade centres and commercial ports; consequently a
large number of people settled in and around these
places. Considering the provincial establishments,
local residents, servicemen and numerous immigrants who
crowded the city for trade and jobs during the middle
of the eighteenth century, which is regarded as the
most glorious period of Murshidabad, the city population
may be estimated at six to seven lakhs in the 1750s.

The famine of 1769-70 reduced the population by
almost half. The removal of the capital to Calcutta
inflicted a further blow in 1772. Since there is no
evidence for any counter increase in the population it
must be assumed that by the end of the century, when
the process of decline of the city was already complete,
the number must have sunk to about two lakhs. No
accurate statistics of population are available before
1829 when the city magistrate reported that the population of the city amounted to 146,176. According to
Adam's report the figure in 1837 stood at 124,804 -
this shows a decrease of about fifteen percent in eight
years. According to the census of 1872 the number then
was only 46,172.[21]

We have no statistics relating to government
establishments nor to any section of the city population from which to assess its composition. It is
however possible to form an idea of the household of the
Nawab and the various grades of officials in the
service of the English East India Company at Murshidabad
after it had assumed the administration. The household
was composed of the members of the Nawab's family,
officials and staff including servants, household
troops, dependants and pensioners. The statement of
Nizamat accounts prepared in 1773 gives the number of
officers and servants of each department of the household from the steward down to umbrella bearers. It

appears that the household consisted of over ten thous-
and people dependent on the Nawab.[22] Under pressure
from Calcutta the number of persons employed in the
household was reduced by almost half.[23] Of the size of
the household of the Nawabs in the days of their independence no details survive, but it can be safely said
that the number of people under the household must have
been much greater than existed in 1773 when the Nawab's
power had declined and the capital had been removed to
Calcutta. It is not possible to ascertain the number of
people employed in the various departments of government
under the Nawabs, but it is recorded that many hundreds
were found superfluous and were omitted from the East
India Company's government structure.[24]

Apart from government departments, the city, as the
capital, became the centre of many other establishments:
those, for example, of the *Kotwal* or the city police
chief; the *Qanungo* in charge of land records and the
Muhtasib or superintendent of the market. It was also
cutomary for the Mughal officials to engage and
support a host of dependants, slaves and servants.
Ahmad Ali Khan, the Daroga of the *Diwan Khana* from the
time of Mir Jafar, for example, left behind him a family
and body of dependents of more than two hundred people
including about 125 slaves and other servants.[25] Among
the leading Muslims there was also some patronage of
culture in the employment of Imams, readers of the
Quran, teachers, musicians and men of letters.[26] Some
also set up madrasa and poor houses to feed the lame,
the blind and the old.[27]

One of the most important contributions to the
growth of the city was made by the landed and commercial
interests. The Zamindars used to maintain in the
capital an establishment of *naibs*, *wakils*, messengers,
peons and other servants required for their purposes;
so did the big merchants and traders. All the foreign
companies had separate factories and besides their own
officials and servants, hundreds were employed as
agents, brokers and workers. The city served as a
manufacturing centre, a market place and as an entrepot. It received goods from the interior and for-
warded them to various places both in and outside
Bengal. The Registers at the Custom House show the
volume of trade handled by the city port. The annual
average custom duties collected at Murshidabad on raw
silk and textiles from 1749 to 1769 amounted to over
two and a half lakhs. This includes only the trade

of those Indian merchants who paid duties. Besides
this there was also a considerable trade in these
articles by the Jagat Seths and others who hardly paid
any duty to the Nawabs.[28] Apart from silk and piece
goods there is a record of the export of copper vessels,
brassware, and ivory work to neighbouring districts and
to the West towards Allahabad, Delhi and Multan. The
main source for the provision of the city was its port
which handled food not only for the human population
but also for thousands of horses and elephants. The
city obtained its food grains from the surrounding
regions. The main items of the import trade consisted
of food grains, salt, spices, betelnut, cotton thread,
iron and various articles of foreign origin. These
were consumed in the city and also distributed to the
countryside through the *bazaars* and *ganjes* around the
city.

As long as it was the capital, a large number of
merchants and bankers along with their numerous agents
settled in the city. Some of these merchants and
bankers owned immense wealth, commanded influence at
the Court and had a great control over the finances of
the country. There were other businessmen who employed
their own moneychangers, brokers, account keepers and
other servants. The bulk of these merchants and
businessmen generally lived in the areas called Mahajan-
tola and Mughaltola, the principal wholesale business
centres of the city. The growth of the town made it
necessary for the artisans, manufacturers and other
professional people to settle there. As the city
covered a wide range of administrative, industrial and
trading activities the great bulk of the city population were occupied in crafts and service industries,
and most of them lived in separate quarters. Some
such quarters are known to us, for example, Jahurtali
(jeweller's ward), Kumarpur (potters' ward), Gowkhana
(milkmen's ward), Katgola (timber market), Chinitola
(the sugar ward), Lakriganj (firewood market), Garowan-
tola (area for the ox carts, and push carts) and
Bakrigali (Kaffle Lane), being called after the names
of the commodities in which they mainly traded. The
main bazar known as the Chauk occupied a central area
of the city. There were several *ganjes* in and around
the city besides places where daily markets were held.
Some of them by their names recall their founders
while others bear the names of those to whom they were
farmed out.

Certain aspects of town planning were not altogether absent in pre-modern times, though not on a
large and well organised scale. Some pattern seems to
have been followed in the location of palaces, forts,
public buildings, mosques, temples, tanks, gardens,
markets and the professional areas of the city. We
have on record the plan on which Farrukabad was built
in 1714 by Nawab Ahmad Khan Bangash.[29] Murshidabad
was not protected by walls, indeed, the only traces of
defence could be found in the Katrajhil which served as
a natural defence during the time of Murshid Quli Khan
and the Maratha rampart constructed during the 1740s
to prevent repeated Maratha raids into the city. The
places known as *baghs* and *baghichas* were not only
pleasure gardens - some of them were also fruit
gardens. There is no doubt that the government
officials and nobles built their houses either at convenient sites in the city or by the river. This perhaps explains the length of the city along the river in
proportion to its width.[30] The main Chauk of the city
seems to have been a well planned undertaking: from the
centre there ran a main street which was again inter-
sected at right angles by other small streets - these
were meant for shopkeepers and traders. There were
also sewers to clear off the water from the area.[31]
Though it is difficult to locate the respective wards
for the weavers, ivory carvers, papermakers, brass-
workers and others it is more than likely that Murshidabad had some craftwise arrangement as was common in
Dacca and in Upper India cities. We have already seen
some instances of separate wards exclusively marked out
for one set of people.

The numerous *ganjes*, *bazaars* and *ghats* not only
suggest that all parts of the city were well furnished
with daily requirements but also that they had a
regular flow of supplies from their extensive hinterland. The water supply to the city, too, was adequate.
The Bagirathi river assured an abundant supply of
water, as did the canals, *jhils* and tanks found in
abundance in the city. Some of the *jhils*, for example,
Kalkapur and Basantpur, were connected with the river
and were well supplied with water all the year round.

We have seen that Murshidabad rose from a small
market town to the position of the headquarters of the
province and by the mid-eighteenth century it was the
most prosperous and populous city in Bengal. However,
in the second half of the century it lost its glory

and importance more rapidly than it had acquired them. There were several reasons for this decline.

After the battle of Plassey and still more after the acquisition of the Diwani in 1765, the East India Company was able to apply administrative pressures in support of its commercial activities. As a result the normal pattern of trade was distorted by the exercise of political power. Apart from the Company's policy the most important cause which destroyed the commercial city was the effect of the great famine of 1769-70.[32] A most destructive calamity over nearly all Bengal, the famine inflicted on Murshidabad the greatest mortality of inhabitants and destruction of its manufactures. Contemporary accounts indicate that in the areas most affected by the famine more than one-third of the population died. The Resident at the Darbar reported to Calcutta during the famine: 'The scene of misery that intervened, and still continues, shocks humanity too much to bear description. Certain it is, that in several parts the living have fed on the dead; and the number that has perished in those provinces which have suffered most is calculated to have been within these few months as six is to sixteen of the whole inhabitants.'[33] He calculated at the worst of the famine in Murshidabad city alone five hundred were dying every day. Charles Grant described the horrors in the city in graphic terms: 'In the capital ... it became necessary to keep a set of persons constantly employed in removing the dead bodies from the streets and roads and these unfortunates were placed in hundreds on rafts and floated down the river. At length the persons employed in these offices died also ... and for a time dogs, jackals and vultures were the only scavengers .... There were persons who fed on forbidden and abhored animals, nay, the child on its dead parents, the mother on her child.'[34]

The amount of depopulation after a year of mortality was really frightful. Many who had escaped death by starvation were taken away by disease which occurred simultaneously, Nawab Saif-ud-daula being among the victims.[35]

Moreover, those who survived were incapable of industry for a considerable time. From government enquiries it could be seen that the silk manufacture of Murshidabad declined after the famine as the weavers, industrial artisans and labourers died in great numbers. The Naib Diwan Muhammad Reza Khan reported that the silk industry could never be revived on its former scale.[36]

The dislocation of economic life had a serious effect on law and order. Many hungry people took to theft and robbery during and after the famine and lawlessness increased on a disproportionate scale with the growing unemployment throughout the northern districts of Bengal.[37] Murshidabad itself even two years after the famine gave the impression of a deserted city and had no proper defence against its consequences. This did not escape the notice of the members of the Committee of Circuit who visited Murshidabad in the middle of 1772 and it greatly influenced their decision for a move of the treasury to Calcutta: 'In enumerating the defects of the present system we omitted to mention the insecurity of the public treasure, and the public records and plunder at discretion before any force could be collected to repel them ... the town of Calcutta is not only sheltered against such danger but the fort offers a most complete security both for public and private property under all circumstances.'[38]

The main object of the Company was to bring the administration under the direct control of the Company's servants. Warren Hastings' policy of centralisation in Calcutta therefore destroyed the political city and also what remained of the financial city of Murshidabad. The transfer of the *Diwani* offices and the *Khalsa* to Calcutta in 1772 was a blow to the position of Murshidabad as the chief city of the province. Not only the *Khalsa* but also the two supreme Courts of Civil and Criminal Justice were transferred to Calcutta. Only the offices of the *Qazi*, the *Kotwal*, the *Qanungo* and the *Muhtasibs* remained in the city for some time.[39] Warren Hastings wrote: 'By these arrangements the whole power and government of the province will centre in Calcutta which may now be considered as the capital of Bengal'.[40]

Murshidabad continued to be the residence of the Nawab, and the seat of the Company's factory, a Custom House, an English resident and of *Nizamat* and *Faujdari Adalats*. But the shifting of the revenue establishment with all its branches and staff dealt a blow not only to the dignity but also to the economic life of the city. The Committee of Circuit rightly commented, after the move to Calcutta: 'The numerous officers and retainers of the Khalsa and of the new Courts of judicature, with all their families, domestics and

dependants will increase the demand for the necessities and conveniences of life, and of course require
a number of tradesmen, artisans. Thus a vast influx of
people will be drawn to Calcutta and with it a great
increase of wealth. The consequence of the Presidency
will be much improved with its population, as it will
lessen that of Murshidabad, which will no longer remain
the capital of the province, having nothing to support
it but the presence of the Nawab, and a few families of
consideration who possessing valuable property on the
spot will choose to continue there.'41
   The trade of Murshidabad had begun even earlier to
be affected by the rise of Calcutta as a new administrative and commercial centre. With the reduction of
the Nawab's powers and forces and the impoverishment of
the nobles Murshidabad declined as a centre of consumption and trade. It ceased to be a lucrative market for
a large number of officials, clerks, servants, bankers
and merchants and assumed the appearance of a district
town. The events of 1773 following the famine in 1769-
70 led to a steady fall in the city's population.
Apart from the officers of the Diwani departments,
those people who were connected with the departments in
an indirect way left for Calcutta to regain their
positions, many others followed to seek new appointments. This migration of population from the city
became a regular feature after the transfer of the
capital. It seems that the people who had come to
Murshidabad from Upper India and beyond the western
frontiers and found employment at the Court left the
city for their homes. An idea of the extent of
unemployment and desertion may be formed from the
contemporary and near contemporary reports: 'The
British rule swept away not only the hopes of those
out of employ and longing to get in, but hundreds of
servants and others, military perhaps especially. The
influx of strangers ceased and a contrary current set
in, drawing away the useless, idle and discontented to
their former homes and haunts.'42
   After the natural calamity of famine, lawlessness,
declining trade and manufactures and the 'man-made
shocks' involved in the transfer to Calcutta of government and headquarters, unemployment and desertion, what
remained of the city? By the end of the century,
travellers could report Murshidabad to be a 'struggling
city in ruins and decay'. Within a decade of the
transfer of the capital from Murshidabad, the Resident

reported that the normal life of the city was disrupted because of the lack of administrative attention - and the monsoon made it worse. Even an official journey of the Governor-General in a palanquin took more than three hours to cover a distance of four miles through the city roads.[43] The city became so unhealthy that its mortality, caused by malarial fever and other diseases, threatened total depopulation. It was not until the early years of the nineteenth century that Government attention was drawn to the sanitation of the city when the European Collectors and officers became victims to malaria and it was realised that the gradual depopulation would involve a heavy loss of revenue in the collection of town duties.[44] A committee for the improvement of the city of Murshidabad was constituted in 1812 but it was beyond its capacity to revive the former glory of the city.

Mohsin, 'Murshidabad in the Eighteenth Century'

1. Caillaud, Journal, 29 December 1759, Orme MSS, IOL, OV 134, p.251.
2. Report, 6 July 1814, Home Misc. 775, pp.201-209.
3. *Statistical and Geographical Report on the Moorshidabad District* (Calcutta 1860), p.8.
4. H.K. Naqvi, *Urbanisation and Urban Centres under the Great Mughals* Simla 1972), pp.130-135.
5. For the importance of this region Philip B. Calkins, 'The Role of Murshidabad as a regional and subregional centre in Bengal' in Richard L. Park (ed.), *Urban Bengal* (Michigan State University 1969), p.21
6. Ghulam Hussain Salim, *Riyas-us-Salatin*, translated by Abdus Salam (Calcutta 1904), p.28.
7. M. Chakrabarti, 'Notes on the Geography of Old Bengal', *Journal of the Asiatic Society of Bengal*, July 1909, p.233. Blochmann has also suggested that the original name of Makhsudabad was derived from the name of a Mughal *mansabdar* Makhsus Khan who spent some time in Bengal during the latter part of Akbar's reign. H. Blochmann, *Contributions to the Geography and History of Bengal* (Calcutta 1968), p.10n.
8. Streynsham Master, *The Diaries of Streynsham Master*, ed. R.C. Temple (London 1911), vol. i, pp.145, 329; and William Hedges, *The Diary of William Hedges*, vol. i, pp. 33, 58-59, 105, 106.
9. *Riyaz-us-Salatin*, p.251.
10. A. Karim, *Murshid Quli Khan and His Times* (Dacca 1963), pp.21, 212 (note 3). The reasons for the transfer of the capital from Dacca have been discussed in K.M. Mohsin, *A Bengal District in Transition - Murshidabad 1765-93* (Dacca 1973), pp.4-5.
11. This Customs House collected duties and controlled the trade and commerce of north-west Bengal - it took away nearly half the jurisdiction of the *Shahbandar* of Dacca. A. Karim, op.cit., p.213.
12. This is discussed in detail in K.M. Mohsin, op.cit., Chapters I, II.
13. W. Hodges, *Travels in India, 1780-83* (London 1793), p.18.
14. J.N. Sarkar, *History of Bengal* (Dacca 1948), vol. ii, p.424.
15. *Riyaz*, pp.282-83; R. Skelton, 'Murshidabad Painting', *Marg*, 1956-57, p.10.

16. Bengal Revenue Consultations, 21 May 1787.

17. This area fits well with some of the early nineteenth century accounts of the city. For example, according to Adam, the city in the 1830s was divided into 19 Thanas containing 373 mahallas and villages.

18. L.S.S. O'Malley, *Bengal District Gazetteers, Murshidabad,* (Calcutta 1914), p.207.

19. A. Karim, *Dacca, The Mughal Capital* (Dacca 1964), p.91.

20. According to J.N. Sarkar, Siyauddin raised the Bengal army to 250,000 (*History of Bengal*, vol. ii, p.424). This may be true for the whole Subah but the army maintained in the city may not have exceeded one lakh. The Nawab's army at the battle of Plassey consisted of 40,000 foot and 16,000 horse with fifty cannon - Major J.H.T. Walsh, *A History of Murshidabad District* (London 1902), p.10.

21. *Report on the Census of Bengal, 1872*, p.102.

22. This is discussed in detail in K.M. Mohsin, op.cit., chapter VI.

23. 'State of the Nizamat Accounts of Nawab Mubarak ud-daula', 23 January 1773, Bengal Secret Consultations, 25 January 1773.

24. B.B. Misra, *The Central Administration of the East India Company*, (Manchester 1959), pp.117-118; see also his *The Judicial Administration of the East India Company in Bengal, 1765-1782* (Delhi 1961), pp.298-299.

25. Murshidabad Factory Records, 6 November 1777.

26. Robert Skelton comments that an independent school of painting - 'Murshidabad style' was developed under the patronage of the Bengal Nawabs - Robert Skelton: 'Murshidabad Painting', *Marg*, 1956-57, pp.10-22.

27. K.M. Mohsin, op.cit., p.250.

28. Orme MSS., O.V.54, pp.21-22.

29. 'The progeny of the rich and nobles received the border part of the town (for the their residence).The sarafs, merchants and craftsmen have been placed in the centre of the town around which a thick and strong mud wall was built. Beautiful gardens have been laid out on all sides of the town. *Neem* trees yielding luxurious shade have been planted in the bazars and lanes. The town from outside looks like paradise and its handsome, tall trees are a heavenly gift granted to the inhabitants of the town. River Ganges flows at a distance of one karoh (kos) in the north. The town has a lofty fort around which mansions of some of the

nobles have been erected.' Quoted in H.K. Naqvi: *Urban Centres and Industries in Upper India 1556-1803* (London 1968), (note 294) from Tarikh-i-Farrukabad, OR. 1718, pp.1,2.

30. See Philip B. Calkins, op.cit., p.26. He argues that neither the nobles nor the merchant-bankers expected their stay to be permanent - hence the lack of substantial buildings.

31. Bengal Judicial Consultations, 10 January 1817.

32. On the other hand Calkins claims that 'it was the British traders and the rivers which destroyed the commercial city and not the British administrators. It is customary to state that Murshidabad began to die when the functions of government began to be transferred to Calcutta. It seems as likely, however, that it was the transfer of trading activities and the eventual change in the course of the river which destroyed Murshidabad.' Philip B. Calkins, op.cit., p.27.

33. *Famine in India* (Extracts), p.27.

34. Quoted in A.J. Embree, *Charles Grant and British Rule in India* (London 1962), pp.35-36.

35. *Siyar-ul-Mutakherin*, vol. iii, pp.25-26.

36. Bengal Public Consultations, 25 May 1772.

37. J.C. Sinha, *Economic Annals of Bengal* (London 1927), pp.98-99.

38. Committee of Circuit Proceedings, p.85.

39. B.B. Misra, *The Judicial Administration of the East India Company in Bengal, 1765-1782* (Delhi 1961), pp.69-70.

40. G.R. Gleig, *Memoirs of Warren Hastings* (London 1841), vol.i. p.263.

41. Committee of Circuit Proceedings, p.84.

42. Gastrell, op.cit., p.11; see also *Siyar-ul-Mutakhkherin*, vol. iii, pp.203-204.

43. Bengal Revenue Consultations, 3 June 1783.

44. Bengal Judicial Consultations, 10 January 1817.

THE CITY OF LUCKNOW BEFORE 1856

Rosie Llewellyn-Jones

Lucknow lies in the province of Uttar Pradesh,[1] in north eastern India, and the town straddles the Gumti, a meandering river which is a tributary of the Ganges. This small river provides one of the few points of interest in an otherwise monotonous landscape. There are only two small hills of note in the city, both on the south side of the river, which appear larger than they are by contrast with the extreme flatness of the surrounding terrain. Much deforestation has taken place in Lucknow, especially over the last century, though the city is still called 'The Garden of India' because of its numerous *baghs* or parks. From the earliest days of Muslim rule in India, when the conquering Ghaznavid nobles swept in from the west, the city of Lucknow has always been regarded as forming part of the province of Oudh,[2] though it was not always the provincial capital. Only when the governor came from Lucknow itself was the capital located there during his term of office, though by the time of the great Mughal Emperor Akbar it appears that Lucknow was recognised as the capital irrespective of the birthplace of the *subahdar*. It also appears that by Akbar's time the governorship of Oudh and the governorship of the city of Lucknow became two separate posts for a short time,[3] but because this was only a temporary measure the term *subahdar* in this article will be taken as referring to the governor of the whole province of Oudh.

Not a great deal of information is available about Oudh in pre-Mughal times. The province was ruled by a series of governors in Sultanate times, who seldom seemed adverse to bettering themselves by opposing the reigning monarchs where expedient. Though Oudh was regarded as part of the Kingdom of Delhi during Sultanate times, plans were made to annex it to Bengal at one point, to make the province independent at another, and it became part of the breakaway kingdom of Jaunpur for almost a century until the then ruler Sa'id Khan was defeated by Ibrahim Lodi.

During Akbar's reign however, the province stabilised and Lucknow became a flourishing town under a succession of *subahdars* who improved and extended the

city. As in other *subahs* of the Mughal Empire, the
subahdars and the other great imperial officials held
their courts after the model of the Emperor's court at
Delhi. With their contingents of calvary, their very
considerable bodies of clerks, superintendents, treasurers and accountants, and their large private households they added very considerably to the wealth and
importance of the provincial capital, drawing to it
bankers, merchants and the agents of the larger land-
owenrs, as well as large bodies of craftsmen, shopkeepers, servants and labourers. They were often on
campaign or on tour with splendid travelling encampments
and individual nobles were subject to regular transfer,
but to the city which they made their capital the consequences were still striking.

The death of the Mughal Emperor Aurangzeb in 1707
marked the beginning of the break up of the Empire and
coincidentally also marked the arrival in India of
Saadat Khan Burhan-ul-Mulk, who was to become the
founder of an hereditary line of *subahdars* or *nawabs* in
Oudh. Saadat Khan (as he was generally called) came
from Nishapur in Persia and was a member of the Shi'a
sect of Islam, the minority sect as opposed to the
Sunnis, who form the majority. Saadat Khan hoped to
find employment at the Court of the Emperor, Bahadur
Shah, successor to Aurangzeb, who was also a Shi'a. By
1722 Saadat Khan had become so successful that he was
sent to Oudh as *subahdar* and he rented some buildings
in Lucknow which were later to form one of the earliest
palace complexes there. When summoned back to the Delhi
Court by the Emperor, Saadat Khan installed his nephew
Safdar Jang as Deputy Governor and Safdar Jang consolidated his position by marrying Saadat Khan's daughter.

In 1728 Saadat Khan was transferred by the Emperor
to the governorship of Agra but he disobeyed and
returned to Oudh, and after that the Emperor, who had
many other problems connected with the decline in
central government, made no further attempt to transfer
Saadat Khan. On the latter's death, Safdar Jang
naturally assumed the position of *subahdar*, and in turn
on his death in 1754 his son Shuja-ud-duala was confirmed by the Emperor in all the posts held by his
father, thus making the appointment virtually hereditary.

By 1761 Shuja-ud-daula had become powerful enough
to attract the attention of the British who were now
pushing into the heart of India from the bases where

they had originally settled as traders of the East
India Company, a commercial concern which combined
business with territorial expansion and political man-
oeuvering in an irresistible force. Shuja-ud-daula had
at one point asked the British for aid 'to settle the
affair of the Empire'[4] (so powerful had he become), but
in June 1763 the Company provoked war with the Nawab of
Bengal, Mir Qasim, and having defeated him repeatedly,
drove him into Oudh. There he persuaded Shuja-ud-daula
and the Emperor Shah Alam to join him in a bid to
reconquer Bengal. In October 1764 that bid failed when
the three, after a stubborn battle were defeated at
Buxar. In Bengal the old Nawab Mir Jafar was restored
- but what was to be done with Oudh? James Mill sums
up the conclusions of Clive and his Council - 'it would
cost the company more to defend the country of the
Vizier [Shuja-ud-daula] than it would yield in revenue,
that Suja oodowlah was more capable of defending it
than the Emperor ... or any other Chief ... and that in
the hands of the Vizier, it might form a barrier
against the Mahrattas and Afghans.'[5] Oudh was restored
to Shuja-ud-daula, and a treaty of mutual assistance
entered into. That treaty laid down that British
military assistance should be paid for, a treaty of
1768 limited the number of the Nawab's own army, and
another of 1773 set a price on each Company brigade he
might requisition. Shuja-ud-daula's successor, Asaf-
ud-daula was required to pay more heavily for an
increased contingent of British troops. The process of
weakening and squeezing would continue until Wellesley,
in 1801, annexed over half of Oudh as the price of his
'friendship'. With this process also went a loss of
internal autonomy. The dominance of the British Resident at the Nawab's court at Lucknow was most
brutally set out by Warren Hastings - 'either the
Resident must be the slave or vassal of the [Nawab's]
Minister or the Minister at the absolute devotion of
the Resident' adding 'he [the Minister] exists by his
dependance on the influence of our Government ... with
the alternative of dissension'.[6] It would later be
cloaked in smoother words and exercised with more
restraint, but down to the annexation of Oudh in 1856
it remained a decisive factor in the politics of the
Lucknow state.
    What the impact of these political events was upon
the fortunes of the city of Lucknow, now demands
attention. The re-opening of the trade routes of the

Ganges valley, but without direct exposure to the East
India Company's commercial pressure, may have had a
stimulating influence for a while, but there is little
evidence of physical expansion in the original area
around and to the south of the Chauk, the main market
place, or in the area which had been developed on the
northern bank of the Gumti. What did change the
physical appearance and layout of the city was the
decision of Asaf-ud-daula, Shuja-ud-daula's son, to move
his capital from Faizabad to Lucknow in 1775. The
palaces and administrative buildings of the Nawabs
added a major eastern sector to the old city, especially between 1805 and 1815 when the low-lying lands on
the southern river bank were built up. With the Nawabs
and the court, the Resident and the Company's brigades
also moved to Lucknow, with their staffs, servants,
bazar shop-keepers and so on, to create a third focus
and another point of active building in the city.
Though the two Company brigades of 1777 or the twelve
infantry battalions, four cavalry regiments and
supporting artillery imposed by Wellesley, or the
smaller post-1801 force were not all stationed at
Lucknow, enough always were to require a considerable
cantonment to house them.

It would be wrong to assume that before 1775 medieval Lucknow was merely a cluster of villages along the
south bank of the Gumti (as some commentators have
done) which were welded together to form a corporate
whole by Asaf-ud-daula and his successors.[7] In fact
pre-1775 Lucknow was a flourishing city exporting
sugar, indigo and cloth, even, to England and Afghanistan, a centre for commerce with a bullion market,
and a place celebrated for its working of copper, which
was gilded, engraved and painted and formed one of the
town's biggest industries.[8] A Jesuit missionary wrote
in 1765 that Lucknow was 'one of the principal towns in
the province of Oud, it is an old and crowded city and
distinguished by a number of remarkable buildings'.
The circumference of the whole city was at that time
four miles round.[9]

Legends claim that the earliest inhabitants of
Lucknow were Brahmans and Kayasthas who lived round
Lakshman Tila, the hill to the south of the Gumti[10]
and that a large shrine on the hill stood until
Aurangzeb, on a visit to Lucknow, had the shrine
demolished and a mosque built there instead, which is
still standing.[11] Unfortunately there have never been

any large scale archaeological excavations in Lucknow,
but a local amateur archaeologist, Shri Amrit Lal Nagar,
has an impressive collection of Gupta statuary and
brick which he has found in and around Lucknow, when
buildings have been demolished or fields ploughed up.

From Sultanate and Mughal days some monuments still
stand, the earliest of which is the tomb of Shah Mina,
a celebrated Muslim mystic who settled in Lucknow about
1450, and whose burying place became a shrine for
pilgrims.[12] Two sandstone tombs stand to the east of
the Chauk (in the present day Nadan Mahal area) which
are undated, but stylistically Mughal, where some of
the Sheikhzadas, the powerful landowning families of
medieval Oudh were buried. The Sheikhzadas owned the
land to the east of the Chauk up to the Lakshman Tila
area, which was later to become the site of a large
Nawabi fort. In 1540, during Humyun's retreat from
Jaunpur, the Emperor is supposed to have camped in the
area to the south west of the Chauk, (near the modern
Abdul Aziz Road) and this would imply that the limits
of the city were then bounded to the south by the
present Akbari gate, since the Emperor's, by its very
size, had to be established on open ground and not
within city walls.[13]

Similarly a tomb to the west of the Chauk, that of
Husain Ali, a commander in Akbar's army, who died about
1600 both marks the probable westward limit of the town
at that time, since Muslims are buried outside cities,
and demonstrates the high quality of provincial work-
manship. Indeed the tomb, which is built of red
sandstone and of small bricks covered with green glazed
tiles and stucco appears to be the earliest surviving
example of the Lucknow stucco which was to become so
widely used in later buildings.

In 1640, two factors, or employees of the English
East India Company (which had been founded in 1600),
were living in Lucknow and buying bales of 'dereabauds'
a kind of muslin, which was being made in the Hasanganj
area on the north bank of the Gumti.[14] They had been
sent up from Surat in Gujarat, then the seat of the
Company's operation in western India and it was to
Surat they despatched their goods. By 1647 a 'house
had been hired at Lucknow for the Company's occasion'
and the factory staff at Lucknow needed strengthening.
The staff was increased and in 1650, Rs.70,000 were
sent to the factors there for buying goods. By then
the 'dereabauds' were being cured or bleached

in the Lucknow factory, and bales of indigo and 'plenty of sugar' were also being sent to Surat.

In 1651 further enlargement of the cloth investment was ordered, but in the next year the factors were complaining of 'want of assistance' and of transport from Lucknow being 'scarce and dear'. In 1653 the Company President at Surat ordered the factory to be dissolved as being 'very remote and chargeable' but it evidently survived until at least 1655 and the Company house was also still there.

During Aurangzeb's reign however, the Farangi Mahal area was given by him to a religious leader[15] and there is no further mention of the British or their trade during the rest of the seventeenth century. Curiously enough the East India Company officials a hundred years later who began to make contact with the early Nawabs seemed completely unaware of the early British traders at Lucknow, and there was no attempt to set up a further British settlement in the Farangi Mahal area,nor so far as can be told, any more trade in 'dereabauds', though obviously from the large sum of money invested in 1650, it had been a factory of some good size, employing a number of local people to work in it.

The site of this factory was the area directly east of the Chauk, still known as the Farangi Mahal, or the 'Foreigners' Quarters'. This area is now a fantastic mixture of old and new walls and houses jammed promiscuously together, and covers a large area. It is still possible to make out some kind of square high walled courtyard with pre-Nawabi houses inside, and the main gateway to the Farangi Mahal courtyard fell down only a few years ago.

The buildings rented by Saadat Khan on his arrival in Oudh as *subahdar* stood on or near the Lakshman Tila, directly south of the Gumti, and were called the Panch Mahala or Five Palaces.[16] The improvements and alterations to these already substantial buildings were to herald the beginning of Nawabi developments in the city and symbolically the Panch Mahala were renamed the Macchi Bhavan or Fish House from the carved fish which decorated the refurbished buildings and which were used by the Nawabs as their insignia on coins etc., the fish being an ancient Persian symbol of royalty.[17] The buildings had been rented from the Sheikhzadas, who owned much of the area south of the river, for the monthly sum of Rs.565 but it is doubtful for how long this rent was paid, and Saadat Khan soon came to

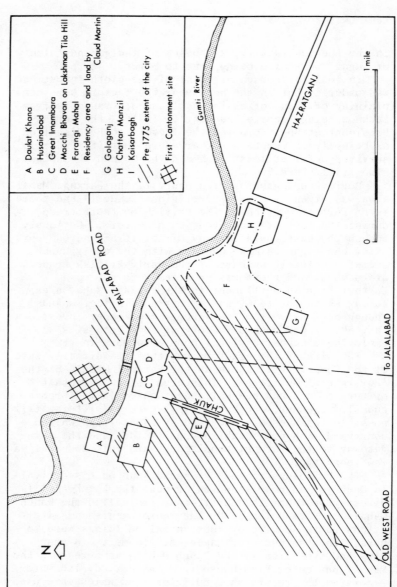

LUCKNOW

A   Daulat Khana
B   Husainabad
C   Great Imambara
D   Macchi Bhavan on Lakshman Tila Hill
E   Farangi Mahal
F   Residency area and land by
       Claud Martin
G   Golaganj
H   Chattar Manzil
I   Kaisarbagh

///   Pre 1775 extent of the city

⊞   First Cantonment site

FAIZABAD ROAD

Gumti River

HAZRATGANJ

To JALALABAD

CHAUK

OLD WEST ROAD

N

0   1 mile

regard these buildings as his own.[18]

In addition to the alterations at the Panch Mahala, Saadat Khan also built various *katras* or *ganjes* to the east and west of the Chauk, and it would be useful to explain here the exact meaning of the term *ganj*, since it is a characteristic of most north India cities, and certainly of Lucknow. The Comte de Modave, who travelled in Oudh between 1773 and 1776 explains it thus - 'Gange is the particular name given to distinguish an enclosure, be it of masonry, of earth, or simple wooden planks, in which one finds housing and the stalls in which are sold the necessities for trevellers, their steeds and their beasts of burden. It is just like a caravanserai. They are constructed either from a charitable impulse or with an eye to profit, for they are hired or leased out, and because of the greater security in these enclosures as compared to totally exposed encampments not only the travellers prefer to sleep there, but many families have established themselves there. I have seen them full of people, and those that would pass for large towns.'[19]

This important passage has been quoted in full because it adds a lot to our understanding of a pre-industrial town if one can visualise a series of these *ganges* clustered together and forming its nucleus. P.C. Mookherjee, writing in the nineteenth century on Lucknow, describes a *ganj* in more detail as a square built round a cross-roads, with two main gates and two smaller ones at the end of each road. There are often bazaar shops with lines of verandahs fronting the main road and private houses at the rear. The walls are pierced on all four sides and there are bastions at the four corners. There is often a tank nearby.[20] Mookherjee also thinks that the *nallas* or stream beds running through the old part of Lucknow formed a natural division between the *ganjes*, which are now raised quite considerably above street level. Many early visitors to Lucknow have commented on the irregular nature of the town, 'the ground is so uneven that one cannot walk about in this city except by detours, climbing up here, going down there',[21] and to the west of the Chauk one still sees buildings or ruins on small clumps of land, which would have been divided during the monsoon by streams running down the *nallas* between them. Abu Talib also comments on the Lucknow hillocks, saying that the ground is 'uneven and the bazaars and streets are narrow and crowded', and he

Rosie Llewellyn-Jones

criticises Asaf-ud-daula for moving from Faizabad (a town to the east of Lucknow), where the first three Nawabs had spent most of their time.[22] Lucknow was certainly expanded, both in pre-Nawabi and early Nawabi times, by the building of various *ganjes* by different *diwans* (ministers) and *subahdars* though it seems fairly certain that the reason for building *ganjes* was the profits which accrued from letting them to families and shop-keepers, rather than 'a charitable idea'. In some cases shopkeepers rented land within the *ganj* from the *diwans* or nobles and built small houses at their own expense, although they had to obtain the approval of the person owning the *ganj* first.[23] New *ganjes* were usually named either after the owner, the landlord, or the traditional functions or occupations of the inhabitants who lived there, so that one finds in Lucknow *Saadat Ganj*, founded by Saadat Khan, *Tikait Ganj*, founded by Tikait Rai, the *diwan* of Asaf-ud-daula, *Loha Ganj*, the iron-workers' area, and *Gola Ganj* where an early arsenal was established (*gola* being a bullet or a cannon ball). It is now necessary to go outside Lucknow to appreciate the original form of the *ganj*, and there is a particularly fine example at Mohun Lal Ganj, to the south of the city, which still preserves one of the original main gateways. Naturally the chaos of an Indian town has broken down the original pattern until often all that remains of most *ganjes* is the name and the central cross roads.

By 1765 Lucknow was a sizeable town, and the first detailed description of it by a European author has this to say: 'the length of this town from Recabganj in the south to Issaganj in the north is a mile and a half [this was all on the south bank of the Gumti] the breadth from Chodaganj in the east to the west is a mile or more. The town is not walled like Adjudea [Ayodhya] and Ganla [Faizabad]. There are a great number of brick houses, but the majority are of lime or mortar, covered with tiles, standing on little mounds of barren land, here and there. The greatest part of the town extends towards the east, and covers an elevated place, the smallest part is in a gorge. The streets are narrow and stinking, because the inhabitants habitually throw all their refuse into the street ....'[24] Apart from the Panch Mahala, the author of this passage, Joseph Tieffenthaler, writes: 'you can also see buildings showing beautiful, even

96

magnificent architecture here and there in the town,
but those are few in number. The market place [i.e.
the Chauk] is narrow and has nothing remarkable about
it. The houses of the merchants are of brick, tall
and solidly built.' He goes on to describe the Gumti,
which could be forded during the summer, and says that
the north bank, too, had 'houses and other buildings
along it'. Tieffenthaler also drew one of the earliest
maps of the city, in which the huge gateway to the
Panch Mahala complex is shown, and the mosque built by
Aurangzeb on the Lakshman Tila. One feels inclined to
place great reliance on Tieffenthaler's descriptions
since he spent at least five years in Lucknow and
touring round Oudh.

During this same period, Shuja-ud-daula was involved
in the enlargement of the Panch Mahala area, already
considerably altered and improved by Saadat Khan, his
great-uncle. The five palaces which gave this site its
name appear to have been merged together at an early
date, so that from the north bank of the river one
large castle-like building stood on the hill, 'like a
chateau, surrounded by walls and with high towers'.
Approaching the building itself one came to 'a great
doorway and a vast forecourt in front of a tall battle-
mented wall supported by arcades, where the tambour
players would sound the drums. [25] The Subahdar [Shuja-
ud-daula] had had much of the battlements and the
apartments demolished and rebuilt in an even grander
style.'[26]

Early pictures suggest that the Lucknow Panch
Mahala resembled quite closely the fort at Faizabad,
said to have been designed and supervised by a Frenchman, although Shuja-ud-daula abandoned it 'as a result
of his natural inconstancy'.[27] Shuja's successors,
however, were more attached to the fort palace at
Faizabad than its creator Shuja-ud-daula seems to have
been, and though Lucknow remained the provincial capital and they did much building there, they spent much
time in Faizabad. The origin of Faizabad and of the
popular name Bangla is rather romantically described
by the Comte du Modave: a *bangla*, he writes,

> is a pavilion of bamboo covered ... with thatch or
> leaves from trees which one constructs in haste
> for some special occasion, like a marriage, a big
> fete, a meeting place during the hunt, or simply a
> meeting place. It is magnificientally adorned with

hangings, with beautiful chintzes, with mirrors and
lustres, etc. One dances there, plays and eats.
The soubas [sic, subahdars] of Laknau had there
thirty years ago one of these banglas put up on the
place that is now Fez-abad. The site on the banks
of the Gogra pleased them. It became a rendezvous
for the Hunt, which gradually became a large town,
which is quite easy in the Indies where one does
not build except of earth, and of the kind which
five or six months can suffice to construct a
town.[28]

But by the Comte de Modave's time it had long been
a substantial town, the nickname origins of which were
concealed by the pleasant fancies of popular etmymology.
Ten years before Asaf-ud-daula moved permanently to
Lucknow, Faizabad could boast a large walled palace,
with 'courtyards, gardens and workshops of all kinds
which formed a separate city within a city'[29] as well
as gardens in the Persian style, four mosques, a chauk
of more than eighty feet in length, closed at each end
by a great gateway with arcades on two storeys, a large
park called the Ranichana with all kinds of animals,
and a *top-khana* or arsenal. But Faizabad suffered a
decline when the Nawabs moved to Lucknow and by 1782
the English writer William Hodges found Faizabad an
almost empty town, though he described the Diwan-i-Am
(the Hall of Public Audience) there as being 'built on
the same plan' as the Lucknow one, but much richer,
but with its painting and gilding 'gone to decay'.[30]

When Asaf-ud-daula moved to Lucknow in 1775 after
the death of his father, all the state business of
dealing with revenue and tax collections moved with
him. The state treasury was here, as were the main
judicial courts, and important prisoners would be sent
to be judged in the capital. Similarly, the business
of government took place here, the ambassadors and
notables from foreign countries would be presented in
Lucknow to the Nawabs, while the headquarters of the
Nawab's armies were also here, the highest officers
living in the palace complex. All these different
functions, judicial, financial, military and diplomatic were centred on the palace complex and there
were different buildings within the complex allocated
to each of these functions. In addition each complex
housed great numbers of servants, not only domestics
but skilled craftspeople concerned with the upkeep of

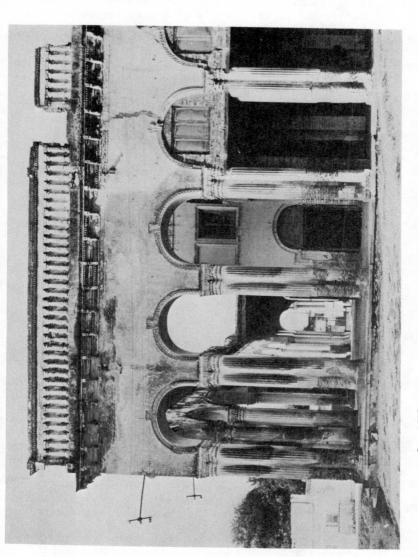

8. LUCKNOW: Asafi *kothi* (Photographed 1975)

the royal buildings and gardens, as well as an army of
administrative staff, clerks, scribes, messengers and
their superintendants. There were also the servants
who ministered to the panoply of state, the royal
coachmen, the personal body guards, the people in charge
of the royal tents and equipment used on hunting
parties, and many others. Artists of all kinds would
also be housed in the palace complexes and some of the
most famous religious buildings of the Shi'a faith in
India were here too, making this area a place of pilgrimage for the spiritual as well as the worldly.[31]

At first the Macchi Bhavan palace complex (the old
Panch Mahala site on Lakshman Tila) was used as the
Nawab's headquarters. Asaf-ud-daula, like his predecessors, greatly extended the area, so that his new
palace there had at least six principal courts, including a *baoli*, which is in reality more like a large
tank, around which arcaded rooms were built for use
during the summer. This is all that remains today of
the palace of Asaf-ud-daula, even the famed Sungi
Dalan or Stone Hall to the east of the *baoli* having
vanished entirely. So too, has the Hasainbagh, a large
garden bordering the river between the Macchi Bhawan
and the Residency.[32]

It was previously assumed that Asaf-ud-daula had the
Daulat Khana palace (his second great complex) built
shortly after his arrival from Faizabad[33] but in fact
the first mention of the Daulat Khana is in 1789[34]
and it was later still that some of the buildings there
were used to house the Nawab's curiousities and
treasures from Europe, and his menagerie of wild
animals.[35] The Daulat Khana complex also includes the
Asafi Kothi, one of the earliest remaining Nawabi buildings, which can be placed on stylistic evidence between
about 1780 and 1790.

Adjoining the old Macchi Bhawan Asaf-ud-daula built
the Great Imambara, a huge religious structure, with its
magnificent gateways, the western one being known as the
Rumi Darwaza or Constantinople Gate, while the eastern
one, which had formed part of the Panch Mahala and
which appeared in Tieffenthaler's 'map', now was
cleverly incorporated into the Great Imambara square.
Lucknow naturally began to expand with the certainty
that the Nawabs would settle there permanently and the
city grew in all directions. To the east it extended
as far as the present day Aminabad, in the south to
Tikait Ganj, in the west to Mahbubganj and to Daulatganj

in the north, where the Gumti makes a wide loop. Far
to the south of the city, probably near the old road
through Jalalabad, a neighbouring town, Asaf-ud-daula
built the Charbagh or Four Gardens, then in the open
country, where the railway station stands today.

The Nawab also established an arsenal to provide
weapons and ammunition for his own troops and in 1776,
a year after his accession, he stated his determination
to have Captain Claude Martin (a Frenchman, but working
both for the Nawab and the East India Company) super-
intend the whole of his artillery and other military
stores as well as his arsenal.[36] Claude Martin left
detailed accounts of his expenses between 1782 and 1784
and records the cost of the 'fixed establishment of the
Vizier's [Nawab's] Arsenal, Poder Mill, Magazin, Laboratory, and hire of these several places' including
hire of 'large Court Yards, Military stores, Rooms,
Houses' etc. and details of the workers he employed,
including 'Bildars, coolies, Carpinters, Smiths,
Mistrees, Armourers, Braziers, Founders, fourteen Men
of different profession, Laskars and a European
writer'.[37] The original site for the arsenal appears
to have been to the sough east of the city, around the
area where Government House now stands, and reaching
as far as the unfinished canal started by a later
Nawab. There is a persistent legend that Government
House (now Raj Bhawan) was in fact Martin's powder
magazine, but this seems doubtful since there is a
later reference to a European style house being built
on the site of Martin's powder magazine on land
purchased from his Estate, and the house subsequently
being demolished when the canal was built.[38] What is
certain is that the whole arsenal was subsequently
moved to Gola Ganj in the area still known as Barud
Khana or Magazine building. This is just to the north
west of present day Aminabad, and the large square
courtyard called Barud Khana is still traceable, though
it is becoming increasingly blurred by hut encroachments.

Descriptions of Lucknow began to appear by Europeans who, while marvelling at the palaces and the
religious monuments were critical of conditions in the
older part of town. The Comte de Modave wrote in
February 1775: 'Laknau is a large and nasty town ...
unremarkable [except for the Panch Mahala which is] a
great building composed of many different parts without
any order, which do not correspond to each other. The

101

mosques are small and have nothing splendid about them
... Laknau after all does not merit consideration save
by its commerce which is quite extensive.'[39] In a
similar vein, William Hodges noted in 1782 that 'the
city is extensive but meanly built, the houses are
chiefly mud and walls covered with thatch and many
considt entirely of mats and bamboos, very few indeed,
of the houses of the natives are built with brick, the
streets are crooked, narrow and the worst I have seen
in India'.[40] In 1786 despite the rapid expansion to
the east of the city, the Chauk was still the principal
street of Lucknow.[41] A report made between 1792 and
1795 describes a journey through the west of the city,
including the Chauk, saying 'the streets all this way
were narrow and dirty, and crowded with bazaars and
poor people',[42] and a description of 1798 elaborates on
this: 'Happening to enter the town at the west end, and
which contains the poor mechanics and labourers of
every sort, I never witnessed so many varied forms of
wretchedness, filth and vice. The street which leads
to the palace is upwards of five miles, more than one
half of which you wade through mire and filth.'[43]

So how much did the arrival of the Nawabi Court in
1775 really affect the city of Lucknow? Comparing the
different functions carried on in the eastern area of
the town, that is the Macchi Bhawan and the Daulat
Khana palace complexes, with those of commercial
interest in the old city, one can sense the feeling of
the 'two cities' manifest in a journey from the east to
the west. Both areas had a high degree of independence
from each other, neither seemed essential for the continuation of the other. The Nawabi palace complexes
and huge religious buildings could just as well have
been constructed in another town of Oudh, like Faizabad
or Cawnpore. Wherever the Nawabi Court had settled it
would have attracted the same crowd of people, the
artists and skilled craftspeople, the intellectual
elite, the poets and painters, soldiers of fortune and
the inevitable hangers-on. It seems equally certain
that the locational advantages of Lucknow as a centre
of manufacture and distribution which had brought
Indian and even European merchants to the city well
before the Nawabs had settled there would have continued to sustain a reasonably prosperous city. What
the arrival of the Court did obviously do, was to
increase greatly the consumer population and so encourage an increase in the number of those who served

them - food vendors, shop-keepers, grain merchants,
bankers, or, more frivolously, silver and gold lace
makers, perfumiers, male and female prostitutes.[44]
   But nevertheless it would be a mistake to imagine
that the old city underwent a complete change after
1775. The very few records extant show that the rich
and complex life of old Lucknow continued in much the
same way, the *shroffs* or money-lenders continued to
flourish, the Mint which had been long established
continued to strike coins, albeit with the Nawabs'
heads instead of the Mughal Emperors', staple industries like tobacco growing, and curing, sugar refining
and the spinning and weaving of cotton continued,
social life revolved around the mosques, the *madrassas*
(the religious schools) and the bazaars, and perhaps,
most important evidence of all, the geography or
physical characteristics of the area remained the same,
so that to quote W.H. Russell, the native city was 'an
aggregate of houses perforated by tortuous paths, so
that a plan of it would resemble a section of worm-
eaten wood'.[45] The 'tortuous paths' of the old city
continued to be peopled with the usual miscellany of
any Indian city, the food sellers, chiropodists,
barbers, itinerant muscians, labourers, people offering
transport, conjurors, metal workers, in fact many of
the trades still met with today in a more ancient form.
The Nawabi fascination with European artifacts also
filtered through to old Lucknow, a good example being
the introduction of lithographic presses at an early
date, which were quickly taken up by business men in
and around the Chauk, so that only eighteen years after
an Englishman, Mr Archer, had been employed on the
Nawab's Lithographic Press in 1831, there were at least
seventeen lithographic presses in Lucknow, which sent
books all over India, and employed a considerable
number of workers.[46] European observers were also
struck, as they still are today, by the number of
beggars, both local and those who came into Lucknow
from the surrounding villages, to be found in the
streets, hoping for charity from the rich of the new
city growing round the Court.
   Occasionally there would be minor upheavals in the
old city when new groups of people moved in, either
because they hoped for work at the Court, or because
conditions in their own area had become bad. A
Residency report of 1828 mentions 'Mewatties' and
different kinds of Sunnis including 'Afghans, Uljas,

Afreedees and Turkay Moghuls who are in the Service of
the State' (presumably as mercenaries), but it is
significant that these newcomers tended to settle on
the outskirts of the old city and set up their own
colonies, the Mewattis, for example living on the south-
western fringe of Lucknow near Talkatora, rather than
in areas within the old city itself.[47]

There are unfortunately no population figures for
pre-1775 Lucknow and no reliable city estimates after
1775 until 1901, although several people volunteered
guesses as to the number of inhabitants of the city.
The earliest estimate was made in 1798 when Lucknow was
said to contain half a million people,[48] but this seems
an unrealistically high figure in view of later
evidence on the Lucknow population. The second figure
is an estimated number of 300,000 in 1800[49] and this is
the same figure which was given fifty-four years later
in a Gazetteer published shortly before the annexation
of Oudh.[50] 300,000 people would have included those
attracted to the splendid Court during the twenty-five
years since its arrival from Faizabad. When the last
Nawab, Wajid Ali Shah, was deposed, the population of
Lucknow fell quite drastically and stabilised at about
250,000 in 1901[51] It was natural that many of the
people who had been servicing the Court, in administration, the maintenance of buildings, as palace servants,
entertainers, military men and courtiers would leave
Lucknow, and in fact the Nawab was accompanied to
Calcutta by a party of faithful followers. But in
addition to this, large areas of Lucknow were physically destroyed by the British after their recapture of
the city following the uprising of 1857. 'Large and
thickly populated areas including the old Bajpei
muhalla and Ismailganj were razed to the ground, a
space of half a mile in every direction being completely
cleared round the old fort.'[52] After 1857 some 50,000
people left the city either driven out by the Mutiny
destruction or following the court. If one assumes
that they represent the number who had been attracted
to the Court when Lucknow was made the effective
capital in 1775 and that the figure of 300,000 given
as the city population in 1800 is a reasonable one,
then the pre-1775 population would be something of the
order of 250,000. It is known that Lucknow was considered a large and extensive town in the 1760's[53]
with a stable population, relatively unaffected by the
later advent of the Court, and it seems not

unreasonable to suggest that when the Court was finally
exiled, the population of the city would again settle
down to approximately pre-Nawabi figures.

To the large and growing late eighteenth century
city with its two elements, the old commercial quarters
and the dazzling new Court attracting people like a
magnet from all over India and beyond by its rich
intellectual life, there was also added a third element:
the British. Unlike the old city and the Court which
functioned to a large extent as two separate entities,
the British quarters in Lucknow were entirely dependent
on the fact of the Nawabi court being established there.
As the British moved up country to deal with the Nawab
Shuja-ud-daula, it became politic for the Nawab to
agree to have about him 'a person of trust', i.e. the
British Resident appointed to the Nawabi Court by the
East India Company.[54] It was not only, however, from
the diplomatic angle that the British gained a foothold
in Lucknow, but also from an astute mixture of business,
both civil and military, carried on more by European
adventurers than by the official British Residents and
their staff. There are a number of reports of Europeans, mostly British and French, involved in the manufacture of arms, guns, cannon and shot, working mainly
for the Nawabs, but occasionally for other nobles in
Lucknow as well. The manufacture seems to have been
something of a cottage industry and in several cases
was carried on in the yards or compounds of the family
house, occasionally it seems, from text-books on how to
manufacture such goods, which implies that the armament
makers were not skilled craftsmen, but adventurers out
to turn a quick rupee.[55] European artists were not
averse to working for the Nawabs either, and ten years
after the arrival of the Court in Lucknow, reports of
the generosity of Asaf-ud-daula had spread to Britain.
Ozias Humphry, a British artist, wrote in 1785: 'I am
assured by Mr Macpherson [the Governor of Bengal] that
a residence of three or four months at Lucknow with
Nabob Vizier [Asaf-ud-daula] will not fail to give me
the fortune I came to seek in India, viz, 10,000 pounds
- of this I am assured by those who are well acquainted
with the state of affairs in these parts';[56] and the
fact that the artist received nothing like the amount
he expected, and that only after protracted negotiations, did nothing to deter others from seeking their
fortune in Lucknow. It is necessary to emphasize
therefore, that during Asaf-ud-daula's time, at least

the British in official positions in Lucknow, as
servants of the East India Company, both civil and
military, were very much in a minority, though the
security of their position and the vast wealth to be
gained either legally or illegally ensured that the
Resident and his close staff lived in great luxury
compared with most other Europeans in the town.

As the position and status of the British increased
in northern India, so too did the power and prestige of
the British Resident in Lucknow, and this is reflected
in the expansion of official and semi-official buildings in the Residency area, which together with the
British Cantonment formed the third 'city' in Lucknow.
Just as the Nawabi judicial court was the central and
most important Court in Oudh, so did the Resident's
own court, for British Transgressors, become paramount
for a time, and there are some fascinating discussions
on the exact function of the Resident, when the British
government at Calcutta tried to define the Residents'
roles. Were they to be seen as traders, diplomats,
soldiers, paternalistic figures to the British and
Anglo-Indian community in Lucknow, religious leaders,
magistrates or glorified clerks?[57] Just as the palace
complex of the Nawabs reflected the many different
functions of an Oriental Court, so did the British
Residency, at different times, reflect all the functions
that the Resident was supposed to carry out. In order
to understand the different areas of Lucknow, it is
important to understand that just as the palace was
more than a palace, so the British Residency was more
than just an abode for the Resident, while the old city
maintained its virtual independence to the west.

The Residency itself (the term is generally used
today to imply the whole of the area incorporating all
the buildings of the British, not just the separate
building where the Resident lived - and this is the
sense in which it is used here), stands to the east of
the Macchi Bhawan on an elevated plain, and apart from
the Lakshman Tila hill, forms the second highest area
in Lucknow, near the river, but immune from flooding.
Here Claude Martin, (the superintendent of the Nawab's
arsenal and general entrepreneur) owned a considerable
amount of land, presumably bought from the Sheikhzadas,
the last recorded owners of the area, and Martin not
only rented out houses to Europeans but sold a good
proportion of the land to the East India Company soon
after the Court moved to Lucknow.[58] By 1778 the East

India Company were so well established there that the
Resident proposed 'erecting a Brick Building for the
purpose of a Treasury' and had a 'plan and elevations
of a Building' sent to him a few months later.[59] This
brick building was to replace a simple hut of bamboo
and thatch which had formerly housed the Company's
wealth, but which had been destroyed in a fire, a large
sum of money lying 'in the open for many days' guarded
by sepoys after the blaze.[60] This first brick Treasury
was itself replaced by a further one in 1851, the ruins
of which are still standing in the Residency. Other
substantial buildings followed the new Treasury so that
by the time of annexation in 1856 the whole Residency
area was almost as built up with intricate mazes and
alleys as the Nawabi palaces themselves.

Even before the Company had established themselves
in Lucknow, however, they had been anxious that no
unauthorised Europeans (unauthorised by themselves,
that is) should remain in Lucknow. As soon as Asaf-ud-
daula succeeded to the position of Nawab, John Bristow,
the British Resident at the Court, sought to have all
non-Company Europeans dismissed from Oudh, because of
fears that the Frenchmen employed by Asaf-ud-daula's
predecessors would poison the new Nawab's mind against
the British.[61] There was also the problem of the
European adventurers who owed allegiance to no-one but
themselves, but were not averse to damaging British
interests if they were paid enough by minor princes or
nobles at the Court. But the fact that John Bristow was
unable to enforce a total prohibition on non-Company
Europeans is shown by a notice that the Nawab was
persuaded to issue in 1788 saying that he [the Nawab]
'does not think it proper to consent to their [the
Europeans] erecting houses or other buildings in his
Cominions and that they must therefore consider themselves as prohibited from doing so'.[62] The Nawab was,
however, not entirely prevented from giving houses or
granting land to a few Europeans, as for example, the
'House upon a large scale with Baths and every comfort,
two large Bungalows and a Bowley [baoli or well]
calculated to raise a great quantity of Water, and an
extensive garden planted with the choicest Trees'
estimated to be worth Rs.50,000 given to one Robert
Beecher, a creditor of the Nawab;[63] and other Europeans
in the Nawab's service also got houses and land. It
also appears that the East India Company were able to
grant permits to Europeans who did not necessarily have

to be personally approved by the Nawab. It is not
always clear who had jurisdiction over Europeans in
Lucknow and Oudh during Asaf-ud-daula's reign and there
are complaints from the East India Company about Europeans who did not have Company passports in the Nawab's
territories and complaints from the Nawab about Europeans with Company passports but without authorisations
from the Nawab. The Lucknow Resident writing to Lord
Cornwallis, the Governor General in 1789, said, however,
that he thought the Nawab would not withdraw passports
already granted by the Company to the Europeans,
provided that they confined their residence to
Lucknow.[64]

By the beginning of Saadat Ali Khan's rule (he was
the brother and successor to Asaf-ud-daula and succeeded him in 1798),[65] several Europeans had built houses
along the banks of the Gumti on land which had been
granted to them by Asaf-ud-daula. These houses became
the property of the builder, regardless of who owned
the land on which they stood, and they could subsequently be purchased by anyone without the Nawab's
consent. Saadat Ali Khan was more concerned than his
predecessor to limit European settlement (and indeed
Company settlement) in Lucknow and he needed no
prompting to supervise foreigners in his capital. In
an attempt to control settlements there, he bought up
every house built by Europeans that came on the market
during his rule, and since there was a rapid turnover
of Europeans, he acquired a great deal of the property.
He also bought some of the land owned by Martin on the
south bank of the Gumti, where Martin had built his
Town House (later named the Farhat Baksh, which was
described when built in 1790 as being *near* the city of
Lucknow),[66] and proceeded to have the whole area
extended and extensively altered to become the Chattar
Manzil palace complex. The development of this area
also included the building of new roads which drew
favourable comments from European visitors, all the
more marked since they also continued to deplore the
narrow and dirty streets of the 'native city' to the
west. In the early 1800s Saadat Ali Khan began to lay
down the road now known as Hazratganj, which ran from
the Dilkusha (one of his country houses) in the south
east of the city, up to the Residency, and this broad
road became the usual route for travellers, ensuring
them a good view of the new and splendid buildings
which sprang up on either side.

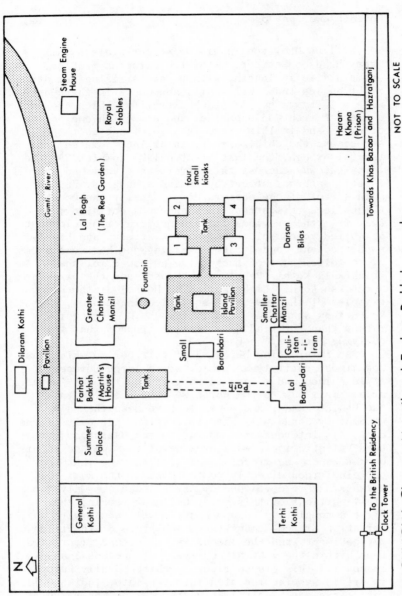

LUCKNOW: Chattar Manzil and Farhat Bakhsh complex

NOT TO SCALE

William Hamilton in his *Gazetteer* praises this
'very handsome street, after the European fashion,
above a mile in length, with bazars striking out at
right angles and a well-built new Chowk in the centre
with a lofty gateway at each extremity, which presents
a Grecian front on one side, and a Moorish one on the
other'[67] and in 1819 there is a reference to this
street and the Chini Bazaar, later incorporated into
the Qaisarbagh, the last great palace complex.[68] The
lofty gateways across this street have vanished, but it
is still a broad street by Indian standards, and the
main street of the eastern city. As for the houses
which lined this street they showed a definite move
away from the previous intense pattern of development
which led to the close and narrow streets and highly
populated and concentrated dwelling and business areas
of the older part of Lucknow. The now demolished
Kankarwali Kothi (Pebble-dash House) and the existing
Nur Baksh Kothi (Light Bestowing House) are both good
examples of the new-style solid looking houses, unexotic
by Lucknow standards, and contained in large gardens
rather than the kind of extensive grounds that the
outlying 'country' houses had.

One interesting building of this period which has
now almost entirely vanished, was a large European
style palace and estate in what is now the Husainabad
area. This was to the north west of the city, near
the Daulat Khana, and seems to have been the only
attempt by Saadat Ali Khan to develop this part of the
city, his interest soon moving to the Hazratganj area.
Lord Valentia included a drawing of this palace in his
book *Voyages and Travels in India*, showing that the
building stood directly to the west of the Rumi
Darwaza square developed by Asaf-ud-daula. Only two
small portions of this great building remain, the
first a completely European style well-house with an
imitation Graeco-Roman stucco sculpture on the triangu-
lar pediment, and the second is the ground floor of a
tomb within the central courtyard of the Husainabad
Imambara. This ground floor, architecturally European
in origin was incorporated into the later Indian building. It seems highly likely that during the reign of
Muhammad Shah (1837-1842) the palace of Saadat Ali
Khan was mostly demolished and the brick re-used to
build the new Imambara and the adjoining courtyards.

It would be useful here to try to define briefly
the difference between the large country houses built

10. LUCKNOW: Dilkusha (IOL)

by the Nawabs, which have already been referred to, and
the palace complexes such as the Daulat Khana and
Chattar Manzil built within the city. There is not
room in a short paper to expound fully the different
aspects of European and Indian ideas on building in
eighteenth and nineteenth century India, but as a rough
guide, one can say that the country houses on the outskirts of Lucknow, such as the Dilkusha (at the end of
Hazratganj) and Barowen (about four miles west of Lucknow) are large, solid buildings surrounded by extensive
gardens, with various outbuildings like stables,
servants' quarters, wells and ice-houses at a distance
from the main building, rather like an English country
estate, whereas the city palaces like the Chattar
Manzil and above all the Qaisarbagh, are all a series
of extensive courtyards where the important buildings
are subjugated to form an integral part of the whole
structure.

There were, for example, at least thirteen separate
buildings in the Chattar Manzil complex, including the
Jewel House, the Tea House, the Looking-Glass House,
the Palanquin House and various store rooms, not to
mention all the passages and corridors that led from
one section to another, and the gardens contained
within the walls of these courtyards. It consisted of
a 'perfect labyrinth of courtyards, inner gardens,
balconies, gateways, passages, verandahs, rotundas,
outhouses and pavilions' wrote one confused observer.[69]
It is particularly unfortunate that in present day
Lucknow one sees a single building, for example the
Chattar Manzil, or the Begum Kothi (recently demolished
to make way for a supermarket), and is told it was the
palace of such and such a Nawab, when in fact it
represents only one building among a great number of
others that went to make up that particular palace
complex. Certainly the house called Farhat Baksh, now
the western wing of the Central Drug Research Institute,
formed only the northern side of an extensive courtyard
with a large tank in the centre that reached to the
small Chattar Manzil and this in turn was only a small
part of the palace of Saadat Ali Khan and the later
Nawabs. It should thus be appreciated that the building of such palace complexes was in fact equivalent to
developing quite large areas of land, with the resulting settlements that would spring up to provide
services that the palaces themselves could not
encompass, like meat markets, and vegetable and

11. LUCKNOW: Chattar Manzil post-Mutiny (IOL)

Rosie Llewellyn-Jones

provision stalls.

The reign of Saadat Ali Khan also saw the British Cantonment moved from its earlier site near the Daulat Khana to Mariaon, almost five miles north of Lucknow. Treaties between the East India Company and the early Nawabs had allowed for Company troops to be quartered in Oudh at the expense of the Nawabs and both these troops and the Nawabs' own troops (some trained by British officers) had been stationed in cantonments on the north and south banks of the Gumti from about 1796 to 1807.[70] A cantonment of this period should be considered as a semi-permanent site covering quite a large area, and containing brick buildings for the officers, with outhouses for the kitchens, stables and servants' quarters, rows of huts for the sepoys (native soldiers) and a good sized parade ground for the troops to exercise on,[71] though the extent of the Lucknow Cantonment is not certain. Nevertheless the bazaars and shops which normally sprang up to provide provisions and services for the troops must have provided a considerable impetus to development on the north side of the river. The initial pressure for the move away from this site seems to have come from the British. By 1807 there were two Company battalions at Lucknow, one on the north and one on the south bank of the Gumti, and there was no room to build more officers' bungalows, since 'the left flank of the present site is Marshy ground and on the right flank the large Bazar'.[72] The British blamed their troops' illnesses on the cramped conditions in which they lived. The men were 'pent up in a small Hindustanee Building within an assembly of Native Huts, and [with] the vile effluvia of such places, it is not surprising' that they became sick.[73] Several sites were suggested for the new Cantonment, but the continuing unease of the Nawab over allowing a new and enlarged British Cantonment is evident in the way he tried to counter every suggestion made by the British. In 1806 the Nawab wrote, on learning the proposed size of the new Cantonment - 'I have seen many Cantonments of the English troops, but have never observed that any one Cantonment occupied as much ground as is now required.'[74]

Finally the British got their own way and building commenced with many stipulations from the Nawab including the following - 'No work like a Fort shall be constructed on that ground besides the Officers' Bungalows and the Magazine for the Artillery, etc' and

114

'the limits of the new Cantonments shall be distinctly
marked out by some durable token' in addition to a
ditch which was to be dug round the Cantonment.[75]
Several commentators after the 1857 uprising were to
remark on the inadvisability of building a Cantonment
so far from the city and the Residency, since the
British troops were too far away to repel an attack in
the city, and in fact during the uprising the Cantonment was devastated and burnt in a single night (not
being defensible), and the survivors limped into the
city to join the Residency for the seige. The building
of the Cantonment meant, of course, that a new road had
to be constructed to lead into the city, and this
followed the line of the present day Sitapur Road,
crossing the Gumti by the pontoon bridge, directly
south of the present day University, and this road was
naturally maintained in 'excellent condition'.[76]
Within the Cantonment itself the roads were metalled.

With the close of Saadat Ali Khan's reign in 1814
it becomes increasingly difficult to plot the expansion of the city. There are plenty of descriptions by
European travellers of individual buildings, and when
they were built, and comparisons between them and the
squalid streets of the old city, but since a list of
buildings cannot properly be included in the general
development pattern of the city, it is only appropriate
to mention here that the next four Nawabs, Ghazi-ud-din
Haidar, Nasir-ud-din Haidar, Muhammad Ali Shah and Amjad
Ali Shah seem to have continued the trend of putting up
prestige buildings to the south and west of the old
city, rather than building *ganjes* as the earlier Nawabs
had done. Developments in the old city are completely
unrecorded in all European writings and Company correspondence - there is for example a vast area of religious buildings to the far south of the city beyond the
unfinished canal started by Ghazi-ud-din Haidar. This
area is called Talkathora and contains a highly
decorated *barahdari* and a large reproduction of the
karbala[77] in a courtyard surrounded by square cells.
There is an elaborate gateway at the entrance to this
complex, built by a minister of Ghazi-ud-din Haidar
(1814-1827), and it would seem that the minister, Mir
Khuda Baksh, commissioned the gateway to an already
existing place of pilgrimage, but no records so far
found have mentioned this site. Had it been in a more
'fashionable' part of Lucknow, i.e. an area where
Europeans visited or lived, it would doubtless have

12. LUCKNOW: Husainabad Bazar gate

become as celebrated as the Rumi Darwarza and the Great
Imambara, but it receives no mention even in modern
guidebooks.

As noted earlier, Muhammad Ali Shah (1837-42) was
responsible for building the Husainabad Imambara and the
great courtyard with its four massive gateways in front
of the Imambara. From east to west through this square
he built the road linking the Husainabad area with the
Great Imambara area, so that the same road runs from
the western Husainabad gate straight through the Rumi
Darwaza, and all along this road with its iron lamp
posts, were elegant one-storey shops and terraces of
European style houses. Only a small portion of the
shops still exist, practically unrecognisable, and most
of the information on this area comes from a large
panoramic painting by a native artist, but in the
Eruopean style, now in Lucknow Museum in a fragile
condition.[78]

It was during the rule of the next Nawab, Amjad Ali
Shah (1842-1847), that the new road from Lucknow to
Cawnpore was finished under British supervision by
Captains Cunningham and Fraser, and later Captain
Fraser also superintended the bridging and metalling of
this road. The Captain had apparently pleased the
Nawab by the way he had erected the Iron Bridge over
the Gumti just to the west of the Residency in 1845/6,
though the idea of such a bridge had been mooted as
early as 1810 and the bridge arrived in sections from
England in 1816.[79]

The last great building project of the Nawabs was
the Qaisarbagh, originally the most extensive of the
palace complexes and now reduced to a totally unrepre-
sentative single courtyard, with only one of the
central buildings still standing. At least two earlier
buildings were cleverly incorporated into the Qaisarbagh complex, the large and splendid palace-cum-prison,
known as Qaisar Pasand, and more commonly as Roshan-ud-
daula Kachahri, and the two tombs of Saadat Ali Khan
and his wife, built by Ghazi-ud-din Haidar, which were
on the site of a house occupied by the latter. The
north terrace of the main Qaisarbagh courtyard has
long since been demolished, but from existing photographs taken in 1858 these two tombs seem to have
formed an integral part of the Qaisarbagh complex and
may even have been entered on one side through the
houses. The buildings and gardens covered a vast area,
from the earlier Chini Bazaar at the west end of

13. LUCKNOW: a gateway in the Qaisarbagh palace complex built between 1848 and 1850 (Photographed c.1858; now demolished)

modern Hazratganj to the Chattar Manzil complex in the
west, and including much of what is now Hazrat Mahal
Park. The Sher Darwaza, now a single detached gateway,
formerly led into a large walled courtyard, only one of
many now completely vanished. W.H. Russell claimed the
area covered by the palace was as large as the Temple
Gardens, surrounded with ranges of palaces, and he
described the courts as opening 'one to the other by
lofty gateways, ornamented with the double fish of the
royal family of Oude, or by arched passages'.[80] A
panoramic photograph taken in 1858 from the top of
Roshan-ud-daula Kachahri gives some idea of the extent
of the area, and also shows quite clearly that there
had been a conscious attempt at 'town planning' and the
buildings and courtyards were not just a haphazard
jumble thrown together as some commentators have
claimed. There is an unsubstantiated report that the
architect of Qaisarbagh was one Chotay Mian, an inhabi-
tant of Lucknow, who later became a notable photo-
grapher, but died in poverty after the 1857 uprising.
Chotay Mian learnt his trade from an Englishman who
brought the art of photography to the city in the
1850s.[81]

Since this paper is concerned only with the development of Lucknow up to the time of annexation in 1856,
there is very little to add, except for two statements
which may inspire someone to start work on recording
the awful devastation that befell the city after the
1857 uprising when the population fell dramatically.
The first is from the Secretary to the Chief
Commissioner to the Governor-General in Council
writing in January 1858 before Lucknow had been recap-
tured from the Mutineers: 'It is not by an indiscriminate massacre of the wretched sepoys that we should
avenge our kindred. Had Delhi been levelled it would
have been well. A stroke like that would have been a
beacon and a warning to the whole of India, and a very
heavy blow to the Mahomedan religion. It is now too
late however. But the Chief Commissioner sees no
reason why that fate should not befall Lucknow. There
ought to be some place which the mutineers may recognise and point to as the monument of their own crime
and of our retribution.'[82] The second is by a Hindu
from Gola Ganj who wrote: 'Moreover, as the spirit of
vandalism is not yet extinct, the edifices, which have
historical association or otherwise any architectural
pretension, are gradually transformed into debris and

14. LUCKNOW: Roshan-ud-daula (June 1859) (IOL)

ruins.'[83] That was written in 1883 and is sadly as apt
now as it was then, except that there are far fewer
Nawabi and pre-Nawabi buildings left now than there
were a hundred years ago.

GENEALOGICAL TABLE: *THE NAWABS OF OUDH*

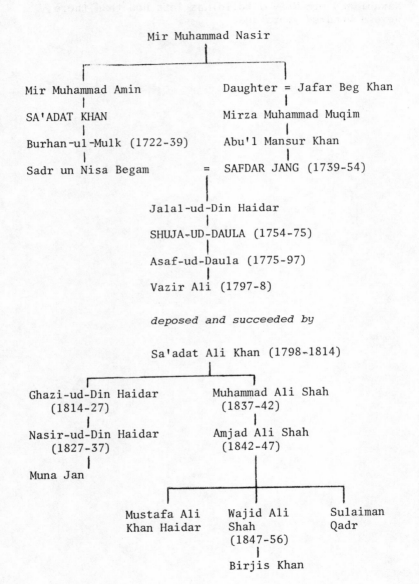

```
                        Mir Muhammad Nasir
                                │
        ┌───────────────────────┴────────────────────────┐
Mir Muhammad Amin                      Daughter = Jafar Beg Khan
        │                                        │
SA'ADAT KHAN                          Mirza Muhammad Muqim
        │                                        │
Burhan-ul-Mulk (1722-39)              Abu'l Mansur Khan
        │                                        │
Sadr un Nisa Begam          =         SAFDAR JANG (1739-54)
                                │
                    Jalal-ud-Din Haidar
                                │
                    SHUJA-UD-DAULA (1754-75)
                                │
                    Asaf-ud-Daula (1775-97)
                                │
                    Vazir Ali (1797-8)

                    deposed and succeeded by

                    Sa'adat Ali Khan (1798-1814)
                                │
        ┌───────────────────────┴─────────────────────┐
Ghazi-ud-Din Haidar                   Muhammad Ali Shah
    (1814-27)                             (1837-42)
        │                                     │
Nasir-ud-Din Haidar                   Amjad Ali Shah
    (1827-37)                             (1842-47)
        │                                     │
Muna Jan              ┌──────────────────────┼──────────────────┐
                Mustafa Ali           Wajid Ali          Sulaiman
                Khan Haidar           Shah               Qadr
                                      (1847-56)
                                          │
                                      Birjis Khan
```

Llewellyn-Jones, 'The City of Lucknow Before 1856'

1. Lucknow since 1947 has been the state capital of Uttar Pradesh, as it had been de facto capital of the United Provinces from the 1920s. From 1856 to 1877 it was the seat of the Chief Commissioner of Oudh whose charge was then merged in the lieutenant-governorship of the United Provinces of Agra and Oudh.

2. Despite a core of continuity, the province of Oudh has been subject to many changes of boundary. The boundaries of Sultanate, Mughal, Nawabi and British Oudh do not coincide.

3. H.R. Nevill, *Lucknow. A Gazetteer*, vol.xxxvii (District Gazetteers of the United Province of Agra and Oudh) (1922), pp.143-144. The *faujdar* or *sarkar* of Lucknow was appointed by Akbar and took orders independently of the governor of the *subah*, at least in the early years of that emperor.

4. Wolseley Haig (ed.), *Cambridge History of India*, vol.iii (Cambridge 1928), p.247.

5. J. Mill, *History of British India*, vol.iii, p. 361.

6. J. Paton, *Abstract of the Political Intercourse between the British Government and the Kingdom of Oude, 1764-1835*, (ed. B. Prasad, Allahabad 1944), pp.44-47.

7. Anon., *Lucknow, the Garden of India* (Lucknow 1928), p.11. And see also John Pemble, *The Raj, the Indian Mutiny and the Kingdom of Oudh 1801-1859* (Harvester Press 1977), p.11. This repeats the myth that Lucknow was merely a collection of villages before 1775 and states (wrongly) that Asaf-ud-daula built the Chauk and the Stone Bridge which crossed the Gumti at Macchi Bhawan. In fact, this bridge was built by Newal Rae, a Minister to Safdar Jang, though the stone coping which gives it its name may not have been added until later.

8. Jean Deloch (ed.), *Voyage en Inde du Comte de Modave* (Paris 1971), pp.183,324. Hereafter Modave, op. cit.; my translation throughout.

9. Joseph Tieffenthaler, *Description Historique et Geographique de l'Inde* (3 vols., Berlin 1786-1788), vol. i, p.256. Again my translation from the original French is used.

10. *Gazetteer of the Province of Oudh* (1877), p. 364.

11. Maulana Sharar, *Guzashta Laknau* (Lucknow n.d.), pp.56,60.

12. Sharar, op.cit., p.55.

13. Gazetteer of 1877, p.365.

14. William Foster, *The English Factories in India* (Oxford), vol.1637-1641, p.278; vol.1642-1645, p.233; vol.1646-1650, pp.122,140,211,338; vol.1651-1656, pp.71, 114,148; 'dereabauds' came originally from the town of Daryabad or Dariabad, a town about thirty miles to the east of Lucknow, hence the name.

15. Two names are quoted for the religious leader who was given the Farangi Mahal by Aurangzeb - according to V.C. Sharma,*Uttar Pradesh District Gazetteer* (1959), p.36, it was the sons of Mulla Qutb-ud-din of Bara Banki who received the buildings, while according to Sharar, op.cit., p.60, it was Mulla Nazam Aladin Sahalvi.

16. Panch Mahala - the term *mahala* or *mahale* which is the plural form of *mahal* (palace), should not be confused with *muhalla* meaning a district or area in a town.

17. P.C. Mookherjee, *Pictorial Lucknow* (Lucknow 1883), p.217.

18. A.L. Srivastava, *The First Two Nawabs of Oudh* (Delhi 1933), p.33.

19. Modave, op.cit., p.142.

20. Mookherjee, op.cit., p.227.

21. Tieffenthaler, op.cit., vol.i, p.256.

22. Abu Talib (transl. William Hoey), *Tafuzzil Ghafi'lin* (Allahabad 1885).

23. Bengal Political Consultations, 19 March 1832, No.54.

24. Tieffenthaler, op.cit., vol.i, p.256. 'The majority are of lime or mortar, covered with tiles' - I think here that Tieffenthaler means the roofs were covered with tiles, not the walls, and that by lime and mortar he probably means unbaked brick covered with a crude plaster.

25. 'Where the tambour players would sound the drums'. This great doorway with the wall supported by arcades was obviously a *Naubat Khana* where musicians and drummers would sit to signal the arrival of a great personage with fanfares. The Naubat Khana, commonly but wrongly translated as 'drum house' was a common feature in great houses, religious buildings and palace entrances, and took the form of a great outer gateway, the thickness of several rooms and often

three or four stories high. Its only equivalent would
seem to be in Elizabethan or Jacobean gatehouses
attached to country houses.
    26. Tieffenthaler, op.cit., vol.ii, p.257.
    27. Modave, op.cit., p.143. It is likely that this
Frenchman was Antoine Polier, a close friend of Shuja-
ud-daula's and an Engineer who had worked for the East
India Company. In 1773 Polier was named as architect
to the Court of Shuja-ud-daula. See Modave, op.cit.,
p.442.
    28. Modave, op.cit., p.145. The Mughals were
originally a peripatetic, tent-dwelling people. The
Emperor Akbar is believed to have spent as much as a
third of his reign under canvas in the great tented
imperial camps set up for royal progresses round the
provinces. These camps were very much as Modave
describes them - full of luxurious tent hangings,
mirrors, carpets, etc, and the outer perimeter of the
camps was marked by two high canvas 'walls' forming a
passage. The early Nawabs, too, spent much time under
canvas, and the tradition was maintained by Asaf-ud-
daula and Saadat Ali Khan with their hunting parties
who would travel for several months during the cold
season from place to place in these tented 'cities'.
Describing such a camp William Blane wrote in 1785-6
'There is a large public Bazar, or, in other words, a
moving town, attends [Asaf-ud-daula's] camp, consisting
of shopkeepers and artificers of all kinds, money
changers, dancing women etc. so that, upon the most
moderate calculation, the number of souls in his camp
cannot be recokoned at less than 20,000.' *An Account of
the Hunting Excursions of Asoph ul Dowlah* (London 1788),
p.8.
    29. Modave, op.cit., p.143.
    30. William Hodges, *Travels in India during the
Years 1780, 81, 82 and 83* (London 1793), p.104.
    31. There are three very useful lists made for the
East India Company of the Servants and the Household
Establishments of the Nawabs; the 1831 list includes
the Personal Troops of the Nawab. They are: The
Nawab's Household Accounts 1780-1783, British Library,
Add. MSS 29093, f.14; Bengal Political Consultations,
30 September 1831, No.54; and Bengal Political Con-
sultations, 13 June 1856, No.172.
    32. Asaf-ud-daula's renovations of the Macchi
Bhawab did not meet with everyone's approval. His
grandmother, Sadrun Nisa Begam, complained to the

Mughal Emperor that 'the Nawab has entirely ruined the
house which Nawab Shuja-ud-daula raised to the highest
pitch of splendour', *Calendar of Persian Correspondence*,
vol.v, 1776-1780, p.189.

33. Sidney Hay, *Historic Lucknow* (Lucknow 1939),
p.13.

34. Bengal Political Consultations, 11 December
1806.

35. Rev. William Tennant, *Indian Recreations* (2
vols., London 1804).

36. *Calendar of Persian Correspondence*, vol.v,
1776-1780, p.25

37. Claude Martin to John Macpherson, 22 February
1785, British Library, Add. MSS 29168, f.103. *Nawab
Vizier* was the full title of the Lucknow Nawabs. The
term nawab (vulgarly nabob) is a Persian word meaning a
governor of a town or district and the word wazir is a
minister of state or prim minister. *Bildars*, shovel
men; *mistris*, carpenters; *laskars*, common soldiers.

38. Correspondence between the India Board and the
Court of Directors of the East India Company, for the
year 1834; Foreign Political Consultations, 3 February
1816, H.J. Clark's petition.

39. Modave, op.cit., p.184.

40. Hodges, op.cit., p.100.

41. Diary of Ozias Humphry, 5 February 1786-19 June
1786, Photostat in the IOL of MS. in Yale University
Library, no pagination.

42. Thomas Twining, *Travels in India a Hundred Ye
Years Ago* (London 1893), p.308.

43. Tennant, op.cit., p.404.

44. Bengal Political Consultations, 8 February
1850, No.150, and other half yearly medical reports
issued by doctors working in the Lucknow Hospitals
between 1 May 1839 and 31 March 1849 in the Bengal
Political Consultations. These reports do not run
consecutively but provide a good picture of the state
of health among the poor of Lucknow. Neville, op.cit.,
see the various reports on crafts introduced during
Nawabi times.

45. W.H. Russell, *My Indian Mutiny Diary* (London
1860), p.106; Bengal Political Consultations, 1 August
1856, No.68.

46. Ibid., 6 October 1849, No.130.

47. Ibid., 22 August 1828, No.11, 13 December, No.
21.

48. Tennant, op.cit., p.404.

49. W. Hamilton, *The East Indian Gazetteer containing Particular Descriptions of Hindostan* (2 vols, London 1828), p.131f. This is also the figure given for the estimated population of Calcutta in 1773, i.e. 300,000 (see Modave, op.cit., p.81), a town founded by the British which expanded rapidly in the eighteenth century. It is doubtful that Lucknow's population would have exceeded that of late eighteenth-century Calcutta even after the influx of people to the Nawabi Court.

50. Edward Thornton, *Gazetteer of the Territories under the Government of the East-India Company* (London 1857).

51. R. Mukherjee and B. Singh, *Social Profiles of a Metropolis (Lucknow) 1954-56* (Bombay 1961), p.11.

52. Gazetteer for 1959, Sharma, op.cit., p.63.

53. Hodges, op.cit., p.100, Modave, op.cit., p.183; Mukherjee and Singh, op.cit., p.11.

54. Home Misc. 345, pp.329-348 quoting from Bengal Secret Consultations, 4 October 1773, Warren Hastings to Nawab Shuja-ud-daula.

55. Bengal Political Consultations, 21 December 1792, Lucknow Resident, E. Otto Ives, writing about the late George Sangster.

56. Letter from Ozias Humphry, 29 December 1785, in the Humphry Collection, Royal Academy Library, London.

57. Bengal Political Consultations, 26 August 1831, No.30. See also, for a discussion of the Resident's position, P.J. Marshall, 'Economic and Political Expansion - the Case of Oudh', *Modern Asian Studies* 9, 4 (1975), pp.465-482.

58. Claude Martin's Will, La Martiniere copy, Lucknow.

59. Home Public Index, 20 July 1778, 28 November 1778, National Archives, New Delhi.

60. Bengal Public Consultations, 28 July 1778.

61. Instructions to John Bristow, the Lucknow Resident - 'he [the Nawab] must make his Election between the French and the English as he cannot be in Amity with one of these Nations without bearing an Emnity to the other', Secret and Military Consultations, 3 April 1773.

62. Foreign Political Consultations, 20 June 1788.

63. Ibid, 9 August 1814.

64. Bengal Political Consultations, 29 July 1789.

65. See the Genealogical table, page 122.

66. *The European Magazine*, vol.xvii (January-June

1790), p.86f.
    67. Hamilton, op.cit., p.131f.
    68. Thomas Lumsden, *Journey from Merut in India to London etc. during the years 1819 and 1820* (London 1822), p.9.
    69. L.E. Ruutz Rees, *A Personal Narrative of the Siege of Lucknow* (London 1858), p.252.
    70. Foreign Political Consultations, 11 December 1806.
    71. Lumsden, op.cit., p.14f.
    72. Foreign Political Consultations, 12 February 1807.
    73. Ibid., 12 February 1807.
    74. Ibid., 11 December 1806.
    75. Ibid., 5 March 1807.
    76. Joseph Fayrer, *Recollections of My Life* (London 1900), p.87.
    77. *Barahdari*, according to Platt's *Dictionary*, is a building with twelve doors, a kind of summer house or garden house. In fact there are often more than twelve doors or arches, sometimes open, sometimes with glazed doors. Such buildings are of one storey, usually with further rows of supporting arches inside, and often elaborately decorated with stucco work. *Karbala* is the name of the place in Iraq where Husain the younger son of Ali was killed and buried. It is also (in India) a Muslim shrine or burying place, the place where the *taziya* is buried (Platts). The *taziya* is a model of a tomb and is associated with the Muharrum or mourning processions of the Shi'as, who commemorate the deaths of the Prophet's family. The Lucknow *karbalas* are supposed to be accurate representations of the tomb of Husain.
    78. Oudh Company Painting, uncatalogued, c.1850, Lucknow Museum.
    79. Foreign Index, 6 June 1846, National Archives, New Delhi. For a fuller analysis of the building of this road, see Robert Varady, 'The Diary of a Road: a Sequential Narration of the Origins of the Lucknow-Kanpur Road (1825-1856)', *Indian Economic and Social History Review*, XV, 2, pp.151-172.
    80. Russell, op.cit., p.193.
    81. Mookherjee, op.cit., p.183.
    82. Secret Consultations, 29 January 1858, 361.
    83. Mookherjee, op.cit., from the preface, (unpaginated).

URBAN PROBLEMS AND GOVERNMENT POLICIES: A CASE STUDY OF THE CITY OF DACCA, 1810-1830

S.U. Ahmed

Historical studies of the towns and cities of India under British rule are still very few.[1] Fewer still are studies of the policy and attitude of the East India Company's government towards the urban problems of the towns of the interior of the three Presidencies, before the establishment of local self-government. An attempt has been made in this article to review this policy and to examine the attitude of the Company to the problems of the mufassal towns of the Bengal Presidency during the early years of its rule. This has been mainly illustrated by discussing the condition and problems of the city of Dacca during the early years of the nineteenth century as a case study.

Mughal policy was to entrust urban administration and police to the *kotwal*. He was the chief of the city police, and his duties included watch and ward. He was also in charge of sanitation, including the establishment of scavengers, who also acted as informers. He was also responsible for the regulation of the market, for the allocation of quarters for butchers, for the maintenance of burial and cremation grounds, for the prevention of social abuses, such as drinking, and for regulating the conduct of the public women.[2] It was mainly the responsibility of the government to build roads, rest-houses, bridges, wells, tanks, drains and the like, but such works were often undertaken as well by the opulent and charitable.[3]

It is impossible to state in general terms for lack of information[4] how diligently and how satisfactorily the *kotwals* performed their duties. It may, however, be expected that in such important urban centres as the administrative capitals, ports and emporia in whose welfare the government had a large stake and where the ruling authorities themselves resided such duties were tolerably performed.[5] Dacca was one such capital city.

From an obscure position the city rose to prominence in 1610 when it was made the capital of the *subah* (or province) of Bengal, Bihar and Orissa. From this time it developed quickly in stature as the metropolis of the province. As administrative and military

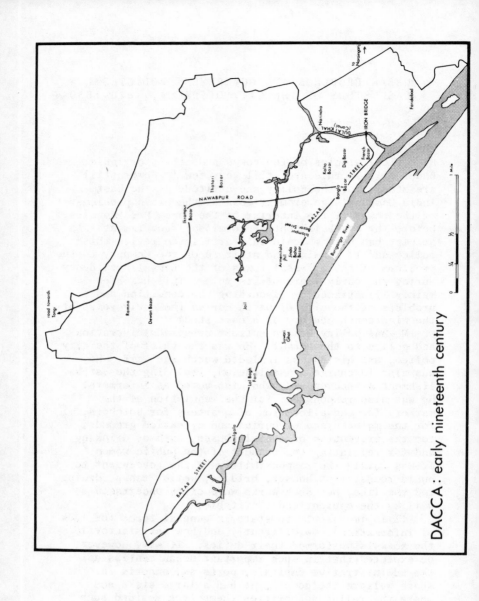

DACCA: early nineteenth century

headquarters of the province the city expanded rapidly
and soon the growth of its trade and commerce and the
flourishing of its world-famous fine cotton goods manufacture brought additional wealth, increased population
and led to its further expansion. Dacca grew into a
large, wealthy and prosperous town to become the queen
of the cities of eastern India.[6]

At the height of its glory and prosperity during
the Mughal period the boundaries of Dacca were defined
to the south by the river Buriganga (on whose northern
bank it is situated), to the north the Tongi bridge a
distance of about fifteen miles, and from Jafarabad on
the west to Postogola on the east - a distance of about
ten miles. However, the city proper was confined to a
much less extensive area chiefly along the ten miles of
the bank of the river and at most two and a half miles
inland to the north. The greater part of the north of
the city consisted of gardens and cultivation and was
sparsely populated. The city was also said to have
contained a population of about 900,000.[7] Many
palaces, mosques, temples, roads, bridges, gateways,
gardens, aqueducts, tanks, markets and *ghats* (landing
places on the river) were built to meet the needs of
the high officials, together with the crowded quarters
of the ordinary people.

By the beginning of the eighteenth century (c.1715-
1716), Dacca had lost its status as a capital which
practically checked its further growth and development.
However, it did not lose its significance as an important centre of administration, trade, commerce and
manufacture for it remained the headquarters of a
regional administration (the jurisdiction of the Dacca
niabat or sub-province of Dacca extended over half the
area of present-day Bangladesh) and its commerce and
manufactures increased by leaps and bounds, largely
through the activities of the European trading companies and other foreign merchants.[8] In 1747 cotton
goods alone worth Rs.28,50,000 were exported from
Dacca so that there occurred no significant decline of
the city.

However, Dacca quickly lost its position as an
important centre of administration and commerce and
manufacture with the disintegration of the Mughal
empire and the rise of the British power during the
second half of the eighteenth century. In 1757 the
British gained military control of Bengal and in 1765
assumed the civil administration of the country. From

16. DACCA: the grand Katra (D'Oyly)

about this time Dacca declined rapidly. Political
power shifted to Calcutta - the rising capital of the
province - which gradually took administrative and
military control over the whole country and increasingly monopolised trade and commerce. Rather later,
the importation of cheap mill-made English cotton
goods ruined Dacca's flourishing textile industry.

In 1765 the city had an estimated population of
450,000[9] and in 1793 was stated to cover an area four
miles long and two and a half miles broad.[10] By 1801
the population had declined to 200,000 and the limits
of the city had shrunk still further from Enayetganj
on the west to Faridabad on the east, a distance of
about three and a half miles, and from Buriganga on the
south to Dewan Bazar on the north, a distance of about
a mile and a half.[11]

Soon after the assumption of direct responsibility
for the civil administration in 1772 the government of
the East India Company began to reorganise the administrative structure of the country. As a result the
city of Dacca lost many of its administrative functions,
and the offices of *faujdar* and *kotwal* who had been
entrusted with police and municipal duties, were superseded by that of the European Magistrate who then became
the chief police officer of the city and district of
Dacca. However, the office of *kotwal* was not actually
abolished and in the administrative reforms of Warren
Hastings in 1782, a *kotwali* establishment was provided
for Dacca consisting of one *kotwal*, sixty *burkandazes*
(armed guards), thirty *pasbans* (watchmen) and ten *doms*
(scavengers) at a monthly cost of Rs.425.[12] However,
the office of *kotwal* increasingly lost its vigour and
power which were steadily taken over by the Magistrate,
so much so that the office became an anachronism. It
was on the advice of the Magistrate of Dacca[13] that
the office of *kotwal* was finally abolished in 1814
under Regulation 13 of that year.

Although the Magistrate replaced the Mughal *kotwal*
he did not expressly assume his municipal responsibilities, and although the government levied town-
duties and house-tax from the urban communities they
were applied mainly to the policing of urban centres
and not to wider municipal purposes.[14]

Consequently municipal functions and the general
improvement of the towns suffered greatly, and in
Dacca in 1810 a group of senior civil servants of the
Company sought to take the responsibility for the urban

problems of the city into their own hands. Shearman
Bird and Edward Strachey, the Judges of the Provincial
Court of Circuit and Appeal, Shearman Bird Junior, the
Magistrate, Charles D'Oyly, the Collector, and John
Pattenson, the Commercial Resident at Dacca, wrote to
government that they proposed 'to form at Dacca under
the authority of Government, an association for the
improvement of the city and its environs'. They added
that in future the association would also include such
'Gentlemen at the station' who might be admitted 'under
the rules of the institution'. Explaining the purpose
of the association they observed that under the former
government there were in the city and its environs
considerable public works[15] such as roads, bridges,
tanks, wells and drains, many of which had been constructed at great expense 'not from a mere principle
of ostentation but for the general good'. Among these
old public works many were now in disrepair, others
had been entirely destroyed, but all those which
existed were 'in a state of progressive decay' owing to
lack of care and maintenance, so that great inconvenience had been felt by the community. It was, therefore, the duty of government to come forward to rescue
those works from ruin and relieve the people from
distress and suffering. Yet in the city of Dacca there
were no proper authorities by whom works of this nature
were cognizable. The Magistrate of the city, they
hastened to add, was indeed the person whom 'matters of
general police' were ostensibly to concern, and the
Judges of the Court of the Circuit had an opportunity
in their periodical reports of bringing such things
under the notice of the *Nizamat Adalat* (the Criminal
Court of Appeal), but it formed no essential part of
the duties of these officers to ascertain and report
the state of public works, to consider 'the inconven-
iences and comforts' of the people at large and to
suggest improvements. As a direct consequence of the
absence of a proper authority entrusted with the welfare of the city and its people, many individuals in
Dacca, they commented, had encroached upon public
lands and thoroughfares by unlawfully constructing
houses and shops upon them to the great detriment of
the public interest, and the city abounded in filth
and nuisances. To stop such practices, to remove
filth and nuisances, to rescue several of the old
public works from total ruin, to repair and improve
others and to construct such new ones as would bring

material advantages to the city and its people, they
said, they wished to form themselves into a Committee
of Improvement, and for such works they asked the
government for the free use of convicts of the Dacca
Jail and a small annual grant. A part of the expense,
they were prompt to add, would be met by 'private
voluntary contribution', and the direction and management of the Committee would be performed by the
members of the association themselves gratuitously.[16]

This first attempt at local improvement under a
municipal body never saw the light of day. The
Governor-General, Lord Minto, rejected the proposal,
arguing that the formation of the Committee would serve
no useful purpose without specific funds and powers.
If the promoters of the association, he replied, had
been hoping to form themselves into a public institution then they were mistaken for he could not permit
them to found such an organisation, 'for such an
arrangement would evidently be too wide a departure
from the general system established for the internal
Government of the country'. He also observed that the
formation of the Committee was unnecessary as several
public authorities had already been entrusted with
those works which they wanted to execute. It was the
duty of the Magistrate of the city to report to
government whenever any existing public works might
require repair. Whether the government would undertake
the execution of such works or not of course depended
upon the availability of funds. It was still more
especially his duty to prevent and abate encroachments
and nuisances, and that of the subordinate officers of
police to report to him all such occurrences for
that express purpose. Likewise, the Judges of the
Provincial Court of Appeal, the Collector of the
District and the Collector of Customs at Dacca, were
not only authorised but required to report and submit
to government through the proper channels their views
'on any question connected with the health and convenience of the community'. It was thus apparent, he
remarked, that there was no want of means of drawing
the attention of government through the established
state machinery to any object of improvement which
might be deemed necessary or desirable. It was also
apparent from the communication, he said, that money
required for the necessary expenditure should be for
the most part provided by government. But he was not
in a position to grant any specific fund for the

improvement of Dacca other than what could be
furnished as routine expenditure of government. Finally
he instructed the Magistrate of Dacca and others to be
more vigilant and active in obviating nuisances and
promoting the public convenience.[17]

It is clear from this reply that the government had
as yet no definite policy for tackling the urban
problems of mufassal towns and certainly no intention
of sanctioning specific funds for public works or of
establishing municipal institutions. Although Minto
was at pains to stress that the police authorities in
the urban centres had been entrusted with municipal
duties, this was not borne out in actual practice. At
least the Magistrate of Dacca did not think that municipal functions were integral parts of his duties-
which explained his being one of the signatories to the
proposal. In any case the Magistrate who was also the
judge of the city had little time to deal with these
problems.

However, the instructions from the Governor-General
to the Magistrate and other officials at Dacca to abate
nuisances and promote public convenience did produce
some desirable effects. Henceforth they became more
concerned to deal with, or at least to bring to the
notice of government the various urban problems. Two
months later in December 1810 Edward Strachey submitted
to government a memorandum on the state of Dacca and
its environs, depicting the sad plight of the town and
furnishing a plan for its improvement which was later
accepted as a model.[18]

In 1813 the Officiating Magistrate of Dacca, James
Oldham, seriously turned his attention to improving
the town. First he undertook to develop the Dacca
Jail and its neighbourhood, clearing the compound and
its surrounds of rubbish and jungle, draining a noxious
marsh and filling in various deep ditches and pits. He
also built a brick wall along the boundaries of the
jail. As a natural corollary to these developments he
then reclaimed and repaired part of the road that ran
northwards from near the Jail towards Tongi Bridge via
Tejgaon where there was still a Factory of the East
India Company. All these works, which greatly improved
part of the northern side of the city were, however,
done solely by the convicts of the Dacca Jail. So
greatly impressed was John Mitford Rees, Judge of the
Provincial Court of Circuit at Dacca, by the results
of this useful employment of the labour of the convicts

that he reported them to government and suggested yet
again the formation of a Committee of Improvement at
Dacca. To forstall any response on the lines of the
Governor-General's letter of 1810 he pointed out that
the heavy judicial and police duties of the Judge-
Magistrate left no leisure for improvement and municipal works, and he made the point that it was vital to
entrust them to a permanent body rather than to
individuals subject to constant postings. Frequent
transfers were a real impediment 'as the work one
Magistrate commences upon is sometimes quitted by the
orders of another who thinks his own plans are better
calculated'. Despite some recent improvements, he
remarked, 'the state of the city in regard to roads,
streets, and nuisances is deplorable - deep pits
covered with jungle and full of stagnant water - piles
of rubbish, clogged drains, broken Bridges and wells
and symptom of Decay appears; the streets are all
irregular, and in many places the people have by
imperceptive degrees encroached upon them by chuppas
(huts) and walls from whence it would be difficult to
dislodge them'. It would be years before many of these
ills were rectified and the condition of the city
improved. Material progress, he said, could only be
achieved if the tasks of cleaning the town and
developing the roads and other public works were
entrusted to a permanent body composed of some
'Gentlemen at the station' and possessing the authority
to use the labour of the convicts. He, therefore,
requested government to set up such a body at Dacca
immediately. He also suggested that as the number of
prisoners in the Dacca Jail was very small - 368 only
of every description - additional prisoners should be
brought from the other district headquarters of the
Division to the city jail whose labour might more
beneficially be utilised in works involving the
improvement of the city. The City Jail, he reported,
could accommodate between seven and eight hundred
prisoners.[19]
This time the government agreed, authorising John
Mitford Rees, John Bardoe Elliot, the acting Judge-
Magistrate, William Rennell, the Collector, and Dr
David Todd, the surgeon, to form themselves into a
'Committee for the Improvement of the City of Dacca
and other places immediately adjacent to the city'.
However, the Governor-General made it clear to them
that the Committee should only be a deliberative body

leaving to the Magistrate the immediate superintendence of the work and the charge of the convicts who might be employed on it and that they should suggest directly to the Magistrate only such work as could be done by the convicts. With regard, however, to work involving expenditure the approval of government must first be secured.[20] The Governor-General also instructed the *Nizamat Adalat* to despatch as many prisoners as possible to Dacca from other districts of the Dacca Division.

The formation of the Committee scarcely constituted a new phase in the policy of government towards the problems of urban centres, still less any new readiness to apply specific funds to urban improvements. It was formulated rather to obviate the practical difficulties arising from the frequent transfers of Magistrates and to make some better use of the labour of prisoners.

However, the child to which government so reluctantly acted as midwife soon died. In September 1814, the Committee wrote to government with a list of works to be undertaken, and recommending the appointment of a full-time Superintendent, at a salary of Rs.390 per month, to supervise them as none of the Committee was in a position to do so in view of the great pressure of their regular official duties. They also requested that the Magistrates of the Dacca Division be again reminded to despatch additional prisoners to the City Jail for the use of the Committee as none had yet been despatched to Dacca. This letter is the only recorded action taken by the Committee during its brief existence. However, the Governor-General in Council rejected the request for a Superintendent of Works on the ground of public economy and warned the members 'not to spend too much time on the matters of the Committee', advising that 'all measures of executing improvement works' must be done by the Magistrate within whose province actually fell the duty of undertaking such tasks.[21] This reply from government seems to have produced a very discouraging effect as the members gradually ceased to take any part in the Committee. The hope that the inhabitants of Dacca would come forward with financial aid also did not materialise, only three individuals making some contribution.[22] Not surprisingly, the Committee soon ceased to function, perhaps with the transfer of its more enthusiastic members.

In August 1817 cholera broke out in the city for the first time in an epidemic form. Fortunately,

however, it did not prove extremely fatal perhaps due
to the treatment provided by the medical authorities.
The Civil Surgeon reported that only 6.6 per cent of
seizures terminated fatally so that out of 1,051
persons attacked, only 69 died.[23] Although the
mortality was not very high, the disease struck terror
into the inhabitants so that many of them left the town
never to return, the re-appearance of the disease in
succeeding years discouraging them from coming back.[24]
It also caused a panic among the European inhabitants
who became alarmed for their safety. At the same time
the medical authorities in the city continued to
express their opinion that the disease could not be
controlled as long as the appalling state of the
sanitation of the city was left unattended. Perhaps
because of such opinions and his own personal experience of the havoc caused by cholera, Judge John Ahmuty
of the Provincial Court of Circuit and Appeal wrote to
government in October 1818 about the deplorable condition of Dacca and suggested measures of reform.
Because of the physical decay and the long neglected
state of the city, he reported, 'epidemic diseases,
which formerly seldom or slightly visited the native
inhabitants at particular periods, are now frequent and
general without adverting to Cholera Morbus which has
already ... decimated the population of India'. It was
thus absolutely essential that measures be undertaken
immediately to improve the condition of the town. He
suggested that the two main streets of the city be
immediately repaired and paved with brick and *surki* or
brick-dust, that all the bridges and drains be
reclaimed and that the jungle, which had been rapidly
encroaching upon the town from the north and east and
which, if not checked and cleared, threatened to invade
and destroy it in time like Gaur (the medieval capital
of Bengal), should be eradicated without delay. He
also submitted a plan of his own for carrying out these
works and requested government to re-appoint a
Committee to execute them, urging that it should
encourage the principal and opulent native inhabitants
of Dacca, including the Greeks and Armenians, to
subscribe towards the improvement of their city.
Meanwhile he pleaded for the Committee to be granted
Rs.6,000 for the repair and paving of the two main
streets, and supplied with the labour of additional
prisoners from the districts for carrying out the
necessary works.[25]

A new Committee of Improvement on the same footing
as the former - the government still refusing to
sanction any grant of specific funds for municipal and
public works - was duly appointed in April 1819 with
John Ahmuty, Shearman Bird Junior, the Judge-Magistrate,
Robert Mitford, the Collector, John Master, the Acting
Magistrate and Register (Registrar) of the City Court
of Dacca, and Dr David Todd, the Civil Surgeon, as its
members.[26] With the formation of this Committee the
work of solving the urban problems and restoring the
public health of Dacca really began.

At first the Committee tackled small improvements
like cutting down the weeds and scrub in and around the
city, clearing ruins and abandoned huts, and cleansing
and sweeping the roads. But in 1822 Charles Dawes was
appointed Magistrate of Dacca; he was one of those
zealous and public spirited British officials of the
early nineteenth century who devoted themselves whole-
heartedly to public service and to works of general
utility. As Magistrate he was also an ex-officio
member of the Committee of Improvement. An 'eccentric
civilian' as a later writer described him,[27] Dawes soon
after taking charge of the city turned his attention to
improving the public thoroughfares and bridges. With
the funds of the Committee and the free labour of the
convicts, he repaired the two main streets of the town.
One of those was the Bazaar Street which ran westwards
from Dulai Khal near Narinda towards Lal Bagh fort and
was about four miles in extent; the other the Nawabpur
Bazaar Street ran from the Company ghat now known as
Sadar Ghat (the principal landing place) on the river
Buriganga in the south to Nawabpur in the north and
beyond the city boundary to Tejgaon bridge and was also
four miles in extent. Only the city portion of this
latter road was, however, repaired and paved. Likewise
Dawes also repaired some other minor streets of the
town. As a further extension of Magistrate Oldham's
works he also repaired and reclaimed the Dacca-Tongi
road up to Tejgaon. He even employed the prisoners in
watering the two principal streets of the city during
the dry months.

In late 1822 he undertook the clearance by convict
labour of the jungle to the immediate north of the
city. After more than three months work, the thick and
almost impenetrable wilderness of Ramna which had been
the haunt of wild beasts and a primary source of
unhealthiness to Dacca was cleared away and 'a large

plain of an oval shape' was gained. The clearance of
this jungle opened up the northern outskirts of the
city and improved the salubrity of those parts of the
town nearest to it by a freer circulation of air. In
early 1823, Dawes also employed the convicts in reclaiming and enlarging the Protestant Burial ground to
the north-east of the city near Narinda.[28] Initially
Dawes was restricted in his work of improvement by his
lack of any considerable resources other than the
convict labour. Fortunately, however, from 1823 funds
were provided in substantial amounts with which many
works of improvements were carried out.

Since the passing of the Chowkidari Act of 1813, the
principle of local taxation to meet a local expenditure,
in this case a house-tax to provide the wages of town
chaukidars or night-watchmen, had been established in
Bengal,[29] and in 1822 government had also agreed to
allow the people of Dacca to spend any surplus from
this fund upon city public works. In 1823, however,
the Governor-General John Adam took the much larger and
unprecedented step of assigning public funds specifically for works of 'general utility' and 'for the benefit
of the population'.

On the eve of his leaving office he recorded a
minute in the Territorial Department on 22 May, frankly
admitting that it was striking that the government had
until then done very little to improve the living
conditions of the people under its rule, and had spent
even less on public works. Although the obligations of
the state in those respects had long been admitted,
there had never been any surplus funds to spend on works
of public utility. On the contrary, he recorded, as the
revenues were deficient, the government had had to
borrow heavily to meet the 'public exigencies'. The
subordinate position of the Government of India had
naturally made it reluctant to allow any increase in
the debt that was not absolutely unavoidable, especially
while the costs of war stretched its resources.
'Indeed', he said, 'until the British supremacy was
fully established over the whole continent, it would
neither have been safe nor prudent to have employed on
such objects funds that might eventually be required to
forward interests of more vital importance'. But the
financial position of the Company had lately improved
substantially so that there was now a surplus in the
Indian revenues.[30] This surplus, he said, could either
be used for relieving the public from burdensome taxes

or be spent on works of general utility for the benefit of the whole population. The subordinate position of the Indian government had rendered it absolutely impossible for him to abolish any item of public revenue without the consent of the Court of Directors. This was why he could not stop the collection of town-duties[31] though he was not insensible to various objections against their imposition. However, he saw no impropriety in immediately assigning the revenues from this source for municipal and public works. Of course the Directors must be informed, but until they decided otherwise the assignment should be continued, for he considered the government 'to be under an imperative obligation to make some special assignment from the superfluities it possesses to promote public works and other objects of extensive benefit to the community'. The principle of such an assignment had already been recognised in the Charter Act of 1813, for in that Act although the Government of India was at the time greatly encumbered with debt and the obligation to reduce it was prominently enforced, special provision had still been made for the assignment of a lakh of rupees per annum for Indian education. 'With this example of anxiety shown by the legislature to make the British rule conducive to the happiness and prosperity of the country,' he observed, 'I think we should fail in duty if we did not endeavour to extend to the community some additional assistance in consequence of the present affluent state of our finances.'

He was particularly struck, Adam said, to see the appalling condition of the roads, bridges and *ghats* on the rivers throughout the country, and the insanitary and insalubrious state of the towns and cities of the interior. Much of the unhealthiness of the urban centres, he remarked, was due to their defective planning and construction. 'In Bengal especially the want of ventilation which arises from the narrowness of the streets, the crowded population congregated in masses of filthy huts, the quantity of trees, bamboos and underwood, the pools, hollow ditches and jheels (marshes) in which the water stagnates and becomes putrid, added to the effect of the heat and moisture of climate, render almost all cities and towns exceedingly unhealthy.' In Calcutta, he said, much had been done by the Committee of Improvement who had had at their disposal the funds raised by a lottery.[32] The impact of their measures on the salubrity of the city was

already apparent, and the results afforded a satisfactory assurance of the extent of the blessings which by a
like course could be bestowed upon the inhabitants of
other cities of the Bengal Presidency. In the city of
Dacca, although a committee had already been established, little had been accomplished for lack of funds,
though as far back as 1810 a valuable memorandum had
been furnished by Edward Strachey on the public works
and improvements required at Dacca. A few thousand
rupees only had at different periods been devoted to
the improvement of the city, but the chief part of
Strachey's plan remained unattempted though to all
appearance highly desirable of accomplishment. Hence,
'the encroachment of the jungle and the accumulation
of the causes of disease (which in Bengal consist
chiefly in the want of ventilation and the miasma of
stagnant pools) threaten the city tho' possessed of
many natural advantages, with a rapidly progressive
decay'. As similar reports had reached him from Patna,
Murshidabad, Gorakhpur and other towns and cities, he
had decided that it would be a very appropriate and
popular measure to assign the duties collected on their
imports for the improvement of public health and the
execution of public works of general utility. Town
duties being local taxes, there could be no reasonable
objections to their use in local improvement works
especially when not required by the state. The management of these funds and the execution of such works
should be entrusted to Committees of Improvement consisting of the principal government officials and
citizens. But he was not interested merely in leaving
the responsibilities of carrying out those works in the
hands of a few amateur bodies lacking special knowledge.
The professional advice of engineers, doctors, scien-
tists and sanitarians was essential. He therefore laid
down that such professional persons, when available,
should be made members of the Committees but that in
all important works their advice must be sought. The
principal works required he said, 'were the excavation
of large and wholesome tanks, the filling up of hollows,
stagnant pools and useless ditches, the construction of
pucca drains and aqueducts, the opening of new streets
and roads, the paving or widening of old ones, the
removal of nuisances arising from particular trades to
the most convenient places and many similar [works]
that must suggest themselves in the circumstances of
particular places'. Adam also hoped that the works

executed by the Committees would eventually contribute
to the economic prosperity of the towns and cities and
he therefore instructed them after meeting the immediate needs of the towns under their charge, to undertake
the construction of roads, bridges and *sarais* in the
neighbouring countryside and indeed throughout the
province, since nothing could more tend to the prosperity of the towns than improved communication in the
country.[33]

On 29 May 1823, a resolution was, therefore, adopted
in the Territorial Department giving effect to Adam's
proposals. It was resolved that from the commencement
of the next financial year town duties would be appro-
priated to public works, the details of their appropriation being settled in the Judicial Department.[34]
It is interesting to note that this resolution in
reality converted the town duties into municipal taxes.
Town duties were in fact in many parts of India
expressly collected for municipal expenditure.[35]

Historians in general have so far dismissed the
governor-generalship of John Adam as a foot-note to the
annals of British rule in India, and even those who
have cared to discuss his reign mention only his
'illiberal' action in expelling James Silk Buckingham,
the editor of the *Calcutta Journal*, for 'undue freedom
of criticism of public officials'.[36] Few Governors-
General, however, did so much in so short a time to
give a new dimension to British policies in India than
Adam in his brief seven months in office. A distinguished civil servant, he proposed the immediate
enlargement of the civil and military establishments.
He particularly wanted to reform the Judicial administration by setting up new courts and appointing more
judges especially at the lower level. At the time the
courts were hopelessly overburdened. The individual
note which he sounded, however, was undoubtedly a call
for more attention to social reforms and public welfare.
Had his period in office been longer the social and
administrative reforms of his successors might more
clearly have been seen to be extensions of his own.

Lord Amherst, his successor, lost no time in giving
effect to his proposals for public works and urban
improvement. In a resolution adopted in the Judicial
Department on 18 September 1823 he decided to set up
Committees of Improvement in all the towns and cities
of the Bengal Presidency where town duties were
collected, and laid down the general principles by

which their conduct was to be guided. Like Adam, he
insisted that the Committees must include scientific
and professional men, wherever possible, and that in
all their major public works the advice of such persons
must be sought. Likewise he laid down that although
the Committees should ordinarily consist of the principal public officials they should have the power to
associate with themselves 'opulent Natives possessing
respectability of character and considerable local
influence' so as to create an interest in the success
of their operations. Generally each Committee should
consist of three members besides a Secretary who
should be entrusted with the duties of executing and
superintending all public works, supervising the office
and keeping the accounts. Some expenditure on office
work had to be incurred and it was unreasonable to
expect the heavy duties of the secretary to be performed gratuitously. But Amherst planned no expensive
bureaucracy that would eat up a large part of the
limited funds and thereby nullify the primary aims of
the exercise, and he limited the personal and office
allowances of the secretary to five per cent of the
town duties collected.

He pointed out moreover, that the limited funds of
several towns would not admit of any separate allowance
to the secretary. At five per cent the receipts at
Patna and Dacca would yield as much as Rs.100 per month
and in other places much less. Since it would be difficult to procure the service of a sufficiently qualified
person as secretary on such a small allowance Amherst
decided that the Junior Member of the Committee in all
these places should 'cheerfully perform the duty of
Secretary' without any personal remuneration as an act
of public service and that the allowance of five per
cent on the annual collections should be applied 'to
the expense of keeping the proceedings and of managing
the detail of the business left to his charge'.

Amherst added little to the works enumerated as
desirable by Adam: bridges and *ghats* and every work
likely 'to conduce extensively to the comfort and convenience of the public or to the Salubrity of the
Town'. However, he instructed that topographical maps
of all towns and cities should be prepared where none
existed, and that their ground level be taken for use in
planning and laying out roads, drains and sewerage.[37]

He resolved that the Committee of Improvement at
Dacca should consist of John Ahmuty, the Senior Judge

of the Provincial Court of Circuit and Appeal, Charles
Dawes, the Magistrate, and Dr George Lamb, the Surgeon,
as its First, Second and Junior Member respectively.
In accordance with the rules laid down Dr Lamb was also
to act as secretary to the Committee.[38]

However, before the new Committee could begin to
function formally in October 1823, Dr Lamb was transferred from Dacca. It therefore became necessary to
appoint a new Junior Member as Secretary. Charles
Dawes who was then in sole charge of the Committee
chose an Englishman, John Carter, to replace Dr Lamb
and asked government to confirm his appointment. John
Carter was a private trader who had lived in Dacca ever
since his arrival in India in 1793.[39] The selection
of a non-official, and a non-technical person at that,
as Member-Secretary was against the general principles
laid down in the government resolution. In the normal
course, the next Civil Surgeon would have been
appointed ex-officio Junior Member-Secretary. However,
Dawes reported to government that Carter's experience
as a businessman, together with his intimate knowledge
of the city and its people and the respectable status
in the town which he had acquired from a residence of
thirty years would not only be of great advantage in
successfully executing the works of the Committee but
would also strengthen its hands in a manner not to be
expected from a newly arrived civil surgeon. Of course,
he said, on all points where the special opinion of a
medical officer would be required, his advice would be
solicited. He also requested that Carter might be
appointed as full-time paid secretary at a monthly
salary of Rs.200. This, he pleaded, was necessary in
view of the considerable work of the Committee and his
own preoccupation with regular official duties. The
appointment of a paid secretary was also contrary to
the government resolution, but he held that the charge
would be much lower than the experience and respectable
position of Carter warranted. Moreover, even after
the payment of the secretary's salary, there would
remain an annual sum of about Rs.20,800 from the town-
duty collections, sufficient for the local works of
improvement.[40] After some discussion the Governor-
General in Council agreed to comply with Dawes'
requests as a special case, and authorised him, in
deviation from the principles laid down in the resolution, to pay John Carter a sum equal to twelve per
cent 'on the funds appropriable to the improvement of

Dacca' as his personal remuneration and charges of
office.[41]

The net proceeds of the town-duties at Dacca at the
time averaged Rs.23,508 per annum, but there was also a
credit balance from the *chaukidari* tax for 1823 of
Rs.4,777 which Dawes also claimed under the grant made
in 1822 to the old Committee of any surplus from that
tax. This government allowed. The new Committee was
thus very fortunate in starting with a substantial fund
at its disposal.

The new Committee for the improvement of Dacca was
all the more fortunate in having two very devoted, hard
working and zealous Magistrates in succession as
Second Member - Charles Dawes then Henry Walters.
Ostensibly the Committee superseded the authority and
took over the urban responsibilities of the District
Magistrate but in practice the Magistrate, ex-officio
Second Member, was the heart of the Committee because
of his unique position as the chief executive officer
of the town. He could, if he so wished, greatly further
the work of the Committee by using his magisterial power
and authority.

The contribution of Charles Dawes amply demonstrated
the central role in the Committee of its Second Member.
He mobilised the Committee for action, set the convicts
of the Dacca Jail who were under his charge to work
clearing and cleaning, and with other hired labourers
set about widening the narrow and tortuous streets.
Dawes seemed to have been partial to the development of
the northern part of the city. Already as we have
mentioned he had repaired and paved the Nawabpur road,
created a spacious plain by clearing the jungles of
Ramna, and reclaimed part of the Dacca-Tongi road which
thenceforth formed a beautiful drive for the European
and Indian habitants of the town who went for an airing
in the morning and evening. However, the Nawabpur road
was very narrow and congested, and it was extremely
difficult to drive carriage and horses through it without endangering the safety of the crowd who thronged to
its shops and bazaars. Dawes therefore decided to
widen this road. However, the bridge near the 'Roy-
Bazaar' (Roy Shaheb's Bazaar) over the Dulai Khal (the
water channel that ran through the heart of the city)
created a problem, being so narrow that carriages could
not cross it without causing frequent accidents. If
the road had to be widened so had the bridge. Dawes
therefore sought and secured permission of government

for expanding the bridge and widening the road. With
the help of the funds of the Committee he set about the
work though it led to legal and other difficulties in
acquiring the side-lands and compulsorily purchasing
the huts and pucca houses which had to be demolished.
The proprietors thus affected were, however, given
adequate compensation. After several months labour
the bridge was enlarged and the Nawabpur road was
widened and paved with brick in its entirety up to the
present railway crossing, becoming a very spacious
thoroughfare much facilitating communications between
the town and its northern outskirts. The newly widened
road also opened up the ill-ventilated muhallas or
wards of Raya Bazaar, Lal Chand Mokim, Umrapur and
Nawabpur along its line and greatly improved their
salubrity by allowing a freer circulation of air.

Dawes also attempted to widen the street which
took off from the Nawabpur road, and then ran westwards
up to the *Chauk* (main city square) and from there went
to Ramna via Nimtoli. This also was then a very
narrow lane, much crowded with huts, and widening
it, he hoped, would open up yet another congested
part of the city and improve communication. But his
colleagues in the Committee disapproved, arguing that
the road was not important enough to require immediate
attention while so many other vital works were left
unattended.

However, Dawes did succeed in accomplishing a great
work to the north of the town with which his name would
remain forever associated. In 1825, as a further step
to develop the newly reclaimed plain of Ramna he laid
out a race course along its edge and enclosed the whole
area with wooden railings. Thus the now famous Ramna
Race Course came into being, a new feature in the landscape of and the life of Dacca. At the extreme north-
west 'half a mile' from the winning post of the race
course he created a small hillock which subsequently
came to be known as 'Dawes' Folly'. The mound was
planted all over with superb fir trees and surmounted
by an apartment built in the Gothic style. Every
morning visitors to the race course assembled at this
hilltop where Dawes used to entertain them with
coffee.[42] He also constructed a new road along the
north-eastern side of the race course connecting it
with the city and planted along the boundaries of the
race course rare trees of various descriptions, some
even imported from Nepal. He also excavated a large

tank in the middle of the Ramna plain near the Kali *mandir*, or temple, supplying water to the people in the neighbourhood.

These developments in the Ramna area marked the beginning of the expansion of the city towards the north which later grew up as the garden suburb of Dacca. Dawes himself built his beautiful bungalow to the north-west of the race course. This bungalow has long disappeared but his race course and the Gothic building on the hill top still survive.

At the same time, while he was developing the Ramna area, Dawes also undertook the extension and improvement of the Dacca cantonment on behalf of both government and the Committee of Improvement. Earlier in the century the cantonment had been transferred from the distant Tejgaon to an area nearer to the city, just north of the Thatari Bazaar or the brass workers' quarters. In 1823, with the outbreak of the first Burmese war, additional regiments were sent to Dacca. This necess-itated the extension of the old cantonment and the building of new accommodation. Under instructions from government Dawes cleared the jungles to the north and west of the old site and laid down new grounds for sepoys' barracks, officers' quarters, cook-houses and parade grounds. He made extensive use of the prisoners in developing the area and showed the same skill and taste in planning and laying out the newly extended cantonment of Dacca as he had displayed in developing the Ramna area. Such was his imagination that he planted all around the cantonment numbers of fir, almond and other 'trees of handsome growth' which in a few years gave the cantonment the look of an extensive park. Within a short time a complex of new military buildings was erected and a new street paved with brick constructed connecting it with the city. Charles Dawes was practically the architect and builder of this new and more extensive cantonment, though much of the work was actually carried out by the Military Department and by his successor, Henry Walters.

Dawes, however, did not confine his activities solely to the northern part of the town. He drained and improved the pestilential *jhil*, or marsh, near Armenitola or the quarter of the Armenians. This Armenitola *jhil*, which was the dead end of a branch of the Dulai river, was one of the black spots of the town. During the rains it was full enough for neigh-bouring villagers to bring their boats to the city

149

through it. But during the dry season it turned into a stagnant pool the receptacle of all kinds of filth and rubbish. People defaecated on its bank and even buried their dead there. It was also a fertile breeding ground of mosquitoes. Dawes turned his attention to reclaiming this noxious marsh, perhaps being urged to do so by the Armenians who had been very friendly with him. To drain the stagnant water and ensure a constant flow of fresh water, he proposed to construct a canal linking the *jhil* with the river Buriganga and, since the canal must cross the line of Islampur Bazaar Street, to build a bridge over it. Government sanctioned both plans.

By early 1826 a canal, extending over 723 feet in length, 18 feet in width and 16 feet in depth, and a bridge also of considerable dimensions, had been completed at a cost of over five thousand rupees. The construction of the canal vastly improved the Armenitola neighbourhood, replacing a large, filthy and stagnant swamp with an ever-flowing water channel which even established a new water link between the Buriganga and the northern parts of Dacca.

Besides the works noted above, Dawes also carried out many other minor improvements like clearing and deepening the drains alongside the principal streets, repairing and developing a few back-streets with earth, turning another obnoxious marsh at Patuatuli into a wholesome tank and so on. He even succeeded in inducing the European and opulent native residents of Dacca to contribute funds for watering the Nawabpur street which grew very dusty during the dry season.

In January 1826, John Carter, the Third Member-Secretary, died. Following his death, Ahmuty and Dawes decided to re-organise the Committee, placing its supervision under more economical management. Instead of re-appointing a well-paid non-official secretary, they recommended to government that the Collector of the District be made ex-officio Third Member-Secretary, entrusting the immediate supervision of the works to a paid Superintendent of Works. These recommendations were accepted and the Collector, Lane Magniac, was appointed ex-officio Third Member-Secretary. A Superintendent of Works was appointed but at a small salary of fifty rupees per month. A small band of petty clerks was also appointed to deal with the paperwork and keep accounts. A regular force of sweepers and cartmen was also recruited for the daily sweeping of the streets and the cleansing of the town. In 1826 the establishment under the Committee consisted of one Superintendent of Works, one *Sirkar* (accountant), one clerk, four *Chaprasis* (messengers or orderlies), twenty cartmen and ten sweepers at a total monthly cost of Rs.104: the first municipal employees of Dacca.

In October 1826, Charles Dawes was promoted Judge of the Provincial Court of Circuit and Appeal at Dacca. Although he retained his membership of the Committee for some time, the effective leadership passed to his successor, Henry Walters, who proved himself equally energetic in urban development.

During the magistracy of Walters, Dacca was caught up in an almost feverish atmosphere of development and improvement. Among the various works carried out by the Committee of Improvement under his guidance, the most lasting were the improvement of the Chauk Bazaar, the widening and paving with brick of a portion of the Bazaar street now known as Islampur Road, and the construction of an iron suspension bridge over the Dulai River near Faridabad Police Station.

The Chauk Bazaar was first established as the *Padshahi* bazaar, or the market for the Mughal nobility and their followers, in the seventeenth century.[44] It was situated between the fort and the River Buriganga where it was conveniently supplied from the water-front. It spread out around a small *chauk* or square which was later enclosed by a wall. During the seventeenth and eighteenth centuries, the Chauk Bazaar grew up as one of the principal centres of trade and commerce in the city. It was linked with the Islampur Road by a small lane on both sides of which shops were also erected, while on the river side merchants built their godowns for grain and other bulky goods. Subsequently the Chauk Bazaar, owing to neglect and lack of supervision, degenerated into a most congested market-place. Shops were irregularly constructed, encroaching even upon the middle of the open square where the daily bazaar was held. The wall enclosing the chauk was also broken down, and much of the lane leading from it to the Islampur Road was similarly encroached upon by shops.

Walters decided to improve and develop the Chauk Bazaar by removing the shops from the square, extending it up to the central police station on the Islampur Road, and rebuilding the enclosing wall. Under his initiative the Committee of Improvement wrote to government seeking permission to carry out the works, stating that 'This measure would be attended with evident convenience and advantage to the inhabitants and to the trade of the city while, by opening an extensive area in the heart of the town, it would provide that free circulation of air which is so essential to its salubrity.'[45]

After receiving permission from government, Walters started to clear the square of all the unauthorised shops, pushing further back, and after extending the area of the square he enclosed it with a parapet wall 860 feet long, 4 feet high and half a foot thick with many outlets. A carriage road around the square was also built and paved with brick. With further improvements, Walters very soon rendered the crowded and congested Chauk Bazaar into a spacious market place with regular lines of shops, adequate drains and other sanitary facilities. He also erected a flag-staff in the middle of the square, and even converted the Chauk Bazaar into an attraction by removing a large old Mughal cannon called Bibi Maziam from the Suwari Ghat[46] on the River Buriganga and installing it on a raised platform near the flag-staff.

As a corollary to the improvement of the Chauk area, Walters then undertook the widening of Bazaar Street running south to it. Although the extent of this work is not clearly known, it seems that he widened and paved that part of the road which extended from the Chauk Bazaar area to its crossing with the Nawabpur Road in the south-east of the city near the Sadar Ghat. This part passed through the muhalla of Islampur. The work proved a great boon as Walters himself later remarked, 'In the Muhulla of Islampore a very great improvement has taken place, and this populous quarter which was sometimes scarcely passable for the throng is now sufficiently open to admit the unobstructed passage of vehicles.'

But the grand work of Walters was the Iron Suspension Bridge on the Dacca-Narainganj Road. Hitherto the absence of a bridge over the Dulai River on this road had greatly obstructed the only land communication between Dacca and Narainganj then a rising place of trade and commerce. As early as 1810, Edward Strachey had suggested in his memorandum[47] the immediate restoration of the old Mughal bridge[48] which was then in ruins. He recommended as well the reclamation and improvement of the Dacca-Narainganj Road itself, then also in disrepair, for he considered the road to be of vital importance to the commercial and trade links

152

17. DACCA: ruins of Tongi bridge (D'Oyly)

between these two places.

By the time Walters became Magistrate, the old
bridge had decayed beyond repair. He therefore decided
to construct a new bridge to replace it under the
auspices of the Committee of Improvement. Since the
expense was beyond the means the Committee he sought
public subscriptions to the work. The people of Dacca
responded generously. The work began in earnest from
1828. Essential materials were imported from Britain
and after two years' labour the new Iron Suspension
Bridge was completed and opened for traffic in 1830.[49]
The bridge became a wonder of the city and a great
boon. It was also, however, the last important work of
Walters in Dacca.

The other significant works which the Committee of
Improvement had accomplished under his guidance were
the reclamation and widening of the Nimtoli Road; the
repair and enlargement of the Nimtol bridge; the
development of the Dacca-Tongi road in its entire
length of fifteen miles up to the Tongi bridge, and the
repair of the Amber bridge near Kairowan Bazaar on this
road; the repair of the Tanti Bazaar bridge,[50] and of
another bridge over the Dulai River; the widening and
developing of the streets running through Ekrampur
Bazaar, Dig Bazaar, French Bazaar, Kalta Bazaar, and
Jinda Bahar Bazaar; the renovation of the Islampur
police station; the construction or repair of sixteen
large public wells, together with the construction of
parapets and railings with pillars around some of
them.[51]

Another very important work which the Committee
had completed was the filling up of a tank known as the
'French-Jheel' near the former French factory at Babu
Bazaar, which over the years had degenerated into a
stagnant and filthy pool. The Committee not only
filled it in but also established a daily market upon
it, letting out the shops. Henceforth the market came
to be called the 'Committeeganj', and yielded a fair
revenue to the Committee.

The various works of public utility and measures of
sanitation carried out by the committees of improvement
since 1819 did produce desirable effects upon the
appearance and health of Dacca, though certainly they
could not control the outbreak of epidemic diseases
like cholera which continued to carry off large
numbers of people almost every year.[52] This was
largely because many of the chief sources of

unhealthiness of Dacca like the polluted water of the
wells, tanks and the river which the people drank, the
improper burial of the dead at unauthorised places within the densely populated areas, and the accumulation of
night-soil were still left unattended to. These were
the problems to which the members of the Committee
were gradually turning their attention in the late
1820s especially under advice from the medical
authorities in Dacca. In February 1828 Dr James
Taylor arrived at Dacca as the city's new Assistant
Civil Surgeon and immediately got himself involved
with the activities of the Committee, taking a keen
interest in tackling diseases and giving a new importance to public health measures.

Much had been achieved to make Dacca a pleasanter
place to live in, so J.B. Elliot, now the circuit
Judge of the Provincial Court at Dacca, reported in
1829: 'It gives me great pleasure to allude to the
operations of the Committee of Improvement,' he wrote,
'which in my opinion have very materially conduced to
the salubrity, convenience and beauty of the city of
Dacca', adding that the achievements of the Dacca
Committee were far greater than those of other
committees except that at Calcutta.[53] The extent to
which the city had undergone development could be
guessed from the fact that in the six years between
1823 and 1829, excluding the expenditure on the Iron
Suspension Bridge, more than one lakh of rupees had
been spent on the improvement of roads, bridges, tanks,
canals, wells, drains, markets and so on.[54] But it was
not only the money but also the zeal, devotion and hard
work of Dawes, Walters, Magniac, Barwell and others
that lay at the root of the improvement of the city
under the Committee's care. Walters became the hero of
Dacca and it is said that when he left the city in 1830,
the rich and the poor of the town alike bade him farewell with tears in their eyes. Indeed, the magistracy
of Henry Walters was the golden age of Dacca's development in the first half of the nineteenth century, and
the older people of Dacca vividly remembered it when
they talked about *'Walter Shaheb ka Amal'* (the period
of Walters) in later days.[55] Walters even became a
part of the city's culture and till recently the
labourers of Dacca used to recite the following canto
while pushing a heavy load -

Walter Shaheb Ne Pul Banaya

Uske Niche Ganj Basaya
Aur Chauk Dhari Kaman Lagaya
Gur Gur Chal ....

(Walters *Shaheb* made the bridge, and under it established a market, and he placed a cannon at the *chauk*;
Oh! Roll on!)[56]

To the misfortune of Dacca and other cities and
towns in the Presidency of Bengal, the improvement
committees did not survive for long. The financial
problems of the East India Company which appeared to be
miraculously over in 1823 reemerged in the late 1820s
with all their threatening consequences. As before it
was the cost of a war that brought the crisis to a
head. This time it was the first Burmese war which
lasted from 1823 to 1826. At the time of his appointment Lord Amherst had been told that there were then
no occasions for further wars and that a period of
peace was expected. But within a month of his arrival
in India, a war broke out with Burma.[57] The war
dragged on till February 1826 bringing much loss of
life and expense.

The costs of this war together with the ever-
increasing expenditure of the civil and military
establishments and the commercial investments depleted
the scanty surplus that the Indian revenues had earlier
achieved so that the Company soon faced the same
financial problems as it had confronted in the opening
years of the century. In 1827-28 the actual deficit in
the Indian revenues amounted to Rs.11,859,541[58] and for
the year 1828-29 a further deficit of Rs.9,120,000 was
estimated,[59] while the public debt grew in 1827-28 by
Rs.83,979,055.[60] As the time for the renewal of the
Company's charter was drawing near, the Court of
Directors repeatedly instructed the Governor-General
in Council to bring the Indian finances into equili-
brium. It was during this dire financial situation
that Sir Charles Metcalfe, senior member of the
Governor-General's Council, suggested the straightening out of the Company's finances through immediate
retrenchments. In his search for economies he left no
stone unturned, and to those expenditures with which
he had no particular sympathy he applied the axe. In
a series of minutes and reports in 1828, he singled out
such items of expenditure and recommended their
curtailment or abolition. One fateful minute dated
28 January 1828 ran,

It is manifest that our expenditure greatly exceeds
our Resources, so much so, that as often as the
weekly returns of subscriptions to the Loan now
open are laid before us, we congratulate each other
on the increase of our debt as affording temporary
relief to present exigencies, although it is
obvious that increase of debt is adding to the
burden of excess of expenditure under which we
already labour. This is a state of things leading
to ruinous consequences, and unless means can be
devised to raise our revenue beyound our expenses,
or to reduce our expenditure within the limits of
our income, our prospects must be considered as
very unsatisfactory and alarming.

Since he did not 'perceive any available means by which
our Revenue can be increased beyond our Expenditure',
he said, 'we are left therefore, to look to reduction
of expense alone, and then comes the question how this
is to be effected.'

One of his recommendations was the 'complete
resumption of the Town Duty Funds for the exigencies of
the public service'. 'This assignment' he remarked,
'was prematurely made at a moment of sanguine expectation of continued financial prosperity. The Public
Service does not now, and cannot within any period that
can be anticipated, admit of such an alienation of
Revenue.' In further justification of his recommendation he claimed

from actual observation, I am convinced, that the
grant of these funds has led to wasteful expenditure, on works which if they could be said to be
improvements are not of a necessary description.
I have seen instances, in which the funds had been
laid out by the local committees, in a manner, from
which no real improvement could rationally have
been anticipated, and which in fact did only
produce deterioration and public inconvenience.
Such extreme cases, of course must have been rare;
but on the whole, fully acknowledging the obligation attaching to Government, to effect every
possible improvement for the benefit of its
subjects, when its resources will allow, I am
satisfied, that the assignment of specific funds
for local purposes tends to produce useless and
wasteful expenditure.[61]

Metcalfe did not substantiate his views by citing any specific example of 'useless' or 'wasteful' expenditure. Our own study of the activities of the Dacca Committee completely contradicts his assertions. It seems unlikely that the other committees had not acted in the main in much the same manner as the Dacca Committee. Even in Calcutta, where Metcalfe might have been able to watch the activities of the Committee more closely, the funds from the town duties had been spent only on most useful works.[62] Some committees may have occasionally misapplied funds or wrongly judged their priorities, but such mistaken judgements were inevitable in any mode of public expenditure. On the whole the reports from the various committees tended to show, as government later also admitted, that the funds had been very usefully spent.[63]

Be that as it may, it secured essential that some means of retrenchment should be found, and Metcalfe, knowing that the resumption of the town-duty funds would meet very few strong opponents and find ready acceptance by the Directors, suggested the measure's immediate enforcement.[64] Lord Amherst, who had himself earlier endorsed the grant of the funds to the improvement committees, found it impossible to support the expenditure any longer and therefore agreed to Metcalf's proposal.

The Directors fully believed what Metcalfe had said and showed extreme concern at his minute. They lost no time in instructing the Governor-General in Council to stop the disbursement of town-duty funds on public works. They even remarked in their despatch of 18 February 1828, 'we very decidedly disapprove of the exclusive appropriation of any particular fund such as Town Duties, the proceeds of the lottery etc. to any particular purposes'. 'Local Assessments', might

> sometimes be expediently resorted to for the purpose of making local improvements, but all the money received by the Government as Public Revenue should be carried to the general account of the State, and disbursed only for objects of general utility. The Calcutta Committee of Improvement has expended in eight years upwards of twenty-five lacs of Rupees.[65] We desire that no more money may be expended under this head without our previous sanction.[66]

The new Governor-General, Lord William Bentinck,

who took office in May 1828, showed himself reluctant,
however, to take such extreme measures, holding that
the Committees had been performing very good work. But
there was no choice; he therefore ordered the dissolution of all the Committees of Improvement with effect
from 1 November 1829, informing them, however, that
'the public exigencies alone have constrained him to
dispense with their further services which the Government has every reason to believe have been beneficially
exerted ... in local improvements and in promoting the
general comfort and convenience of the public'.[67]
    The order from the government came as a great shock
to the members of the Dacca Committee who deeply
regretted that the instruction to abolish the Committee
had come at a time when several works of major importance for improving public health and the economic life
of the city had yet to be attended to. In their
letters to the government through the Divisional
Commissioner of Dacca dated 9 October 1829 and 5 July
1830, Barwell and Walters also voiced their fear that
in the absence of a local Committee and of a regular
fund of a substantial amount much of what had been
achieved in improving the state of the city would soon
be undone.[68]
    The government, however, though otherwise unmoved,
did on the recommendation of the Committee authorise
the Magistrate of Dacca to maintain a 'scavenger establishment' at a monthly cost of Rs.150 for the cleansing
of the town.[69] This was understandably a very small
amount considering the needs of the city, which in 1830
was still nearly 41 square miles in extent and contained a population of nearly 75,000.[70]
    The first phase of the government's involvement in
the urban problems of the country thus ended abruptly
though not ignominiously. The financial problems led
to the discontinuance of funds set aside for public
expenditure but the obligation of the state to care
for the welfare of the urban centres and their
inhabitants was recognised and firm principles of
policy were also laid down for which credit must go to
the Governor-General John Adam. Later, with the
improvement of the Company's finances and after
pressure from local officials, funds would again be
released for the development of the towns, and new
Committees founded. Meanwhile, however, the condition
of the city of Dacca worsened. Soon after the
dissolution of the Committee, Henry Walters also left

159

Dacca, and with his departure a chapter in the history
of Dacca's urban improvements came to an end.

The fears of Walters and Barwell about the future
state of the city proved only too well founded for in
the following decade neither a Committee nor funds were
provided, and many of the improvements did indeed slip
back into disrepair so that Dacca once again degenerated into a filthy and insanitary place.[71]

Ahmed, 'Urban Problems and Government Policies: A Case
Study of the City of Dacca, 1810-1830'

1. For a general discussion of the lack of historical studies of the towns and cities of the Indian
sub-continent see Kenneth L. Gillion, *Ahmedabad - A
Study in Indian Urban History* (Berkeley and Los Angeles
1968).

2. See Paramatma Saran, *The Provincial Government
of the Mughals* (2nd ed., Bombay 1973), pp.158, 214-
215, 332-335; Bankey Bihari Misra, *Administrative
History of India, 1834-1947* (Bombay 1970), pp.591-592;
Hugh Tinker, *The Foundations of Local Self-Government
in India, Pakistan and Burma* (London 1954), p.17.

3. Saran, op.cit., pp.384-407.

4. Ibid., pp.214-218; see also Misra, *Administrative History*, pp.591-592, for a brief comment.

5. For a general account of Ahmedabad during the
Mughal period, see Gillion, op.cit., p.15f.

6. See Abdul Karim, *Dacca, The Mughal Capital*
(Dacca 1964); Ahmad Hasan Dani, *Dacca - A Record of its
Changing Fortunes* (Dacca 1962); S.M. Taifoor, *Glimpses
of Old Dhaka* (2nd ed., Dacca 1965).

7. Syud Hassain, 'Echoes from Old Dhaka' in *Bengal
Past and Present*, iii (April-June 1909), quoting
Rahman Ali Taish, *Tarikh-i-Dhaka*.

8. See Karim, op.cit., chs.iv and v.

9. James Rennell's estimate quoted in N.K. Sinha,
The Economic History of Bengal, vol.ii (Calcutta 1968),
p.228.

10. Ibid., p.227.

11. Report of the Judge-Magistrate of Dacca, John
Melville, 3 November 1801, Home Misc. Series, 456 (F),
287-89; Melville, however, wrongly computed the
distances. Thus he calculated the distance between
Enayetganj and Faridabad as seven miles and that between Buriganga and Dewan Bazaar as two and a half
miles. Compare this with the *Revenue Survey Map of
Dacca*, 1859.

12. Bankey Bihari Misra, *The Judicial Administration of the East India Company in Bengal 1765-1782*
(Delhi 1961), p.332.

13. Letter from the acting Magistrate to Government
of Bengal, 14 May 1814, in Bengal Criminal Judicial

Consultations (henceforth BCJC), Range CXXX1, vol.40, No.42; 10 June 1814.

14. Misra, *Administaative History*, p.592.

15. For illustrations of some of the finest relics and public works of Dacca, see Sir Charles D'Oyly, *Antiquities of Dacca* (London 1812-27).

16. Letter and enclosure, Shearman Bird and others to Government of Bengal, 11 October 1810, BCJC, CXXX, 22, 18 and 19, 30 October 1810.

17. Government of Bengal to Shearman Bird, BCJC, CXXX, 22, 20, 30 October 1810.

18. Edward Strachey to Government of Bengal, BCJC, CXXXLLL, 58, 24, 22 April 1819.

19. J.M. Rees, report, 6 December 1813, BCJC, CXXXL, 34, 2, 19 March 1814.

20. Government of Bengal to J.M. Rees, BCJC, CXXXL, 34, 6, 19 March 1814.

21. Government of Bengal to Committee of Improvement, BCJC, CXXXL, 47, 16 September 1814.

22. Magistrate of Dacca to Provincial Court of Circuit and Appeal, in J. Ahmuty to *Nizamat Adalat*, 13 October 1818, BCJC, CXXXLL, 58, 24, 22 April 1819.

23. See First Annual Report of the Sanitary Commissions for Bengal, for 1868, II, 103.

24. Acting Magistrate of Dacca in Provincial Court of Circuit and Appeal to *Nizamat Adalat*, 28 August 1818, BCJC, CXXXLLL, 34, 9, 11 September 1818.

25. Ahmuty to Government of Bengal, 13 October 1818, BCJC, CXXXL, 58, 24, 22 April 1819.

26. Government of Bengal to *Nizamat Adalat*, BCJC, CXXXL, 58, 25, 22 April 1819.

27. 'Dacca, the ancient capital of Bengal', *Friend of India*, 4 March 1876, 197.

28. Magistrate of Dacca to Government of Bengal, 31 January 1823, BCJC, CXXXV, 44, 29, 6 February 1823.

29. For the background of this Act, see B.B. Misra, *The Central Administration of the East India Company 1773-1834* (Manchester 1959), pp.361-367.

30. The net surplus of revenues in 1822-23 amounted to Rs.8,000,000; Adam's minute para.111.

31. Town duties were established in Dacca by the order of government under Regulation X of 1801. They were levied at first at the rate of 4 per cent upon certain articles of imports of the town and later reduced to 22 per cent in 1810 (Regulation X).

32. The mode of raising funds through a lottery was first introduced in Calcutta in 1817: see Misra,

Administrative History, pp.568-569.

33. Minute of the Governor-General, 22 May 1823, Bengal Judicial Proceedings, CXXXV, 62, 37, 18 September 1823.

34. Ibid., Resolution of the Governor-General.

35. See Gillion, op.cit., pp.110-116, et passim.

36. See, for example, Percival Spear, *The Oxford History of India* (Oxford 1958), p.586.

37. A topographical map of the city of Dacca based upon a survey was first prepared as early as 1819. Unfortunately this map could no longer be traced. The next topographical map was prepared in 1859.

38. Resolution of the Governor-General, BCJC, CXXXV, 62, 38, 18 September 1823.

39. See, *The East India Register and Directory for 1823* (2nd ed., London 1823), p.155.

40. Charles Dawes to Government of Bengal, 30 October 1823, BCJC, CXXXV, 68, 22, 4 December 1823.

41. Government of Bengal to Charles Dawes, BCJC, CXXXV, 68, 23, 4 December 1823.

42. See above, note 27.

43. Government of Bengal to Committee of Improvement, BCJC, CXXXVI, 36, 42, 3 December 1824.

44. For further details see Karim, op.cit., p.33f; Taifoor, op.cit., p.41 et passim.

45. Committee of Improvement to Government of Bengal, 16 November 1826, BCJC, CXXXVII, 56, 9, 7 December 1826.

46. This was the landing-place reserved for the Nawab in the Mughal times.

47. See above, p.136.

48. For an illustration of the remains of this bridge see D'Oyly, op.cit., Drawing no.16 of the India Office vol.x, 706.

49. 'On the day the finishing touch was given to the bridge, an elephant was with great difficulty and after a good deal of persuasion, made to walk over it, to test its stability and strength ....'; see above, note 27.

50. For an illustration of this bridge before repair see D'Oyly, op.cit., Drawing No.20.

51. Report of the Committee of Improvement dated 5 July 1830; BCJC, CXXXIX, 55, 12, 12 October 1830.

52. Between 1822 and 1826 cholera appeared in the city in epidemic form; in 1825 420 persons died of the disease. However it declined during the next nine years; for details see *Annual Sanitary Report of*

Bengal for 1868, part ii, 103.
  53. J.B. Elliot to *Nizamat Adalat*, 6 February 1829, BCJC, CXXXIX, 24, 46, 2 April 1829.
  54. John Gerant, Magistrate of Dacca, to Government of Bengal, 6 September 1836, BCJC, CXLI, 4, 187, 27 December 1836.
  55. Editorial note, *Dacca News*, 27 December 1856. In gratitude the Dacca Municipality later named a street in the eastern part of the city after him. Walters Road still bears his name.
  56. Azimuachan Haider, *Dacca: History and Romance in Place Names* (Dacca 1967), p.38.
  57. P. Spear, op.cit., p.586, and Lawrence Kitzan, 'Lord Amherst and the Declaration of War on Burma, 1824', *Journal of Asian History*, IX, 2 (1975), pp.101-127.
  58. Report of the Accountant-General, 15 June 1829, *Bengal Financial Consultations* (henceforth BFC), CLXI, 73, 1, 22 September 1829.
  59. Accountant-General, report, 26 February 1828, BFC, CLXI, 67, 1, 28 February 1828.
  60. Accountant-General, report, 15 June 1829, BFC, CLXI, 73, 1, 22 September 1829.
  61. Minute of Sir Charles T. Metcalfe, 28 January 1828, BFC, CLX, 2, 21 February 1828.
  62. The following is a statement of the receipts and disbursement of the town duty collections by the Calcutta Committee of Improvement for the year 1826-27.

Receipts	Disbursements		
Sicca Rs.55,712-3-4	A. Regular charges:		
		Sicca Rs.	As. Ps.
	1.'Raising Water'	5583-	2 - 1
	2.Watering roads	17615-	2 - 3
	3.Lighting streets	8347-	5 - 1
	4.Paving roads and Constructing Drains	7628-	8 - 3
	5.Sundry charges	2833-	10 - 4
	B. Disbursements or improvement and repair works	9197-	9 - 4
	C. Balance	4513-	14 - 0
Sicca Rs.55,712-3-4		55712-	3 - 4

Abstracted from the statements submitted by the Magis-

trates of Calcutta to Bengal Government, 20 November
1827, BCJC, CXXXVIII, 33, 44, 29 November 1827.
   63. See below.
   64. It is significant that when Metcalfe, an
experienced civil servant, suggested several measures
of retrenchment in this minute he took great pains to
reassure the Governor-General in Council that no
dissatisfaction would be created among the civilian and
military establishments. With regard to the town
duties he proposed their resumption without showing any
anxiety about the consequences: the interests of
bureaucracy would not be harmed.
   65. This includes funds raised by lotteries.
   66. Separate General Despatch to Bengal, 18
February 1828.
   67. Resolution of the Governor-General in Council,
BCJC, CXXXIX, 31, 6 22 September 1829.
   68. Barwall and Walters to Government of Bengal, 9
October 1829, and 5 July 1830, BCJC, CXXXIX, 32, 24,
20 October 1829, and CXXXIX, 55, 12, 12 October 1830.
   69. Government of Bengal to Commissions of Dacca,
BCJC, CXXXIX, 32, 25, 29 October 1829.
   70. For an account of the city and its population
in 1830 see Henry Walters'Census of the City of Dacca',
Asiatic Researches, XVII (Calcutta 1832), pp.534-558.
   71. For an account of the city of Dacca in about
1840 see James Taylor, *A Sketch of the Topography and
Statistics of Dacca* (Calcutta 1840), pp.363-371, et
passim.

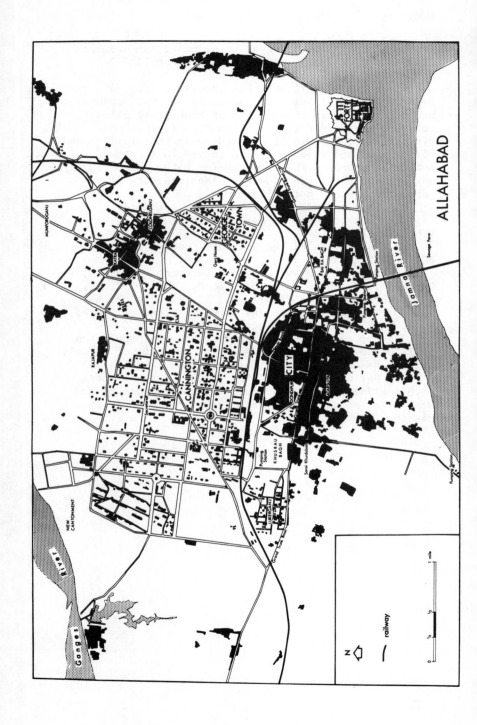

ALLAHABAD

ALLAHABAD: A SANITARY HISTORY

J.B. Harrison

The centres of population as first known to me
presented an appearance of much neglect. The local
officials of supreme authority, as a rule, gave
little thought to sanitary conditions, often spoke
of their occasional visits to the less public
quarters of a town or city as dangerous to health,
a duty most safely performed under the influence of
a lighted cheroot, or with the aid of an occasional
pinch of powdered camphor, as a defence against the
prevailing unwholesome atmosphere. In the old days,
indeed, I have walked with many authorities in
unwholesome lanes of a city site - to their display
of much disgust, holding of noses, and rapid
departure to a place of purer air. But never could
anything of evidence be discovered, favouring the
idea that the authorities were in any measure to
blame for this condition of things. Plainly,
indeed, the view was expressed that, if the natives
chose to live amidst such insanitary surroundings,
it was their own concern. And how they managed to
do it without greater penalty of death, than seemed
apparent, was a frequent cause of expressed
surprise.

As a fact, however, the local authorities of
those days had as little knowledge, or thought, of
the true death penalty of a city or town, as of
their true position as the peoples' defenders
against insanitary conditions. Conditions not born
of any desire or fault of the people, but inseparable - until the authorities shall interfere with
decision for their remedy or prevention - from the
life circumstances of many families closely
associated.

At the present day I have good reason to believe
that much of this spirit of apathy, or unwillingness to acquiesce in long-established malpractices
or insanitary evils, has given place to an ardent
desire for improvement ....[1]

C. Planck
Sanitary Commissioner
North-Western Provinces, 1868-1885

The purpose of this paper is to sketch an answer to the
questions raised by Dr Planck's valedictory survey -
under what impulses and under whose pressure did
attitudes to sanitary matters change, to what evils did
awakened official zeal address itself, with what understanding, and with what effect, and finally, how the
general public responded to this concern and activity -
using Allahabad as principal source in estimating 'the
true death penalty of the city'.

In England the pressure for sanitary and public
health reform can be traced back to the early nineteenth
century and to the quite unprecedented growth of towns
- growth ranging from 47 per cent for Manchester and
Salford, 60 per cent for West Bromwich, to 70 per cent
for Bradford in the single decade 1821 to 1831. The
resultant breakdown of sanitary arrangements, and of
efficient water supply, coupled with often gross overcrowding led to a reversal of the downward trend in
mortality rates. Though the reversal was only slight,
it was dramatically peaked in 1831-2, 1848-9, 1854 and
1867 by outbreaks of cholera, which 'struck down many
hundreds of thousands of victims, killing tens of
thousands',[2] and did so with an unpleasant disregard of
social class. Among the poorer classes, moreover,
typhus, always endemic, also assumed alarming epidemic
proportions, in 1826-7, 1831-2, 1837 and 1846. One
response was a flurry of temporary activity by local
authorities in years of alarm. Another, of more permanent importance, was the prosecution of a series of
major enquiries: in 1838 by Drs Southwood Smith, Arnott
and Kay, employed by the new Poor Law Commission to
study the 'constantly acting causes of destitution and
death' in London;[3] in 1842, on a national scale by
Chadwick, who to the 1838 material added reports from
his Assistant Commissioners, from the medical officers
to Boards of Guardians, and from local doctors, to
construct his Report on the Sanitary Condition of the
Labouring Population of Great Britain; in 1844 a Royal
Commission on the Health of Towns; and 1869, in
response to medical criticism, the Royal Sanitary
Commission.

The conclusions set out by Chadwick were

That the various forms of epidemic, endemic, and
other disease caused ... by atmospheric impurities
produced by decomposing animal and vegetable
substances, by damp and filth, and close and over-

crowded dwellings prevail among the population in
every part of the kingdom....
    That the formation of all habits of cleanliness
is obstructed by defective supplies of water.
    That the annual loss of life from filth and bad
ventilation are greater than the loss from death or
wounds in any wars in which the country has been
engaged in modern times.
    That the ravages of epidemics and other diseases
do not diminish but tend to increase the pressure
of population.
    That these adverse circumstances tend to produce
an adult population short-lived, improvident,
reckless, and intemperate, and with habitual
avidity for sensual gratifications.[4]

Having skilfully played upon pocket, sympathy and
fear Chadwick proceeded from diagnosis to remedy: 'The
primary and most important measures, and at the same
time the most practicable and within the recognised
province of public administration, are drainage, the
removal of all refuse of habitations, streets and
roads, and the improvement of the supplies of water.'
And to this statement of objectives he added the
riders that sanitation should be entrusted to 'responsible officers qualified by the possession of the
science and skill of civil engineers', and to 'a
district medical officer independent of private
practice',[5] both supported by 'uniformity in legislation and in the executive machinery'.[6]
Chadwick's findings were confirmed by the Royal
Commission on the Health of Towns, and his pleas by the
Royal Sanitary Commission's proposals that the unsys-
tematised sanitary laws and jurisdictions should be
made 'uniform, universal and imperative'.[7]
With varying degrees of delay and of acceptance of
Chadwick's bland statement that public interest should
override private property rights where health and
sanitation were concerned, legislation followed. In
1848 the first comprehensive Public Health Act was
passed and a General Board of Health was established.
It was made imperative upon local bodies to appoint a
surveyor and an inspector of nuisances, to make public
sewers and require owners to provide house drains, to
cleanse streets and fill up offensive ditches, and to
provide adequate supplies of water, if necessary from
local authority water-works.[8] London had to wait until

1855 for its Act for the better Local Management of the
Metropolis, the establishment of a central Board of
Works, and provision for the appointment of Medical
Officers of Health and Inspectors of Nuisance by ves-
tries and local boards. But in the next decade
further acts were passed against the adulteration of
food and drink, to prevent pollution of the Thames, to
make vaccination compulsory, to establish isolation
hospitals, and to control Artisans' Dwellings[9] while
in 1871 and 1875 the Local Government Board Act and
the Public Health Act provided for expert central
review of local enforcement of a consolidated body of
health regulations.[10]

The Public Health Act of 1875 established bye-laws
of general application, prescribing minimum housing
standards. The Royal Commission on Housing in 1885 led
in 1890 to a Housing Act which not only raised those
standards, but gave local authorities power to recon-
dition existing houses and to clear away slums.
Together with legislation covering working conditions
in factories, shops and homes, these acts sought to
provide an adequate environment. The Boer War, however,
revealed an alarmingly poor physique among army
recruits, and the report of the Duke of Devonshire's
inter-departmental enquiry into physical deterioration,
published in 1904, led to a wider range of legislation
- the Open Spaces Act in 1906, the Act establishing
the School Medical Service in 1907 and the Maternity
and Child Welfare Act of 1919 - which added a new
dimension to the idea of public health.[11]

What had been a late element in the evolution of
sanitary policy in Britain - the spur of military
needs - was in India the starting point of serious
concern. The importance of sanitation to the army,
established and publicised by the Crimean War, was
confirmed by the Mutiny in which the losses by illhealth had vastly outnumbered those incurred in combat.
As a result of that experience, and of the great
increase in the size and cost of the British element in
the post-Mutiny army in India a Royal Commission on the
Health of the Army in India was appointed. It reported
in 1863, not only upon directly military matters such
as the duties and diet of European troops in India,
their barracks, hospitals and cantonments, but also
upon the sanitary state of Indian towns and cities.
As the Report put it, 'It is indeed impossible to
separate the question of health, as it relates to

troops, from the sanitary condition of the native population, especially as it regards the occurrence of
epidemics ....'[12]

The 1863 report led directly to the creation of a
Sanitary branch within the Home Department of the
Government of India, and to the appointment of Sanitary
Commissioners and Assistant Commissioners to the subordinate governments under a Sanitary Commissioner to
the Government of India. The impulse behind these
appointments is made manifest in the form of the
Sanitary Commissioners' annual reports which opened
always with sections on the European Army and the
Native Army before dealing with the General Population.
And when submitted to Parliament, the Report on Sanitary Measures in India was accompanied not by a review
from the Local Government Board, but by a memorandum
from the Army Sanitary Commission at the War Office.
Nor was the military bias thus imparted redressed, as
it would have been in Britain, by powerful professional
bodies, such as the Institute of District Surveyors,
the Institute of Civil Engineers, or the British
Medical Association, for in India these professions
were largely in the military hands of officers of the
Royal Engineers and the Indian Medical Service. The
administration of civil hospitals and dispensaries,
and of jails, medical attendance on government servants
and responsibility for public health was entrusted to
I.M.S. Officers on loan to Government. Even the 'civil'
surgeon' to be found in every district was an officer
liable at any moment to recall to military duty.[13] The
direction taken by medical research in India was long
influenced by military needs, whence the attention to
typhoid, which killed European troops, rather than to
consumption which carried off the sepoy, or the treatment of V.D., which kept the equivalent of three regiments permanently in hospital, as a military but not a
civilian problem.

Military interests were not, of course, the sole
determinants of public health policies in India. In
the North-Western Provinces and later in the Punjab,
as the annual sanitary reports make very clear, the
mortality and illhealth which overtook the cultivators
in districts brought under canal irrigation, quickly
became a matter of deep concern to revenue officials,
and to the medical authorities.[14] No less clearly, in
Bombay, Karachi and Calcutta the interests of trade -
and of the world community - were brought to bear

when plague broke out in these ports.[15] And in every
town with a considerable body of European civilians,
official or non-official, some sort of station committee came into existence to secure a minimum standard of
health and comfort, for themselves at least. Calcutta[16]
with its Justices of the Peace appointed in 1794, its
Lottery and its Fever Hospital Committees, and from
1847 its Board of Improvement Commissioners might lead
the way - both in the size of its sanitary problems
and the amount of taxation and effort deployed for their
solution - but by 1853-54 the Station Committee at
Allahabad had four dispensaries in action in the native
city, Katra and Daraganj, the cost defrayed from the
Magh Mela fund,[17] and two years later it reported an
expenditure of Rs.700 a month on conservancy from the
proceeds of the Chaukidari Tax.[18] Indeed, as early as
1827, Fanny Parkes had described Allahabad as 'pretty
and well-ordered, the roads the best in India', with
station ice-pits, but also with both a leper and a
blind asylum supported by public subscription.[19]
     Such local effort lacked funds, lacked direction,
continuity and professionalism, and failed to involve
even the 'respectable natives' of the town, except by
way of an occasional consultation or appeal for subscriptions. In 1861, however, post-Mutiny financial
embarrassment led Wilson, Finance Member of the Government of India, to propose a transfer of responsibility
for roads and public works to local bodies and the
grant of a corresponding power to raise taxes locally,
a shift towards decentralization which Lawrence was to
follow by transferring the costs of town police, and
Mayo of local education and medical services to local
authorities.[20] In 1861 the Allahabad magistrate accordingly sounded out leading townsmen on the subject of
local taxation - and found 'an almost universal feeling
in favour of octroi. The only objectors were a few of
the large traders'.[21] In 1863 a municipal committee
was appointed, under Act XXV of 1850, to deal with
police, conservancy and town improvements. In 1867 the
the civil station and city were amalgamated for municipal purposes, while in 1868, under the North-Western
Provinces Municipalities Act, six wards were demarcated
and the and the elective principle introdued. At the
same time an octroi tax was levied on a scheduled list
of commodities on imports into the city: a tax which
remained the chief source of municipal income well into
the next century.[22]

In the same period the Royal Commission on the
Health of the Army in India had authoritatively
identified the sanitary problems in towns such as Allahabad, in a series of trenchant vignettes: 'The habits
of the natives are such that, unless they are closely
watched, they cover the whole neighbouring surface with
filth ....' 'There is no such thing as subsoil drainage
.... Neither latrines nor urinals are drained. For all
purposes to which drainage is applied in this country,
as a means of preserving health, it is unknown in India!'
'There has .... been no application apparently of any
modern improvement, as regards either the examination
of water sources or the means of collecting or distributing water for use for stations, bazars or towns
.... the present condition of the water supply ... is
unquestionably a predisposing cause of disease, especially during the prevailing seasons of cholera, fever,
dysentry and other zymotic diseases.'[23] The remedies
were clear - those which Chadwick had prescribed for
the equally insanitary state of British towns[24] -
improved water supply, drainage and cleansing. Once
these were introduced the health of troops would
necessarily improve, while freed of the burden of illhealth the natives, too, would become 'better and
abler men, women and children for all the purposes of
life'.[25]
The appointment of a Sanitary Commissioner to the
Government of India, and of a staff of provincial
commissioners provided the supervisory organisation
which could press for these reforms, with authority,
expertise and continuity. What is more, by their
instructions, the new commissioners were required to
concern themselves solely with the native population:
the traditional areas of I.M.S. concern - Army cantonments and the European occupied Civil Station -
remained entirely in army hands.[26] When in 1878 the
office of Superintendent-General of Vaccination was
absorbed into that of Sanitary Commissioner, the
Superintendents of Vaccination were also appointed
Deputy Sanitary Commissioners. Their new duties were
to spread vaccination, to monitor birth and death
registration, to preach sanitation and to report to
District Magistrates any disease-provoking conditions
noted in towns met with on tour, and to suggest
remedial measures. (This last duty, they were warned,
must be done personally 'no subordinate officer of the
department being permitted at present to inspect or

report upon the sanitary condition of any town or village.')[27] I.M.S. jealousies had limited the range of work open to the new service - but with the happy effect of compelling attention to conditions in the Indian city and town. The new men, moreover, were competent professionals, who in many cases acted, as the Medical Officers of Health appointed in Britain had done, as active reformers. The village, town and city bazaar had otherwise only seen humble creatures of little standing - the vaccinators[28] and the native doctors, products of the Agra or Calcutta Medical Colleges, who in 1855 were thought highly paid at Rs.25 per month.[29] The Sanitary Commissioners could command attention to their views.

But what were their views? Dr Planck sets them out for us in his first annual report as Sanitary Commissioner in 1868:

> *Typhoid Fever.* This form of fever is due to a poison of animal origin, as malarial fever is due to a poison of vegetable origin. I write in the simplest words for the advantage of non-professional readers, and the prevalence of contagious fever is always found to be in close relation to the imperfect manner in which sewage matters are removed.
> *Malaria.* Malaria [literally Bad Air] is believed to be rather heavier than pure air, and to be more prevalent, or men less able to resist its effect, in the early morning hours. It is therefore very desirable that all who can should sleep on a surface well raised above the ground.
> *Malarial Fevers.* ... the principal causes of which are the undrained condition of the sites of towns or villages, or their dranage into excavations which neighbour upon, or often exist in, those centres of population, so as to form large collections of stagnant water.
> *Cholera.* There are two circumstances with reference to this fatal form of disease, which recent research would appear to have established.
> 1st - That the disease is most prevalent in places the air of which is tainted by fermenting or decomposing animal excrement.
> 2nd - That the germ or contagium of the disease is found in the dejections of cholera patients, and especially in the characteristic rice-water discharges.

The proper precautions are therefore to clear away and
prevent accumulations of house refuse, disinfecting
any large collections of impurities before they are
disturbed; 'especial cleanliness must be enforced in
sewers, drains, foul ditches, sewage ponds, slaughter
houses, and places where beasts are kept', and 'care
must be taken that the brick work of all the wells is
in good repair, and that every well from which drinking
water is taken has its mouth surrounded by a low wall'.

> *Dysentry and Diarrhoea.* .... where malaria abounds,
> where conservancy is neglected, where coarse and
> ill-cooked food is often eaten, deaths from
> dysentry and diarrhoea will often occur in fatal
> form.
> *Smallpox.* It is I think well known to all educated
> persons, that small-pox has ... in all probability
> no other mode of communication than from one person
> to another .... Therefore it fortunately happens
> that an efficient method of preventing its
> prevalence has been discovered in vaccination ...[30]

Two things stand out from this lengthy extract -
the inadequacy of Dr Planck's understanding of the
mechanics of disease, and his firm grip upon many of
the practical precautions to be taken to avoid conta-
gion. His use of the phrase 'germ or contagium'
reminds us that though he was writing ten years after
Pasteur's work on fermentation, and eight after Lister's
demonstration of the value of antiseptics, it was still
to be another eight years before Koch isolated the
anthrax bacteria and produced his postulate that
specific diseases were caused only by specific
bacteria.[31] Not for another thirty years would the
role of insects in transmitting plague, kala azar and
malaria be established. But, as the Army Sanitary
Committee, reviewing the excited report of the isolation in Indian cases of the same *bacillus typhosus* as
had been tracked down in Europe, rather grumpily
observed, given the new identification the old sanitary
measures had still to be pressed home.[32] What those
measures were Dr Planck already in many cases knew when
he first surveyed Allahabad, the city in which his headquarters were established, in 1868.

In 1868 the boundaries of Allahabad enclosed a
great blunt wedge of land, six miles long by four miles
broad, hemmed in on three sides by the Ganges and the
Jamna, whose confluence made the town a sacred place

of pilgrimage. The city proper, a square mile in
extent, straddled the Grand Trunk Road and so north to
the Jamna. South of the city, across the East Indian
Railway, spread the formal grid-iron of Cannington, the
new civil station, where the classical Secretariat was
under construction. And round that again, in a great
arc touching the Ganges to east and north, lay the
Fort, remnants of the old civil station, and two new
sprawling cantonments - in which were embedded Daraganj,
Sheokothi and Katra, pilgrim centres and bazaar. It
was a vast site, most of it standing high, with ample
well-water. Since 1853 the population had grown by
35,000 to 106,000 in 1868 and it would go up by as
much again by 1873. (In January of each year, at the
time of the Magh Mela, the population was for some
three weeks swollen by perhaps 100,000 pilgrims, a
figure vastly exceeded every twelfth or Kumbh Mela
year.) Of the municipal revenue of Rs.96,000,
Rs.11,000 went on conservance, Rs.37,000 on road maintenance, tree planting and such works as drains,
culverts and latrines - in all half the total budget.[33]
    The contrast between city and civil station - north
and south of the railway track - was striking. The
city had two or three main streets of fair width, but
from these a labyrinth of smaller and smaller lanes led
off into the interior of the muhallas, many of which
still had gates to seal off the whole block at night.
There were several mandis for grain, fodder, etc, one
or two considerable serais, and a townscape of mixed
pucca and kutcha housing[34] given distinction only by
the Mughal Khusru Bagh and Khuldabad Sarai. Houses
looked traditionally inward and with space already
limited were growing upwards. The civil station, laid
out by the Commissioner Thornhill in 1858, was a grid-
iron of regular broad roads, those nearest the station
already metalled, with newly planted avenues of trees,
framing bungalows which stood in two, three and even
ten acre compounds. Though the numbers in the civil
lines were always larger than expected, since many
bungalows were in multiple occupation, and the long
low ranges of servants' quarters were often in part
let out to artisans or labourers, while the coach-
houses and compounds were leased to ekka-drivers,
petty shopkeepers and stall holders, the contrast in
density between the European and Indian wards of the
city was still extreme.
    So, often enough, was the contrast in the servicing

and sanitariness of the two parts of the municipality.
Thus, on roads and surface drainage, Dr Planck reported
in 1868 that though the city was fairly swept, and the
main roads well made 'but their side-drainage is
faulty; many of the by-roads are unmade, and almost
impassable in the rains. ... in a sanitary point of
view the urgent requirement in this city is for the
creation of an efficient surface drainage system ...
every hole or excavation now existing being at the same
time filled up.' He went on, 'The Civil Station,
inhabited by the European community, has been covered
in all directions with very good roads; its drainage
has been carefully attended to; ... and I would urge
that the same attention should now be given to the
city, where men congregate and much business is
done.'[35]

    The metalling of the roads, scarified and then
re-dressed every four to six years with rammed kunkur,
and their regular watering to bind the surface and lay
the dust was an expensive business,[36] made more so as
the side ditches were made pucca with brick. Between
1873-4 and 1882-3 the yearly average on maintenance
and petty repairs of metalled roads was over Rs.24,000,
and that exclusive of road watering, sweeping and
drainage. This represented a tenth of all municipal
expenditure.[37] (The one bright spot in the roads
account was provided by the road sweepings, which in
the age of the horse, found ready sale as fuel for
brick-kilns, while these were still permitted within
municipal bounds,[38] and thereafter were taken by the
army for the improvement of their great sweep of grass
lands to the south of the Civil Lines.)[39] By far the
larger part of this outlay was upon roads outside the
city proper, while as is clear from the covert criticism of Devon, the Municipal Engineer, in 1900 maintenance was weighed out upon racial grounds, rather than
upon those of weight of traffic or the needs of trade.[40]
As for the minor interior lanes of the city muhallas,
these had to wait for attention until the devastating
outbreak of plague in 1902, when an emergency grant of
Rs.15,000 for paving and Rs.20,000 for draining those
lanes 'where plague has broken out or is likely to
break out', was made by the Lieutenant-Governor in
person. The Collector reported 'This work has been
received with extraordinary satisfaction by the people
and applications for further work are constantly
received, but have unfortunately to be rejected.'[41]

The other recurring expenditure by the municipal
authorities - and the most urgently necessary - was
upon conservancy. No more trenchant comments were
passed by the Royal Commission than upon this subject,
it figured largely in every Sanitary Commissioner's
report on the state of towns and villages, it obtruded
itself upon everyone's attention, and if inadequate was
the major cause of that 'death penalty of a city'. On
the outskirts of the city, where the cover of standing
crops, the ravines running down to the river, tanks or
old brick fields invited it, what Dr Planck described
as open-air conservancy was practised, a 'daily offering of impurity exposed on the surface of the earth'.[42]
This villagers' habit always created a 'nuisance', and
as the theories of bacterial infection gained acceptance, created alarm too, as a source in the dry weather
of infectious dust and in the rains of polluted water.
The one effective action to which alarm led, however,
was the forcible removal of native villages and hamlets
from within the civil station and cantonments 'to
preserve the health and life of the remaining and more
important section of the community'.[43] The prime
example of this was the uprooting in 1901 of the
village of Nimi Bagh, as an insanitary eyesore, much
too close to Government House.[44]
One gut reaction to popular but insanitary habits
was thus to attempt to stamp them out by use of bye-
laws, fines or compulsory acquisition powers. The more
constructive response was to find alternative modes of
sanitation adapted to urban conditions. The simplest
answer was to define an area which might be used for
defecation, and to appoint sweepers - or to allow pigs
and cattle - to keep the enclosures clean.[45] On his
first Allahabad inspection Planck noted several such
fenced enclosures provided on the outskirts of the
city as latrines.[46] The next stage was to build
latrines and urinals of a kind more familiar to the
European mind, and more appropriate to the dense building pattern of the city. Almost endless inventiveness
was displayed by sanitary officials and by amateur
enthusiasts in devising new types of latrine, some,
such as those at Cawnpore, being quite palatial:

> These latrines are in the shape of a double row of
> cells with a wide passage between, cells and
> passage covered by one roof. The passage is the
> sweepers' domain, and by it impurities as they

collect can be deodorized by means of earth and
removed to the carts, the lower or receptacle part
of being open towards the passage. The whole
structure, 90 feet long by 20 feet broad, is of
brickwork .... a separate residence for sweepers is
provided, so that they need never be absent.[47]

At the other extreme was the simple structure of
timber clad with iron sheeting mounted on wheels so as
to permit it being moved daily over another set of
trenches. In between came a whole variety of latrines,
some open some roofed; some of brick set in lime - or
since this was attacked - set in mud mortar; some
tarred, some coated with dammar; some to Dr Bellew's
Bombay pattern, others in the Lucknow style, and yet
others in the widely copied railway functional which
became the norm in Allahabad.[48]

By 1881 there were 34 public latrines in the city
and 12 in Katra-Colonelganj, while in 1888-9 no less
than 11 kutcha city latrines were rebuilt in burnt
brick, stone floored, and with ashlar seats, with
sweepers' houses attached, and the total had risen to
56 public latrines.[49]

But no number of latrines would be of any use
unless they were kept clean - the first need, as Dr
Planck insisted, was to make them 'acceptable to the
Indian people .... unless the municipal authorities
of a town are prepared to ensure this amount of cleanliness, they had better not waste their money in providing latrines at all'.[50] The ideal solution in
financial no less than aesthetic terms, was to employ
the water-closet system. On no point had Chadwick been
more emphatic than this, arguing that the great barrier
to urban conservancy, the expense and annoyance of hand
labour and cartage, could only be met in great cities
'by the use of water and self-acting means of removal
by improved and cheaper sewers and drains'.[51] That
solution was not open to Allahabad before the twentieth
century. Meanwhile reliance had to be placed upon
two measures - the use of dry earth, spread over the
whole latrine and thereafter freshly applied as the
latrine was used to deodorise the faeces and absorb the
urine, and secondly the regular and speedy removal of
contents.

Private household latrines in the city and bazaars
took two traditional forms - the *sandas*, or well-
latrine, and the *Mugli* privy. The *sandas* was a dry

well, as much as 30 to 40 feet deep, sunk in the courtyard of the house, closed with timber or stone, leaving
a small hole in the centre. The *Mugli* privy as described by the Secretary of the Agra Municipality was
'the cupboard or chest form of latrine, which opens by
a shutter on to the public street',[52] designed to permit its being cleaned from outside by the sweeper without his entering the house. Both merited the criticism
of the Government of India: 'There is every reason for
suspecting that the chief disease causes in all Indian
towns are to be found within the walls which enclose
the compounds and houses.'

The obvious danger from the *sandas* lay in its
usually being sunk in the same courtyard as the well
from which the drinking water of the family was drawn.
When the first chemical analysis of wells was undertaken in Allahabad in 1891 very few were found to be
uncontaminated, and many of those in the city were
declared dangerous to public health.[53] By the early
1880s official pressure was being applied to secure the
discontinuance of the use of *sandas*es. Act III of 1894
then provided all the authority necessary to compel
closure, and empowered the municipal authority to enter
houses to inspect their sanitation and required them to
undertake such inspection systematically.[54] In 1898
the Special Health Officer for Allahabad, Surgeon
O'Connor, could report that some 70 *sandas*es had been
filled in on his order, though householders had
objected, including some who were members of the Board.
No prosecutions, however, were instituted 'for continuing a habit that seems to have been in use with
them for probably over two hundred years or more'.[55]

The dangers of the *Mugli* privy were even more
obvious:

> Connected with almost every house is an open
> square pit ... situated either beneath the wall of
> the house itself or just on the margin of the pub-
> lic roadway; in many instances the family latrine,
> a small dark cupboard-like place, stands inside
> the house, near to the pit to which the latrine is
> connected by a short drain. The condition of
> these drains and their cesspools ... is, in a sani-
> tary point of view, very sad. They are approach-
> able only with disgust, contain impurities, long
> since collected there, and present a state of
> things which calls urgently for amendment.

In some instances, the family retiring place in the better sort of houses is situated near to the top of the house, and is then connected to the cess-pool below by a narrow [open] channel running down the face of the house outside.[56]

When in exercise of its powers under Act XV of 1883 the Allahabad Municipality drew up new bye-laws, it included one declaring that 'no Mughli Privies opening on any road, lane, street or public place should be sanctioned'. In June 1889 the Working Committee instructed those members of the Board in charge of conservancy in their wards to enforce this provision.[57] When in July 1889 Dr Ohdedar, as conservance member ordered a certain Masnad Ali to remove his 'Moghli paikhana', he was overruled by the Board,[58] but though rights in existing property were thus respected, permission to build new or alter old houses was made conditional upon the provision of an improved latrine - 'the privy must not be a Mughli privy, but one with a good door',[59] or more specifically, 'the privy should be made pucca and *kadamchadar* according to the new specifications'.[60]

Upon what precise pattern the mainly European and Anglo-Indian occupants of the Civil Lines bungalows arranged their sanitation is not clear - thunderboxes for the bungalow, served by the sweeper, and some sort of latrine in the compound for the servants seems to have been the pattern. What is certain is that sanitation was in general appallingly neglected. Dr Planck recorded how the bungalow was served in 1868: '... house conservancy is left entirely to the management of the sweepers, who as a general rule ... throw out impurities into any convenient place not far from the house and leave them to dry up. If any man should doubt this as too horrible to believe, I think he would be wise to investigate the circumstances of his own house.'[61] As for the servants, crowded to the rare of the compounds, they were often left ill- or unprovided for. T.N. Ghose, the conservancy member for the ward, reported in 1885 that 'many of the landlords in the Civil Station, although served with notices to repair and construct latrines and supply buckets to the latrines have failed to do so'.[62] And if they did provide latrines, they seem rarely to have used the household sweeper to keep them clean. Major Chaytor White, I.M.S., reported scathingly in 1908 upon the Civil Station:

> At present in many cases no provision is made by
> house owners for serving private latrines in com-
> pounds. The servants often club together and pay
> for the survices of a sweeper or pay the bungalow
> sweeper something for his services. In large com-
> pounds the proprietor may let out servants' houses
> separately - the rent of the bungalow being thereby
> reduced. The consequence is that all and sundry
> occupy these compounds and the state of the
> latrines is most unsatisfactory. Under Act I of
> 1900 Municipal Section 91 (1) powers are given to
> compel house-holders to keep the latrines in
> order. Notices have been served times without
> number on various house-holders, but they are
> treated with contempt. The compound of the Alla-
> habad Club on which I made a special report is in
> a deplorable condition: the latrine accommodation
> is totally inadequate .... Notices have been
> served but nothing has been done. In England when
> a notice to abate a nuisance is served a reasonable
> time is given for the improvement and if on visit-
> ing the Sanitary Inspector finds nothing has been
> done no second chance is given. I consider that
> the Municipality is far too lenient and that in
> future proper fines should be inflicted. It has
> been suggested to me that a sanitary tax of Rs.2/-
> a month levied per private latrine which should
> include the service of the latrine ....[63]

However, when a special sub-committee of the Board
reviewed Chaytor White's report, they opined that it
was not advisable to undertake municipal cleaning of
the private latrines in the Civil Station.[64]
The immediate condition of latrines, public or
private, depended upon close and energetic supervision
of the persons in charge of them, the conservancy of
the municipality as a whole upon willingness to spend
money and to organise in a business-like fashion. It
was a considerable task and required a small army to
perform it, even in 1870-71:[65]

City	Rs.	Civil Station	Rs.
9 Jemadars	1,200	1 Head Inspector	1,440
1 Bukshee	300	1 Jemadar	120
2 Chuprassies	120	2 Chuprassies	120
		10 Beldars	480

City	Rs.	Civil Station	Rs.
240 Sweepers and		40 Drivers	2,440
Mehtranies	8,600	40 Assistants	1.920
50 Drivers	3,000	40 Sweepers and	
		Mehtranies	1,680
		2 Domes	130

The force thus assembled had then to be equipped with
some hundreds of vehicles - country carts for the
sweepings, heavy iron filth carts for the product of
the latrines and cask carts and hand barrows for the
daily 30,000 gallons of sullage water and urine, together with a few donkeys to carry paniers through the
innermost lanes.[66] The disposal of the road sweepings
- some 3,000 cubic feet or perhaps 100 tons a day - has
already been noted. The disposal of the sewage remains
to be considered.

For a while the city sewage was trenched on ground
close to the latrines,[67] and until it was discovered
that it was a prime carrier of the germs of enteric
fever the urine was used to water Alfred Park,[68] but
for most of the period both were carted to municipal
trenching grounds outside the city. This was the
system early used in Cawnpore and seems to have been
modelled thereon. Shallow trenches were opened, filled
with sewage, lightly covered with soil and left for a
season. They could then be let, at high rents, to
cultivators. The problem was to secure long-term
possession of the land, which required an astute
purchase,[69] and to keep conservancy cattle strong
enough to haul the immensely heavy filth carts in the
hot weather and the rains over many miles of roads.
Years of famine or heavy monsoon always saw conservancy
approach the point of collapse.

In Calcutta the problem had been solved by building
a municipal railway in 1867 which ran through the city
collecting refuse from street depots and carrying it to
the Square Mile in the Salt Lakes.[70] In 1887 Allahabad
investigated the possibilities of a tramway, sending
plans and estimates 'to Capitalists at Home'.[71]
Nothing came of this, and the tramway languished until
in 1905 a syndicate applied for an electric tram and
lighting licence - the tramway to double as a conservancy and passenger system. The Collector thereupon
went over to Cawnpore to examine the conservancy
tramway and incinerators there. He was discouraging
and the electrification scheme fell through.[72]

Meanwhile Allahabad had got a water-works, the possibility of water-borne sullage and sewage disposal had opened up, and eventually a considerable part of the city's output was pumped across the Jamna by Schone's Ejectors and used to irrigate farm land there.[73]

The system, first in operation in 1917, had come just in time. In 1909 it was noted that the supply of sweepers, on a monthly pay of Rs.4 a man and Rs.3 a woman, was barely adequate.[74] Two years later rising prices had created a serious problem: 'the Mohalla sweeper finds his hereditary calling no longer provides a decent livelihood. The poorer classes in the city are in consequence seriously embarrassed how to get their houses cleaned.'[75] By 1918 it was clear that the sweeper force was now 'stationary, if indeed not thinning through various outlets to cleaner labour open for untouchables in a town growing under modern conceptions of life and labour'.[76]

Since enteric and cholera were suspected to be water-borne diseases the Royal Commission had drawn particular attention to the dangers of polluted water - shallow contaminated wells, tanks into which a soiled urban surface often drained, rivers which might prove as treacherous a source as the polluted Thames.[77] This concern was reflected in Allahabad by an attempt - abortive - to discourage the use of river water taken from below the dhobi ghat,[78] by orders for regular cleaning of public wells[79] and by the listing of tanks in which the washing of animals was prohibited.[80] More positively, from 1883 or a little earlier consideration was given to the possibility of providing a piped water supply. Curiously enough the main arguments adduced in favour of such a supply were that without it surface drains could not be adequately cleaned and the profits of a sewage farm would not be realised, and that supplies for road-watering would also fail.[81] The minimum cost, Rs.15½ lakhs, was felt, however, to be prohibitive. Nevertheless in 1889 plans were submitted to government and approved, and a loan applied for.[82] By 1890 tenders had gone out and contracts had been placed, and the following year saw pumping begun.[83] Almost at once petitions came in from inhabitants in the city muhallas[84] for the laying of pipes in their lanes, and individuals even offered to lay street mains at their own cost if they might then be allowed a house connection. By 1894 a million gallons a day were being supplied, to houses or street stand pipes,

and for the great Kumbh Mela of that year temporary
pipes were run out for the use of the pilgrims. Since
the valuation of all the houses in the municipality and
their assessment to water-tax had gone off quietly and
without too large arrears, the scheme might seem to
have been a success.[85] From a sanitary point of view,
moreover, the result was most encouraging. The municipal analyst reported that the purity of the water
supplied was very satisfactory, and as the range of
the mains extended it was possible to speed up the
process of filling in the polluted tanks. The analyst
was also required to begin the testing of public and
then of private wells.[86] In 1881 Markham, as President
of the Municipality, had blandly declared 'the quality
is good, and the supply ample'.[87] As analysis proceeded more and more were found to be polluted, and
notices to clean or close them were sent out[88] - and
then when re-analysis found them still tainted, power
was taken under Act XV of 1883 prohibiting their use
for drinking purposes.[89]

Within a very few years, however, second thoughts
about the sanitary advantages of a good piped water
supply had emerged. The North-Western Provinces and
Oudh Water Works Act, Act I of 1891, under which
Allahabad operated, had taken careful note of all those
legislative failures under which London had laboured in
respect of its water-supply. It had firmly required
the Municipal Board to supply 'pure and wholesome
water sufficient for the use of the inhabitants for
domestic purposes': there would be neither the
scandals of cholera-bearing water such as the Lambeth
Company had supplied, nor the cutting off of all
supplies on Sundays which Jephson has so deplored; nor
indeed would it be possible for the remissness of a
landlord to imperil his tenant's water supply, since
the latter could compel the former to arrange for water
to be brought into the house.[90] But what it had failed
to do was to prescribe a drainage system capable of
dealing with the mass of new water poured into the
city. Water at the stand pipes was free, and piped to
the house, was still kept deliberately cheaper than
well water brought up by bullock power.[91] The conservancy department had seized upon the opportunity to
install scours from which to flush surface drains,
into which sullage water was increasingly diverted.
By 1898 the District Magistrate was reporting 'owing
to the introduction of the filtered water supply the

want of proper drainage is being felt more and more
each year',[92] and two years later the municipal
engineer noted, 'Very few houses have proper arrangements for carrying off waste water, in consequence of
which a large percentage of water percolates into walls,
floors and ground near water taps and damp unhealthy
areas are found all over the city.'[93] It was well that
the 1891 Water Works Act had been followed by Act III
of 1894, the North-Western Provinces Sewerage and
Drainage Act.

Of the drainage system of Allahabad, Dr Planck had
this to say in 1879: '... the street drainage of the
city is unsatisfactory. There is no system, and no
funds exist to create one. The surface drainage, of
both the city and the civil station, is delivered
chiefly into deep pools or tanks'. The main sewerage
artery, the Ganda nala, running from the railway
station right across the city to the Jamna was reasonably described as 'a noisome ditch everywhere, with
crawling fetid contents'.[94] As late as 1896 the road
side drains in parts of the Civil Station were described as 'nothing better than elongated earthen
cesspools'.[95] Every year some drainage black-spot was
tackled - but never to an overall plan.

It was the growing problem created by the new
water-supply which compelled rethinking. First the
Health Officer, Surgeon-Captain Davidson, demanded a
large-scale survey and mapping of the city, forward
planning of building and drainage, and tight control of
both.[96] He was told that with Rs.96,000 annual
interest payments on the water-works loan no more
could be done. Instead in 1900 a list of no less than
58 minor drainage works was drawn up, to be tackled
piecemeal as funds could be spared. Under the pressure
of the municipal engineer, however, a basic survey of
levels was begun in 1904,[97] and this was enlarged at
the instance of the Sanitary Engineer to Government
into a full drainage system. After reference to Mr
Lane Brown, M.I.C.E., who added his professional
weight - and fees - to the scheme, the project finally
got under way in 1913: a triumph for the influence of
the expert, a heavy burden on municipal finance.[98]

The last sanitary problem to be successfully
tackled in London was that of overcrowding, whether of
persons or buildings. The only early triumph there
had been in the control of lodging-houses, tackled by
an Act of 1851. But that act became the model for

Bengal Act IV of 1871 to control lodging-houses for
pilgrims at Puri, and upon that in turn was built Act I
of 1892, dealing with lodging-houses in the North-
Western Provinces and Oudh. Initially this was applied
to Benares and Hardwar, but not to Allahabad - an odd
omission when a Kumbh Mela was due, and when Planck had
drawn so compelling a warning from the last great
Allahabad Kumbh in 1882:

> The houses generally overcrowded, many of them quite
> full of people lying, at night time, in pretty close
> order whereever shelter from the sky could be
> obtained. Rooms, verandahs, out-houses, temporary
> shelters of mats ... all accommodating, to their
> utmost, their *quota* of people.
>
> Surface cleanliness neglected, the drainage-
> ways choked with sweepings, chiefly large leaves in
> which food had been purchased - moistened with much
> refuse water used for cooking or washing, with
> great suspicion of urine admixture. Attached
> private retiring places, generally in one corner of
> the courtyard, overflowing with impurities .... A
> condition of things always deplored by the house-
> holder, but excused upon the plea that sweepers
> could not, at this time be found to effect the
> usual business of cleanliness.
>
> The water of the wells, stirred up by ceaseless
> drawing, slightly discoloured and of unpleasant
> odour....

All of which was but preparation for the last scene, at
the station, of the struggling and then weary crowd of
pilgrims, from which 'in every day of its existence,
cholera cases were carried away ....'[99]
However, what government had not prescribed, the
municipality took to itself. Despite the objections
of pandas and the Daraganj dharmsalas Lodging-House
inspectors were appointed and the law imposed, a
recognition that once a year the municipality had a
special duty larger than that owed to its own
citizens.[100]
To the overcrowded conditions under which many of
those citizens lived it chose, indeed, to turn a
selectively blind eye. If the District Magistrate
McNair pointed to the crowded Atarsuiya or Dundipur
areas of the city, Brownrigg, the Commissioner,
splendidly replied,

I do not think that the Allahabad City can be said
to be seriously congested. There may be some overcrowding in the two Mohallas ... but I doubt if it
is of such a nature as to require heroic measures.
Every large town is bound to have some parts which
are more or less congested.

As to providing model 'bastis' for the poor, I
do not believe for a moment that any plan of this
kind would meet with success. It seems to me
altogether utopian. What many persons, though, in
Allahabad really would like is cheap houses,
detached residences, where Government servants
could live ... something after the fashion of
Lukerganj.[101]

The outcome of the Brownrigg attitude took two
forms. Insanitary overcrowding in Rajapur was dealt
with by evicting the inhabitants of 'this little pest-
hole from the heart of the civil lines'.[102]   And to the
model settlement for Government Press employees,
Lukerganj, was added the early Mumfordganj and the
George Town Extension which provided for the senior
clerks of the Secretariat and for professional men
retreating from the dangers of plague in the city.
The *Indian People* was happy to applaud this action to
deal with 'this most pressing need of Allahabad ...
congestion in the Civil Lines'.[103]

But attention to the problems of the city could not
long be withheld. In December 1883 Austen Chamberlain
had re-opened the question of slum clearance and
working class housing in Britain with a sharp attack on
the Torrens and Cross Housing Acts, 'tainted and
paralysed by the incurable timidity with which Parliament [deals] with the sacred rights of property'. *The
Times* joined in the attack on overcrowding in 1884 and
the Royal Commission on the housing of the working
classes was appointed whose work was to issue in
Housing of the Working Classes Acts in 1886 and 1890.[104]
In Bengal an amending Act VI of 1881 gave the Commissioners of Calcutta power to acquire bustees in order
to improve them, while far more extensive legislation,
Act II of 1888 and Act III of 1889 imposed improvement
of bustees upon owners, or in default upon the municipality and provided for driving roads and lanes of
standard width through such areas.[105]   Add to this the
example of the Bombay Improvement Trust's work, and
nearer to hand, that of the Aminabad improvement in

Lucknow,[106] and some action in Allahabad on similar
lines became inevitable.

The final impetus was given, perhaps, by the
Sanitary Conference at Naini Tal in September 1908. In
January 1909 a trust deed was executed in favour of the
municipal board at Allahabad, empowering an Improvement
Trust to open up the most crowded areas of the city by
making new roads, and to provide sanitary houses for
the displaced population. An initial grant of
Rs.125,000 was made by government to set going what
was expected to be a self-supporting operation.[107] A
whole series of operations followed, under the chairmanship of Professor Stanley Jevons of Allahabad University, most notably the driving through of Hewett Road,
Crosthwaite Road, Sheo Charan Lal Road and Zero
Road,[108] relieving the pressure on the Grand Trunk
Road, undoing in part the ills caused by the presence
of three railway systems driven into the heart of the
city, and slicing through the heaviest concentrations
of working class population. These measures, and those
later initiated by the Allahabad Improvement Trust
refashioned in 1919 by the United Provinces Town
Improvement Act VII of 1919, were on the whole
financially successful - the Hewett Road frontages
sold for sums that astonished everyone.[109] They did
do something to cope with the traffic of a city which
had much more than doubled in forty years. They did
let in that light and air on which sanitarians placed
so much stress - though in a crude way, which as was
later admitted would scarcely have secured the approval
of the generation of 'organic' town planners such as
Patrick Geddes.[110] What they did not do, of course,
was to provide satisfactorily for the slum dwellers who
had lost their homes. The new model townships - Bai
ka Bagh and its successors - ended up in middle-class
hands, as Collector Hopkinson had foreseen.[111]

19. ALLAHABAD: Sewered, paved and lit corner of Bharti Bhavan Muhalla

Harrison, 'Allahabad: A Sanitary History'

1. *Eighteenth Annual Report of the Sanitary Commissioner of the North-Western Provinces, 1885*, pp.60-61 (hereafter Sanitary Report NWP).
2. M.W. Flinn (ed.), *Report on the Sanitary Condition of the Labouring Population of Great Britain* by Edwin Chadwick, 1842 (Edinburgh 1965), p.8 (hereafter Flinn).
3. Sir George Newman, 'The Health of the People', in H.J. Laski, W.I. Jennings and W.A. Robson (eds.), *A Century of Municipal Progress, 1835-1935* (London 19 1935), p.159 (hereafter Newman).
4. Flinn, p.423.
5. Flinn, p.424.
6. Flinn, p.425.
7. Newman, p.160.
8. H. Jephson, *The Sanitary Evolution of London* (London 1907), p.45 (hereafter Jephson).
9. Jephson, pp.184-218.
10. Newman, p.160.
11. Newman, p.168.
12. *Royal Commission on the Health of the Army in India, 1863*, p.77 (hereafter *Health of the Army*).
13. H.H. Dodwell (ed.), *Cambridge History of India*, vol.vi, (Cambridge 1932), p.365.
14. Parliamentary Papers: *Report on Sanitary Measures in India in 1886*, vol.xx, Cd.5533, p.10 (hereafter *Sanitary Measures*).
15. *Sanitary Measures in 1897-98*, vol.xxxi, Cd. 9549, p.162.
16. See S.W. Goode, *Municipal Calcutta* (Edinburgh 1916) for a full study.
17. Commissioner of Allahabad to Nazul Committee, 20 April 1861, Commissioners' Records, Basta 78, File 13, Serial 98 (hereafter CR). The Magh Mela is the annual Pilgrim Fair at the confluence of Ganges and Jumna at Allahabad in January and February. Every twelfth year there occurs the greater and more suspicious Kumbh Mela.
18. Magistrate to Commissioner, 28 June 1861, CR, Basta 78, File 4, Serial 116.
19. Fanny Parkes, *Wanderings of a Pilgrim in Search of the Picturesque*, vol.i. pp.72-3 and 206.

20. See H. Tinker, *The Foundations of Local Self-Government in India, Pakistan and Burma* (London 1968).
21. Magistrate to Commissioner, 28 June 1861, CR, Basta 78, File 4, Serial 116. In Calcutta the house-tax was the mainstay of municipal finance - Goode, *Municipal Calcutta*, pp.51-61.
22. H.R. Nevill, *District Gazetteers of the United Provinces of Agra and Oudh XXIII, Allahabad* (Allahabad 1911), pp.143-4.
23. *Health of the Army*, pp.82-94.
24. Just how dirty British towns were may be judged from the evidence of the Provost of Inverness: 'There are very few houses in the town which boast of either water-closet or privy, and only two or three public privies in the better part of the place exist for the great bulk of the inhabitants. Hence there is not a street, lane, or approach to it that is not disgustingly defiled at all times....' Quoted in Flinn, p.116.
25. *Health of the Army*, p.81 - approvingly quoting Sir Charles Trevelyan.
26. First Sanitary Report NWP, 1868.
27. Eleventh Sanitary Report NWP, 1878.
28. Ibid.,'"Vein-opener", "needle-pricker" etc. are the names by which the vaccinator is designated in the bazar and sensitive to ridicule as our Indian fellow-subjects are, it requires the pressure of considerable poverty to enlist respectable recruits.'
29. Dr James Irving to Magistrate, 12 December 1855, CR, Basta 78, File 13, Serial 23. 'I fixed 25 Rupees as being the rate of pay allowed to the Native Doctors educated at the Calcutta Medical College ... but should 25 rupees be reckoned too much for the Native Doctor the services of an inferiorly qualified man could be secured for 12 or 15 rupees.' [per month]
30. First Sanitary Report NWP, 1868.
31. See Newman.
32. *Sanitary Measures in 1889-90*, vol.xxiii, Cd 6501, pp.151-155.
33. First Sanitary Report NWP, 1868, para.29.
34. That is housing of fired or sun dried brick and pise. The bricks were either made on site or in brick-fields west of the city. Brick was the building material of the civil station too, though classically clad in stucco.
35. First Sanitary Report NWP, 1868, para.33.
36. The *Report on the Administration of the Allahabad Municipal Board, 1887-8* (Allahabad 1888)

(hereafter Municipal Administration) records the first
use of a steamroller. Roadwatering done by hand by
bhisties with water-skins cost Rs.372 a mile in 1888-
89, but less than Rs.100 a mile by 1894 when water-
carts had largely replaced bhisties.

37. Municipal Administration, 1882-3, para.45.
38. Ibid., 1879-80, pp.7-8.
39. Ibid., 1889-90, p.14.
40. Ibid., 1899-1900, para.94.
41. Ibid., 1901-02, para.46.
42. First Sanitary Report NWP, 1868, para.102.
43. Ibid., para.36.
44. Collector to Commissioner, 4 January 1901, CR,
Dept. VIII, 1901-02, File 9.
45. See for example the report on Riwari, in
Gurgaon district, *Report on the Sanitary Administration
of the Punjab for 1870* (Lahore 1871), p.39.
46. First Sanitary Report NWP, 1868, para.33.
47. Ibid., para.393.
48. Municipal Administration 1916-17.
49. Ibid., 1888-9, p.17.
50. First Sanitary Report NWP, 1868, para.389.
51. Flinn, p.117.
52. Agra Municipality to Government NWP, 15 March
1869, NWP General (Sanitation) Proceedings, 17 April
1869, No.2.
53. Municipal Analyst to Municipal Board, 7 April
1892, NWP General (Municipal) Proceedings, August 1892,
No.49.
54. *The United Provinces Code* (4th ed., Calcutta
1906), vol.ii.
55. Municipal Administration 1898-99.
56. Sanitary Commissioner to Government NWP, 6
October 1868, NWP, General (Sanitation) Proceedings,
17 April 1869, No.2.
57. Working Committee Proceedings, Allahabad
Municipal Board (hereafter Working Committee), 1 of 27
June 1889.
58. Working Committee, 19 of 28 July 1890.
59. Ibid., 17 of 19 May 1892.
60. Ibid., 21 of 20 August 1908.
61. First Sanitary Report NWP, 1868, para.103.
62. Working Committee, 14 of 12 November 1885.
63. Sanitary Commissioner to Municipal Board, 17
February 1908, CR, Dept. XXIII, File 63, Serial 3.
64. Municipal Board to Commissioner, 11 March 1908,
CR, Dept XXIII, File 63.

65. NWP General (Municipal) Proceedings, 9 July 1870, No.211.
66. Municipal Administration 1916-17, p.XVI.
67. Municipal Administration 1891-92.
68. Sanitary Commissioner to Municipal Board, 10 September 1907, CR, Dept XXIII, File 63, Serial 2.
69. Municipal Administration 1879-80, pp.4-6; ibid., 1881-82.
70. Goode, *Municipal Calcutta*.
71. Municipal Administration 1886-87.
72. Ibid., 1904-05, p.9.
73. Ibid., 1912-13, p.8.
74. Ibid., 1908-09, p.7.
75. Ibid., 1910-11, p.10.
76. Ibid., 1917-18, p.12.
77. *Health of the Army*, pp.89-93; see also H.J. Dyos, *Victorian Suburb* (London 1961), pp.143-45.
78. Working Committee, 14 of 8 August 1885.
79. Ibid., 11 of 3 December 1885.
80. Ibid., 14 of 19 April 1886.
81. Municipal Administration 1882-83, p.13.
82. Ibid., 1888-89, p.25.
83. Ibid., 1890-91. The water-works were opened by the Viceroy.
84. Working Committee, 6 of 11 May 1892. This records a letter from Lala Jagat Narain 'offering to lay a watermain in the street on which he resides, on condition that he may use the pipe for connecting all his houses in the mohulla'.
85. Municipal Administration 1893-94.
86. Working Committee, 23 of 6 October 1892.
87. Municipal Administration 1880-81.
88. Working Committee, 15 of 3 November 1892.
89. Ibid., 7 of 22 December 1892.
90. *The United Provinces Code*, vol.ii, (4th ed., Calcutta 1906).
91. Working Committee, 4 of 8 December 1892. The Army Sanitary Commission commented 'The drainage works, which are the necessary complement of a water-supply will tax the resources of these [NWP] cities and towns for their completion, but completed they must be if the introduction of the water supply is to prove an unmixed benefit to the public health.' *Sanitary Measures in 1895-96*, vol.xxix, Cd 8688.
92. Municipal Administration 1897-98.
93. Ibid., 1899-1900.
94. Twelfth Sanitary Report NWP 1879, para.124;

Thirteenth Sanitary Report 1880, para.97.
    95. Municipal Administration 1895-96.
    96. 28 July 1897.
    97. Municipal Administration 1904-05, p.8.
    98. Ibid., 1911-12, para.32.
    99. Fourteenth Sanitary Report NWP 1882, paras.197 and 208.
    100. Municipal Board to Commissioner, 11 March 1909, CR, Dept XXIII, File 41, Serial 4.
    101. Commissioner Brownrigg to UP Govt., 3 August 1908, CR, Dept XXIII, File 98.
    102. Commissioner to Collector, 9 September 1911, CR, Dept XXIII, File 98.
    103. *The Indian People*, 19 January 1908.
    104. See Jephson, pp.293-343.
    105. See Goode, *Municipal Calcutta*.
    106. UP Govt to Commissioner, 25 August 1909, CR, Dept XXIII, File 98.
    107. UP Govt to Commissioner, 20 January 1909, CR, Dept XXIII, File 98, Serial 43.
    108. Municipal Administration 1912-1913, para.12; Ibid., 1913-14; H.S. Jevons, *Preliminary Report on the Improvement of Allahabad* (Allahabad 1920).
    109. Municipal Board to Commissioner, 14 December 1912, and reply of 16 December 1912, CR, Dept XXIII, File 98.
    110. The Improvement Trust Sub-Committee of the Municipal Board appointed in 1908 discussed the opening up of the city and construction of parks and open spaces with Professor Gedes and the map of proposals they prepared 'was drawn with his general approval'.
    111. Hopkinson to Commissioner, 11 June 1909, CR, Dept XXIII, File 98, Serial 96.

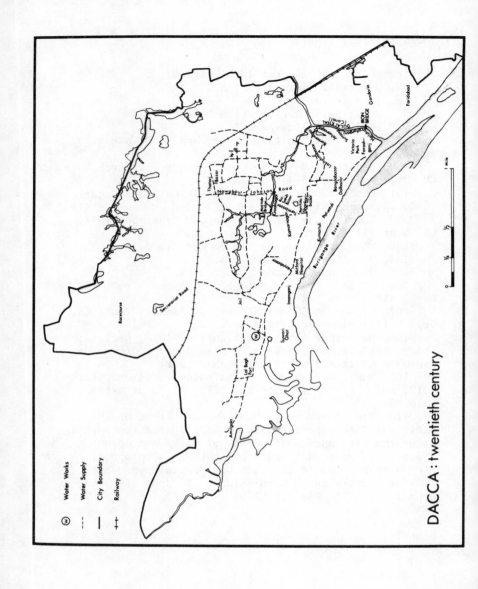

Water Works

Water Supply

City Boundary

Railway

DACCA: twentieth century

THE CITY OF DACCA, 1921-1947: SOCIETY, WATER AND ELECTRICITY

Nazia Hussain

The city as a subject for study has attracted
researchers from various fields who have developed
approaches emphasizing different features of urban life.
It has become increasingly apparent that the city is a
complex phenomenon and that no aspect of it should
properly be studied in isolation. To select just two
topics - the growth and distribution of population in
Dacca in the years 1921 to 1941 and the pattern of
water and electricity supply provisions in the city -
for discussion in this paper, is therefore necessarily
rather artificial, though not, it is hoped, without
significance.

Dacca is an old city and bears all the traces in
its physical lay-out of its history, whether as a
trading and manufacturing centre or as an administrative
capital or sub-capital, and in the detail of house
style and neighbourhood of its history under Hindu,
Muslim and British rulers. The existence of a substantial Hindu town is evident from the place names of
the city - it is this which occupies the half-moon
between the Buriganga river and Dulai Khai (canal).
The main Hindu settlements were Patuatuli, Kumartuli,
Jaluanagar, Banianagar and Goalnagar; and these, as
Dani and S.M. Taifoor argue, accommodated the craftsmen and businessmen of the city. The principal
markets are comemorated in the names Lakshmibazar,
Banglabazar, Shankaribazar and Tantibazar.[1]

During the whole of the seventeenth century Dacca
experienced great industrial and commercial prosperity.
The weaving of muslins secured imperial patronage. A
large number of foreign traders settled in Dacca and
the Portuguese, the Armenians, the Dutch, the English
and the French established their factories in the town
near the Banglabazar and the Babubazar area. This
location eventually increased the importance of Banglabazar which had been ursurped by the Chauk during the
hey-day of the Mughals in Dacca.

Dacca's expansion and development was seriously
interrupted when the capital of Bengal was transferred
to Murshidabad in 1717. When the British administration took over in 1765, the city had shrunk from the

maximum limits earlier recorded, and the new administration added little to the existing structure.
Rennell's map of 1780 shows large areas as under trees
and gardens - though whether this had or had not always
been true it is impossible to decide - while the river
frontage was by then only some four miles long. By
1824 when the city had been over-shadowed by the rise
of Calcutta as the main administrative, military and
commercial base of the East India Company in Bengal,
the decay of Dacca was much clearer. Bishop Heber
described the city as merely the wreck of its ancient
grandeur having two-thirds of its vast area filled with
ruins and jungles. Despite such decline, however, the
city population was recorded by Heber as 300,000 Hindus
and Muslims living in 90,000 houses. In the absence of
any formal census records, this seems too large a
figure to be accepted without dispute. However it is
universally accepted that Dacca was a big city during
the Mughal period. Bishop Heber's account would seem
at least to confirm that.[2]

In the first census of 1872 the population figure
for Dacca city was recorded as 69,212. This was,
however, the population within the municipal area of
six square miles, which was much smaller than the area
described by Heber and other foreign travellers. From
1872 onwards a steady growth of population was recorded
in the census reports.

Decennial population of Dacca City 1872-1941[3]

Year	Population	Year	Population
1872	69,000	1911	109,000
1881	79,000	1921	119,000
1891	82,000	1931	139,000
1901	90,000	1941	213,000

The localities of Wari and Gandaria on the eastern
side of the city came into existence in the nineteenth
century together with the Topkhana, the Purana Paltan
and Naya Paltan associated with the British military
establishment. In the present century this old cantonment area was given over for the residential
purposes of the city people. In 1905, Dacca was
reincarnated as the provincial capital and the seat of
the Government of Eastern Bengal and Assam, though
only to be relegated to the more obscure position of a
divisonal headquarters again in 1911. During this
short period of glory the foundation of the modern

Ramna area was laid.[4] This area was developed to
accommodate the new offices and residential houses for
the officials.

All this new development, it will be seen, had
occurred to the north of the old city. The river had
tended by this date to change its main course away from
the Mughal, westward limits of the city, while in 1885
the East Bengal railway had reached Dacca connecting
the city with Narayanganj, the centre of the jute trade,
and with Mymensingh in 1886.[5] The new governmental
areas or Civil Lines, and the fashionable area of Ramna
were both north of the railway. This trend has vastly
accelerated since 1947, assisted by the growth of new
forms of transport, the bicycle, the car and bus, and
the cycle- and motor-rickshaw.

Some of the developments that took place in the
twentieth century had their origin in the last century.
The laying out of the racecourse in 1825 by the
Collector, Mr Dawes, was actually the start of the
development of this area under the British in the
twentieth century. In the 1870s the British removed
their administrative headquarters from the old fort to
the Johnson road which is the southern end of the
Nawabpur road. This road assumed great importance from
that time onward. The municipality (which came into
existence in 1864) remained continuously engaged,
through-out the nineteenth century, in developing
areas near this road by filling the low-lying parts in
Islampur, Tantibazar, Kamarnagar, Goalnagar and Rai
Saheb Bazar.[6] The Nawabpur-Johnson road with the
District Court at the southern end and the Rest House
and Government House at the other grew to be an even
more important thoroughfare in the twentieth century.
The Fulbariah railway station on the offshoot of this
road, the railway workshop and quarters in the same
vicinity, and the University of Dacca created in 1921
near its northern end all contributed new elements to
the importance of this road. A number of shops for
fashion articles gradually grew up on either side of
the road.[7]

From the sources available it appears that in the
Mughal period the Muslims were overwhelmingly the major
community in the city. Bishop Heber in a letter from
Dacca on 13 July 1824, stated that even then three-
fourths of the inhabitants were Mussalmans with the
Hindus as the next largest community and a handful of
Greeks, Armenians, Portuguese and Christians.[8] However

Nazia Hussain

given the size of the old Hindu city and the predominance of Hindus later in the nineteenth century one
could reasonably doubt the accuracy of the accounts of
European travellers regarding the population composition
of the city. The travellers probably noticed public
and religious buildings and the more imposing houses
visible from the main thoroughfares. Their impression
about a city is not objectively accurate, as a census
is, but socially subjective. If, however, the accounts
of the foreign travellers are to be accepted this
would imply that during the British period the communal
structure of the city population was reversed, since
all the twentieth-century figures make the Hindus the
larger community.

Numbers of Hindus and Muslims in Dacca, 1901-41[9]

Census	Hindus	Muslims
1901	51,247	41,728
1911	59,994	47,295
1921	69,145	49,325
1931	79,906	57,764
1941	129,233	82,921

It was in the 1911-21 decade that the growth in Hindu
numbers began to outpace that of Muslims. The Hindus'
dramatic advance recorded in the 1941 census is open to
considerable suspicion, but that the Hindus were
decidedly the larger community after 1921 is quite
certain. In 1947 in the wake of the partition of India,
however, many Hindus left for West Bengal and many
Muslims from West Bengal and other parts of India moved
into Dacca. At no point was there any significant
number of persons in the city who where neither Hindu
nor Muslim.

A number of factors might have been responsible for
the shift in the communal balance in the Dacca city
population during the British period in so far as it
occurred. The movement of the capital to Murshidabad
and still later of independent Muslim authority to
Lucknow and Hyderabad doubtless led to some migration
by Muslim military and service families and of those
specialist artisans who served the Muslim Courts and
nobility. The decline of the cotton industry may also
have reduced the Muslim weaver element in the city
population. On the other hand, the revival of Dacca
in the later nineteenth century as a commercial and
administrative centre may well have attracted Hindus

200

in a disproportionate number, dominant as they were in
the commerce of Bengal and leaders in the acquisition
of the English language and the technical qualifica-
tions required.[10]

Dacca city attracted more people when it acquired
the status of a provincial capital in 1905. The
increase in the city population during 1901-1911 was as
much as 21 per cent.[11] However, the annulment of the
partition of Bengal in 1911 and the influenza epidemic
of 1918[12] adversely affected the growth rate which
declined between 1911-1921 to only half that of the
previous decade.[13]

The establishment of the Dacca University as a
compensation for the annulment of partition did
attract a number of East Bengali people, but most of
the students and teachers nevertheless were Hindus.
The Hindus in Bengal were already much ahead of the
Muslims in education, and it was only natural perhaps
that they should constitute the majority of the
teachers, though not quite so expected that the bulk of
the students should have been Hindu too.

The censuses of 1931 and 1941 recorded a 15.2 per
cent and 54 per cent growth rate in the city population.
The latter figure seems to have been inflated: Muslims
accused Hindus of deliberately increasing their numbers
for political purposes, and Hindus made similar
accusations against Muslims. But the fact remains that
the city population had been increasing steadily, all
the seven municipal wards sharing in this growth.[14]

Spatially, Dacca city is now roughly divided into
two halves by the railway line running from the north
to the south east. The area to the south of the railway line may be called the old town and the rest is
largely of post-independence construction.[15] It is
with the old town and its seven municipal wards that
we shall be concerned in this paper. The most dense
settlement was along the banks of the Buriganga river
and the main road running parallel to it, at a distance
of two to three hundred yards, where many of the houses,
close packed, were three storeys high. Wards 5,2,1,4,
7 and 3 were in that order the most dense of the city,
and all of these included portions of this old river-
based settlement though extending northwards also into
the less closely-packed areas. Ward 6 marked the
other end of the spectrum, being least heavily populated and lacking any section of the congested part of
the city. Three wards were predominantly Hindu; in

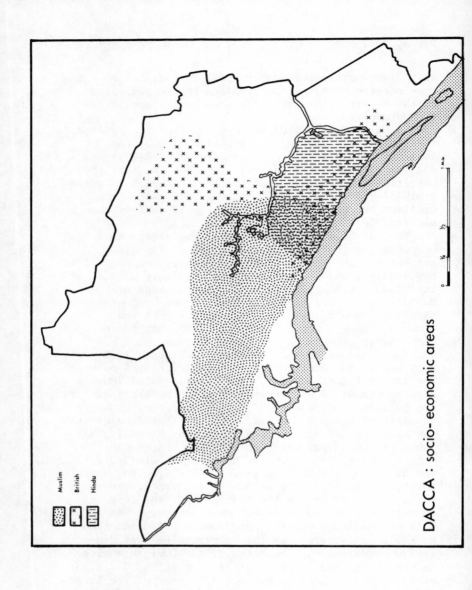

DACCA : socio- economic areas

Muslim

British

Hindu

ward 2 they formed 76.1 per cent, in ward 3, 75.9 per
cent, in ward 1, 68.8 per cent, of the inhabitants.
Two wards were almost equally divided between the
Hindus and Muslims, Hindus forming 52.4 per cent in
ward 7, and 50.0 per cent in ward 5. Muslims predom-
inated in wards 4 and 6 where only 31.4 per cent and
36.8 per cent respectively were Hindus. The total
number of Christians in Dacca according to the census
Reports of 1921 was 710, most of them being found in
ward 1. People belonging to the other religions were
no more than 279.[16]
Three of the most densely populated wards were in
the heart of the town near the business centres on
Nawabpur Road and Johnson Road and on Mitford and
Waterworks Road. The distinctive house pattern of
these areas, with narrow street frontages and very long
buildings running back from the shop fronts, was
particularly noticeable in the Tanti Bazar and Shankri
Bazar areas. The shopkeepers lived, as in mediaeval
towns, on the premises. The whole of the central wards
were typical, in their dense development, of a pedes-
trian city with businessmen, their clerks and their
porters all within walking distance of their place of
work. The hackney carriage was still the commonest
form of transport and a slow one, in this period, with
the bicycle as supplement. Living near the business
centre saved people both time and money. The pattern
is seemingly as typical of the Muslim- as the Hindu-
dominated wards.
Trade and commerce with the banking associated with
an old capital, together with administration, were the
main functions of Dacca city.[17] In the areas dominated
by the Hindu community the principal names of the
commercial elite were Basak, Das, Roy and Saha.
The Basaks were traders mainly in jute, rice and
oil.[18] They were also metal button manufacturers,
booksellers and publishers. They owned a number of
cloth and stationery shops on the Nawabpur Road[19] and
in Patuatuli.[20] Like the Basaks, the Dases were also
engaged in the jute business.[21] But unlike them they
were horn mother-of-pearl button manufacturers and
dealers in photographic materials, crushed food and
forage.[22] They were also engaged in printing and
publishing, hardware and timber-business and also in
meony lending. They were concentrated in Nawabpur
Road, Faridabad, Walter Road,[23] Chauk Bazar,[24] Ampatti
and Lalbagh.[25] The Roys who owned two newspapers, *The*

203

East and the *Dacca Gazette*,[26] were also hardware merchants. The Bengal Zamindary and Banking Company dealing with loans, banking, estate management, land development and agency business was jointly owned and run by the Roys and Dases, with Gangulys, Pakrashis and Mukherjees as the partners. This was located on the Johnson Road.[27] Their other business concerns were situated in Armanitola and Mughaltuli, further west in the old city.[28] The Sahas were druggists, cloth merchants, dealers in coal, paint, varnish, colours, machinery, hardwares, spices etc. They were also engaged in the printing or publishing business. Their shops were located mainly in Babubazar on Waterworks Road and in Islampur.[29] The names of Mukherjee, Ghose, Kundu and Banerjee were also to be found as merchants and traders in the city.

If the trade and commerce of the city was largely in Hindu hands so were the major industries. Textile firms such as the Gupta and Company Hosiery works at Patuatuli, Das and Brothers at Farashgang, Dey Sarkar and Company at Wari and Basu Rai Chaudhury in Faridabad were all owned by Hindus.[30] The Boolbool Soap factory, the first toilet soap factory in Dacca, was also started by a Hindu. It was located in Gandaria, though this was also a residential area.[31] More surprisingly Babu Sachindra Nath Ghose, a Calcutta graduate, started a tannery works in the city and a shoemakers' colony in the Lakshmi Bazar area. A number of shoemakers were already living there - all of them Hindus - and more came thereafter to concentrate on this area, a nice example of the way persons of similar craft and religion cluster in one place.[32] The major factory industries of Dacca like the Madan Mohan Iron Works,[33] Desha Bandhu Sugar Mills, the East Bengal Sugar Mills, Prasanna Match Factory, Hardeo Glass works,the Dhakeswari glass factory, the Boses' glass works, the Alexandra Steam Machine Press, the Narayan Marine Press, the Wari Printing Works, the Bijaya Press and the Provincial Press were again all owned by Hindus. Most of the owners of these industries lived in Dalbazar,[34] Nayabazar and Tantibazar,[35] congested parts of the city, because of cultural tradition and social habit.

Among the Muslims by contrast there were hardly any industrial entrepreneurs. The Nawabs of Dacca owned a small factory in Karmartuli, though this was working at a loss because of the greater popularity of

David and Company's ice factory in Narayanganj.[36]
Muslims also owned the Islamic Press and the oldest
brick factory in the city, that of Jalfikar and Company.
There were more than 7,000 industrial workers in
the city in 1931:[37] they constituted roughly five per
cent of the city's total population. The majority of
them was Hindu, most of them living in the wards
nearest to the factories and so within walking distance
or in one case living in workers' barracks attached to
the mill.
On the lowest rung of society were the beggars,
vagrants, prostitutes and their procurers. In 1911 a
total number of 17,844 such people was recorded in the
census in the district of Dacca.[38] In 1921 the
district is reported to have had 18,299 people as
beggars, vagrants and prostitues,[39] but between 1921-31
their number declined to 9,610. There was no particular
area for beggars and vagrants. They were homeless
people and lived in the open verandahs of offices,
houses, shops, the railway and steamer stations, near
mosques, temples, *mazars* (graves of Muslim saints),
and on the streets. They were virtually everywhere in
the city. The prostitutes, however, were concentrated
in the Badamtoli area very near Absau Manzil, the palace
of the Dacca Nawabs. About the religion of these
classes no data is provided by the sources: Muslims
commonly held, however, that most of the prostitutes
and procurers were Hindus.
Although, as can be seen, some large-scale factory
industries had been introduced in the city, the bulk
of the manufactures was still in the hands of industrial
craftsmen and artisans whose homes were residences-cum-
workshops. A large number of people was engaged in
weaving, in the conch-shell industries, horn-carving,
gold and silver work, soap manufacturing, leather,
bamboo and cane work, the making of fishing nets and the
production of caps, brass and bell metal products,
pottery and so on.
Dacca's distinctive industries, cotton spinning and
bleaching, the weaving of muslin and embroidery, were
exclusively confined to the homes of industrial artisans and their families. Although Dacca's famous
muslin industry had almost died in the nineteenth
century, in handloom manufactures the city remained one
of the principal centres of the Province till the first
quarter of the twentieth century.[40] The Tantibazar,
Bhiti Azimpur and Nawabpur areas accommodated most of

the city's weavers. The cotton weavers were locally
known as Tanties, Jugis and Jullahas, and of these
only a small minority, the Jullahas, were Muslims. The
areas in which they were concentrated thus went by their
craft name. They had been living and working in this
area from a long time past.

Next to weaving, conch-shell cutting was the most
important industry in Dacca. This was an old industry
'with its roots and tentacles dug deep into the social
and domestic life of the Bengal people'.[41] Its close
connection with Hindu religion, sentiment and practice
kept the industry alive. The people engaged in this
industry were all Hindus. The workers were locally
called 'Sankharis' and lived in the heart of the city,
in 'Sankhari Patti' or 'Shankharibazar', the colony or
market of the conch-shell goods manufacturers. They
typically combined their residence and workshop in the
same place. About the housing condition of this area
the District Gazetteer of 1912 stated,

> the houses here have a very narrow frontage with
> a quite disproportionate depth. The most extreme
> instance of a characteristic which is common in a
> greater or a less degree to all the houses in this
> Bazar is to be found in a well built masonry
> dwelling which in 1909 was inhabited by a family
> of eight persons. This extraordinary structure
> had a depth of 55½ feet and a uniform breadth of
> 3 feet 4 inches only. Another curious house is
> 60 feet deep, 27 feet high and only 6 feet wide.
>
> These houses are well built and kept in
> excellent repair but very little light or air can
> penetrate into the curious little cave-like
> chambers of which they are composed.[42]

This pattern remained unchanged during the period under
review.[43]

In the horn carving and country soap manufacturing
industries, the artisans were all Muslims. The
workers in the former industry used to manufacture
horn combs, buttons, toys, knife blades and so on.
They lived mainly on the river front at Amligola,
Churihatta and in the Nawabgarj area[44] west of the
Mughal Lalbagh. About where the soap makers lived
and worked, there is some doubt. The District
Gazetteer of 1969 states that they lived mainly in
Farashganj and Faridabad.[45] Islam says that they
were from Narinda, Burbur Bazar and Imamganj.[46]

However, Babubazar and Imanganj were Muslim majority
areas in this period, located near the river, with two
big markets of their own. The city map of 1912-15 also
shows considerable areas of poor thatched housing in
these areas. By contrast Narinda was a much richer
area, of *pakka* housing, in which no thatched houses are
shown at all. These areas do not seem likely centres
for such a trade and for such poor people. Of Faridabad
and Farashganj the former was a very sparsely populated
area. For a particularly smelly, unpleasant industry
like soap boiling this might séem appropriate. Farashganj, however, seems to be a more likely place where
this business or industry could grow. There were
several bazars or markets around this locality and it
was also a Muslim majority area. One of the reasons
why these industries did not attract the Hindus doubtless was because animal fat was commonly used as an
ingredient of the country soaps. However, we should
not stretch the factor of religion too far when all the
shoemakers of Lakshmi bazar were reported to be Hindus.
There was of course some difference between the raw
materials used by the Hindu shoemakers and the Muslim
shoemakers of Dacca. The former group only used
chrome leather imported from Calcutta, whereas the
Muslim Chamars and Rishis (the shoemakers' local names)
used local leather.

Another occupational group concentrating in a
particular locality was the carpenters. They were
locally called 'mistris' or 'Sutradhars'. They too
lived mainly in the Farashganj areas and near the
Sutrapur market. These places were along the Dolai
Khal, the semi-circular canal flowing across the city,
and it was probably for the easy supply by water of
the raw materials that his location was chosen by this
occupational group.

Patuatuli and Kumartuli were yet other examples of
localities having largely one occupational group. The
inhabitants were overwhelmingly Hindu Kumars (potters).
They used to make earthen statues of the Hindu Gods
and Goddesses and also earthenware jars and pots, for
day-to-day use.[47]

Thatharibazar, Kansharibazar, Nawabpur and Islampur
were known for brass, copper, and bell metal wares.
The artisans were locally known as 'Kansharis'. Except
for Islampur these areas were predominantly Hindu. The
metalwares were also more commonly used by the Hindus
in Bengal. Even if personal experience did not tend to

confirm the fact, it would seem certain that most of those workers were Hindus.

Gold and silver work was a well-known craft in Dacca. The gold and silversmiths were the descendants of the muslin weavers who after the decline of the Muslin industry, took up gold and silver work and excelled in this field also. There were 548 males and seven females recorded as engaged in the jewellery and ornament making industries in the city in 1931.[48] A large majority of them were Hindus, mainly concentrated in the Tantibazar, Nawabpur and Islampur areas.

Tailoring and book binding were the main trades taken up by the Muslims. Their workshops were mainly in Banglabazar, Sadarghat and Nawabpur - strategically placed for contacting customers in the old city and civil station - though with scattered representation throughout the seven wards of the municipality. Their residences do not seem, however, to have been located in any one particular area. The same may well have been true of the drivers of the hackney carriages and carts, who were nearly all Muslims. But if it is a fact, as some people are strongly inclined to believe, that they were mostly drawn from the Kuttis, the native Bengali Muslim labouring class, then of course their concentration can easily be located in Banglabazar area.[49]

Clearly there were also large numbers of people engaged in such occupations as milk production, oil pressing, poultry rearing, the making of bidis (country cigarettes) and the manufacture of cane and bamboo baskets, mats and furniture, just as there were publishers and book-sellers, stationers, musical instrument makers, and so on. They might be one community or another, or both, and were not grouped spatially in one particular quarter, but with barbers, washermen, domestic servants and the like were found everywhere in the city.[50]

Among the very low income groups the scavengers and sweepers, who were regarded as untouchables by the caste Hindus, lived in a group in the periphery of the city. Their main colony was near the railway line towards the north.

Since Dacca was a capital or a sub-capital for Bengal the other major groups of occupations were the administrative and professional. Those who served government or entered the professions, the (western) educated, were often rent-receivers also, and formed the Bhadralok.[51]

Lawyers formed one of the major professional groups in the educated middle-class of the city. In the province as a whole the number of people engaged in the legal profession was very large compared to that of the other provinces of India. This profession flourished in Dacca, there being no dearth of civil and criminal cases in that region. It appears that 'everything that could be litigated about was eagerly litigated by these people'.[52]

In 1905 the city of Dacca had 128 vakils and pleaders. This number excluded an enormous number of kazis, law agents (locally known as 'muhuris'), mukhtyars and petition writers who were also engaged in the legal profession. Of these 128 pleaders, however, only two were Muslims and the rest were Hindus.[53] By 1911 their number had risen a little to 144 of whom only three were Muslims.[54] (The census of 1911 recorded a total number of 1,464 people engaged in the legal profession in the district. This number covered lawyers of all kinds, including kazis, law agents, mukhtyars, petition writers and so on.)[55] *Thacker's Indian Directory* listed as many as 267 pleaders in the city of Dacca by 1921. The bar in the city was still dominated by the Hindus, depsite the period of partition: except for Moulvi Osman Bhuiyan and Abdul Siddique, all the pleaders were Hindus.[56] The next decade saw a continued increase in the numbers of those the legal profession despite the slump. In 1931 the city had 946 people engaged in this profession. In comparison we may note that Howrah city had a much smaller number of lawyers, a mere 287, in 1931.[57] *Thacker's Indian Directory* for 1940-41 records some 321 people in Dacca as pleaders alone of whom 19 were Muslims. This is the first significant increase in the number of Muslim pleaders to be recorded.[58]

People with law degrees often showed an interest in politics too. Many of them sat on the Municipal and District Boards. Some became famous in provincial politics also. Mention may be made in this connection of Khawaja Nazimuddin, M.A., C.I.E., Bar-at-Law, who was the Chairman of the Municipality from 1923 to 1930, and later rose to the position of the Chief Minister of Bengal.[59]

Doctors formed another professional group in the city. In 1911 the district was recorded by the census as supporting 3,704 males and 389 females engaged in medicine.[60] Under this heading come the medical practitioners of all kinds including dentists, occulists, veterinary surgeons, midwives, vaccinators, compounders, nurses, masseurs etc. In 1931, the city had about 400 registered and unregistered medical practitioners, a figure which excluded the miscellaneous categories included in the 1911 figure. Due to the non-availability of the complete statistics it is difficult to be certain about whether the number represents an increase or decrease. Looking at the steady increase in the number of lawyers, one could, however, assume that there was no reason for a decrease in the number of doctors.[61]

University, college and school teachers formed an important and articulate class of professional people. They were, as a class, not as well organized as the other two groups already mentioned. Nevertheless many of them were politically active and socially respected. In 1911 the district had 2,593 males and 93 females working in this field.[62] In 1921 the number had risen to 3,430 males and 252 females[63] and in 1931 to 4,354 males and 498 females when the city had 472 males and 41 females so employed.[64] Like the legal, the medical and teaching professions were also dominated by the Hindus. Till the partition of India in 1947, the University of Dacca had a majority of Hindu teachers.[65]

A large number of the middle-class people in the city were engaged in what the Census Reports called Public Administration.[66] The number of engineers, architects, surveyors, artists, sculptors, musicians, publishers etc., was small.[67] But, whereas the Army could not attract a single soul, no less than 1,096 men were found as police in the city.[68]

The sources consulted do not show any remarkable segregation in the residential pattern among the professional groups mentioned above. Except for the University, and a few institutions like Dacca College and Engineering School, nearly all the educational institutions were located near the city centre. As the teachers were not provided with any residential quarters by the schools and colleges, they lived wherever accommodation was available. Therefore, no teachers' colony grew up at any particular area.

Some Hindu lawyers and doctors seem to have preferred to live in Wari, which was outside the city centre, a new 'quality' area, but the one considerable example of segregated housing was provided by the

railway quarters which in Dacca, as elsewhere, were
provided for all levels of the service by the railway
company itself.

The picture that emerges from the above discussion
is that there was no rigid segregation in the residential pattern of the middle-class professional groups
on the basis of occupation.

Some commercial groups and artisans who were
continuing hereditary traditional occupations were,
however, concentrated in particular areas. Their
concentration created a natural residential segregation
from the point of view of religion also, since particular crafts were so often traditionally associated
with a particular community.

Despite the fact that Dacca experienced serious
communal riots in 1905, 1926, 1941, and 1942, the
population remained fairly mixed. This suggests that
the city did not have very rigid residential segregation by community.

It has been indicated in the above discussion that
the city had more than one past. The names of the
Muhallas and markets - Shankaribazar, Tantibazar,
Goalnagar, Banglabazar, Kumartuli, Bairagitola,
Patuatuli, Kagajitola, Islampur, Begumbazar, Nayabazar,
New Mughaltuli, Purana Mughaltuli, Farashganj, Urdu and
Chauk Bazar - record its pre-Mughal as well as its
Mughal past. A traveller approaching the city from the
west would notice little that marked the presence of a
third past - the British. Although many of the old
structures on the bank had been swept away by the
river, the western and middle section of the eastern
side of the city still gave a strong impression of the
Hindu and Mughal past. Between Lalbah fort and the
eastern end of the Old City marked by the Dulaikhal only
the Water Works, east of Lalbagh fort, Water Works
Road, Mitford Road heralding the Mitford Hospital, the
steamer station and the Northbrook Hall could be called
British. The east-west axis of the main road running
for about two miles parallel to the river Buriganga
was Indian.

The north-south axis, which was new and British,
was also about the same length. This ran from Sadarghat, situated on the riverbank, towards Government
House and the racecourse, the southern and northern
parts of the road being known as Johnson Road and
Nawabpur road respectively. This road was marked by
the Eden Girls' School, the Baptist Mission Church,

the Bank of Bengal, a cluster of schools and colleges,
that is Pogose School, Collegiate School, the Normal
School, Jagannath College and so on, and then in formal
well-spaced sequence the Munsif's Court, the Judge's
Court, the Registration Office, the Collectorate Office
and Magistrate's Court, with Victoria Park to mark
the approximate crossing part of the two axial roads.
The scale of the buildings and even more of the walled
compounds in which they stood, presented an exaggerated
contrast with the crowded houses and shops of the
Shankaribazar just to the west. The abandoned sepoy
lines, the racecourse and the Dacca Club standing at
the other end marked this axis off as British and
different from the indigenous one.

This example of European architecture and town
planning stood upon a wedge of ground which in the 1859
map appears still comparatively open. The modern lay-
out of spacious and walled residential bungalows of
Wari was also made possible because that space was too
open. The coming of the railway line in 1895 added to
the northward shift, forming a distinct boundary
between the old and the new Dacca which grew up in the
twentieth century. Considerable new constructions took
place in the wake of the partition of Bengal and during
Dacca's short span of life as a provincial capital
between 1905 and 1911. The new Secretariat, Curzon
Hall, Government House and a number of western-style
residential bungalows with spacious compounds grew up
along the new straight roads, Minto Road, Bayley Road
etc. This formally planned Ramna area, already well
supplied with trees and gardens became a much praised
model. The area was further developed when the
University was started in 1921 and the students' Halls
and hostels were opened. This was an added element
that distinguished this growing westernized part from
the old and in many ways traditional part of the city.

Although only the northern part of the city looked
distinctly British, the rest of the city was not quite
outside the British influence and activities. There
had been no remarkable change in the spatial arrangement of roads, bazars and housing. There had, however,
been new patterns superimposed upon the old map - that
of telegraph poles, water-mains and electric light
poles, the last two of which can briefly be touched
upon.

Dacca was peculiar among the Indian cities in that
both her water and electricity works were gifts, not

212

the results of municipal or government enterprise.
Both these important civic amenities were provided by
the Nawabs of Dacca and both were free services
initially. The Dacca municipality accepted the cost of
maintaining them. The number of electric and kerosene
oil lights in the city at the close of the year 1935-36
was 1,066 and 869 respectively. Although the street
lighting absorbed a sizeable portion of municipal
expenditure every year, the municipality was not able
to levy any lighting rate until 1948.[69]
    The generosity of the Nawabs in providing the
capital costs of the two schemes was not disinterested,
but was a recognition of favours granted by and hoped
for from the government.[70] The purposes of the street
lighting were clearly visible at night. Then the vast
circuit of the empty racecourse away to the north-west,
Secretariat road (in front of what is now the Dacca
University), the surroundings of the Government House,
of the Rest House, of Curzon Hall and of the Engineering School formed a great pool of glittering light.
From it there ran a thin thread of light southward
along Nawabpur road, to a second rather less imposing
pool round the courts, the educational institutions
and Victoria Park spreading out east along the Municipal road beyond the Roman Catholic Church, and south
before the Ahsan Manzil between Farashganj and the
river. From there westwards upstream virtually the
whole city was dark or dimly oil-lit, except for a
line of bulbs along Mitford road, which terminated
with the lamp-posts round the Chaukbazar. The six
lamp-posts round the crowded Chauk contrast with the
twelve round the almost empty Bank of Bengal, Collegiate School and Victoria Park compounds and nearly one
hundred round the racecourse and Curzon Hall, largely
unpopulated areas. The lights very obviously
burned brightest in the areas where they were more
likely to be observed by British official eyes.
    Electric lighting of the streets may have seemed a
frivolous amenity, especially when there was one
policeman on the payroll for every 35 adult male
citizens of Dacca. But the waterworks, built in 1878,
a quarter of a century before the power station, had
as their civic purpose an improvement in the sanitation
and health of the crowded city proper. It is of
interest, therefore, to see how the network of mains
was laid out by the municipal authorities. This may be
traced, with occasional uncertainties, from the 1912-15

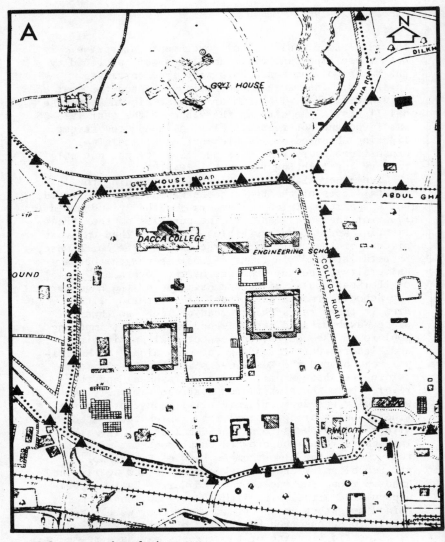

DACCA : supply of electricity

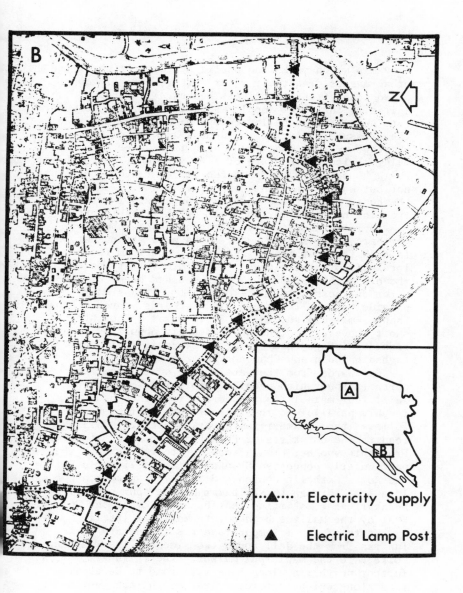

B

N

▲···· Electricity Supply

▲ Electric Lamp Post

Nazia Hussain

city map which marks the public hydrants at which the
urban masses drew their water. There were of course
piped connections to private houses.[71] Although
initially the water supply was a free service, a water
rate had later to be levied by the municipality under
the pressure of increasing demand and the chronic
shortage of municipal funds. In 1935 water tax was
being levied at the rate of five per cent, where there
was a house connection and two per cent where there was
not but where a hydrant was within reach.[72] However,
the house connections must have been less important
than the hydrants for the bulk of the inhabitants.

Whereas the generating station was in the new,
northern suburbs, the water-works were sited near
Lalbagh fort, at the highest point upstream for an
intake from the Buriganga. This meant that whereas
the old Mughal centres to the west had been left in
utter darkness, without electricity, it was easy to
provide water. Two spurs ran westwards, through Atosh
Khana, Amligola and Sheikh Sahib Bazar. They stopped
short, however, of the quite densely populated Hajari-
bagh, Nazirbagh, Enayetganj, Nawabganj, Kasimnagar,
Baghsainuiddin and Chaudhurybazar areas.

Eastwards from the waterworks, apart from a
northern spur which provided amply for the central
Jail, four main lines fanned out from the Chauk
roughly parallel to the line of the river. One
followed the Islampur (waterworks, Mitford, Farashganj)
road to the outskirts of Farashganj where it stopped.
From this another branch took off to run through the
particularly congested Shankaribazar to Victoria Park,
the Roman Catholic Church and School compounds and back
in a loop through Lakshmibazar with a spur north from
Shankaribazar, skirting Tantibazar to cross the Dulai
Khal by the Malitol bridge into Malitola itself.

North of the Islampur road the second arm of the
fan ran from the Jail round two sides of the Training
College to the municipal market. The third arm, still
further north ran along Bankshall road to Nawabpur
road along which it turned first south then west again
along Cemetery Road to the Wari 'suburb', to loop back
through Goalpara and also further north, through Than-
taribazar. There it met, on the Nawabpur road, the
last arm of the fan which had run through the much
less dense Aga Sadekbazar, Siddirbazar, Alubazar and
Seukhanidhi market areas south of the railway.

The pattern which the water mains made was

216

obviously dictated in part by geography and engineering
north of the Hindu city within the Dulai Khal, where
there was another large mass of waterways, sometimes
quite broad. Their presence required that the mains
stopped when they reached them, went round them or
crossed them where they narrowed by the far bridges.
Thus the second arm of the fan stopped when it reached
the spreading waterway at the municipal market, the
third crossed it at the Bankshall road bridge, the
fourth went round it to the north.

Engineering problems dictated that where possible
the mains should follow straight roads. The constant
turns and twists of the lanes and alleyways of the
dense old quarters and bazars were a great problem with
constant junctions and corners. Whereas the electricity poles could zigzag their way above ground from
Panitola to Rai Sahib bazar, the line of hydrants
rarely left the main roads.

However, it does also seem that means and influence,
rather than need, played a part in dictating the areas
to be supplied with water. The deprived areas were not
always exclusively inhabited by one particular community. Religion as a determining factor does not seem to
have been important - except perhaps in the short run
of piping to a hydrant to serve the Jami Masjid.[73] (Of
course the fact that religion and caste were closely
associated with occupation does mean that if occupations
have a high or low economic status then allocation by
income group takes on an indirect communal or caste
colouring. As in other cities of India[74] caste/occupa-
tion groups often remained together instead of moving
into the less crowded parts of the town.) It was,
then, areas with a high proportion of Kachcha thatched
houses - Faridabad or Kaltabazar, for example - which
were quite without water hydrants, as were Halsharafat-
ganj and Sutrapur market in the eastern end of the old
Hindu city. There were two hydrants in the wealthy
businessmen Dalbazar area in the main Farashganj Road,
but none in the very congested Farashgang area proper.
There is in fact a most striking contrast between the
low income areas of Shankribazar - the conch shell
cutters' quarters - and the congested areas of Tantibazar, Kamarnagar, Goalnagar, Pannitola and Sutranagar
which shared three hydrants, on the one hand, and the
model suburb of Wari, with its straight roads and
large compounds, which had nine hydrants for scarcely
a hundred houses, on the other hand. 'Nothing in fact'

remarked the *District Gazetteer*, 'could be greater than the contrast between the amenities of Wari and the squalid discomfort of the remainder of the town'.[75]

TABLES

Population in Dacca City in each Municipal ward in 1911 and 1921, along with the density per acre in 1921.

Ward No.	Population 1921	1911	Density per acre 1921
1	23,308	21,000	39.1
2	15,800	15,000	64.7
3	22,122	19,000	25.3
4	22,015	20,000	27.9
5	9,429	9,000	81.8
6	12,093	11,000	18.5
7	13,133	12,000	26.0

Figures are rounded to the nearest thousand.
Source: *Census of India*, 1921, vol.v, part i, p.109.

General and English literacy in Dacca City by religion, 1931.

	Total Population	Literate	Literate in English
All religions	139,000	71,000	22,000
Muslims	58,000	16,000	5,900
Hindus	80,000	33,000	16,000

Figures are rounded to the nearest thousand.
Source: *Census of India*, 1931, vol.v, part i, p.175.

Hussain, 'The City of Dacca, 1921-1947: Society, Water
and Electricity'

1. Ahmad Hasan Dani, *Dacca a record of its changing
fortunes* (Dacca 1962),p.7; S.M. Taifoor, *Glimpses of
Old Dhaka* (Dacca 1952), p.6; Abdul Karim, *Dacca the
Mughal capital* (Dacca 1964), p.29.
2. Bishop R. Heber, *Narrative of a Journey through
the Upper Provinces of India* (London 1828), vol.i.
p.141.
3. Figures are rounded to the nearest thousand. See
Census of India, 1872, Bengal, p.107; ibid., 1881,
Bengal ii, p.529; and ibid., 1941, vol.iv, Bengal,
p.18.
4. Munshi Rahman Ali Taish, *Twarikh-i-Dhaka* (Dacca
1910), pp.313-314.
5. M. Atiqullah and F. Karim Khan, *Growth of Dacca
City, population and area* (Dacca 1965), p.10.
6. Grenfell Radduck, *Towns and Villages of Pakistan*
(Karachi 1964), p.76.
7. Dani, op.cit., p.89.
8. The figures mentioned in the paper are of the
Dacca *Katwali* which is a slightly bigger area than that
of the Dacca Municipality. See Heber, op.cit., vol.ii,
p.341.
9. *Census of India*, 1901, Bengal, vol.vi-B, p.34f;
1911, vol.v, part ii, p.20f; 1921, vol.v, part i, p.117;
1921, vol.v, part i, p.117; 1931, vol.v, part i, pp.490-
491. Figures for Dacca city in 1921 include 1,017 males
and 533 females in Dacca cantonment and Ramna civil
station.
10. Ibid., vol.iv, pp.94f. Dacca with its excellent river communications was a natural collecting and
distributing point for the commerce of all Eastern
Bengal, and with its steamer and rail connections with
Calcutta was naturally attractive to the Hindu commercial classes.
11. Ibid., vol.v, part i, p.108.
12. Government of Bengal, *The Land Revenue
Administration of the Presidency of Bengal, 1917-18*,
p.1.
13. See above, note 11.
14. S.N.H. Rizvi (ed.), *East Pakistan District
Gazetteer, Dacca* (Dacca 1969), p.81. In general

Dacca's growth rate was faster than most towns in
Bengal.

15. The Ramna Civil Station with its large open
spaces including the Racecourses, by far the least
densely populated part of the city, was not one of the
municipal wards during the period under review, 1921-
1947.

16. *Census of India*, 1921, vol.v., part i, p.109.

17. According to the 1931 Census, of the 33,073
male workers in the Dacca City, nearly 10,000 were
engaged in trade, including banking and insurance and a
further 2,000 were cashiers and accountants. Public
Administrators accounted for 6,000 or more.

18. *Thacker's Indian Directory* (Calcutta 1901),
Mofussil Station, p.778.

19. Ibid., 1921, p.123.

20. Ibid., 1911, pp.159-160. Some of the Basaks,
Roys and Dases had substantial landed property and
were recorded as zamindars in Thacker's Directories.

21. *Thacker's Indian Directory, 1901*, p.778.

22. Ibid., 1921, p.123.

23. Ibid., 1901, p.123.

24. Ibid., 1911, p.129.

25. Ibid., 1901, p.123.

26. Ibid., p.778; 1911, p.160.

27. Ibid., 1931, p.143.

28. Ibid., 1911, p.160.

29. Ibid., 1901, pp.160,778; 1911, p.124; 1931,
p.143.

30. Chaudhury, M. Islam, *The Regional Geography of
Dacca* (Aligarh 1944), p.124.

31. Ibid., p.126. Later a number of up-country men
came and settled there as shoemakers. Some of the
indigenous shoemakers lived in Malitola and Nawabpur.
See the East Pakistan District Gazetteer, p.205.

32. Islam, op.cit., pp.125-126.

33. Ibid.

34. Dalbazar lies between Poddar's Ghat and Bairagitola.

35. *Thacker's Indian Directory*, 1921, p.124.

36. Islam, op.cit., p.133.

37. *Census of India*, 1931, vol.v, part i, p.91.

38. Ibid., 1911, vol.v, part ii, p.306. The
figures given are for the whole of the district, but it
seems probable that a very large portion of the meti-
culously accurate total was to be found in the city.
Since it is stated that the total also includes

receivers of stolen goods and cattle-poisoners, both
of whom seem unlikely to have readily reported their
presence to the census officials, perhaps the figure
may be taken as an approximation. The unexplained
halving of the number between 1921 and 1931 may be
treated with a similar scepticism.

39. Ibid., p.151.

40. Later on cheap mill-made cloth posed a threat to
the handloom industries.

41. A.T. Weston, quoted in Islam, op.cit., p.114.

42. *Eastern Bengal District Gazetteer*, vol.v, *Dacca*
(Allahabad 1912), p.457.

43. *East Pakistan District Gazetteer, Dacca*, p.201.
This District Gazetteer also described the housing
condition of these people in exactly the same way.

44. Islam, op.cit., p.116.

45. *East Pakistan District Gazetteer, Dacca*, p.202.

46. Islam, op.cit. p.116.

47. Ibid., p.119.

48. *Census of India*, 1931, vol.v, part i, p.110.

49. Rudduck, op.cit., p.74. The Kuttis are
generally believed to be crossbreeds between Afghans,
Mughals and the natives. Later on they also took up
cycle-rickshaw pulling.

50. The 1931 Census records 1639 males and 890
females as engaged in domestic service - most of them
presumably living in their employers' houses - but the
figures seem improbably low. See *Census of India*, 1931,
vol.v. part i. p.306. It is now generally believed
that there was a large concentration of washermen in
the Fuller Road area. The Bengali meaning of the word
'Fuller' is Dhoba or washerman.

51. See for details J.H. Broomfield, *Elite conflict
in a plural society: Twentieth century Bengal* (California 1968), pp.1-20; see also *Bengal District Administration Report 1913-1914* (Calcutta 1915), p.166.

52. See John Beames, *Memoirs of a Bengal Civilian*
(London 1961), p.284; and also S.G.Panandikar, *The
Wealth and Welfare of the Bengal Delta* (Calcutta 1926).

53. *Thacker's Indian Directory*, 1905, Mofussil
Station, pp.827-828.

54. Ibid., 1911, p.159.

55. *Census of India*, 1911, vol.v., part ii, pp.296-
297.

56. *Thacker's Indian Directory*, 1921, Mofussil
Station, pp.122-123.

57. *Census of India*, 1931, vol.v, part i, p.139.

221

58. *Thacker's Indian Directory*, 1940-41, civil
divisions, pp.19-20.
59. Khwaja Nazimuddin became the Chief Minister
of Bengal in 1943. See Kazi Ahmed Kamal, *Politics and
Inside Stories* (Dacca 1970), p.123.
60. *Census of India*, 1911, vol.v, part ii, p.297.
61. Ibid., 1931, vol.v., part i. 140-141.
62. Ibid., 1911, vol.v, part ii, p.299.
63. Ibid., 1921, vol.v, part i, p.324.
64. Ibid., 1931, vol.v, part i, p.142.
65. The total strength of the teaching staff in the
thirteen departments of the University of Dacca between
1921-25 was 122 of whom only 24 were Muslims; an over-
wholming majority was Hindu, with a few European
Professors and Readers; see, *The Dacca University
Calendars* for the years 1921-24, pp.215-217. Of 20
Professors and Readers at the University between
1930-1933 as many as 16 were Hindus; see ibid., for
the sessions 1929-1933, pp.8-9. The Muslim students
were also small in number as they formed only about 19
per cent of the total number of students at the
University in 1921. They constituted not more than 29
per cent in 1925. See the Vice Chancellor, Sir P.J.
Hartog's *Address delivered at a meeting of the Court of
the University of Dacca on 25 November, 1925*.
66. See *Census of India*, 1911, vol.v, part ii, p.291;
1931, vol.v, part ii, p.132; 1941, vol.iv, p.125.
67. The city had 37 males under the heading architects, surveyors, engineers and their employees (not
being state servants), 73 as musicians (other than
military), actors and dancers. See ibid., vol.v, part
ii, p.145.
68. Ibid., p.135.
69. The street lighting absorbed 10.1 per cent of
the total municipal expenditure in 1932-33. See *Bengal
Administration Report*, April 1935, p.209.
70. In order to celebrate the conferment on his
father of the title K.C.S.I., by the British government,
Nawab Ahsanullah Bahadur contributed a large sum of
money and the electric installation was opened on 7
December 1901.
71. Hridaynath Majumdar, *Reminiscences of Dacca*
(Calcutta 1926), p.61. Hridaynath Majumdar, a retired
Dacca City pleader, recalled that it was allowed on
payment of a monthly tax of Rs.4 per hydrant plus the
initial costs of pipes, hydrants and reservoirs.
72. *Proceedings of the Government of Bengal, Local*

Self Government Department, April 1935, p.197.

73. There had been three Hindu and three Muslim Chairmen and the same proportion of Vice-Chairmen of the Municipality between 1885 and 1915.

74. See Kenneth L. Gillion, *Ahmedabad, a study in Indian Urban History* (Berkeley and Los Angeles 1968) pp.123,125.

75. *East Pakistan District Gazetteer, Dacca*, p.457.

LIFE IN THE MUFASSAL TOWNS OF NINETEENTH-CENTURY BENGAL

M.S. Islam

When Robert Lindsay, a young civilian newly arrived in
Bengal, was first appointed as Collector of Sylhet in
1775 he considered himself fortunate to be thus
stationed in the very first instance at the 'City of
Chunam'. He proceeded immediately to report to his
new station. On his arrival the great men of the town
received him at the river *ghat* with a spectacle of
'boats dressed out for the occasion'. At the close of
the rite of reception Lindsay expressed his wish to see
the city. However, when taken round, he was dismayed
to find that the 'City of Chunam' was 'only an incon-
siderable bazar or market place'.[1] Since others, like
Lindsay, may begin by viewing our mufassal towns through
the glass of imagination and so be disappointed at the
sight of reality we shall begin our discussion with a
description of the size and nature of urban Bengal in
the nineteenth century.

Questions of urbanization and urban settlement are
essentially quantitative ones.[2] But for the pre-census
period in Bengal, that is for most of our chosen
period, quantitative evidence is rarely available. The
desultory data occasionally found for a specific period,
place or area are of little help because they are
neither continuous nor reliable enough for any satisfactory regional analysis. Even the decennial census
data found from 1872 onwards are of uncertain value
because of the ambiguities of urban place as a category.
The self-governing municipalities which were accepted
as urban centres often included surrounding villages and
hamlets in unknown numbers. However, even if this is
ignored, the 1872 census still gives a total urban
population for the five Bengal Divisions of Burdwan,
Presidency, Rajshahi, Dacca and Chittagong of only
1,823,597. In 1901 that figure had increased by
721,469 to 2,545,066.[3] But while in thirty years the
absolute growth in urban population had been of the
order of 25 per cent, the growth in urban as a percentage of total population had risen from 4.8 to five
per cent.[4] Urbanization had scarcely proceeded at all.
Peach has found the same situation at all-India levels:
'The effect of urbanization in the West was that not

only did the large majority of the population live in
towns, but the *numbers* living in rural areas decreased
as well. In India, it has produced a huge aggregate of
urban population but it forms only a small proportion
of the whole; while towns grow, the rural population
seems nowhere to diminish.'[5]

In the absence of regular demographic data we are
unable to chart the rate of urbanization in the earlier
part of the nineteenth century. However, the five per
cent urban figure recorded in 1901 precludes any considerable growth rate and might indeed conceal some
deurbanization. (That towns like Dacca and Murshidabad lost population in the early decades is well
attested. What is not so clear is whether there was
an overall loss within the region or only a transfer of
population from declining to growing centres.) There
is the further question, moreover, whether the five per
cent is to be accepted as a valid indicator of
urbanization in Bengal. The 1901 Census comments: 'The
ordinary town in Bengal is usually, to a great extent,
urban only in name, and many of the Mofussil Municipalities are either overgrown villages, or contain on
their outskirts considerable areas of purely rural
character.'[6] It was argued in the Census report that
if such rural inclusions were subtracted from the gross
urban figure, then the actual urban population would be
'less than half the figure entered'.[7] The cadastral
survey of the Faridpur and Madaripur towns made by
J.C. Jack, which revealed that 'in each case considerable portions of the surrounding agricultural country
have been included within the Municipalities',
certainly supports the Census view.[8] Another example,
which demonstrates how rural areas came to be included
within urban boundaries, is provided by Barisal town.
In the *Thakbast* or demarcation survey of 1859 the area
of the town was about three square miles.[9] But when
the Barisal municipality was created in 1869 the boundary of the town was extended to enclose a further
three miles 'just in order to increase the collections
from the taxes'.[10] Barisal's was by no means a unique
case of villages being incorporated to make municipalities which by the Census were then defined as towns -
the 1872-73 *Bengal Administration Report* declared that
the municipalities were all 'actually half towns and
half villages'.[11] It can thus be concluded that in
1901 only 2.5 or 3 per cent of the Bengal population
lived in towns. The mufassal towns were just tiny

islets in a vast rural ocean, arms of which ran deep inland. The number and size of these urban dots enumerated at the three decennial censuses of 1871, 1881 and 1891 were as follows:

Table I

Statement of Number and Size of Towns in Bengal in 1872, 1881, and 1891[12]

Description of Towns with Inhabitants from	Number of Population		
	1872	1881	1891
5,000 to 10,000	179	146	121
10,000 to 15,000	42	49	38
15,000 to 20,000	8	14	18
20,000 to 50,000	23	22	28
More than 50,000	11	11	10

Settlement of Mufassal Towns

The word *mufassal* is a relative term meaning inferior or subordinate in relation to *sadr* or headquarters.[13] Calcutta is thus *sadr* in relation to Dacca; whereas Dacca is *sadr* in relation to its dependent town Manikganj. The *mufassal* towns we are going to discuss are those which are essentially district and sub-divisional towns with populations below the 50,000 mark. The great, populous cities like Calcutta, Dacca, Howrah or Chandranagar are deliberately excluded from our consideration on the ground that functionally and structurally, and as regards physical layout, forms of construction, social organization, modes of governance, technological complexities, and heterogeneities, the great cities present an urbanism of a distinct type which differs fundamentally from that of the *mufassal* towns. But that is by no means to say that *mufassal* towns share no common characteristics with such cities, which form one extreme of the urban continuum; the difference is mainly in the level of services they provide. In the hierarchy of human settlement the *mufassal* towns really lie between the villages and cities. Here we find the justification for studying *mufassal* towns independently of cities or villages.

Urbanization is always an inter-related and interdependent process involving a complex series of changes. In a given society and economy, changes in one settlement set up pressures and demands requiring readjustments in other sectors. If the old social and

settlement structure is sufficiently elastic it may
adjust to the tension. If not, it will break under
the strain.[14] In Bengal, under the impact of British
conquest and rule, the urban structure of the old
regime did break rather than adapt.

The types of towns and cities found immediately
before the establishment of British rule may broadly
be classified into four groups; the great metropolitan
cities, the zamindari towns, the European factory towns
and the 'transient' *mufassal* towns.

In a pre-industrial traditional society like that
of Bengal, a largely subsistence economy with under-
developed monetary and marketing systems and made
less mobile by the caste system, city growth on a
large scale could hardly be expected without state
patronage and protection. Under the Mughal system the
seat of power was also the seat of favour, grace and
consumption. Seekers of fortune, of security and of
a market were drawn to the palace complex as officers
and soldiers, officials and clerks, bankers, merchants
and craftsmen who all 'crowded inside the city walls'.[15]
Dacca and Murshidabad were such cities in Bengal.
Urbanization did not end at that level: the same process of urban growth was repeated on a smaller scale
round the establishments of Mughal *faujdars*, *qanungos*,
qazis or *shahbandars*. Small provincial towns like
Chittagong, Rangpur and Hugli thus sprang up with
government establishments as their foci.[16]

The towns of the second group were built up under
the patronage of the landed aristocracy. The great
zamindars, maharajas and rajas ruled over extensive
areas not only as holders of their own very great
estates but as administrative overlords of the smaller
zamindars of their neighbourhoods, empowered by the
Mughals with military, police and judicial functions
in addition to their revenue duties.[17] In consequence
they had to maintain large establishments of armed
retainers, police and revenue peons, bookkeepers,
treasurers and clerks. To cater to the needs of
these troops and officials came shopkeepers, artisans,
craftsmen, entertainers and mendicants, the resultant
aggregations turning the *rajbaris*, or residences of
the great zamindars, into considerable towns. Among
rajbari towns the most prominent were those of
Burdwan, Natore, Dinajpur, Birbhum, Nadia and Bishna-
pur. In eastern Bengal the two major *rajbari* towns
were Rajnagar in Dacca district, founded by Rajvallab,

and Chandradip in Bakarganj which was the capital of
the ancient ruling family of Bakla. Both these cities
had been washed away by shifting rivers before the
advent of British rule, while the zamindaris themselves
were swept away under the operation of the permanent
settlement.[18] Just as the Mughal metropolitan cities
had their auxiliary para-military provincial towns so
the great zamindari *rajbaris* had their dependent towns
established at the headquarters of the large *parganas*.
These *kachahri* towns were often set up at important
trade and communication centres, their purpose being
not only to oversee the collection of land revenue,
but also to levy tolls on passing boats and *sair* or
internal customs from the established *hats, bazars* and
ganjs.

The third group of towns in pre-British Bengal was
founded or extended by the various European trading
companies and grew round their factories. Most prominent of these factory towns were Calcutta, Chandranagar,
Chinsura, Kasimbazar and Malda in western Bengal and
Lakshmipur, Jagdia, Komarkhali in eastern Bengal. The
investment process of the European companies pulled
large numbers to the factory areas - merchants and
brokers, sorters, packers and porters, bakers, ship-
wrights and so on - which ultimately grew into towns
and cities.[19]

The last group of pre-British towns in Bengal were
the transient *mufassal* towns, which, like the frequent
alluvions and diluvions along the great rivers, were
formed by one transient political current and swept
away by the next. Such towns were first remarked upon
by Mackenzie, the Judge and Magistrate of Bakarganj,
when he was making s survey of the *hats, bazars* and
ganjs of southern Bengal in 1816.

About the rapid rise and fall of these towns
Mackenzie remarks:

> The natural course in this country is that the
> market first attracts the people and then the
> people the market. It is astonishing how these
> Hauts and Gunges, in spite of everything, spring up
> sometimes in inconceivably short periods of time
> into *Flourishing Towns*, like exhalations, when well
> regulated under a sensible superintendence, while
> the wrong-headed avarice of a different management
> reduces them in a much shorter time to deserts and
> ruins.[20]

In his explanation of the shifting nature of these
towns, Mackenzie argued that rivalry between neighbouring zamindars was the principal cause of the fall of
newly emerged towns, with internal mismanagement and
exactions as next in importance. We lack sufficient
documents to make any authoritative judgement. What
may perhaps be said is that Bengali society at the
rural level was not as insular and immobile as has been
thought; under favourable social, economic and political conditions people were prepared to make the move
from countryside to city, however painful the wrench to
traditional social ties this might be.

We have outlined the nature of pre-British urbanism
in Bengal in order to see more clearly the developments
under the new regime. The changes were likely to be
extensive since power was seized by an alien race,
politically and technologically superior enough to
ignore the institutions of the conquered and to
introduce laws and institutions more in accord with
their own interests and genius. Change was the more
drastic because initially the East India Company's
servants, however good at drawing out balance sheets,
bills of exchange or bills of lading, were ignoramuses
in the art of territorial administration. In the
twenty years they took to learn the craft, native
institutions and social structures suffered a cata-
strophe. Within less than a decade of the permanent
settlement of 1793 all the great zamindaris had been
destroyed.[21] Their fall, following the dismantling
of much of the Mughal nawabi structure, precipitated
the steep decline of most of the pre-British towns,
Dacca, Murshidabad, the *rajbari* towns and their
dependencies. Towns which had once hummed with
activities lost their population and disappeared under
the encroaching jungle.[22] To cite just two examples:
Dinajpur town was said by Buchanan to have had a
population of between 25,000 and 30,000 at the
commencement of British rule, and even more in the
time of the last great raja, but by 1809 this had
fallen to only 15,000.[23] The mother of the Nadia raja
reminded the government in 1813 that Navadip which was
once the 'cultural capital of India' was now like a
graveyard in consequence of the fall of the family.[24]
Even in Burdwan, though the zamindari was saved, the
city was considerably reduced once the raja had been
shorn of all his powers and establishments beyond
those necessary to a rent collector.[25]

The fall of the Mughal government led to a corresponding fall of the Mughal metropolitan cities which, in turn, led to the decay and disappearance of their dependent towns in the *mufassal*.[26] A little later the factory towns too began to decay as the English East India Company wound up its trading side, and for political reasons limited the commercial freedom of the other European factory powers. This, and the industrial revolution in Britain and the commercial revolution of free trade led to a drastic curtailment of Company investment and then to the closing down of factories. Thousands of persons who had been attracted to the factory towns lost their occupations, returned to agriculture and left the factories deserted.

British rule, however, did not come like a one-eyed monster only to destroy towns and cities; it had a constructive side too. The new system of administration and land tenure to which the country was exposed was capable of producing a new pattern of urbanization, more broad-based and more generally distributed. The entire country was divided into a number of conveniently sized districts which became pivotal elements in the administrative structure. Every district had two establishments - judicial, headed by the Judge, and executive, headed by the Collector. Each establishment was manned by a considerable body of officials and subordinates. In addition there were at district headquarters bodies of police, sepoys, messengers and functionaries of various government departments, together with the staff of private business houses. Pleaders, *mukhtyars*, and revenue agents, other by-products of the new system, came to district head-quarters to earn their living, and there too came litigants in search of justice. To supply the needs created by the presence of the courts and *kachahris* came shopkeepers, artisans, merchants and manufacturers, servants of all sorts and professional men in variety. With the building of quarters to house both officials and those who had come to serve them the original rural settlements were transformed over time into towns.[27] It would not be too rash to generalize and argue that almost all the district and subdivisional towns of Bengal, some old *rajbari* towns excepted, had their origin in the new British system of administration.

In the pre-industrial, mainly subsistence economy of Bengal, government, as holder of power, was the

major creator of services - and where services were
provided there people gathered. This had happened
during Mughal days and dependence on the state long
continued under British rule. How greatly a district
town depended on the presence of government establishments was dramatically illustrated by the fate of
Bakarganj and Natore towns when they lost their *sadr*
status. In 1801 the *sadr* of Bakarganj town was transferred to the village of Barisal, which thereupon grew
into a town while the old town of Bakarganj sank into
a village *hat*.[28] Much the same happened when the *sadr*
of Rajshahi district was transferred from Natore,
already decaying with the disintegration of the Rajshahi Raj, to the twin village of Rampur-Boalia (the
later Rajshahi). The latter grew, the former was
reduced to a mere bazar until the establishment of a
subdivisional headquarters there in the 1860s partially revived it.[29] Emphasising the role of government
in the making of district towns, Westland cites the
further example of Jessore, not previously great,
but 'a town which depends for its character almost
entirely upon the cutcheries and their surroundings,
and which would be little more than a second or third
class bazar if they were not there.'[30] In short, most
mufassal towns were fundamentally service towns, born
of the British system of district administration.
Unfortunately the baby, after its birth, often did not
grow much for many years. Only a meagre diet of
government establishments was provided since the
Company restricted its role to the collection of a
fixed revenue and maintenance of law and order. Under
such circumstances the stunted district towns scarcely
outgrew their sister villages. It was not until the
Crown took over from the Company and government
responsibilities were expanded to include education,
sanitation, health, local self-government and the
development of communications and industries that
better nourished towns could really grow. As they
enlarged, in numbers and functions, they at last
acquired the heterogeneity, sophistication and complexity to differentiate them from their surroundings.
As Ravindranath Tagore noted: 'Years ago the villages
and towns, like Siamese twins, were indistinguishable
and inseparable. But now the town is recognizable and
it has developed its own identity.'[31]
     In modern Europe and America many towns grew as a
result of industrial development and reflected the

changes in socio-economic relations which such
development induced. But in Bengal urbanization was
mainly the outcome of administrative actions. Its
parallels are found in colonial Africa and Latin
America where towns were planned and founded for
administrative purposes and to allow the 'isolated
colonists to breathe'.[32] There was one difference,
however. The Spaniards built with a sense of perman-
ence and the towns they founded were regularly planned.
The merchant government of Bengal lacked any such sense
and in any case lacked the means to found planned
towns, having tied its financial hands in 1793. The
creation of inviolable private property in land further
restricted the creative power of government. Indeed,
until the 1830s, the government was so indifferent to
town planning and development that even its own
officials and offices were accommodated as far as
possible in privately-owned rented houses.[33] The
lay-out of *mufassal* towns thus owed nothing to conscious
town planning and everything to local topography, land
ownership and social formations. Town development took
its natural course, clustering round the place of power
and activities, the 'central place', and round the main
bazar. Throughout the Company's period the central
place or core of the town was formed by the courts and
kachahris - the founding factors of most *mufassal*
towns. The *thakbast* surveyors of 1859 thus record the
civil or *kachahri* area as the centre of the town, with
business and residential areas in mixed form as
peripheral settlements.[34] It was in the last quarter
of the nineteenth century that the centre of gravity
of *mufassal* towns shifted from the court precinct to
the business areas with the growth of population, of
communications, trade and commerce and secondary
industries, and the steady rise of an educated middle
class. This shift in area significance found
political expression in the Swadeshi Movement which was
organized at district levels mainly by this new urban
middle class.[35]

The most remarkable physical and social characteristic of the settlement system of the nineteenth
century *mufassal* towns of Bengal was provided by the
para or segregated blocks into which every town was
socially and spatially divided. Some of the common
descriptive names applied to the residential blocks -
Munshipara, Keranipara, Munsifpara, Senpara, Kayastha-
para, Brahmanpara and Maulvipara - demonstrate the

area separation of various religious, social and
occupational groups which produced the mosaic of
neighbourhoods that together laid out the social map
of the town. The *para* pattern of urban settlement in
the *mufassal* first came to official notice when the
district gazetteers and the record of rights required
by the 1885 Bengal Tenancy Act were under preparation.
The author of the Rangpur Gazetteer thus notes: 'There
is a tendency among the Hindus and Muhammadans to
form separate paras or quarters; thus Keranipara and
Senpara are chiefly occupied by the former while
Munshipara and Mussalmanpara are strongholds of the
latter.'[36] Even Chittagong town with its relatively
long urban tradition, where some communal heterogeneity
might have been expected, was residentially segregated,
almost entirely on the basis of caste and kinship.[37]
When the record of rights was being prepared for
Comilla town in 1890 it was found that many inhabitants
had long ago mutually exchanged their rights for the
sake of 'living nearer to their relations and *jatis* or
caste groups'.[38]

Clustering together in groups on the basis of some
agreeable common factor seems to accord with universal
habits of urban settlement. But Bengal *para* segregation differs greatly from the more usual segregation
which is based fundamentally on occupation and status.
The unique style of Bengal *para* segregation can best
be understood by looking at the original settlement
process.

The first batch of people who came to settle in the
new Company towns as immigrants were the office *amla* or
native ministerial staff. It was they who heralded the
rural-to-urban movement. In consideration of the very
low pay and extremely backward communications of that
period, Company policy was to recruit staff normally
from the same district as the town and on the basis of
a recommendation by and security from someone already
in government service, where possible. The native
amla could thus use their contact with the authorities
to secure employment for their own relations and kinsfolk. Once in service a man would try to become a gold
mine, bringing younger members of the family to town,
giving them some education and practical training and
ultimately securing jobs for them. These newcomers,
when once established, tended to build or rent houses
in the same *para* as the 'headman', who thus acted as
queen bee to a hive. As an example there is the case

of the father of the nationalist leader Bipin Chandra
Pal. The father was a court munshi at Bakarganj in the
1850s. Bakarganj was a ten days journey from his home
district Sylhet but problems of distance did not act as
a deterrent to his family building role. He brought
amny people from his home district and provided them
with work in Bakarganj. Bipin thus records in his
memoirs: 'My father's quarters were surrounded by a
cluster of huts, which formed a small colony of our own
people from Sylhet, who had gone with my father in
search of their fortunes. Some were my father's
relations; many were his neighbours and retainers.'[39]
When Bipin's father was transferred to his home town,
Sylhet, he got an even better opportunity to help his
own people to move to town and he set up 'a colony of
his own men'.[40] Such rural-urban movement along the
lines of kinship, caste and region was sustained by a
complex pattern of social behaviour. Periodic visits
to the villages, especially at times of religious
festival, created occasions for recruiting further
urban immigrants. Such urban immigration through
friends and relatives is not, however, to be taken as a
purely Bengali phenomenon. In varying degrees it is
found everywhere, though most notably in societies
undergoing the transformation from a pre-industrial
state to modernity.[41]

To the *para* settlement system a new element was
added from the mid-nineteenth century. In the new
phase of immigration not only surplus agricultural
labour was involved. The zamindars, taluqdars and
other superior tenure-holders, whose hold on rural
society was largely loosened by the process of sub-
infeudation which alienated the zamindars from their
peasantry and by the Tenancy Act of 1885 which established peasants' rights in land, now began the townward
move. On the one hand the changed agrarian conditions
pushed landholders out of their traditional social
positions while on the other improved urban services
pulled them towards the cities. Thus pulled and
pushed most landholders thought it prudent to build an
alternative residence at least at the district *sadr*
town, if not in the metropolis.[42] The zamindars' immigration was of special significance not only
socially but spacially too. The residential areas
they occupied were as big or small as their wealth and
status permitted or dictated. But invariably their
residences were marked off from those of the generality.

A zamindar must have an area exclusively his own and
its periphery must be occupied by his 'creatures' in
'a complicated network of clientage held together by
ties of loyalty and interest'.[43] In adopting a name
for a particular zamindari *para*, care was always taken
to choose one which would tell people unmistakably
which estate that particular *para* represented.

It seems that by the 1870s in Bengal the usable
city space was already mostly occupied and that
bustees or slums were emerging in most *mufassal*
towns.[44] The marginal land hitherto used as open space
or for garbage was not taken over by poor squatters
so creating the slum conditions characteristic of
nineteenth-century urbanization all over the world.
The emergence of such slums in the *mufassal* towns in
this period, however miserable their condition, is
indicative of the development of an atmosphere of
competition and of mobility, both important traits of
urbanism.

With the changes over time in the settlement
pattern there also went changes of architecture and
artifacts. The basic unit of the *para* was the *bari* or
house. Every house consisted of several huts built
round an oval-shaped compound or *uthan*.[45] Each hut
served the purpose of a room in a modern house, with
kitchens and lavatories separate from the main living
huts. The building materials were indigenous natural
products, bamboo, straw, reeds, the tough grass called
shan, cane or timber.[46] Till the later nineteenth
century masonary buildings were rare, as the *thakbast*
and revenue surveys (1850-1865) reveal.[47] The
furniture was of as simple a nature as the houses.
Rich and poor used much the same furniture, the
principal items being the cane or split bamboo mats
used for sleeping and sitting on, low wooden stools,
and the *shikas* or hanging holders which served as
alternatives to cupboards. Western furniture such as
chairs, tables, cupboards, sofas and beds crept into
urban households only in the latter half of the nineteenth century. When Bipin Chandra Pal's father first
bought some old furniture from an outgoing European
judge at a public auction, the young Bipin was
astonished. He notes in his memoirs, 'My father
unconsciously introduced a very great innovation ....'[48]
But traditional furniture and building styles soon
came to be rejected, especially by those who had a
western education and came into wider contact with

Europeans. By the end of the century the traditional
furniture, if not the houses, had given way to European
models. No urban family, however poor, lacked at least
a chair and table.

As has been indicated, the social formation of the
town was *para*-based and every *para*, because of its
kinship and caste elements, had a distinctive identity
to which the *para* people attached much importance.
The social values of the *para* were expected to be
upheld by all its members. But the very uniformity of
thought and conduct which was required became a cause
of discord when champions appeared of different values.
Social ambition also fired rival claimants for the
leadership of their little circles.[49] Every *para* thus
had several factions each trying to establish its
influence over the whole *para*. Intra and inter *para*
leadership conflicts led to polarisation of public
opinion into groups with distinct competing leaders.[50]
Such factionalism was always at its height at times of
religious festivals or fairs and at municipal elections.

Till the last quarter of the nineteenth century the
focus of every *mufassal* town was the court-*kachahri*
which, as the basic factor in the growth of these towns
played the most important role in shaping the social
structure and life of the town. The type of judicial
and revenue system introduced by the Company's government, coupled with the insignificance of industrial
enterprise throughout our period,[51] accorded the court-
kachahri a unique position, from which all favours and
disfavours flowed. The court was the focus not only
of town-dwellers, but of all the inhabitants of the
district. Life in and around the court was therefore
one of the main themes of literature, local newspapers
and bazar gossip in nineteenth century Bengal. Both
in real life and in fiction parents are found adopting
ambitious names for their children, such as 'Judge Mia',
'Fateh Munshi', 'Deputir Bap', 'Peshkarar Ma' and so
on, which indicate the attitude of contemporary society
to the court complex. To become a court amla was
considered to be the greatest success a native could
then achieve. When Mir Musharraf Hussain, a famous
nineteenth century writer, was born the family astrologer forecast that he was born under such a lucky
star that he was sure to become a court munshi like
his maternal uncle. It was a considerable misfortune
that his star made Musharraf a postmaster instead.

The government was conscious that to keep the
people respectful to authority, which at district
level culminated in the court, some institutionalised
ceremony should be maintained to distance the one from
the other and district judges were so advised. The
proceedings of the law courts were conducted with
solemn ceremonial.

During this ceremony the court police kept themselves alert in order to maintain the grave silence
and decorum of the occasion, the swinging bamboo staves,
known to contemporaries as Regulation sticks, six foot
long, being always ready to descend upon the heads of
anyone found negligent in observing the rules of
conduct. When the *mufassal* town was small and simple
and the court was its nucleus, this ceremony was an
important daily distraction for the people - and one
from which the visitor could form an idea of the
augustness of the British raj.

Any description of court life, especially of early
nineteenth century Bengal, remains incomplete without
some reference to the *amla* or native ministerial staff,
who allegedly wielded the real power behind the facade
of ceremony. It was common gossip round the court that
the judge was a mere figurehead and that the actual
power was exercised by the *amla*. 'The amlah are the
middlemen', to quote an experienced civilian, 'through
whom all business must be transacted and whose goodwill it is even more important to secure than that of
the hakim himself .... The *serestadar* who allows the
case to be placed on the role, the *peshkar* who reads
it, and the *mohurrir* who writes the deposition, must
all be consulted and appeased. From their houses and
with his deceitful counsel on his lips and in his
memory, the complainant comes into the court and tells
his tale.'[52] Nabin Chandra Sen, a nineteenth century
deputy magistrate fully corroborates the above account.
In his memoirs he records:

> My father was a *peshkar* to the Judge of Chittagong
> in the 1850s. In rank he was next to the *seres-
> tadar*; even then he appeared to be so powerful
> that in the morning and evening the drawing room
> was crowded by various classes of people who sought
> to meet him for advice and help. Among them were
> litigants, merchants, Hindustani cloth vendors,
> shopkeepers, job seekers, etc. They used to
> fondle me warmly and give me sweets in the presence

237

of my father.[53]

Mir Musharraf Hussain, Nabin Chandra's contemporary, also speaks of the court *amla*, especially his uncle who was a court munshi at Rangpur. The barber who went to Rangpur to give the news of his birth, Musharraf records, was said to have been so lavishly rewarded by the visitors in his uncle's drawing room that he at once became rich.[54]

Stories about the undue influence of the *amla* over their alien masters abound in contemporary books and newspapers. George Campbell dismissed these allegations as absurd: 'The undue influence of these men over their superiors is ridiculously magnified by those who nothing about it. Popular grievance-mongers, people who have lost their suits, and Europeans who are not permitted to do as they like, represent a state of things which could only arise if either the "Omlah", as they are called, possessed supernatural powers or their superiors were absolute idiots ....'[55] Campbell had passed most of his life in Upper India, however, and had little or no practical experience at local levels in Bengal. If the problem was perhaps less extreme than sometimes assumed, to deny that it existed is to go to the other extreme. The *amla*'s pay was low, job security was small, and the prospects of promotion were permanently barred. Under such conditions their genius tended to seek irregular outlets and to develop the art of influencing superiors as a way of fulfilling their ambitions. The strategy of the 'Sleek velvet-tongued amlah' was to proceed subtly, invisibly, keeping a long-term aim in view.[56] Only a very wide-awake civilian could ultimately escape their net or write with any conviction, as Lindsay proudly did, 'I saw I was on the point of becoming a cypher dependent on a black amlah', on the assumption that he had escaped.[57]

There were, moreover, many reasons why civilians should have become indifferent to their duties and ready to hand over weary routine to their *amla* while they retired to their typically nineteenth-century pleasures - hunting, racing, gambling, womanizing or drinking.[58] The system of frequent transfers destroyed many civilians' interest in their work. In Campbell's view, mentally everyone was preparing for the next transfer before even being settled in the current assignment; the judiciary was made something of

a dumping ground for failures. The reigning service
philosophy was: 'if a civilian is fit for nothing,
better make him a Judge and get rid of him'.[59] For the
court-tied judge, moreover, the climatic conditions and
the absence of amenities also made for lethargy and
inattention.[60] Against slackness the local press was
ready to protest, as when the *Dacca Prakash* appealed to
government 'to make some strict rules for those who are
inattentive to their duties, who regard but little the
convenience or inconvenience of others, and consider
their own comforts as most important.'[61] The higher
authorities were aware of the problem, issued occasional circulars urging civilians to be 'more punctual
in their attendance at court',[62] and punished the
erring by despatching them to distant districts -
'penal stations' as they were popularly called. But
then the communication gap itself became the greatest
security against the detection of negligence, while to
clear the arrears of work the civilians would extend
a long rope to their *amla*. The latter used their
advantage to the full.[63]

Wily *amla* were not the only creatures against whom
the civilian had to be on his guard. Equally malevo-
lent, as the social group which feathered its own nest
at the expense of society, were the *mamlabaz* or
chronic litigants and the coached professional
witnesses. Through practice they acquired so much
dexterity in instituting and pursuing false cases that
in a case between rival *mamlabaz* both would be in a
position to produce completely convincing witnesses
and exhibits. Faced with such a situation, so one
story went, the judge retired to his ante-chamber and
determined the case by the highest throw of the dice.
The judgement was so satisfactory that henceforth all
cases were decided by him in this way.[64] The story
may be apocryphal but it points to the widespread
assumption amongst most Europeans about the morals
prevailing in the court arena and the perfection in
mendacity to which the *mamlabaz* had attained. Unfortunately most European officials formed their impression
of the Bengalis in the courts, the most common or only
meeting ground between them. Their conclusion was that
all Bengalis were liars. Hence when after 1863 a
system of agricultural exhibitions was started in the
mufassal towns, designed to encourage 'improvements'
of all sorts, one of the prizes was reserved for
'anyone who can bring to an Agricultural Exhibition

a Native who does not tell a lie'.[65]
    The Cornwallis Code had produced many social
results of far reaching significance. The rise of a
specialised professional lawyer class was one of those.
Before 1793 there were *vakils* but not in the sense of
a recognised profession with legally defined functions.
Lawyers, as specialised professionals, were new to
society, and like most other innovations, the legal
profession was also initially disliked by the people,
nor were lawyers sure of their roles in the socio-
political system. In this fluid condition the legal
profession attracted very few men of 'respectability
and character'. Besides the pleaders there were other
legal practitioners called *mukhtyars*. Though not
licensed by law, the *mukhtyars* attended the courts and
did most of the attorney work at nominal fees. They
were men of practically no education and substance.
About them the correspondent of the *Dacca Prakash*
writes from Chittagong in 1864, 'Many of the Mukhtars
are of the lower order of Muhammedans who till the
ground in the morning, and at 10 o'clock dress their
hair and go into court. They take a few pice or annas
for their labour.'[66] The Calcutta High Court, after
its establishment in 1858, allowed the High Court
advocates and vakils to visit *mufassal* courts and take
up original and appellate cases there. This mitigated
the isolation of *mufassal* legal society. The establishment of contact with the Calcutta legal class and
Act XVIII of 1879, which required all lawyers to know
English and to have passed a law examination, greatly
improved the status of the lawyer class. The same two-
way traffic between Calcutta and the *mufassal* courts
had a far reaching significance not only professionally
but politically also. Lawyers moved throughout the
country in pursuit of their profession and thus had a
view of the country as a whole. No wonder that
lawyers, equipped with this knowledge and also with
professional freedom, emerged as the natural leaders
of New Bengal.[67]
    So far we have been dealing with the various con-
stituent elements of the court society - *amla*,
officials and lawyers who, in fact, represented the
functional aspect of the court. As an effect of their
work we find a regular standing crowd in every court
compound which deserves attention from social
historians just because the crowd was regular, and
had its own method of formation and action. As an

adjunct to the British system of judicature this crowd
had been a regular phenomenon ever since the establishment of the district courts. But no arrangement was
originally made to give them shelter from rain and sun:
'Do we not give stamp duty and court fee? Why should
we not be provided with even a thatched shed to protect us from rain and sun?' asked a discontented
suitor when he was sweating under the scorching sun.
His fell-sufferer replied grimly: 'My poor friend,
remember two things when you come to court. First,
you must not speak of honour, and second, you must not
think of comfort.'[68] The bureaucrats, however, solved
the problem by planting the low growing variety of
banyan tree in the compound of every *mufassal* court.[69]
Its sprawling roots and branches served as benches and
roof for the whole crowd. The measure was so successful that the government later decided to plant banyan
trees in the compound of all public offices and places
where the problem of mass visiting and waiting was
involved.[70] Banyan trees thus appeared as the
principal ecological characteristic of public offices
and authority in the *mufassal*.

Let us glance at the assortment of people under
the banyan tree. It was a world in itself. *Vakils*,
mukhtyars, revenue agents, *muharrirs*, scribes, litigants,
witnesses, touts, hawkers, vendors, beggars, mendicants,
astrologers, preachers, advertisers, baids (physicians),
barbers, pickpockets - all had their representatives in
the heterogenous banyan tree crowd. The nucleus of the
crowd was formed by the litigants who, since they were
supposed to have money in their pockets, were the focus
of all the others. The way the litigants were courted
by all classes of people under the banyan tree is well
described by 82 year old Irfan Munshi of Barisal Town:

> Pleaders, mukhtyars, their agents, come to the
> litigant to make him their client; touts come to
> tell him who is the best pleader at the bar; *amla*
> come to tell him that the Saheb never takes a
> decision without consulting them, so they should
> be remunerated if he wants a favourable decision;
> thus everybody's aim is to fleece him as much as
> possible. Beggars, mendicants, sannasis, fakirs,
> all come to bless him for a pice or even for a
> cake brought from his village home. The astrologer
> is there to tell him his future; preachers come to
> remind him of his past sins. His sinful past and

hazardous future, he is promised, will all be
corrected if the preachers and astrologers are
remunerated enough. Professional witnesses come
to him to volunteer their skilled services, for a
fee. Vendors, hawkers come to sell their merchan-
dize. Pickpockets are always watching him for
half a chance, agents of highway and river dacoits
are gathering intelligence to swoop on him on his
way home; agents of prostitutes come to tell him
who is the most beautiful one in town. A man
becomes rich only to go to court and he goes to
court to become poor again. New riches go to
court to keep the court people alive.[71]

The litigants were thus lost in the court milieu.
While everybody's eyes were on the litigants the
latter's eyes, or rather ears, were fixed on the court
call. They were never sure when they would be called
for a hearing. That depended on the mood of the *amla*
and also on the magistrates whose presence was always
uncertain. Till their cases were announced the banyan
tree was their only shelter. The position of the
waiting litigants is well described by the mid-
nineteenth century writer   Peary Chand Mitra in his
satirical social novel entitled *Alaler Charer Dulal*,
or The Rich Man's Pampered Son:

Barada Babu, Pani Babu and Ramlal are rich people.
So they must have cases in court. They sit on a
satranj or coloured blanket which they have brought
from home for the purpose. It is not certain when
the call for their hearing will come. The office
amla approach them for a douceur. They say, 'Give
us good money, we shall arrange for a quick call
and a decision as well'. Next comes a vakil and
says to Barada Babu, 'Give me sufficient money, I
have well trained witnesses with me. Their witness
never fails.' Office time is at ten in the morning,
and it is now past two o'clock, but the magistrate
is not yet come. No one knows when he will come.
The impatient suitors at last approach an Acharya
or astrologer and say, 'Here is your fee; will you
be good enough to read the stars and tell us
authoritatively when will the magistrate come?'
The learned Achnarya reads the stars and declares,
'No, the Magistrate Bahadur will not come to the
office to-day. The Stars indicate that he is

sleeping at home.'
    The believers left the court for home. But
alas! the magistrate came at last. It was then
three o'clock.[72]

A description of the crowd scene remains incomplete
without some reference to entertainers and to shrines.
A group of entertainers would keep the crowd in good
spirits. These entertainers may be classified into
two groups: commercial entertainers and pure professionals. In the absence of effective literacy and
of any good communication system the best method of
advertising goods was by word of mouth and for that
the best place was the court compound where people
from all parts of the district daily gathered and
returned home carrying the thoughts and fashions of the
town to the remotest villages. The mode of advertisement was to sing attractive current songs punctuated
by enticing speeches advertising goods or services.
The most common objects of advertisement were medicines
of indigenous origin, discovered through a 'dream',
'divine message' or 'accident'. These medicines were
claimed to have the power of curing a wide range of
ailments from the most ordinary cough to the dreaded
cholera.[73] There were also professional entertainers
who expected some tips from the crowd for their
performances. It was they who used to draw the
greatest crowds. The most common of their performances
were songs, spiritual and mundane, story-telling
accompanied by music, the playing of musical instruments, especially the flute and *behala* or violin,
the demonstration of card tricks, acrobatics, jugglery
and magic, and the performance of monkey shows,
cockfighting and *ghatu nautch* or dances by boys in
girls' costumes.
    Musical recitals of the great myths and spiritual
songs were usually performed at the compound of the
shrine, of which every *mufassal* court had at least
one. Though most of these shrines emerged with the
development of the courts every such shrine was given
an enticing history to attract suitors who sought help
not only from the *amla* and other authorities but also
from the great 'spiritual souls' in the shrine of the
compound. Interestingly, most of the court shrines
were universalist in outlook. People of all religions
and castes were allowed to visit them. That was
necessary to maximise the income of the court *amla* who

were universally the patrons and supervisors of these shrines.[75]

Landholders and litigants, old officials and the new class of lawyers, and all the hangers-on whom they attracted, thus gathered round the court-*kachahri*. The little administrative world that made up the *mufassal* town of the early nineteenth century thus progressively grew into a truly urban centre providing multiple attractions for immigrants. But the people came to visit the district or subdivisional headquarters not only for litigation and registration purposes: increasingly they came also for education, in search of health, a career or for recreation. To make a career possession of a traditional education was now of no help. To enter into the official world one must have an English education, and the town was the best place in which to find it.[76]

The number of students at the 25 public seminaries in Bengal in 1835, was only some five hundred.[77] Three decades later the number of students at all levels of education from primary to college had risen to about one and a half millions, one-third of whom came from Bengal's *mufassal* cities and towns, Calcutta being excluded.[88] The tiny urban islands thus contributed quite disproportionately to the new education. Moreover most of the higher education was provided in the towns. In growth terms this meant the building of new schools, of hostels and playgrounds; the employment of teachers, instructors, clerks and peons; the printing of books, journals and periodicals; the establishment of book and stationery shops, sports goods shops, tailoring shops, and so on. What Sir Richard Temple called 'a stir of thought and movement in the national mind'[79] also meant a stir in the worlds of property and commerce.

The increasing student population made the towns more colourful and noisy than before. A local intellectual of Jessore town observed in 1887 that 'even two decades ago there were few students in the town, but now roads and maidans were filled with strutting youngsters and the sound of reading aloud was heard from every home, even after midnight'.[80] Burning the midnight oil was imposed on students partly by the job prospects held out to them if they could achieve good results in the examinations, and partly by the school teachers who had a considerable personal interest in producing good results and enrolling more

and more students in the schools they served. The
salaries of teachers under the education system evolved
after 1854, were not determined upon a fixed pay-scale.
Instead Zillah schools were classified into first,
second or third class according to the number of
students enrolled and their performance in the examinations. The salaries of teachers increased or
decreased according to the movement of the student
roll and the average examination results. Under such
competitive circumstances teachers tried to mould the
academic life of their pupils, frequently making
surprise visits to their pupils' homes to ensure their
devotion to study and exerting their authority as
freely there as they did at school.[81] As the urban
middle class and its associated individualism grew,
however, the traditional authority of teachers over
their students declined. The first complaint of this
decline in authority was made by the teachers themselves when they found that their students were more
influenced by political activists than by themselves.[82]

With the expansion of Western education, Western
medicine also secured a rapid acceptance among the
masses, especially in the towns. The indigenous
medicine administered by Vaids and Hakims held sway
till the mid-nineteenth century. Thereafter, in
consequence of Western education and the provision of
social services by the missionaries, the traditional
medicine gradually gave way to Western medicine, and
by the 1870s even the rural people were said to
prefer it.[83] Health thus became an additional factor
in the movement of people to the cities which
provided the facilities for modern medicine. In view
of the much greater supply of trained doctors coming
from the Bengal medical colleges than there was a
demand for in the Government health services, the
obligatory employment of all students who passed out
successfully from medical colleges was discontinued
in 1874. That measure forced Indian medical students
to start private practice, and for that a *mufassal*
town was decidedly a better place in which to seek
success than Metropolitan Calcutta where there were
said to be enough doctors to cut each other's
throats.[84] Private medical practice was certainly
not an easy or lucrative profession in Bengal until
the beginning of the twentieth century when the
traditional medicine was almost totally routed, in the
towns at least. Till then the private doctors of the

mufassal towns used to supplement their modest income
by dealing in drugs and drinks. The drug houses of the
nineteenth century *mufassal* towns were all owned by
doctors, many of whom, of course, acquired them as
dowries from their fathers-in-law.[85]

Whereas such traits of urbanisation and specialisation, complexity or heterogeneity had mostly been
wanting in the first half of the nineteenth century
when *mufassal* towns were just emerging from their rural
surroundings, by the last quarter of the century these
newly emerged towns had developed distinctive person-
alities. They had become regional centres for
education, health, recreation, creative activities,
social and political movements - and centres, too, for
a new 'stir of thought'.[86] This stir had been
silently and steadily effecting a break with traditional rural ties creating a tension in the urban-
rural relationship. The village was losing its
attraction, it was the older generation which still
held fast to its values. Ramhari, a character in a
social drama of the 1870s, is described as buying a
house in Jessore town. His move brings a sharp
reaction from his old mother who says reprimandingly:
'We have been Bhadralok in the village for generations,
how could you dare to buy a house in town? Do you mean
to take to town life? Impossible. At least impossible
for me.'[87]

This conflict was to be expected. The village,
which for so long lived unaffected and unchallenged
by any rival value system, was now exposed to a kind
of urbanism which threatened not only the traditional
economy, but also the institutions and wisdom that
the villagers had been accustomed to follow without
question. Villagers were now required to cast off
their self-imposed isolation and visit the towns for
justice, education, health, employment and a market.
It was a painful change to have to make. Thus we find
that at first only a male member was allowed a temporary move to town. His family remained in the village
after his departure and to share with his kinsfolk the
fortune that he was to earn in the town. Such an
absolute bar against allowing the family to accompany
the husband to town was too rigid to sustain, but
even at the end of the century we find that the percentage of women to men living in towns was still low.[88]
Henry Beveridge makes the point, citing the example of
Barisal town where he was the Magistrate:

The town is largely occupied by the professional
classes, such as pleaders and attorneys, and their
servants. They are only temporary residents, and
hence at times when the courts are closed, such,
for example, as the Durga Puja holiday, the town
is almost deserted. As the pleaders and shopkeepers do not make the town their home, there are
comparatively very few women in it, and even of
these a large proportion are prostitutes.[89]

In 1809 Francis Buchanan enumerated five hundred
prostitutes in Dinajpur town which was then said to
have a population of about fifteen thousand.[90] That
would mean that of every thirty persons, male and
female, young and old, one was a prostitute. Diwan
Kartika Chandra Roy, an early nineteenth-century
writer, argued that prostitution in those days was a
socially acceptable institution, so much so that
'grandfather, father and son all used to visit
prostitutes without any sense of moral guilt or
inhibition, and never felt embarrassed if they happened
to meet each other in the cottage of the prostitute.
During Durga Puja it was rather considered a desirable
thing to visit a prostitute.'[91] Prostitution was,
however, of two distinct types. One class was that of
the *bais*, who were not prostitutes in the ordinary
sense of the term but cultivated courtesans, at once
specialists in sex, in the arts and in sophisticated
good manners, higher class hetaira as in Greece, whose
favours went to the wealthy but also to those who
were culturally competent to appreciate their accom-
plishments. Many of the *bais* were very rich.[92] The
principal attraction of the *bais'* houses was the
nautch, originally confined to performance in royal
and great zamindari courts. After the British take-
over, and the fall of the great zamindars, the *bais*
were released from royal exclusiveness and thrown into
a wider world. The change probably affected their
professional excellence, but they now attracted much
wider audiences, composed of office *amla*, lawyers,
merchants and absentee landlords, in the towns. What
was the nautch like? From Hur Chander Dutt, a mid-
nineteenth century witness, we get a graphic description. The dancing hall, Hur Chander says, was spacious,
carpeted and full of murals. There were projecting
mirrors fixed on the walls. The light was 'dim but
decorous and dignified'. The dancing girl 'comes

attired in the finest and most gorgeous muslins
bordered with lace, sweeping the ground and parting and
closing sensuously at each movement. She begins her
song in a very light, low voice, gradually raises her
voice and ultimately comes to a climax. At intervals
she kneels at the feet of one or other of the audience,
then rises again to renew the dance. First she starts
dancing, after a while she starts singing; the songs
are principally in the Hindustani dialects.'[93]

Besides the *bais*, there were many ordinary
prostitutes in every *mufassal* town, and they found
most of their patrons among the office *amla*, pleaders
and shopkeepers.[94] The social attitude to prostitution
is reflected in the hitherto unpublished memoirs of
Ganiur Raja Chowdhury, a zamindar living in Sylhet
town in the last decade of the century,[95] who wrote
that the death of his wife in 1892 made him so upset
that 'all the prostitutes of Sylhet town were not
enough to console him'. So he proceeded towards Dacca
'to live in the midst of the prostitutes of high
standard and recover from the mental grief'.[96]

From the last quarter of the nineteenth century,
with the growth of the theatre, amateur and professional, in Bengal, alternatives to the nautch began
to appear.[97] But in Dacca, as late as the 1890s,
Ganiur Raja Chowdhury heard members of the public
cursing Nawab Abdul Ghani because he had spent ten
thousand rupees on a balloon flight across the river
Burhiganga. The public sentiment was that instead of
arranging so absurd a thing he should have spent the
money on a proper *bais* nautch which would have given
him a lasting reputation as a patron.[98] Rural
resistance to innovation and to the introduction of all
things of (westernising) urban origin was even stiffer.
Country people jeered at a townsman visiting the
village who showed off his urban habits, by wearing
western dress, for example, or by smoking cigarettes
or cigars. Ramkrishna Mukherji, a character in a
contemporary satirical drama depicting the rural-urban
dichotomy, is portrayed as having acquired his education in town together with many urban habits. When he
returns to his village home (Bikrampur in Dacca
district) with shirt, trousers and spectacles, all
the villagers gather to condemn his fall. He tries to
get married, but no Bhadralok will agree to marry his
daughter to him because he has lost his caste by adopting new habits. Ramkrishna then throws out a challenge

that he will not marry till he has 'civilised' all
these rural rustics. But he cannot keep his vow. He
soon discovers his 'mistake' and gives up all his
unacceptable habits. He is accepted into the *samaj* or
society only when he had made a public apology for his
cultural heresy.[99] The writer did not have the
courage to make his urban representative succeed
because in the rural-urban dichotomy the village still
held the dominant position, though its influence was
receding fast.

In some respects, indeed, village attitudes continued to dominate the towns, as in attitudes to
sanitation. The more the *mufassal* towns grew in size
the more unhealthy they became. By the 1880s all the
Bengal *mufassal* towns were found by the Sanitary
Commissioner to be utterly filthy, havens for cholera,
smallpox and malaria.[100] Town dwellers, carrying their
country habits with them, showed little interest in
improving the abominable public environment they were
living in. When Kirkwood, the Magistrate of Chittagong built several public latrines and asked the
people to use them instead of defiling their surroundings, the public reaction was violent. It aroused
such horror among the people that one night they
assembled and burnt all the privies one after another
and demanded the immediate transfer of Kirkwood, 'the
bad magistrate'.[101] Their stated objection to the
privy system was that since the privies would be used
by all people, irrespective of caste or creed, they
would defile their caste purity. Religious prejudice
doubtless played a part in their insurrection. But
probably more significant was that they suspected
that a sanitation tax would follow their acceptance of
the privies, and they were unwilling to pay the cost
of urban improvement.

How suspicious the village people were of all
things of urban origin is well indicated by their
reaction to the Agricultural and Industrial Mela (or
Exhibition) that government organised once a year in
every district town from the 1860s onwards. Its
declared aim was to achieve a closer mutual understanding between town and country, through which
social and economic progress was to be attained.[102]
But people interpreted these *melas* as a weapon to
destroy the distinctions of caste. Some even suspected that 'people are to be compelled to purchase
vegetables only from shops set up by Government and

that those who manifest the greatest Agricultural skill
are to be sent to other colonies to cultivate the
soil'.[103] Such a response to urban initiatives long
prevailed. In nineteenth century Bengal urbanisation
no more than kept pace with rural growth and so it
failed to create that massive rural-to-urban movement
observable in contemporary Europe and America. Consequently rural values survived undefeated. As Lambert
observes 'urban-based changes ... quickly lose their
impact when spread over the vast number of villages
that have to be affected'.[104]

   To sum up, the urbanisation found in nineteenth
century Bengal was basically linked to the system of
administration that was introduced by the British.
Most of the district and subdivisional towns had as
their nucleus the establishments of the judge and
collector, and since they were primarily administrative
towns, their growth was strictly conditioned by the
size and range of government establishments. This
partly explains why urban growth was so slow during
our period. In the absence of large scale industrialisation the urban centres failed to create a rural-to-
urban movement such as happened in contemporary Europe
and America. Thus most towns grew only in proportion
to the growth of government and other public bodies.
The social life of the town was accordingly dominated
by the service elites until the emergence of professional classes as social leaders towards the last
quarter of the century. As urban population growth
was moving quite in parallel with the rural growth,
and as the urban population still formed less than
five per cent of the total population at the close of
the century, the towns failed to influence their rural
hinterlands to any significant extent. It is however
also true that the *mufassal* towns were silently laying
the foundation of a new modern outlook as opposed to
rural traditionalism. Internally these towns were
undergoing a quite rapid transformation and moving
towards greater sophistication and specialisation.
With the steady growth of new forms of communication
in the twentieth century they would achieve a nation-
wide urban unity in matters of social change and
modernisation.

Islam, 'Life in the Mufassal Towns of Nineteenth
Century Bengal'

1. Robert Lindsay, *Oriental Miscellanies: Comprising Anecdotes of an Indian Life* (Wigan 1840), p.27.
2. Such terms as urbanisation, urbanism, city and
town have been used in their most general sense, and
without any specialist overtones from sociology or
urban geography.
3. *Census of India, 1901*, Bengal, Part III, Table
III.
4. Ibid., Report Volume, p.27.
5. G.C.K. Peach, 'Urbanisation in India' in R.P.
Beckinson and J.M. Houston (eds.), *Urbanization and its
Problems* (Oxford 1968), p.297.
6. *Census of India, 1901*, Bengal, Report, pp.480-
481.
7. Ibid.
8. J.C. Jack, *Final Report on the Survey and
Settlement Operations in the District of Faridpur,
1901-1914* (Calcutta 1916), p.19.
9. *Thakbast Survey Field Book for Barisal Town*
(Collectorate Record Room), p.7.
10. Henry Beveridge, *The District of Bakerganj*
(Reprinted by Barisal District Council 1970), p.327.
11. *Bengal Administration Report, 1872-3*, p.115.
12. *Census of India, 1901*, Bengal, Report, p.138.
13. See H.H. Wilson, *A Glossary of Judicial and
Revenue Terms* .... (London 1955).
14. Neil J. Smelser and S.M. Lipset (eds.), *Social
Structure and Mobility in Economic Development* (Chicago
1964).
15. John E. Brush, 'The Morphology of Indian
Cities'. in Roy Turner (ed.), *India's Urban Future*
(Berkeley 1962), p.65.
16. Hughli owed much of its early growth to the
Portuguese. During the Emperor Shahjahan's time it
came under the Mughal imperial city system.
17. See Shirim Akhtar, *Role of the Zamindars in
Bengal, 1707-1772* (PhD thesis, London University 1973).
18. Sirajul Islam, 'The operation of the Sunset Law
in Dacca District', *Journal of the Asiatic Society of
Bangladesh*.
19. See Sushil Chaudhury, *Trade and Commercial*

Organisation in Bengal, 1650-1720 (Calcutta 1975).
    20. A. Mackenzie to Government, 21 September 1816,
Civil Judicial Proceedings, 24 January 1817, No.16.
    21. See Sirajul Islam, Permanent Settlement in
Bengal: A Study of its Operation 1790-1890 (Dacca 1978).
    22. See especially M.A. Laird (ed.), Bishop Heber
in Northern India: Selections from Heber's Journal
(Cambridge 1971) and R.M. Martin, The History,
Antiquities and Statistics of Eastern India (London
1833), vol.iii.
    23. Francis Buchanan, Geographical, statistical and
historical description of the District of Dinajpur
(Calcutta 1833).
    24. Bengal Revenue Consultations, 15 January 1814,
No.25.
    25. W.B. Bayley, 'A Statistical View of the
Population of Burdwan ...', Asiatic Researcher XII,
(Calcutta 1816).
    26. See K.M. Mohsin, A Bengal District in Transi-
tion: Murshidabad, 1785-1793 (Dacca 1973) and Shari-
fuddin Ahmed, The History of Dacca City, 1840-1885
(PhD Thesis, London University 1978).
    27. See Bengal District Gazetteers: Noakhali by
J.E. Webster (1911), p.106; Khulna by L.S.S. O'Malley
(1908), pp.179-180; Mymensingh by F.A. Sachse (1917),
p.154; Rajshahi by L.S.S. O'Malley (1916, p.179;
Rangpur by J.A. Vas (1911), p.147.
    28. Henry Beveridge, The District of Bakerganj,
p.327.
    29. L.S.S. O'Malley, Bengal District Gazetteer:
Rajshahi, p.179.
    30. James Westland, A Report on the District of
Jessore (Calcutta 1871), p.250.
    31. Ravindranath Tagore, Jibansmriti [Memoirs]
(Viswa-Bharati 1962), p.10.
    32. J.M. Houston, 'The Foundations of Colonial
Towns in Hispanic America' in R.P. Beckinsale and
J.M. Houston (eds.), Urbanisation and its Problems,
p.352.
    33. See Civil Judicial Proceedings, 25 September
1807, No.26; Criminal Judicial Proceedings, 10 October
1822, No.9; 16 March 1826, No.16; 1 February 1827, No.
15; 28 June 1827, No.13; 11 January 1827, No.20 and 16
August 1827, No.21.
    34. See Thakbast Survey Field Books, Collectorate
Record Rooms, Bangladesh.
    35. Sumit Sarkar, The Swadeshi Movement in Bengal,

1903-1908 (New Delhi 1973).
    36. J.A. Vas, *Bengal District Gazetteers, Rangpur District* (1911), p.146.
    37. L.S.S. O'Malley, *Bengal District Gazetteers, Chittagong District* (1908), p.52.
    38. Cummings, Settlement Papers on Pargana Roushanabad (1890), No.19, Comilla Rajbari Record Room, Comilla.
    39. Bipin Chandra Pal, *Memoirs of My Life and Times*, vol.i, 1857-1884 (Calcutta 1973), p.42.
    40. Ibid., p.34.
    41. See Gideon Sjoberg, 'Rural-Urban Balance and Models of Economic Development' in Smelser and Lipset, op.cit., pp.235-261.
    42. Absenteeism was not a new social phenomenon. As a by-product of the permanent settlement it began from the closing years of the eighteenth century. But then it was largely confined to those new zamindars who purchased lands at auction sales but found it difficult to live on their estates, either because rural society rejected them as upstarts, or because their purchases were of scattered estates. See Sirajul Islam, *Permanent Settlement in Bengal* (Dacca 1978).
    43. Nilmani Mukherjee, *A Bengal Zamindar: Jaykrishna Mukherjee of Uttarpara and his Times, 1808-1888* (Calcutta 1975), p.397.
    44. *Report on the Administration of Bengal, 1874-1875* (Calcutta 1876), p.142.
    45. Frances Buchanan, *Dinajpur*, p.74.
    46. Montgomery Martin, *Eastern India* III, pp.488-489.
    47. See, for example, J.E. Gastrell, *Geographical and Statistical Report on the District of Jessore, Fureedpore and Backergunge* (Calcutta 1868), p.35, and Robert E. Smart, *Geographical and Statistical Report on the District of Tipperah* (Calcutta 1868), p.4.
    48. Bipin Chandra Pal, *Memoirs*, vol.i, 1857-84 (Calcutta 1973), p.42.
    49. R. Carstairs, *The Little World of an Indian District Officer* (London 1912), p.26.
    50. Nilmani Mukherjee, *A Bengal Zamindar*, pp.396-398.
    51. See Iftekharul Awwal, *Industrial Development of Bengal, 1900-1937* (PhD thesis, London University 1978).
    52. Anon, 'A Young Civilian at Mofussil Court', *Calcutta Review*, vol.33 (1859), p.59.
    53. Nabinchandra Sen, *Amar Jiban Katha* [Sketch of my Life], (Calcutta 1907), p.15.

54. Mir Musharraf Hussain, *Amar Jibani* [My Life], (Calcutta 1908), p.100.

55. George Campbell, *Modern India* (London 1952), p.294.

56. Anon, 'A Young Civilian', p.56.

57. Robert Lindsay, *Oriental Miscellanies*, p.39.

58. *Government of Bengal Proceedings (General Dept)* for December 1863, p.66 - summaries of Native Press Reports.

59. George Campbell, *Modern India*, p.280.

60. Resolution, Governor-General in Council, 23 April 1821, *Civil Judicial Proceedings*, 23 April 1821, No.5.

61. *Dacca Prakash*, 21 January 1864.

62. *The Bengal Gazette*, 22 December 1864.

63. A Member of the British Indian Association, *The Affray Bill and the Criminal Administration of Bengal* (Calcutta 1864), p.36.

64. Anon, 'A Young Civilian'.

65. Bengal Proceedings, General Dept - Art and Industry, December 1863, p.72.

66. *Dacca Prakash*, 5 May 1864.

67. See Samuel Schmitthener, 'A Sketch of the Development of the Legal Profession in India', in *Law and Society Review*, vol.iii, Nos.2 and 3 (November 1968 - February 1969), pp.337-382.

68. Panchanan Das, *Bicharer Prahasan* [A Travesty of Justice] (Dacca 1869), p.18.

69. Government of Bengal Proceedings in the Department of Public Works and Cess, February 1872, B Proceedings 1-3, (Dacca Secretariat Room, Dacca).

70. Government of Bengal Proceedings, Judicial in the Public Works Branch, March 1889, B Proceedings 11-13, (Dacca Secretariat Room, Dacca).

71. Oral interview with Irfan Munshi, a zamindari munshi at Barisal town since 1902. His father and granfather had been court munshis.

72. Tekchand Thakur (Peary Chand Mitra), *Alaler Gharer Dulal* (Calcutta BS 1264), pp.1-3.

73. These 'medicines' were also advertised in the local periodicals, and leaflets about them are also found in old *puthis* and books. The Bangla Academy, Dacca, has made a collection of such literature.

74. Oral interview with Irfan Munshi.

75. *Census of India, 1901*, Bengal, Report Volume, pp.178-179.

76. A description of the cityward movement for

education is given in Kalikinkar Chakrabarty, *Banger Parichay* - Introducing Bengal (2 parts, Calcutta 1873).

77. *Report of the General Committee of Public Instruction, Bengal Presidency* (Calcutta 1837), p.1.

78. *General Report on Public Instruction for 1881-2* (Calcutta 1881) p.14.

79. Minute by the Lieutenant Governor, Sir Richard Temple, 14 January 1875, in *Report on the Administration of Bengal, 1874-75* (Calcutta 1876), p.94.

80. Benoy Behari, *Shedin Ar Edin* [Life Yesterday and Today] (Jessore 1887), p.11.

81. Ibid., p.17.

82. The following Bengali Tracts record the increasing disobedience of the younger generation towards their elders and the way in which new values were upsetting the raditional relationship between students and teachers: Prasad Das Goswami, *Amader Samaj* [Our Society] (Srirampur 1895); Chandra Shekhar Sen, *Ki Halo?* [What is Happening?] (1895), Girish Chandra Sen, *Atma Jiban* [My Life] (Calcutta 1907).

83. Anon, *A short account of the village of Joinsar* (Dacca 1875), India Office Library Tract 524, p.10.

84. A Doctor, *Doctor Babu* (in Bengali) (Calcutta 1875), p.3.

85. Ibid.

86. Bengal General Proceedings, May 1873, pp.4-5.

87. Pramanathan Biswas, *Shasuri Bau* [Mother-in-law and Daughter-in-law] (Calcutta 1879), pp.27-28.

88. *Census of India, 1901,* Bengal, Part II, table V.

89. Henry Beveridge, *Barkerganj,* p.329.

90. Francis Buchanan, *Dinajpur,* p.79.

91. Diwan Kartikeya Chandra Roy, *Atmacharita* [Autobiography] (new edition, BS 1365). He was the diwan of the titular raja of Nadia in the early nineteenth century.

92. Francis Buchanan, *Dinajpur,* p.27.

93. Hur Chundur Dutt, *Bengali Life and Society* (Calcutta 1853), India Office Library Tract 164, pp.8-9.

94. Sibnath Sastri, *Ramtanu Lahiri O Tatkalin Banga Samaj* (erd ed.), p.40.

95. His memoirs were discovered among the family papers by Muntasir Mamun, who published them in part in the Dacca Weekly *Bichitra,* 22 September 1978.

96. Ibid., p.36.

97. See Vrajendranath Vandyopadhoy, *Bangla Nattay Shahitter Itihas 1795-1876* [History of the Theatre in Bengal] (Calcutta BS 1346).
98. Ganiur Raja Chowdhury, *Memoirs*, pp.38-9.
99. Kaliprashanna Chattyopadhya, *Bau-Babu* [Wife and Babu] (Dacca BS 1312), p.26.
100. Bengal Sanitary Commissioner to Government of Bengal, 15 April 1880, April 1880, Appendix IV.
101. Chittagong Divisonal Commissioner to Government of Bengal, 25 May 1876, Bengal Municipal Proceedings, September 1876, pp.105-106.
102. Bengal Proceedings General Department, March 1864, p.1
103. Rangpur Dikprakasa, 10 December 1863 (Bengali Weekly) in Bengal General Proceedings, July 1864, p.41.
104. Richard D. Lambert, 'The Impact of Urban Society upon Village Life', in Roy Turner (ed.), *India's Urban Future*, p.117.

THE LOCAL ORGANIZATIONAL BASIS OF SOCIAL RELATIONSHIPS AMONG HINDUS IN CALCUTTA IN THE LATTER PART OF THE NINETEENTH CENTURY

John McGuire

Although the exact size and nature of the population of Calcutta in the latter half of the nineteenth century is a matter of conjecture, there is little doubt that the majority of its inhabitants were Hindu. For example, according to the *Census of the Town of Calcutta, 1881*, which is considered fairly reliable, Hindus represented approximately two-thirds of the 405,019 residents.[1] Indeed, from its inception in 1690, when it was founded upon a small group of villages, which were mainly occupied by Hindu weavers,[2] Calcutta had provided a focal point for settlement by Hindu merchants, traders, clerks, artisans, and landed property owners, and, as it developed into the administrative capital of India, civil servants, teachers, lawyers, and doctors.

These Hindus tended to settle in the northern section of the city[3] and this influenced the development of north Calcutta, which gradually came to resemble a number of large villages linked together by narrow laneways and by imposing *rajbaris*, temples and *atisalas*.[4] Physically, in fact, as it developed, it retained elements of rural Bengal. Economically, too, this section of Calcutta was characterised, in parts, by certain features of rural Bengal; for it was in the process of changing from a system based on a pre-capitalist mode of production to one based on a capitalist mode of production. Indeed, although there had been a systematic development of merchant capital, there was only a limited development of other forms of capital.

As a result of this process of transition, Hindus in Calcutta had two alternative means of survival. They could in the local system obtain their living within a *jajmani* form of exchange, or they could, in the larger system, exact a wage from the market economy. Whereas the local systems were based on a reciprocal exchange of services arising out of a hereditary social status that had been gradually transferred to Calcutta, the larger system was part of an emerging capitalist economy in which services could be bought and sold in the market.

This essay is an attempt to describe the organizational basis of Hindu society in the former context. It is primarily concerned, therefore, not so much with the emerging class system as with the remnants of a pre-capitalist system. Moreover, owing to the lack of detailed data, it is only possible to describe this system in general terms. Yet, given this limitation, it could be argued that an analysis based on a series of case studies of the agnatic lineages of the most powerful Hindu families in Calcutta in the nineteenth century[5] provides a broad understanding of the social relationships upon which this system was based.

Certainly it is clear that when Hindus migrated to Calcutta they had to adapt to a society which was much more complex than the one from which they had come. Indeed, there is little doubt that many of them experienced difficulties in making this adaption. For instance, it has been widely documented that Hindus in Calcutta retained strong ties with their ancestral villages and returned home regularly to fulfil social obligations.[6] Still, the fact remains that they were all bound to Calcutta for at least part of the year. What remains unclear, however, are the ways in which they adjusted to this more complex environment.

This question has, of course, been the subject of much debate, for while there is evidence to demonstrate that Hindus were divided into numerous castes and sects, there is also evidence which indicates that cleavages occurred within a common ideological framework. In the latter context, Dumont has argued quite powerfully that Hindus were ideologically bound together by the belief in a social hierarchy in which Brahmans assumed a pre-eminent position.[7] Very broadly, this belief was based on the concept of inherited permanent sin which gave rise to the idea of superior and inferior roles in society and which, as a result, led to a dominant-deferential situation in all social interactions between Hindus.

Predictably, the most powerful Hindu families in Calcutta attempted to assume the superior roles within this sytem. Like Hindus in other parts of India, they did so by imitating Brahmanical social organizations. In this respect, they endeavoured to define more clearly their kinship structures by adopting a ceremony called *parvana sraddha* in which obligations were offered up to a common ancestor. In

this ceremony, all those who offered oblations of
water to a common paternal ancestor (up to fourteen
degrees away) referred to one another as *samanodakas*;
all those who offered partial oblations of *pinda* to a
common paternal ancestor five degrees away referred to
one another as *sakulya*; and all those who offered full
oblations of *pinda* to common ancestors up to three
degrees away referred to one another as *sapindas*.[8]

Membership in each of these groups carried with
it certain rights and duties in institutions and customs such as adoption, marriage and inheritance.
For example, a Hindu could not marry into a family that
belonged to any of these groups; nor could he adopt a
son from outside them. His position as heir was
similarly governed by these ties; a *sapinda* assuming
precedence over a *sakulya*, and a *sakulya* over a *samanodaka*. Generally, if he could afford it, he was
expected to provide food and shelter for the less fortunate of his kinsmen. In this respect, the most
powerful Hindu families provided focal points in these
kinship networks, for they were able to support large
numbers of individuals. The Dey family of Simla, for
example, maintained a small colony of kinsmen in their
household, while the Datta family of Nimatala supported
a large number of their household.[9] In addition, other
families, like the Sens of Kalutala, provided employment for kinsmen in their family enterprise. In so
doing, they fulfilled a variety of functions of which
the most clearly defined were those that were
determined by the *sapinda* relationship.

Those individuals who referred to one another as
sapinda formed the Hindu family in the broadest sense.
Generally, they fell into agnatic and cognatic groups;
the former of which assumed precedence over the
latter. As a cognatic *sapinda* (commonly referred to
as *bandhu*), a Hindu inherited the duties that his
mother had held in the paternal family, but he did not
pass these duties on to his children. Yet there were
some instances where a *bandhu* relationship took precedence over the paternal one. For example, the son
of a daughter stood before a brother because only the
bandhu relation was capable of offering *pinda* to the
individual when he had died. Such complicated customs
occasionally played an important role in the restruc-
turing of Hindu families. For instance, when Ashutosh
Dey died without any patrilineal descendants, his
fortune went to the sons of his daughter (Mitras of

Simla),[10] and, as a result, they assumed much more
powerful positions in Hindu society. Cases like this
were rare, however; for Hindus without male heirs
usually adopted a close relative.

Indeed, the agnatic relationship, which was hereditary, was usually much more important than the
cognatic one, which was terminal; for it ensured that
the deceased would continue to be incorporated in the
pinda offerings of future generations. In the widest
sense then, the Hindu family could range over seven
generations in that those who offered *pinda* could
rightly expect to receive similar offerings from their
own sons, as well as their grandsons and great grandsons on the patrilineal side. However, the family of
worship rarely functioned as one unit in other respects.
Most of the Hindu families, for example, tended to
divide their property equally among their sons, or, if
they had no sons, among their adopted sons.

However, division in property did not necessarily
carry with it division in household. In a number of
cases, three generations lived in the same household
and ate in the same kitchen. Furthermore, in such
cases, although various individuals might have owned
property, they allowed the right of management to be
vested in the head of the family. In certain instances
this situation led to quarrels within the family and to
the formation of new households. The Tagores of
Pathuriaghata and of Jaransanka, for example, were part
of the same family of worship in the latter half of the
nineteenth century, but had split into separate households at much earlier dates.[11] Similarly, the Malliks
of Pathuriaghata and of Chorevagan were members of the
same family of worship during the period under discussion, even though they had divided into separate
branches in 1821.[12]

This pattern of sub-division tended to repeat
itself, so that a family of worship usually consisted
of members from a number of households. For example,
the Tagores of Pathuriaghata separated into two households in 1885, when Surendra Mohan left the parent body,
headed by his elder brother Jarindra Mohan, and formed
a new branch of the family.[13] Sometimes this cleavage
led to a complete duplication of family functions in
all matters except those relating to the *parvana-
sraddha*. In other instances, they simply resulted in
the duplication of a few functions, and in important
questions such as marriage the separate households

acted as a corporate unit.

The leading Hindu families in Calcutta also adopted more complex Brahmanical kinship structures. In particular, many of them drew up *gotras*. In so doing, they attempted to establish exogamous social structures which were popularly defined as containing all those Hindus who were patrilineally related to a common ancestor and who could, as a consequence, be identified by a common patronym. In practice, however, Hindu patronyms did not coincide with *gotras* or, indeed, with *jatis* or castes. Among the leading Hindu families, for example, there were Sens who were Daksina Radhi Kayasthas, Radhi Vaidyas and Saptagram Suvarnavaniks.[14] In fact, various sources indicate that most of the powerful families changed their patronyms from generation to generation. The Ballabhs of Bagbazar,[15] the Devs of Sobhabazar,[16] the Deys of Simla,[17] the Malliks of Barabazar,[18] the Malliks of Pathuriaghata[19] and the Mitras of Kurmatala[20] had altered their names at least once, and in most cases more than that.

Presumably then, these families, in conjunction with the *ghattaks* whom they hired, wielded great influence in creating these *gotras*, especially over families who claimed membership in their *gotra*. Nava Krishna is said to have acquired a very influential position among his kinsmen by performing such a task for the Daksina Radhi Kayasthas.[21] The Setts acquired a similar influence when they compiled 23 *gotras* for the Tantavaniks later in the nineteenth century.[22]

If the *gotra* represented the highest organizational form based on exogamy, then *jati* represented the highest organizational form based on endogamy. Between these two organizational forms, there lay various other groupings, the most widespread of which was that of *kula*. As with other levels of organization, most Hindus modelled their *kula* rankings upon those employed by Brahmans. In so doing, they ranked themselves along a scale ranging from Kulin at the top, to Maulik at the bottom; a classification system which was ostensibly introduced by King Vallala Sena in the middle of the twelfth century.[23] For example, the Daksina Radhi Kayasthas divided themselves into three major *kulas*, while the Saptagram Suvarnavaniks formed two such groupings.

Although it is not known at what dates these classification systems began to take effect, they probably did not occur among the *jatis* of which the

leading Hindus were members until the second half of
the eighteenth century; for it was during this period
that Nava Krishna endeavoured to formalize the *kulas*
of the Daksina Radhi Kayasthas by compiling, with the
aid of *ghattaks*, the 'Kayastha Kulagrantha' in which
the ranks of Kulin families were fixed.[24] Given that
the Daksina Radhi Kayasthas were one of the most
Brahmanized *jatis* in the latter half of the nineteenth
century, it is doubtful whether any other *jati*, except
the Radhi Vaidyas, had formally divided into *kulas*
prior to the latter half of the eighteenth century.

Once such a structure had been established, leading
Hindu families of inferior, and thus suspect, *kulas*
could firmly establish their social status within the
jati by means of marriages with Kulin families.[25]
Certainly the leading Daksina Radhi Kayastha families,
like the Dattas, the Devs, the Deys and the Sinhas,
improved their Maulik status by marrying members of
their families to Kulins. In order to do this, they
had to give part of their wealth to the Kulin family
concerned, in exchange for a measure of high social
status which the latter inherited. Ram Dulal Dey, for
example, married his five daughters to high ranking
Kulins each of whom received, among other things, a
house (worth 10,000 rupees) and 50,000 rupees.[26]
However, as wealthy families were rarer than Kulin
ones, they could afford to impose rigid standards in
selecting Kulin sons-in-law or daughters-in-law.
Ashutosh Dey, for instance, rejected Dwarka Nath
Mitra - a high ranking Kulin and one of the outstanding
scholars in Bengal in the 1850s - as a potential
husband for his grand-daughter because Mitra was
physically unattractive.[27]

Jati structures, like *kula* organizations, were
also based on Brahmanical models. Hindus endeavoured
to demonstrate that their *jatis* belonged to one of the
twice-born varnas, or failing that, at least, to a
clean Sudra rank; a sign that they had inherited a
high social position in Hindu society. The leading
Hindu families played a major role in this process
by introducing into their *jatis* such customs as the
wearing of sacred thread, *pujas* and prayers used by
Brahmans, and, as has been demonstrated, kinship and
kula structures similar to those of the Brahmans.
They endeavoured to substantiate these innovations by
reference to historical sources such as Vedic
writings, and by publishing *jati* histories in which

they attempted to relate the origins of their *jati* to
twice-born varnas.[28]   They also sought to reinforce
these claims by securing government recognition, and
by obtaining favourable judgments on their status
from one or more of the authoritative *samajes* of
pandits.[29]

They achieved government recognition by having
members of their *jatis* admitted to the Sanskrit College.
When the government established this college in 1823,
only Brahmans and Rarhi Vaidyas were admitted. By
1863, however, all of the leading Hindu families in
Calcutta had managed to have members of their *jatis*
admitted to the college as students, and subsequently
as teachers.[30] The Dev family, for example, was
primarily responsible for securing the admission of
Kayasthas to that college in the late 1840s, when it
used its influence with the government to have
members of its family accepted there.[31]

In addition to securing government recognition of
their claims, most of the powerful Hindu families
attempted to secure a favourable *vyavastha* on the
status of their *jati* from one of the celebrated
samajes of pandits, the four most important of which
were those of Nadiya, Tribeni, Vikrampur, and Bakla.[32]
In particular, they sought the acknowledgement of the
orthodox Sakta pandits who resided in Nadiya.[33] For
example, in the late eighteenth century, Krishna
Kanta Nandi asked the Nadiya *pandits* for their support
when the Pandas of the Jagannath Temple in Orissa
refused to accept his gifts because he was unclean
Sudra. Nandi received a favourable reply from the
Nadiya *pandits* and, as a result, his gifts were
accepted by the Pandas.[34] There is little doubt that
Nandi, who was one of the richest and most powerful
Hindus in south-west Bengal, used his influence to
secure this *vyavastha*. Indeed, although the *pandits*
declared him to be a Tili (oil merchant) which they
claimed was a clean Sudra, it would seem that this
group was, in fact, part of the Teli (oil manufacturing) *jati* which was ostensibly unclean.[35] In short,
leading Hindus, like Nandi, were capable of improving
the status of their *jati*, or, at least, of certain
members within it. It is significant, in fact, to
note that all the *jatis* to which the leading Hindus
belonged were, by the end of the nineteenth century,
classified as twice-born or clean sudra by the orthodox *pandits* of Nadiya.[36] All, that is, except one.

Unlike other *jatis*, the Saptagam Suvarnavaniks
remained unclean in the eyes of the Sakta pandits in
Nadiya, even though its members were among those
respectable *jatis* who established the Hindu College in
1817,[37] and who founded the Dharma Sabha in 1830.[38]
Indeed, Ram Gopal Mallik, a leading Saptagram Suvarnavanik, was the first *pradhan* of the latter organization.[39] The Saptagram Suvanavaniks, moreover, gained
admission to the Sanskrit College both as students and
as teachers, and, like other *jatis* to which leading
Hindus belonged, followed a policy of Sanskritization;
the Malliks of Pathuriaghata, for example, having
introduced the sacred thread into this *jati* in 1862.[40]
Why then did this *jati* fail to achieve the rank of Tili
for instance?

There are a number of possible answers to this
question. Perhaps the most obvious reason is that they
were rich merchants by tradition and were thus the
object of jealousy among other Hindus, in much the
same way as the Marwaris in Calcutta are today.
Indeed, in spite of the fact that representatives of
this *jati* were among the most charitable of all
Hindus in Calcutta, they were the subject of proverbs
such as

> A sonar [Saptagram Suvarnavanik] will rob his
> mother and sister; he will filch gold even
> from his wife's nose ring; if he cannot steal
> his belly will burst with longing.[41]

Yet is doubtful whether this was the most important
reason. Unlike most other *jatis* in Calcutta, the
Saptagram Suvarnavaniks virtually all belonged to one
religious sect; namely the Vaishnavas, who paid homage
to the Gossain Brahmans.[42] As a result, few, if any
of them, acknowledged the orthodox Sakta *pandits* in
Nadiya and the *pandits*, in turn, had no interest in
promoting the social status of their *jati*. On the
contrary, the Saptagram Suvarnavaniks were referred to
disparagingly by the *pandits* of this school.[43]
Presumably, if some of the powerful Hindu families in
this *jati* had, like those of other *jatis*, offered
expensive gifts to the Nadiya *pandits*, the situation
might have been different. Yet the Saptagram
Suvarnavaniks cannot be classified as inferior simply
because the Nadiya *pandits* held a low view of them.
Public opinion among Hindus was too diverse for that.
Indeed, it is difficult to see how one opinion,

though influential, would have prevailed in Calcutta
where a large number of Hindus were Vaishnavas.

Generally then, Hindus built up local ties by
introducing social relationships based on Brahmanical
models ranging from small kinship organizations to *jati*
itself. In this way, they helped develop a set of
rules which provided the basis of a larger Hindu
community. Yet the question remains: how exactly did
they ensure that the functions which these relationships implied were fulfilled?

Within the context of the family, they attempted
to achieve this by creating a set of clearly defined
roles which were determined by age, sex and generation.
Normally, the most significant role was filled by the
eldest male of the first generation; an individual
who was called *karta*.[44] The other roles were
hierarchically ordered according to generation and age;
the eldest member of each generation, for example, was
referred to as *dada* by his brothers. Although the
women deferred to the male members of the household,
they had a parallel structure among themselves. The
eldest woman of the first generation, who was
usually the wife of the *karta*, was known as *ginni*;[45]
and the eldest member of each generation was called
didi by her sister. In fact, there was a specific
term for each possible interaction which might occur
within a family. To give an example, the youngest
brother of a husband's father was known as *chhota
thakur*, but only by the wife of an elder brother's son.
The Hindu family, then, represented a very complex
structure in which behaviour was, for the most part,
pre-determined.

Of course, in so far as the Hindu family operated
at different organizational levels, an individual
could be *karta* in one situation and a younger brother
in another. For example, in 1857 Kali Krishna Dev
performed the role of *karta* in the junior branch of the
Dev family, but Radha Kanta Dev, the head of the
senior household, filled that role in matters relating
to the family of worship. When Radha Kanta died in
1867, his position as *karta* in the senior household
was assumed by his eldest son, Rajendra Narain. His
position within the family of worship, on the other
hand, was inherited by Kali Krishna, who was next in
line within that group.[46]

This structure, although not so clearly defined,
was also the model for Hindu social relationships

which operated in the larger societal organizations.
Indeed, it provided the means through which the leading
Hindu families related themselves to their more distant
kinsmen and to sections of their *kulas* and *jatis*. It
was, however, less effective as an integrating agency
in the higher levels of organization.

Certainly there is little evidence to suggest that
jatis acted as tightly knit groups in the latter half
of the eighteenth century. In this respect, the most
powerful Hindu families tended to play a divisive role;
for once they had accumulated large capital holdings
they tended to purchase the most significant roles
within their *jatis* for themselves and thus disturbed
the prevailing structure.

The Devs, for example, bought the position of
gostipathi in the late eighteenth century. Nava
Krishna, the founder of the Dev family, gave a large
sum to the Sinha family of Gopinagar, so that his
grandson, Radha Kanta, could marry the daughter of the
leader of the latter family, and thus assume the role
of *gostipathi* which the Sinhas had held.[47] The
functions which this role implied, however, could only
be fulfilled so long as *jati* fellows accepted the
gostipathi in question. In this case, other powerful
Daksina Radhi Kayasthas challenged the right of the
Dev family to hold that position. The Dattas of
Hathatala, for instance, refused to accept its
rulings, and they carried a large number of Daksina
Radhi Kayasthas with them.[48] Similarly, the Roys of
Andul rejected the leadership of the Devs on the
question of caste.[49] In 1841, in fact, there was a
cleavage within the Dev family itself over the
subject of leadership, that occurred when one faction
endeavoured to outcaste the other.[50]

Conflict among the powerful Hindu families of
various *jatis* over leadership roles continued
throughout the period under discussion. For example,
in 1875, when the Sett and the Basak families joined
together to legislate on the question of dowries in
Tantavanik marriages, their decision was disallowed by
a number of *jati* fellows.[51] In 1878, when the
Malliks of Pathuriaghata called a meeting to formalize
certain customary laws for the Saptagram Suvarnavaniks;
they were not supported by all of the powerful
families within their *jati*,[52] in spite of the fact
that they had claimed the position of *pramanik* among
the Saptagram Suvarnavaniks since the eighteenth

century.[53] When these divisions are added to the
others which presumably occurred among these *jatis*
throughout south-west Bengal, it seems unlikely that
jatis were highly organized at any time in the latter
half of the nineteenth century.

But the struggle for power among the powerful
Hindu families was not the only factor that prevented
jati fellows from uniting under one head. In many
cases religious beliefs cut across *jatis* and precluded
them from functioning as corporate units.[54] Unfortunately, there is inadequate data to demonstrate
exactly how religious belief affected social organization of Hindus in Calcutta; yet there is evidence to
show that it was quite often important in determining
marriage and other social relationships. For instance,
Vaishnavs, like the Bose family of Simla, refused to
eat with Saivites, like the Dey family of Simla, even
though they belonged to the same *jati*.[55] Similarly,
the Dey family severed its ties with the Datta family
of Hathatala, when the latter negotiated a marriage
with the family of Ram Gopal Ghose, a professed non-
believer.[56]

Owing to these internal cleavages, the *jatis*, as a
whole, were never homogeneously Sanskritized.
Certainly there is no way of determining the rate at
which Sanskritization occurred within the various
jatis. Generally, however, powerful Hindu families
from non-Brahman *jatis* had been involved in Sanskritization within their respective *jatis* from as early as
the second half of the eighteenth century. Yet
Sanskritization was not summed up in one such change,
nor within one short period; and in many cases was
never fully effective within the *jati* as a whole. For
example, in the 1840s, the Roy family of Andul introduced the sacred thread into the Daksina Radhi Kayastha
jati, but by 1885, and, indeed as late as the end of
the nineteenth century, many members of this *jati* did
not wear the thread.[57] In fact, by the end of the
period under discussion, the Radhi Vaidyas were the
only *jati*, apart from the Brahmans, themselves, to
have become almost completely Sanskritized.[58]
Presumably, they achieved this because they had pursued a policy of Sanskritization for a long period,
and because they were a relatively small *jati*. In
addition to the internal cleavages which prevented
jatis from being fully Sanskritized, there were
external difficulties; for the *jati* members concerned

had to convince other Hindus that their claims were
justified. Yet there is little evidence to suggest
that the different *jatis* fitted neatly into the main-
stream of a Hindu ideological system. On the contrary,
there is ample evidence that competition of this kind
between members of various *jatis* led to conflict rather
than to consensus. Indeed, while the powerful Hindu
families endeavoured to establish a high place for
themselves in the system of varnas, few of them were
prepared to accept the similar claims of others. In
many cases, this feeling was manifested more generally.
For example, in 1869, Bhola Nath Chunda wrote that

> antipathy between a Kayest [Kayastha] and a
> Bunya [Suvarnavanik] is as strong as between
> a Hindoo and Mussulman.[59]

While it is doubtful that all Kayasthas and all
Suvarnavaniks felt this way about one another, it is
highly probable that there existed a lack of consensus
over questions of *jati* among these two groups;
especially as they both contained a number of the most
powerful Hindus in Calcutta. Similar examples indicate
that there was no specific set of rules which Hindus of
different *jatis* could follow when interacting with one
another. Unlike Hindus in *mufassal* communities, those
in Calcutta were part of a much larger group of
individuals many of whom were newly arrived and not
all of whom were permanently resident in the city.
They were thus faced with the difficulty not only of
performing different roles, but also of adapting to
a much wider range of social relationships. Moreover,
because they had to do this in a situation where no
one authority prevailed, it was hardly possible for a
tightly knit Hindu community to evolve.
  Nonetheless, in so far as the hierarchical concept
of life remained the essential belief of Hindus in
Calcutta, the leading Hindu families were able to
build up a wide range of stable relationships around
themselves, even though they were unable to fix their
positions firmly within the Hindu community. As has
been noted, they did this in the first place among
kinsmen and *jati* fellows. They also did this among
other Hindus by imitating the behaviour of the
traditional *mufassal raja*. Ideally, in performing
this role, they were endeavouring to fulfil the
function of a Kshatriya king as the ruler and
protector of Hindu society.[60] In Calcutta, during the

period under discussion, the leading Hindus were
naturally severely restricted in this respect; for not
only were they subject to a colonial regime, but they
were also competing with one another for such a
position. Yet their behaviour was based on this model.
    There were various ways in which they imitated the
model. They built or bought themselves large houses
which resembled and, indeed, were often referred to as
rajbaris.[61] Yet they used these houses not just as
symbols of traditional *rajbaris*, but as centres of a
large number of social interactions of which the
leading Hindu families, and, more especially, the
kartas within the families were the focal points. As
has been indicated, the *kartas* stood at the top of a
set of hierarchical social relationships which existed
between their kin and their *jati* fellows.
    The same individuals assumed a similar relationship
with other Hindus who were bound to their families;
Hindus who could be broadly classified as Brahmans or
non-Brahmans. Of these two, the former were the most
important, for they defined the ritual ranking of other
Hindus by the manner in which they interacted with
them. If, for example, a Brahman refused to take
water from another Hindu, he was stating, in effect,
that he considered that individual to be *acchal* and
thus of lower hereditary status. If, on the other
hand, he accepted water from a Hindu he was acknowledging his *jalchal* or respectable hereditary status.[62]
    The most powerful Hindu families felt that it was
imperative to come within the latter category; for they
could not otherwise claim to fulfil the function of a
raja which by definition covered a wide range of
interactions with Brahmans. Like all Hindus from
respectable *jatis*, they were expected to have *purohits*
at every family ceremony from the *jala karma* to the
sraddha; and *gurus* at all initiation ceremonies in
which religious advice was required. All were
supposed to feed other Brahmans at these ceremonies and
to support *pandits* who were pursuing Sanskrit learning.[63]
As has been indicated, of course, not all of the leading
Hindu families were served by all Brahmans. Nonetheless,
each of these families could refer to one Brahman *jati*
which would serve it. For example, while those who
were Saptagram Suvarnavaniks were unable to obtain the
services of Radhi Brahmans, they were able to secure
the services of a large number of Daksina Vaidika
Brahmans.[64]

Yet the leading Hindu families were, themselves, not prepared to accept the services of all Brahman *jatis*; nor, for that matter, of all members within one *jati*. For example, the Saptagram Suvarnavaniks only paid homage to those Daksina Vaidika Brahmans who were Vaishnavas. In fact, as has been noted, they did not honour Brahmans who were orthodox Saktas. As a result of this situation, a growing number of Saktas in search of gifts were converted to Vaishnavism during the period under discussion.[65] Indeed, the leading Hindu families were able to employ their wealth to gain the services of even the highest Brahman *jatis*. For instance, the Tagores, who, as Pirali Brahmans, had been rejected by the Radhi Brahmans at the beginning of the nineteenth century, were receiving recognition from the highest ranking members of this *jati* by the end of the period under discussion.[66]

In one context then, the relationship between the leading Hindu family and the Brahman can be seen as a power struggle. Yet, significantly, it was a struggle within an ideological framework. Each sought to fulfil an ideal within society but could not do so without the support of the other. To perform their priestly functions Brahmans needed material goods, whereas to perform their kingly functions the powerful Hindus needed priestly services. This situation was clearly evident in the wills which were drawn up by the powerful Hindus. For example, when Kristo Mohan Basak died in 1878, he left a will which stated that his trustees were

> to spend suitable sums at the annual sraddha or anniversary of my father, mother, and grandfather as well as of myself after my demise on the feeding of the Brahmin and the poor. To spend suitable sums for the annual contribution to the Brahmin Pandits holding tolls or native schools for the diffusion of Sanskrit learning in the country at the time of Doorga Pujah. To spend suitable sums for the perusal of the Mahabharat and Puran and for the prayer to the God during the month of Kartick.[67]

Basak belonged to the Tantavanik or traditional weaver *jati*, and was hardly the ideal Hindu to perform the Kshatriya role. Yet he saw himself as the protector of Hindu institutions, and, more importantly, so did the Brahmans who benefited by his gifts and who provided religious services in return.

The most powerful Hindu families were also related through *jajmani* ties to such non-Brahmans, as *jhis*, *khansamas*, *sirkars*, *napits*, and *dhobas*. Their relationship with those servants were, of course, partly determined by the market economy. Nonetheless, they selected servants to fulfil traditional roles and the behaviour which marked the master-servant relationship was highly ritualized.[68] A *napit*, for instance, would not wash clothes or mix with Hindus who did. He would, however, shave the members of the chief family prior to any religious function and convey news of happy events to kinsmen of the family. In return for these services, he would receive, in addition to his own wage, various gifts of a traditional nature. When he carried good news from the chief family, for example, he received presents such as shawls, silk, and brass vessels from both kith and kin.[69]

In addition to these specific roles, the most powerful Hindu families provided the means for more general forms of social relationships among Hindus in Calcutta, for they supported the charitable works, the temples, and the *pujas* which helped to bind the Hindus together.[70] For example, they established *atisalas* where mendicants could obtain food and lodgings. In times of general crises, they fed thousands as, for instance, the Malliks did during the famine of 1866.[71] They also spent large sums in constructing temples and other religious buildings in Calcutta and in holy centres such as Brindaban, and in caring for existing temples. The Mar family of Jaunbazar, for example, set aside 3,000 rupees per year for the preservation of temples which it had built.[72]

Undoubtedly, however, the most important function of these powerful families among Hindus in Calcutta was to provide elaborate celebrations during *pujas*. In fact, these families were expected to fulfil this role when they were celebrating both family ceremonies such as weddings and major festivals such as Kali Puja and Durga Puja. The Pramaniks of Kasaripara, for instance, fed thousands of Hindus on the annual occasion of Durga Puja.[73]

Among the Hindus of Calcutta in the latter half of the nineteenth century then, the most powerful families provided focal points for social relationships which were largely remnants of a pre-capitalist system. Thus, they helped to create a cluster of overlapping

localized systems in the north of the city where each
Hindu assumed a postion in the hierarchy according to
his relationship with the *karta* of one of the powerful
families. Inevitably, as the result of urbanization,
these relationships became increasingly more diffuse
and difficult to identify, and conversely, of course,
the emerging class system became progressively more
apparent.[74]

Acchal A Hindu from whom a Brahman will not accept water.
Atisala A guest-house.
Bandhu A matrilineal kinsman.
Chhota-thakur Husband's younger brother.
Dada Elder brother.
Dhoba A washerman.
Didi Elder sister.
Ghattak A Brahman who arranges marriages.
Ginni Woman in charge of Hindu household.
Gostipathi Caste-leader.
Gotra Lineage relationship by descent from a common male ancestor.
Guru A Brahman priest who provides advice on social and religious questions.
Jajmani A socio-economic relationship based on a tradition or a custom.
Jala-karma A Hindu birth ceremony.
Jalchal A Hindu from whom a Brahman will accept water.
Jati An endogamous group. Frequently referred to as a subcaste.
Jhi A female servant.
Karta The male head of a Hindu family.
Khansama A male servant.
Kula Social rankings within *jatis* based on birth. A set of clans.
Lakh One hundred thousand.
Mufassal Rural area.
Napit A barber.
Pandit A Brahman scholar.
Parvana-sraddha A ceremony in which an offering for ancestors is made.
Pinda Funeral cake.
Pradhan Chief.
Pramanik A caste leader.
Puja A religious festival.
Puja-dalan A household temple.
Purohit A household priest.
Raja A title given to Hindu chiefs.
Rajbari A palace.
Radhi West
Sakulya A patrilineal kinsman within five generations.
Salagram A household deity.
Samaj A society.
Samanodaka A patrilineal kinsman within fourteen

generations.
Sapinda A patrilineal kinsman within three
   generations.
Sirkar A manager.
Sraddha A funeral ceremony.
Tol A sanskrit school.
Uttara North.
Vyavastha A judgement.

NOTES

McGuire, 'The Local Organizational Basis of Social
Relationships among Hindus in Calcutta in the latter
part of the Nineteenth Century'

1. H. Beverley, *Report on the Census of the Town
and Suburbs of Calcutta, 1881* (Calcutta 1881), Table
iv, v.
2. C.R. Wilson (ed.), *The Early Annals of the
English in Bengal* (Calcutta 1895), vol.i. pp.127-128.
3. *Administration Report of the Calcutta
Municipality for 1877* (Calcutta 1978), pp.3-4;
Beverly, op.cit., Table ix, xxiii.
4. See, for example, Calcutta, Municipal Assess-
ments, 1857; "Charitable Institutions", *Administration
Report of the Calcutta Municipality for 1884-85*
(Calcutta 1885), pp.2-3.
5. Various indicators were used to draw up a list
of these families. See John McGuire, 'Some Problems
Relating to the Collection and Reconstruction of Data
for a Quantitative Study of Political Leadership',
*Bulletin of Quantitative and Computer Methods in
South Asian Studies* No.1 (June 1973), p.20; 'Political
Leadership Among Hindus in Calcutta: 1857-1885',
Unpublished Ph.D. Thesis, University of London, 1976,
pp.29-32.
6. See, for instance, Beverley, op.cit., p.42.
7. Louis Dumont, *Homo Hierarchicus* (London 1970).
8. *Calcutta Review*, vol.iii, (1971), pp.255-256;
P.N. Bose, *Hindu Civilization Under British Rule*
(Calcutta 1895), vol.ii, pp.123-124.
9. S.C. Bose, *The Hindoos As They Are: A
Description of the Manners, Customs and Inner Life of
Hindoo Society in Bengal* (2nd and Revised ed., Calcutta
1883).
10. L.N. Ghose, *The Modern History of the Indian
Chiefs, Rajas, Zamindars etc.* (Calcutta 1881), vol.ii,
p.78.
11. James W. Furrell, *The Tagore Family* (London
1822), p.17.
12. L.N. Ghose, op.cit., vol.ii, p.60.
13. *Bengalee*, 26 September 1885.
14. See John McGuire 'Political Leadership Among
Hindus in Calcutta: 1857-1885', Unpublished Ph.D.
Thesis, University of London, 1976, Appendix A. It

is interesting to note that S.N. Mukherjee in his
'Class, Caste and Politics in Calcutta, 1815-38', in
Edmund Leach and S.N. Mukherjee (eds.), *Elites in
South Asia* (Cambridge 1970), p.47, classifies
Rajnarayan and Rupnarayan Sen as Kayasthas when, in
fact they were Saptagram Suvarnavaniks.

15. Mukherjee, loc.cit. makes a similar error in
classifying this family as Vaidya when, in fact, there
is little doubt that it was Daksina Radhi Kayastha;
for L.N. Ghose, op.cit., p.74, lists it as such, and,
more importantly, it was related by marriage to the
Mitras of Bagbazar.

16. N.N. Ghose, *Memoirs of Maharaja Nubkissen
Bahadur* (Calcutta 1901), pp.4-5.

17. Grish Chunder Ghose, *Ramdoolal Dey* (Calcutta
1868), p.2.

18. P.N. Mullick, *History of the Vaisyas of Bengal*
(Calcutta 1902), p.107.

19. Ibid., p.120.

20. *An Account of the Late Govindram Mitter 'Naib
Zamindar' in Mr. Howell's Day and of his Descendants
in Calcutta and Benares* (Calcutta 1869), p.12. Hereafter this publication is referred to as *Govindram
Mitter.*

21. N.N. Ghose, op.cit., p.173.

22. Nagendra Nath Seth, *Kalikatasha Tantu-Vanik
Jati Iitihas* (Calcutta 1951), pp.195-196.

23. N.K. Datta, *Origin and Growth of Caste in
India* (Calcutta 1965), vol.ii, p.5.

24. N.N. Ghose, op.cit., p.174.

25. J. Bhattacharya, *Hindu Castes and Sects*
(Calcutta 1896), p.179.

26. S.C. Bose, op.cit., p.72.

27. Ibid., p.48.

28. See, for example, P.N. Mullick, *History of the
Vaisyas of Bengal* (Calcutta 1902).

29. See, for example, Kissory Chand Mitter, 'The
Kassimbazar Raj', *Calcutta Review*, vol.62, No.113,
(1873), pp.94-95.

30. *General Report of Public Instruction for
Bengal 1862-63* (Calcutta 1863), Appendix A, p.305.

31. Subul Chandra Mitra, *Isvar Chandra Vidyasagar*
(Calcutta 1902), p.219.

32. Gura Prosad Sen, *Introduction to the Study of
Hinduism* (Calcutta 1893), p.218.

33. P.C. Bagchi (ed.), *The Second City of the
Empire* (Calcutta 1938), p.23.

34. Mitter, loc.cit.
35. Hitesranjan Sanyal, 'Continuities of Social Mobility in Traditional and Modern Society in India: Two Case Studies of Caste Mobility in Bengal', *The Journal of Asian Studies*, vol.xxx, No.2 (February 1970), pp.315-339.
36. See, for example, Bhattacharya, *Hindu Castes and Sects* (Calcutta 1896).
37. *Calcutta Christian Observer*, vol.i, No.2 (July 1832), p.70.
38. Brajendra Nath Banerjee (ed.), *Samvadpatre Sekaler Katha* (Calcutta 1949), vol.i, p.301.
39. Ibid.
40. *Hindoo Patriot*, 8 September 1862.
41. H.H. Risley, *The People of India* (Calcutta 1908), Appendix I, xi.
42. Bhola Nauth Chunder, *The Travels of a Hindoo* (Calcutta 1869), vol.i. p.36, vol.ii, xvii.
43. Bhattarcharya, op.cit., pp.198-199.
44. Bose, op.cit., pp.2-3.
45. Ibid., p.3.
46. *Sadharani*, 19 April 1874.
47. N.N. Ghose, op.cit., p.175.
48. Grish Ghandra Ghose, op.cit., pp.35-38.
49. *Samvad Prabhakar*, 29 April 1842.
50. *Calcutta Christian Observer*, vol.x, No.104 (Old Series) (January 1841), pp.67-68.
51. *Hindoo Patriot*, 11 January 1875, 18 January 1975.
52. N.N. Laha, *Suvarnavanik: Katha O Kirti* (Calcutta 1940-2), vol.ii, pp.152-191. Over 1000 Saptagram Suvarnavaniks attended the meeting, but they did not include all the leading Saptagram Suvarnavaniks in Calcutta.
53. L.N. Ghose, op.cit., p.51.
54. For a general division of some of these groups see H.H. Wilson, *Essays and Lectures* (London 1862), vol.i., Section iii, pp.30-33.
55. L.N. Ghose, op.cit., p.228.
56. Grish Chunder Ghose, op.cit., p.38.
57. H.H. Risley and E.A. Gait, *Census of India 1901, vol.i India* (Calcutta 1903), p.541.
58. Bhattacharya, op.cit., p.160.
59. Chunder, op.cit., vol.i. p.40.
60. For a theoretical discussion of this concept see Louis Dumont, 'The Conception of Kingship in Ancient India', *Religion-Politics and History in India*

(The Hague 1970), pp.62-89.

61. The Seal household, for example, had over 140 rooms. See Calcutta Municipal Assessments, 1857, Book 47, p.37.

62. Sen, op.cit., p.35.

63. Ibid., pp.52-53.

64. Risley and Gait, op.cit., p.542.

65. *Bhattarcharya*, op.cit., p.471.

66. Ibid., p.124.

67. P.G. O'Kinealy (ed.), *The Calcutta Law Reports of Cases Decided by The High Court Calcutta* (Calcutta 1878), vol.i, p.567.

68. Bose, op.cit., pp.14-18.

69. *Bhattacharya*, op.cit., pp.306-7.

70. See, for example, 'Religious and Charitable Endowments of Bengali Zamindars', *Calcutta Review*, vol. ccxxi, (1900), pp.88-99. vol.ccxxii, (1900), pp. 223-249.

71. *Hindoo Patriot*, 9 July 1866.

72. *Calcutta Review*, vol.ccxxi, (1900), pp.88-89.

73. Panchanan Roy Kabuatirtha, *Pratasmaraniya Tarachnath Pramanick* (Midnapore 1937), p.10.

74. This problem is examined at length in J. McGuire, 'Political Leadership Among Hindus in Calcutta: 1857-1885', Unpublished Ph.D. Thesis, University of London, 1976.

THE MUSLIMS OF LUCKNOW - 1919-1939

Sarojini Ganju

Lucknow derives its significance as a focal point for the study of Muslims in an urban framework from its antecedents, as a Muslim capital during the reign of the Shia Nawabs of Oudh. In 1775 A.D. the seat of government of the Nawabs was transferred from Faizabad to Lucknow, and with the establishment of the court Lucknow flourished as the centre of a culture, the idiom of which was overwhelmingly Muslim, and the dominant manifestations of which were expressed in a subtlety of language, a specialization of craftsmanship, and a refinement of dress and etiquette. It remained the prime city of the province until 1856, when the kingdom of Oudh was annexed by proclamation by the British, and the last king of Oudh, Wajid Ali Shah, was deposed. With the successful crushing of the revolt of 1857, and the shifting of the centre of governmental activity from Lucknow to Allahabad, Lucknow entered a period of decline, but the character and culture of the city continued to bear the stamp of Nawabi days, even in the twentieth century.

This paper attempts to evaluate the extent to which elements from the historical and religious background of the city continued to affect the fabric of society that had generated this culture; and to illustrate how the past exerted an influence on the perception of the Muslim citizens of themselves, both within and outside the community.

Broadly speaking, the paper is divided into two sections. In the first the structure of the Muslim society of Lucknow is examined in terms of the size and character of its population, the nature of its distribution within the city, its occupational structure, and the nature of its leadership; then, various levels of political activity in the city are discussed in order to determine the degree to which traditional factors affected the Muslim politics of the city, and to illustrate the dynamics of that society.

In terms of the composition of its population, one perceptible historical effect was that Lucknow remained a stronghold of the Shia sect. This did not mean that they were numerically preponderant, just that they were

279

more heavily concentrated in Lucknow than the norm.
However, since the annexation of Oudh the proportion
of Shias to Sunnis had declined, perhaps owing to the
disappearance of the influence of the Royal Family.
In 1901, 84 per cent of the Muslim population were
recorded as belonging to the Sunni sect.[1] Muslims
throughout the period constituted slightly over a
third of the city population (in 1921, 88,797 of a
population of 240,566 were recorded as Muslims, in
1941, 137,481 of a population of 387,177)[2] a ratio
which seemed to have remained fairly static from
Nawabi days.

Another visible effect of that period was the
fact that in the city the muhallas which had the
highest concentration of an exclusively Muslim population were located in the section which had earliest
been built by the Nawabs, around the Chauk (e.g. the
muhallas of Deorhi Agha Mir, Chikmandi, Golaganj,
Kashmiri Muhalla). The sheer number of mosques in this
area also indicates where the Muslim centre of the
city had been situated. It is necessary to point out,
however, that though there may have been areas of Hindu
or Muslim predominance in the city in the period under
discussion, spatial segregation was not ghetto-like,
and there were many muhallas in which the distribution
of the Hindu and Muslim populations was fairly propor-
tional.[3] Under the Nawabs, the Chauk had been the
nucleus of the old city, a residential area, the area
in which were located the handicraft workers - silversmiths, chikan embroiderers etc.- and, no less important in the context of the social life of Lucknow, the
prostitutes.[4] The fact that this area retained its
essentially Muslim and multi-purpose character into
the twentieth century must be explained by the fact
that most of these crafts were organized on a family
basis, that certain areas had come to be associated
with certain occupations, and also perhaps that the
demand for the products of these craftsmen remained
highest within the locality. It may also have shown a
general unwillingness of the Muslims to move into new
areas, and, indeed, the two newest wards of the city,
Hazratganj and Hassanganj, showed the thinnest concentration of Muslims. With the establishment of British
rule, two new hubs of activity grew and developed -
Aminabad and Hazratganj. The former was a melange of
an indigenous retail shopping area, with food and
vegetable markets of different kinds; the latter was

the area in which most of the modern banking, insurance and government offices were situated, and it also developed into a retail shopping centre which had branches of various European concerns, chemists, etc. Lucknow displayed a striking contrast between a densely populated indigenous section and a large Anglicized part, which supposedly is characteristic of all cities with pre-British origins.[5]

The imprint of the Nawabi period was not only evident in the physical distribution of the Muslims in the city, but also in the nature of the occupations they pursued. With the balance of population as it stood it is but natural to have expected that the Hindus would outnumber Muslims in most occupations; that they do not always do so is significant, and certain trends become apparent. In the census of 1911, the occupations of slightly over 50 per cent of the Muslim population in Lucknow are described under the category of 'Preparation and supply of material substances'. They dominate in the textile industry, particularly in the production of lace, as embroiderers etc., but not in cotton ginning, cleaning, spinning. They are also preponderant in the manufacture of articles of dress and toilet, especially as tailors; in the 'industries of luxury and those pertaining to arts and sciences' - as bookbinders, manufacturers of beads, bangles, toys, musical instruments, as printers, composers of music etc. Apart from two firms, the perfumery of Asghar Ali and Mohammad Ali established in 1839, and the tobacco manufacturing firm of Ahmad Husain Dildar Husain, the involvement of Muslims in the trade of the city was confined to small-scale activity.[6] They dominated the trade in clothing and toilet articles, in tobacco, opium and ganja, in hides and skins, and as butchers, but were almost completely absent from the class that was involved in money-lending and brokerage. Certain elements of this pattern of urban occupational distribution seem to characterize the Muslim provincial population at large, for instance, their overwhelming preponderance in the textile industry; however, their absence from participation in money-lending is at variance with the provincial figure, which suggests that most of those who lived off banking and money-lending were Muslim. One wonders whether the sanction in Islam against usury operated more strongly in Lucknow, which was the centre of Muslim influence, than in areas which were not so directly under the influence of the court. To a large extent the fact that a higher proportion of Muslims than Hindus lived in towns, and therefore followed more urban pursuits can explain these trends, but it is clear that these professions were geared to the demands of a court, and were perpetuated by an elite that maintained the pleasure-cum-leisure-oriented existence of its forebearers.

The feudal structure under the Nawabs of Oudh was probably also responsible for the dominance of Muslims in the category of agents and managers of landed estates, amongst those who derived their income from land, and their absence from the category of cultivators. Also, the fact that a much higher number of Muslims than Hindus were completely unproductive and survived on inherited wealth or pensions, and as beggars, vagrants and prostitutes, can almost certainly be attributed to the disappearance of the Oudh court.

How far did the Muslims respond to the new occupational opportunities that resulted from the establishment of British rule? They took hardly any advantage of the employment opportunities offered by the post office, telephone and telegraph services, and had little to do with the construction of roads and railways, though in the railway and administrative services they were represented, and in fact recruitment took place on the basis of communal ratios. In the professional categories Muslims outnumbered the Hindus in the categories of medicine and instruction, which would seem to indicate that at least in Lucknow until 1911 they were no more backward than Hindus; the latter did, however, dominate in the field of law, though in terms of the distribution of the population the figure was by no means disproportionate.[7]

New employment opportunities must have been created in the period under discussion, with the building of a railway workshop, and the gradual shift of governmental offices from Allahabad to Lucknow, but the Census of 1931 suggests that there were no really significant shifts in the occupational pattern of Lucknow.[8]

The impact of British rule did not foster much economic change in Lucknow because of the very nature of its impact. Unlike Calcutta, where administrative changes, the development of a market in land, and the growth of industry disrupted the traditional economy, in Oudh the bolstering of an essentially feudal element in making land revenue arrangements and the lack of industrial development meant that the structure of the economy remained feudal. But even within the limited sphere of economic activity created by the British - the post office, the construction of roads and railways - the Hindus were predominant. This may have been because the Hindus were more pragmatic in their approach to British rule; perhaps also the Muslims wanted to resist the changes being imposed on them by an alien culture. Certainly this was the case in nineteenth century Calcutta where the Hindus dominated socio-economically, and where 'the vast majority of Muslims had neither the inclination nor the skill required for the type of administrative posts open to the Indians, nor for the areas of economic activity which received a new impetus under the British.'[9]

The Muslim community may have shown great internal economic differentiation, but there were ties of solidarity that cut across class lines: the domestic servants were dependent on their masters, the artisans on their patrons. To whom did authority accrue in this situation? It is evident that the participation of the small artisan, petty shopkeeper, or domestic servant in the activities and administration of the city would, in the colonial context of local self-government, be negligible. The people who would be able to exercise some power and influence would be those who could parley on some level with the government, those important within the community's own institutional framework, or the wealthy or educated person who could make his influence felt in a certain area. In the Muslim community wealthy traders were few, so this usually meant the landowners, taluqdars or zamindars, the ulama, the old aristocracy - who were heirs and dependants of the Nawabs of Oudh - and the newly emerging class of Western-educated lawyers and doctors.

The taluqdars, Hindu and Muslim, owned large estates, particularly in the Lucknow and Faizabad divisions, but often resided in the city. Many were descendants of the 'little kings', autocrats or heads of local lineages, who had managed to establish local rule in the Nawabi period.[10] After the Mutiny land had been restored to them by granting them *sanads,* and the government had bolstered their position even further by giving some of them the power to deal with revenue disputes and act as Deputy Magistrates, and by introducing primogeniture. The British Indian Association formed in 1861 was the organ through which they communicated with government, and they were given a meeting place and town residence in the Qaisarbagh Palace in Lucknow.[11] As a group the taluqdars contributed one-sixth of the total revenue of the province, but they were conscious of their dependence on government and staunchly supported British rule.[12] Under the British, they still regarded themselves as 'natural leaders' of society, as they had not grasped the implications of the change in the nature of the landlord-tenant relationship from a paternalistic to a legalistic one. It was not until the thirties, when the position of the taluqdars was increasingly challenged by the professional clases that they began to organise themselves politically.

Lucknow's survival as the cultural centre of Oudh can to a large extent be attributed to them. They were responsible for the maintenance of the Nawabi life-style - the continued patronage of poets and musicians, the *mushaira*, the nautch parties, the wearing of finely-embroidered cotton Angarkhas and caps that could cost the sight of several workmen.[13] In a sense, Lucknow's renewed importance in the twentieth century owed a great deal to them. Though Sir Harcourt Butler, the Lieutenant Governor of the United Provinces (1918-1921), emphatically refuted the suggestion that the transference of the Council Chamber from Allahabad implied an eventual permanent shift of the Secretariat to Lucknow, this was exactly what did happen: there was no secret about his predilection for Lucknow - 'the city of parks and palaces', 'the centre of learning and literature' - and his sympathy for the taluqdars.[14] The taluqdars were responsible for much good that was wrought in the city. They contributed liberally towards the establishment of educational institutions: they raised Rs.25,000 annually for the support of Canning College,[15] and when in the early twenties it was decided to establish Lucknow University they donated Rs.30 lakhs towards its foundation.[16] The latter institution owed its origin to an idea originally mooted by the Raja of Mahmudabad, which was taken up by Sir Harcourt Butler, who was also a close friend. Ironically enough, though the taluqdars may have contributed to social and educational progress by helping to establish institutions, as a group they

did not particularly encourage Western education among
their own kind. The low figure of enrolment at Colvin
Taluqdars' School, a school meant for the sons of
taluqdars, would indicate this. The prevailing ethos
seemed to be that Western education would be pointless,
as they in fact would not have to earn their living,
and stress continued to be laid on Urdu, Arabic and
religious education. It should be mentioned, too, that
the taluqdars were possibly the only class in the city
that could have used their capital to encourage and
develop industry. That they did not do so was another
reflection of their traditional and patrician mode of
thinking and functioning.

As an influential body of men the taluqdars were
always represented on the Lucknow Municipal Board, on
university councils, and on various other organizations,
but direct participation in municipal politics was rare,
as they considered it beneath their dignity to behave
like 'horse-traders' and fight for votes.[17] Indirectly,
however, they could influence municipal politics as
many of the city-based lawyers who were active partici-
pants depended on them for their work.

However, it was as individuals, rather than as a
group, that the taluqdars made their greatest impact
on the rest of the community. The Raja of Mahmudabad,
for instance, was conspicuously active. He could
appeal to the ordinary Muslim in the street by riding
at the head of a procession,[18] and to the newly
qualified lawyer Choudhry Khaliquzzaman by keeping him
employed as Education Secretary when Vice-Chancellor
of Aligarh College - a job with 'hardly any work' plus
'Rs.350 a month with horse and carriage'.[19] He helped
to support the Sunni ulama of Firangi Mahal, endowed
numerous schools, had money distributed to beggars
each time he came to Lucknow.[20] He generally refrained
from anti-governmental activity after Sir Harcourt
Butler was appointed Lieutenant-Governor of U.P., but
when guided by conviction he would stir up agitation.
He defied the attitude of his fellow taluqdars and was
responsible for the 'Simon, go back' black balloons,
which were floated into a reception given in honour
of the Simon Commission in Lucknow by the British
Indian Association.[21] Men like him derived their
position from birth, privilege and wealth, but it
seems unlikely that they would have maintained it
without some intrinsic quality.

A section of the Muslim community that retained

prestige but had a limited sphere of authority or influence, were the descendants of the dependants and pensioners of the Court of Oudh. Provision had been made for their maintenance in the endowment established as the Husainabad Trust, money which had been deposited with the British resident in the reign of King Muhammad Ali Shah, and the interest of which was dispensed monthly to pay pensions.[22] On the death of a recipient these pensions were divided among the heirs of the deceased; this process had reduced some pensions to mere pittances, and may of these people were extremely impoverished. In 1913, there were 1,661 *wasikadars* in Lucknow; this figure must have increased considerably by 1939. These people made little or no effort to adapt to the change in circumstances that befell them, considered it derogatory to earn their own living, and rather than do so sold what little land they possessed, and became increasingly indebted to the Rastogi money-lenders by pawning their jewellery. In the early decades of the twentieth century the government grew alarmed at the 'straitened means and illiterate condition of many of these wasikadars' as they became progressively poorer, and began to encourage them to take to Western education by granting them scholarships.[23]

Some semblance of cohesion was given to this group of people by the formation of the Oudh Ex-Royal Family Association, and the Oudh Wasikadars and Political Pensioners Association. Apart from the context of petitioning government against Home Rule, for representation on the Legislative Councils, and about the management of Trusts, they were rather ineffectual organs.[24] The British to a certain extent propped them up by giving them token representation on various boards and committees and thus helped them to cling to the myth of their own importance. The *wasikadars* dwelt very much in the past, and their attitude to the changes that were taking place around them is exemplified by the fact that some of the Nawabs who claimed to be direct descendants of the Royal Family held darbars at least until the early 'twenties.[25] In reality, however, they were voices crying in the wilderness, though nostalgia could and did arouse some, particularly the Shias, to react to them.

The pronouncements of the ulama carried much weight, particularly among the poorer section of the Muslim community; political participation in a movement

or the settlement of disputes often depended on their
intercession.   In Lucknow their influence was height-
ened by the fact that it was the centre of ulama of
various schools.   The Sunni school of Farangi Mahal
could trace its origin to the Nawabi period, but two
new schools had come to be established, the Nadwat-ul-
ulama in the 1890s, and the Dar-ul-Muballaghin in 1931.
The former was established as an institution to combine
the best of Islamic and western learning, the latter
was a militantly anti-Shia seminary.[26]   The issues that
roused the ulama were fundamentally of a religious
nature - the fate of the Khilafat, or the future of
Palestine - and they could whip up the enthusiasm of
the masses on these issues.   In politics, their primary
interest was the fate of Islam rather than the control
of legislatures or the attainment of self-government,
but neither the politicians nor the government could
ignore the potential influence with which these men
could sway the masses.

Apart from these elements that derived their
influence from an appeal to tradition, birth or ritual
status, a new middle class was emerging of Western-
educated lawyers, doctors and government servants,
who also attained powerful positions within the
community.   Though to a certain extent their social
influence was based on the fact that they belonged to
specific professions, patronage often played a role
in their advancement.   In the city the municipality
served as their political stepping-stone and platform.

An example of the rise to prominence of a member
of this class can be found in the career of Choudhry
Khaliquzzaman, who was Chairman of the Lucknow Municipal Board three times, 1923-26, 1929-32, 1936-45,
an active member of the Congress, and in the late
1930s of the Muslim League.   His father had been a
naib tahsildar; he himself was educated at the
Government School in Lucknow, then at Aligarh
University.   After university he found a patron for
some time in the Raja of Mahmudabad, and then established his own practice by alternately being junior
to his uncle, Mohammed Nasim, who was one of the
leading practitioners of the Oudh Bar, and to his
uncle's son, Mohammed Wasim.   He joined the Congress
in 1916, and was a member of the Reception Committee
of the Congress Session held in the same year.   From
then on he was active both in city and provincial
level politics.[27]

This class of men shared a common educational background and interest in political activity with their Hindu counterparts. They started off as champions of a class, but over a period of time through constantly being in the public eye - on managing boards of schools, as office-bearers of trade unions, as members of municipal boards - they emerged as public spokesmen, and finally, as defenders of their own community. It was this class of men who were caught in the mid-1930s (with the passing of the Government of India Act of 1935, the formation of a Congress Ministry in U.P., and the re-organization of the Muslim League) between their identity as Muslims in a minority province, and as nationalist politicians. Some, indeed, tried to keep a foot in both camps - for example, Khaliquzzaman himself, or Syed Ali Zaheer. When this stance ceased to be possible Khaliquzzaman opted for the Muslim League, Syed Ali Zaheer for the Congress.

Initiative for any form of political activity within the community stemmed from one or more of these elites, but there was little solidarity, and factionalism made itself evident even within these groups. The taluqdars and professional classes shared a common cultural matrix with the Hindu members of their class, and for the major part of our period their political attitudes were dictated more by class than communal interests. Often they were at odds with the ulama and the descendants of the Royal Family who tended to associate themselves with retrogressive movements.

In the following section certain issues that involved the Muslims of Lucknow, either exclusively or in their interaction with the Hindus, are chosen as the framework within which to examine the extent to which traditional factors continued to affect the nature of political activity within the city, and also to analyse how the various levels of leadership came into conflict or allied with one another. It should be mentioned that the stress is on the internal structure of city politics rather than on relations with provincial or national politics.

The Nawabi heritage of a complex of institutions and customs was a field in which various elements of the Shia leadership tried to maintain or establish

dominance. Any attempt at reform represented a threat
to the prestige or influence of the ulama, or the Oudh
Ex-Royal Family, and was resisted. Government, as
administrator and final arbiter, was wary of disrupting
traditional practices, and invariably this resulted in
the maintenance of the status quo. To choose one
example, a Bill introduced in the Legislative Assembly
by the Shia lawyer, Syed Ali Zaheer, in 1935, to reform
the administration of the various trusts set up by the
Nawabs was met by a great deal of opposition from the
Shias in the city. The Trusts had a wide range of
functions, which included the distribution of pensions
and of money for pilgrimages, the upkeep of the Asafud-
daula mosque, and supervision and provision for the
celebration of festivals. The Bill sought to democra-
tize the administration of the trusts; it was based on
the contention that since the whole Shia community
was affected by it they should have a voice in the
administration. According to the stipulation made by
the founder of the trust, the trustees were to be
selected from descendants of the Royal Family. That
the Oudh Ex-Royal Family Association came out vehe-
mently against the Bill is not at all surprising as it
undermined their influence within the community, but
what is, is that the very people whose welfare the
Bill sought to improve claimed that the change was
against the founder's wishes, that it went against the
Islamic Law of Trusts. This was clearly an indication
of the amount of influence that the Oudh Ex-Royal
Family could still bring to bear: the various meetings
held among the Shia residents, which resulted in the
despatch of memorials to government, were organized
by them. What seems equally clear is that the implications of the Bill were not explained or not understood. That the Bill was stopped was due in no small
measure to the public opinion that the Oudh Ex-Royal
Family had been able to arouse.[28] But the same Bill,
introduced by the same lawyer, was passed after Independence - perhaps a reflection of the change in their
position vis-a-vis the community.

We may now turn to the Shia community's relationship with the Sunni community of the city, in the
context of the Shia-Sunni riots of the late 'thirties.
In the post-1937 era, when many other cities in U.P.
were convulsed by communal riots, Lucknow remained
singularly immune to them, but was the scene of
sectarian riots. How and why did a traditional

rivalry persist in modern day politics?

In addition to the doctrinal disagreement, the roots of this rivalry in Lucknow must have lain in the dominant position occupied by the Shias under the Nawabs. This was underlined by the scale and manner of their religious festivals. Asaf-ud-Daula is reputed to have spent from Rs.5 to 6 lakhs during the Muharram.[29] With the disappearance of the Nawab's court, their influence must have gradually declined, and as they were a minority, the fear, or perhaps the reality, of Sunni domination began to take hold. It has been suggested that land in the city was passing from Shia to Sunni hands,[30] but evidence is lacking.

However, it was under British rule that the rivalry was in a sense institutionalized, and consequently intensified. The agitation of the 'thirties, though on a much larger scale, bore some resemblance to an earlier conflict in 1905, when for the first time the Shias and Sunnis were made to take their *tazias* to separate *Karbalas* during Muharram, and the Sunnis to impart a distinctive quality to their celebration recited the *Madh-e-Sahaba* (praises of the first four Caliphs). Rioting ensued, and a government committee, known as the Piggott Committee, was appointed to make an inquiry. On the basis of their findings it was agreed that the recitation of the *Madh-e-Sahaba* verses during *tazia* processions should be prohibited in public places on Ashra, Chehlum and 21st Ramazan. The government passed an order to that effect, an order which represented a victory to the Shias.

The issue was re-opened in 1935 when two Sunnis courted arrest for inciting their co-religionists to disobey these orders. The following year the Sunnis applied to the local authorities to be allowed to take out a *Madh-e-Sahaba* procession on the Barawafat (the Prophet's Birthday), and on being refused permission they began to take more direct action. Every Friday there were processions reciting the *Madh-e-Sahaba*, in spite of prohibitory orders from the District Magistrate. This state of affairs continued for over three months, and many arrests were made. The Sunnis petitioned the Governor for permission to recite the *Madh-e-Sahaba*; the Shias petitioned him because such recitation offended their religious susceptibilities. Shia and Sunni leaders tried to reach a settlement and failed. Then the government appointed another committee - the Allsopp Committee.[31]

Meanwhile, the Sunnis called off their agitation, and those arrested were released.

But relations worsened after the publication of the Allsopp Committee report in March 1938. This upheld the conclusions of the earlier Piggott committee. The Sunnis, dissatisfied, pressed the government for permission to allow the recitation of the *Madh-e-Sahaba*, under threat of a civil disobedience movement. This was instituted in March 1939, and the government began to consider a concession to Sunni demands. This unleashed intense rioting between the two communities. Then the government issued a communique allowing the Sunnis to recite the *Madh-e-Sahaba* every year in procession on Barawafat day. The Shias thought that they had the authority of two committees, and the practice of thirty years, in support of their position. They began a civil disobedience movement - the *tabarra* (criticism of the Caliphs) agitation - and very large numbers went to jail.[32]

For most of the Muslim masses who participated in this agitation, the issue only had a religious dimension - they were protecting the tenets of their faith - and indeed, this was how most of the ulama perceived the issue, and why they urged the masses to act. In fact, in the first phase an *alim* from Dar-ul-Muballaghin played a fairly important role in initiating the movement. The elites reacted on a religious plane as well, but there were political overtones that accentuated and perpetuated the controversy.

Neither the Sunnis nor the Shias presented a united front. Though all Sunnis may have sympathized with the demand for the public recital of the *Madh-e-Sahaba*, the more educated Sunnis wanted to achieve this right by presenting some form of demand to government. It was the local Ahrari party 'which was numerically very weak, and contained no man of even moderate social position in its ranks' that decided to initiate the *Madh-e-Sahaba* processions. When they were arrested, others replaced them. The people in the bazar were attracted to the movement in increasing numbers. It seems, too, that the movement was encouraged by political interests; it was believed that 'Choudhry Khaliquzzaman has exercised a pernicious influence taking pains to stiffen Sunni opinion'.[33] In the context of the impending elections of 1937, which Khaliquzzaman, a Sunni politician, was fighting from Lucknow city on the Muslim League ticket, this would seem to make sense.[34]

But after 1937, it seemed that the Congress used the issue. The *Madh-e-Sahaba* agitation was revived largely under the leadership of Maulana Husain Ahmad Madani, who was a member of the U.P. Congress Committee. The desire to conciliate the Sunnis would seem to be an adequate explanation for the change in the government's position; but it has also been suggested that there was an agreement between the Maulana and Pant, the Congress Premier of U.P., that if the former would support Pant's resolution against the Congress President, Subhas Chandra Bose, at the Congress session at Tripura, then a claim for public recitation of the *Madh-e-Sahaba* would be acceded to.

The Shias reacted unanimously against the government's communique in 1939 - the masses and the ulama on a religious basis, and the more Westernized elites for political reasons. The latter belonged to one or other of two organizations, the Tanzeem-ul-Momineen, and the All-India Shia Political Conference. The former was formed in the wake of the *Madh-e-Sahaba* agitation, in May 1938, to protect the social, political and religious rights of the Shias. It was a militant body, which in fact threatened to start the *tabarra* agitation even before the issuing of the government communique; it was basically an anti-Congress organization, and claimed that the Congress was out to impose the domination of the majority section of the Muslims on the minority, and to secure the maximum number of votes it could at elections. Diametrically opposed to this was the All-India Shia Political Conference, which had always taken and maintained its pro-Congress position. Throughout the *tabarra* agitation it issued no resolutions supporting it, but offered the Ministry its mediation in order to bring the agitation to a close; as this was refused it felt that the only weapon that was left was direct action.[35]

However, the politicians had probably overreached themselves and were hard put to find a solution, as the agitation dragged over a long period. Various attempts were made at reconciliation, but sporadic riots continued to occur, and it was not till the following year that the agitation lost momentum.

The various attitudes adopted by the Muslims in the Shia-Sunni conflict would indicate that the community was politically very segmented. How did they project

themselves as a group vis-a-vis the Hindus of the
city? In Lucknow communal relations were generally
harmonious. In an age when it was difficult to dissociate communal politics from what was happening in
the wider arena of provincial/national politics, why
did Lucknow remain immune to communal outbreaks?

In Lucknow, there was no marked socio-economic
differentiation between the two communities, and as
has already been stated there had not been any major
dislocations in the local economy, unlike other U.P.
cities. Also, though there may not have been much
fraternization at the lower rungs of society, for
generations there had been areas in which both
communities lived and accepted each other. At the top
Hindus who belonged to the professional and administrative classes did not come into conflict with their
Muslim colleagues, as they belonged to the Brahmin,
Kashmiri Brahmin and Kayastha elites, who had also
been service communities under the Nawabs. They
shared the language and the life style of their
Muslim colleagues.

At the municipal level, what is striking is the
degree to which compromise and harmony remained the
keynotes of political behaviour whenever any issue
arose which could have upset the relations between the
communities on the Board and occasionally even when
political interests were at variance. Though the
separate representation provided for in the U.P.
Municipalities Act was first received by the Hindus
with a complete boycott, an amicable settlement in
Lucknow caused the government to raise the number of
members from 30 to 36. There was also an unwritten
understanding that a Muslim chairman would alternate
with a Hindu one, and that Shia and Sunni constitu-
encies would be defined.[36] Even when Khaliquzzaman
began openly to support the creation of Pakistan, and
the life of the Board was extended during the war,
Hindu members of the Municipal Board continued to
support him.[37]

Throughout the period under discussion there was
only one small communal outbreak in Lucknow - over the
issue of temple music in a certain park disturbing
Muslim prayers. That it occurred at all was probably
due to the fact that ripples from a similar riot in the
neighbouring village of Amethi were felt in Lucknow.
Religious leaders and politicians from Lucknow became
involved in the incident, and several public meetings

were held in Lucknow which aroused communal passions.
Though in the city a settlement was quickly
arrived at, on the Municipal Board the issue of whether
the park could be used as a meeting place for prayer
remained a bone of contention between the extremist
Hindu party and the Muslims for some time. From
attempts to settle the issue, however, it is clear that
the problem had acquired a political dimension as well.

For instance, when a Hindu member of the Board
tabled a motion that Muslim prayers should not be
offered in the park as it contravened a municipal bye-
law, the Chairman, Khaliquzzaman, managed to influence
Hindu members, and there was unanimous agreement not
to support the motion.[38] This caused the Hindu and
Muslim members great unpopularity; the next municipal
election was fought on this issue and resulted in a
Board with strong Mahasabhite tendencies among the
Hindus. When permission was asked to hold prayers in
the park, the eleven Hindu members voted against the
resolution, the eleven Muslim members for the resolution, and the Chairman, a Hindu, tossed a coin.
Unfortunately the decision went against the Muslims and
led to their resignation from the Board. This was more
a matter of election tactics, rather than a reaction of
affront, as they were put up to it by the Raja of
Salempur and Chaudhuri Niamatullah who hoped to oust
the Chairman and put in their own man.[39] When the same
question came up under the new Municipal Board elected
in 1929, which was under the Chairmanship of Khaliquzzaman, the decision of the Board was against
permission being granted to the applicant to hold
prayers in the Aminabad Park and no heat or venom was
attached to the issue.[40] It would seem that on the
Board, on the whole, emotional unity was more important
than political divisions.

It seems that in the study of cities with pre-
British origins it is important to assess the extent
to which features from the past persist in the environment. Not only does this reveal the nature and degree
of social change that has occurred within the society,
but it also throws light on certain physical aspects
of the city, and on the configuration of relationships
that explain the particular manner in which city life
is carried on. It may also serve as an aid in the
classification of the cultural function that the city
performs.

In Lucknow, both the structure of Muslim society

and its functioning maintained a considerable influence
from the past in the period under discussion. The
community seemed either unable, or unwilling, to
dissociate itself from the legacies inherited from the
Nawabi era. Also, the establishment of British rule
did not foster much change as there was no major
disruption of the economy: the taluqdars were maintained, there was little industrial development, and
Lucknow did not thrive as an educational centre until
the second decade of the twentieth century. If the
classification of 'orthogenetic' and 'heterogenetic'
could be applied to communities instead of cities, the
Muslims of Lucknow would probably merit the 'orthogenetic' label, as they give the overall impression of
being conscious bearers of their culture.[41]

Ganju, 'The Muslims of Lucknow - 1919-1939'

1. *District Gazetteers of the United Provinces of Agra and Oudh*, vol.xxxvii: *Lucknow* (Allahabad 1904), hereafter referred to as DGUP, p.68.
2. *Census of India*, 1921, U.P. part II, p.34; *Census of India*, 1941, U.P., p.38f.
3. *Census of India*, 1921, U.P. part I, appendix E.
4. O.H.K. Spate and Enayat Ahmad, 'Five Cities of the Gangetic Plain - a Cross-Section of Indian Cultural History', *Geographical Review* , vol.xl (1950), pp.260-278; Mirza Ruswa (trans. Khushwant Singh and M.A. Husaini), *The Courtesan of Lucknow* (Delhi 1961), p.33.
5. J.E. Brush, 'The Morphology of Indian Cities', in Roy Turner (ed.), *India's Urban Future* (Berkeley and Los Angeles 1962), p.58.
6. C. Khaliquzzaman, *Pathway to Pakistan* (Lahore 1961), p.9.
7. *Census of India*, 1911, N.W.P. and Oudh part II, pp.578, 630, 656, 682, 704.
8. *Census of India*, 1931, U.P. part I, p.405.
9. S.N. Mukherjee, 'Class, Caste and Politics in Calcutta, 1815-1838', in E. Leach and S.N. Mukherjee (eds.), *Elites in South Asia* (Cambridge 1970), p.49.
10. P.D. Reeves, 'Landlords and Party Politics in the United Provinces, 1934-7', in D.A. Low (ed.), *Soundings in Modern South Asian History* (Berkeley and Los Angeles 1968), pp.261-291.
11. T.R. Metcalf, *The Aftermath of Revolt. India 1857-1870* (Princeton 1964), pp.154-162.
12. On the taluqdars of Oudh, Butler Papers, India Office Records MSS Eur. F116/75.
13. A. Hosain, *Sunlight on a Broken Column* (London 1961), p.33.
14. Butler, reply to a deputation of citizens from Allahabad, 23 July 1921, MSS Eur. F116/75; reply to farewell address presented by members of the Lucknow Municipal Board, December 1921, MSS Eur. F116/92; cp. S.H. Butler, *Oudh Policy, the Policy of Sympathy* (Allahabad 1906).
15. DGUP, p.130.
16. Butler, speech at the laying of the foundation stone of Lucknow University, 19 March 1921, MSS Eur.

F116/91.

17. A. Hosain, op.cit., p.256.
18. Intelligence Dept Records, Lucknow, 1926.
19. C. Khaliquzzaman, op.cit., p.35.
20. F. Robinson, *Separatism among Indian Muslims, the Politics of the United Provinces' Muslims, 1860-1923* (Cambridge 1974), p.419; C. Khaliquzzaman, op.cit., p.6.
21. C. Khaliquzzaman, op.cit., p.92.
22. Deputy Commissioner to Commissioner, Lucknow Division, 24 April 1935, U.P. Secretariat Records, Local Self-Government Dept., File 142.
23. Commissioner, Lucknow Division to Chief Secretary, U.P., 24 September 1912, U.P. State Archives, Political Dept., File 42.
24. Proceedings of a meeting of the Oudh Ex-Royal Family Association, 13 November 1917, General Administration Proceedings, part A, February 1918; Local Self-Government Dept., File 142, passim.
25. Interview with Mirza Mohammed Jafar Husain (formerly Secretary, All-India Shia Political Conference), 3 March 1975.
26. I.H. Qureshi, *Ulema in Politics* (Karachi 1972), p.233; P. Hardy, *The Muslims of British India* (Cambridge 1972), p.245.
27. C. Khaliquzzaman, op.cit., pp.5,13f,35,38,148.
28. Husainabad and Allied Endowments Administration Bill, 1935, Local Self-Government Dept., File 142.
29. J.N. Hollister, *The Shi'a of India* (London 1956), p.156.
30. Interview with Sri B. Tandon.
31. Report of the Allsopp Committee, pp.1-21, U.P. Gazette Extraordinary, 1938.
32. Note on Lucknow Shia Sunni controversy, National Archives of India, Home Dept., Political File 5/6/39.
33. Governors' Reports, U.P., 7 June 1937.
34. C. Khaliquzzaman, op.cit., p.151.
35. *History of the All-India Shia Political Conference* (Lucknow 1941), passim.
36. Interview with Syed Ali Zaheer, December 1974.
37. C. Khaliquzzaman, op.cit., p.149.
38. Ibid., p.71.
39. General Administration Dept., 1927, U.P. Secretariat Records, File 503.
40. Annual Administration Report, Lucknow Municipality, 1928-9.

41. R. Redfield and M. Singer, 'The Cultural Role of Cities', *Economic Development and Cultural Change*, iii, 1 (October 1954), pp.53-79; M. Singer, *When a Great Tradition Modernizes. An Anthropological Approach to Indian Civilization* (London 1972), pp.6-9, et passim.

AN URBAN MINORITY: THE GOAN CHRISTIAN COMMUNITY IN KARACHI

Raffat Khan Haward

For well over a century there have been Goans in Karachi - since the British conquest of Sind in 1843, or, as the Goans themselves believe, since an earlier time. Throughout these years, and especially since 1947 when for a while it became a capital city in addition to being a major port, Karachi has been actively growing and sharply changing. But though the social context and external constraints within which they have had to operate have altered drastically, the Karachi Goans have survived as a notably successful minority. It will be argued that they have done so because of their control of highly valued educational and health services and their possession of indispensable skills, and that the control of these assets has been dependent upon the preservation of a collective ideal of Goan identity.

The Growth of the Community[1]

In 1839 forces of the Bombay army of the English East India Company occupied Karachi, then no more than a primitive trading settlement,[2] as a base for war in Afghanistan. With the army and its supply train came Goan clerks and camp followers. In 1843 Sind was conquered and annexed to the Bombay Presidency, Karachi becoming a garrison town, administrative centre and port for the new possession.[3] Subsequently the abolition of inland duties in Sind, the creation of an effective police force, the improvement of roads and the introduction of the Indus Flotilla Steamship Company operating up river to Multan greatly developed trade within Sind.[4] The opening of the railway linking Karachi to Kotri on the Indus in 1861 and of the Multan-Lahore railway line in 1865, tapping the trade of the Panjab, led to the steady development of Karachi as the port of the whole Indus valley.[5] The cotton boom in western India and the Panjab at the time of the American Civil War, the opening of the Suez Canal in 1869 and the harbour improvements which by 1873 had made Karachi an all-weather ocean port, established the city yet more firmly as a major commercial centre.[6]

KARACHI

In 1844 trade through Karachi was worth some Rs. 2,250,000 - in 1874 some Rs.33,500,000.[7] The 14,000 inhabitants of 1843 grew in 25 years to nearly 60,000.[8] Among the immigrants were more Goans, serving as clerks and other lower-echelon staff in government offices, in the army and in business, and as cooks, tailors or personal servants.

The concentration in two main areas of these immigrant Goans led to the founding of Catholic churches to minister them. The chapel dedicated to the Sacred Heart of Jesus at Kiamari served the port, its parishioners being employed in the port area, customs and shipping companies and as suppliers to ships crews in port,[9] while St Patrick's Church, the later Cathedral, first built in 1845 in the Cantonment, served the camp area.[10] The baptismal registers for St Patrick's for 1863 record that out of a total of 98 baptisms, 34 were of Goan children. Of the fathers of these 34, seven were cooks, seven clerks, five soldiers in the native infantry (probably bandsmen), four were apothecaries, four musicians, together with a baker, a butler, a ship's steward, a bugler, a hospital attendant and a deputy postmaster. The Goans here, as elsewhere in British India, made their way by filling in the interstices in the occupational structure. But if structurally and culturally marginal to the society with which they had to interact, they were a cohesive minority. The parish structure was one organizing principle. But as early as 1869 enough Goans were present in the city for a suggestion to be mooted that a reading room and library be set up for the development and improvement of the Goans. A secular organization thus appeared alongside the religious organizations active under the aegis of the Church, one which was the precursor of the Goan Portuguese Association.[11]

From 1878, when the last link in the railway system connecting Karachi with the Panjab and Delhi was completed, the city enjoyed even more dramatic growth. Karachi could now compete successfully with Calcutta and Bombay, and from the canal colonies established in the Panjab from 1895 onwards wheat poured down to Karachi.[12] By 1913, with 13 steamer berths at work at times handling over a million tons of wheat in the one year, Karachi was the biggest wheat exporting port in the British Empire.[13] There were 104 British and Indian business firms in the

25. KARACHI: St Joseph's convent and high school

city, a dozen banks, as many shipping companies, and a
range of ancilliary industries, steam flour mills,
cotton presses, tanneries and a wide range of local
service industries. By 1913 the population of Karachi
had reached some 160,000.[14]

Goans, Parsis, Marwaris and Gujaratis arrived from
western India in waves, and among the Goans not only
middle and upper class immigrants but an increasing
influx of working class immigrants too. This was not a
haphazard or purely individual movement, but was
organized through a characteristically Goan innovation,
the Coor (*Kur*). These Coors, or workers' residential
clubs, were first founded in Bombay.[15] Several
functions were served by them, there and in Karachi:
they were an employment agency monitoring the supply
and demand of labour by a network of intelligence
within the city, they transmitted demand to the
village, and they provided living quarters to the
newly arrived immigrant while he made his initial
forays into the city. The Coors were also socialising
transit zones, and it was here that the qualities
rewarded by the occupational structure were taught to
newcomers - by, for example, the creation of the
stereotype of impeccable honesty. The Coors, by
reassembling a familiar environment of village- and
caste-mates with whom to share the experience of city
life, made the transition easier for the newcomer and
prevented both anomie and deviancy. Each Coor had an
altar with the Sacred Heart enthroned, and the Goan,
cut off from his old moorings, was kept within the fold
of Catholicism until ties had formed with his new
parish. Even when the migrant had found employment and
his own housing he still maintained Coor ties during
his leisure hours and during the annual village Saint's
feast-day. These Coors sprang up in a section of
St Patrick's parish where there is still a lane called
the Goan Clubland, though with the cessation of
immigration the Coors are now all but defunct. The
Goan identity was also conserved and morale sustained
by the maintenance of ties with Goa. While immigrants
were content initially to occupy such niches as were
available, even menial ones, their status as respectable *Gaunkars* and *Bhatkars* back 'home' was sustained
by remittances to the family, by visits to Goa, and by
generous donations to the village Saint day celebrations, so that when the donor died he might be carried
in procession with the special banner which was to

honour those who had supported village feasts.[16]

Parish and Coor provided the setting within which
traditional family and neighbourhood structures could
be maintained or reconstructed. Catholic practices and
rituals were observed and the Goan caste system
expressed in the choice of marriage partners and in
membership of caste-based clubs. But the Jesuits who
were in control of the ecclesiastical district of
Karachi also built the schools for which St Patrick's
parish is still famous.[17] Education in a city growing
as Karachi was doing provided the community with the
means of upward mobility. In 1896 the St Patrick's
registers record 50 Goans of the parish, of whom 10
were cooks, three were tailors, and 22 were clerks,
but there were also three medical practioners, three
teachers, two engineers, plus an assistant surgeon, a
guard, an inspector and a foreman on the North-Western
Railways. In 30 years or so there had been a sharp
rise in the status and educational level of the Goans
appearing in the church registers. By the turn of the
century favourable economic conditions and the absence
of constraints had led to several Goan business enterprises being started, the major ones of which were to
be converted into public limited companies with leading
Goans as their chairmen.[18] Apart from this success in
commerce, Goans profited from the British policy of
increasing Indianisation of the civil services. Goans,
educated, literate in English and possessed of the
attributes of reliability, had the appropriate quali-
fications. And once in authority Goans were able to
operate a system of patronage favourable to their
fellows.

The period from 1914 to 1946 was an unsettled one,
with recessions in the trade of Karachi caused by the
first world war and then by the world-wide inter-war
slump.[19] However, the continued expansion of
irrigation in the Panjab and the opening of the great
Lloyd Barrage in Sind in 1932 led to a revival, though
cotton replaced wheat as the major commodity handled
by the port, some 10,000 bales in 1932, 350,000 in
1934.[20] In the second world war Karachi became an
important supply base for the Near East fronts and a
major ship repair port.[21] The separation of Sind from
the Bombay Presidency in March 1936, and the establishment of Karachi as the capital of the new province,
were a further fillip, especially for employment in
government services. The population of Karachi rose

26. KARACHI: St Lawrence Church, Cincinnatus Town

from 217,000 in 1921 to 337,000 in 1941 and the 1930s
saw the largest wave of Goan immigration ever.[22]
    The rise of population led to a major expansion of
the built up area in Karachi north-eastwards over what
had been government garden land towards the Lyari
river (the new Lyari Quarter and Garden Quarters) and
eastwards over the old cantonments, with outlying
suburbs at Kiamari and Clifton on the coast and at
Drigh Road near the airfield.[23] In this shift the
Goans participated. Even before the first world war
the increase in Goan numbers and their economic and
professional stratification had led to horizontal
mobility. Many left the crowded vicinity of the
Sadar Bazar area and of St Patrick's, now called the
'cooks' and butlers' parrish', and settled in larger
houses in Catholic colonies. The most notable of
these latter was Cincinnatus Town, established when
government garden land north of Lawrence Road to and
beyond the river was released for housing. Part of
the Garden Quarter was bought by the Goan community on
the initiative of Pedro F. D'Souza and was carefully
laid out with good roads, spaciously set bungalows, a
market, school and church, the whole being named
Cincinnatus Town after Cincinnatus D'Abreo, founder of
many Goan enterprises.[24] The Town served as physical
symbol of the success of the community, now highly
stratified and with a well-articulated elite. There
were so many eminent Goans that several streets in the
area were named after them. The Garden Quarter was
also formed into a new parish, that of St Lawrence
whose church, in the Islamic style with Mughal domes
and arches, dominated the area.[25] The cleavages
within the community to which such new settlements
gave visible expression were also given institutional
form in the two clubs, the Goan Portuguese Association
and Goan Union Hall, the first created by and for the
upper-class, high caste Goans, the second for the
lower classes.[26]
    The 1930s were a time of change for the Church too.
In 1935 Dutch Franciscans took over the Mission, and
in the same year Karachi was separated from the Bombay
Archdiocese and made a *Missio Independens*.[27] As a
counterpoise to the many secular and social associations in the community, the Church started and
encouraged many pious associations, such as the Legion
of Mary, Sodalities for men, women, boys and girls,
the Apostleship of Prayer, and the League of Night

Adoration, as a means of committing them to their
parochial community. Welfare organizations were instrumental in creating a consciousness of community.
Membership of these organizations and the social clubs
overlapped in many cases. The result was that the
social and religious life of the Goans remained well
structured. In 1937 the Franciscan Friary was built
in the city.[28] This meant an increase in vocations,
most of them Goan. The papal encyclical *Maximum
Illud* declared that the ultimate aim of missionary
endeavour was the formation of a native clergy. As a
Karachi Goan priesthood was trained to take over its
own territory, the Church became more and more
identified with the community, intensifying the
involution and synonymity of the two.[29] (The priesthood also provided yet another means of social
mobility.) While there were signs of emerging class
distinctions, of an elite being formed with incipient
cross-cultural upper-class qualities as wealthy
Westernized Goans drank or played cricket with the
British and upper-class Parsis and Hindus, other
forces were thus strengthening community solidarity.

The most modern period in Karachi history began in
1947. The immediate consequences of the partition of
British India, of the British withdrawal and the
emergence of Pakistan were drastic in the extreme.
Karachi, the chief port, became for some years the
capital also of the new Dominion. The city developed
into a major industrial centre, its 41 industrial
plants of 1947 rocketing within twenty years to over
3,000, producing a quarter of the total output of
West Pakistan.[30] The population, under 400,000 in
1947, was over a million by 1951, nearly two million
by 1961.[31] A great outflow of Hindus, many of them
business or professional men, took place, along with
a great influx of Muslim refugees, more often peasants,
artisans or labourers. In the years that followed
independence there were two wars, and repeated changes
of government and transformations of the constitution.

Briefly, partition opened new opportunities for
qualified Goans to fill the vacancies caused by the
exodus of Hindus. And though Goans, as members of a
non-Muslim group, suddenly had the legal status of a
minority thrust upon them, there were many reassur-
ances that this would have nothing to do with the
business of the State. Prosperity continued, much new
building took place, Goan resources in land and

property increased several-fold in value, and new
community housing societies were set up. But links
with Goans in India became difficult after 1961, when
Goa was incorporated into the Indian Union, Goans in
Pakistan were almost cut off from their homeland.
Goan immigration to Karachi stopped. Though new
parishes were being created in Karachi, uncertainty
and underemployment was leading to Goan emigration,
and older parishes recorded a fall in numbers: between
1960 and 1973 those in St Patrick's fell from 9,000 to
7,870 and in St Lawrence's from 2,977 to 2,071.[32]
Since many of those moving out were young people a very
visible vacuum was created - St Lawrence's parish has
become what one Goan describes as 'an old peoples'
home'.

Minority Status and Marginality

For Karachi Goans partition was a turning point. Before
1947 Roman Catholic Goans had formed a category of
persons, to use the terminology of Parsons and Shils,[33]
albeit a bounded one since no outsider could acquire
the territorial definition of being 'from Goa' though
he might become a Roman Catholic. They had optimised
their cultural attributes, achieved economic prosperity
and thrown up an elite which mediated with the over-
arching system.[34] (The success of that elite encouraged other Goans to operate within the system which had
led to its emergence and thus to produce more clients
for the elite patrons.) But in the open atmosphere of
British rule in India the community had felt no need to
reduce the social distance between its members, inhibit
the emergence of class or wipe out the internal
cleavages of caste.

After 1947, however, Goans in Karachi were driven
to evolve from a category into a collectivity. Whereas,
earlier, Goans had shared with all other communities in
India the experience of subjection to an alien British
rule, after partition they became a tiny minority among
the vast body of Muslims for whom Pakistan had been
designed as a homeland ruled according to the
principles of Islam. The constitution of Pakistan
proclaimed equality for all citizens, but Islamic
tradition prescribed for non-Muslims the status of
zimmis,[35] those excluded from politics, tolerated in
only a limited range of occupations, allowed only a
handful of personal rights. Recent election

campaigns have shown how attractive such orthodox views can be, the emphasis changing from one government and one draft of the constitution to another.

The ambiguity of the non-Muslims' position in Pakistan is sharpened by the pressures within the new state to reduce or eliminate regional, ethnic, linguistic and cultural divisions. Urdu has become the 'standard' language, a Sunnified Islam the 'official' religion, and a whole range of cultural items have become *Awami* or 'national'. Implicit in remaining Christian is a refusal to convert and therefore a rejection of this new identity. According to context Christians are seen as interlopers, reminders of colonial domination, unqualified to belong because they escaped the suffering and sacrifices of partition, and potentially treacherous, even though they may also be seen as *Ahl ul kitab* (People of the Book),[36] and as 'the only honest people around'.

Moreover in all situations of change and/or frustration any group which is different and appears to be doing well becomes vulnerable to being made a scapegoat, either as a result of public propaganda (for example letters to the editor making spurious allegations of missionary or fifth column activities by non-Muslims) or individual bullying (for example the daily cheating of Christian housewives by Muslim shopkeepers).[37]

In a metropolis such as Karachi many groups, less privileged members of the majority community, may seem to be as distinct and as discriminated against as the Goans. What is different is the way in which the relationship between 'them' and 'us' is conceived. The poorer Muslim always sees himself as part of the entire machinery of the society in which he lives. The Goans feel themselves to be outside or marginal to that society. Marginality as a concept may thus be useful in understanding their cognitive map and their reasons for choosing certain patterns of behaviour.

Barth,[38] Gist and Wright[39] have identified certain aspects of group marginality - the existence between groups of barriers, customary or legal, which prevent members of one group qualifying for inclusion in another, even though they are in some sort of functional relationship, and the one group sees the other as an object of emulation or identification. These barriers are preserved by discrimination on one side and pressures against betrayal on the other. In the Goan case the barrier areas which demarcate their cultural marginality are found in five important ascriptive criteria: language, territoriality, religion, family organization and familial values, and a distinctive life style.

Sometimes these configurations are dictated by religious dogma, for example the Roman Catholic prohibition of cross-cousin marriage which is the preferred form of marriage among Muslims. Other diacritica are adhered to in spite of disincentives; dress, for example, is thus an emotional indicator of identity. The wearing of the European frock is seen by Muslims as not only provocative, but also a flagrant violation of the Islamic norms of *sharm o haya*, modesty and chastity, and of *purdah*, which means not only the seclusion of women, but also decently covering the body. The mini-skirted Goan girl walking through the bazars has to run a gauntlet of stares and remarks which are frequently hostile. What is significant is that the wearing of a certain style of dress by a certain section of its women makes the whole community reprehensible - and that Goans persist in this pattern of behaviour.

Language is similarly an instrument of communication, a symbol of identity and a barrier. Goans pride themselves on being the principal repository of English in Karachi, though historically this was not their heritage but that of the Anglo-Indians. There was a conscious effort on the part of aspiring Goans to forego Konkani and learn English, as this was a means of achieving status within the community, or rather of making language irrelevant as an indicator of status. (The Portuguese spoken by some old families and the speech of the less-educated Goan are replete with distinctive colloquialisms.) In the ironing out of sharp differentials of lineage and caste within the community language has been decisively important. In this instance the ethnic bond based on language can be viewed as either an evolved or a deliberately created unity based on a language other than the mother tongue. In any event English is now part of the 'Western' cultural tradition which the Goan claims as his own.

English continues to be important to Goans because it is an invaluable asset when competing for jobs in the crowded middle ranges. But it is also a link with upper class Pakistani society, which considers English an essential social attribute in spite of government

efforts to make Urdu the official language. This is
one of the few points of Goan emulation of or identification with that society. Finally, English is the
Goan's passport for emigration to the West, an important psychological refuge. One of the reasons for
leaving Pakistan given by emigrant Goans was their
fear of the compulsory teaching of Urdu or Sindhi in
the schools - a threat to English and hence to their
own identity. Acculturation in Urdu or other
Pakistani languages is so firmly resisted that many
Goans prefer to use sign language in dealing with
shopkeepers and servants.

The community's territorial heritage, signalled
by Portuguese surnames and the label 'Goan', is also
cherished. Hostile relations between Pakistan and
India since partition have placed severe restrictions
on communications between Karachi and Goa so that a
whole generation has grown up with only very limited
contact with Goa. Ties, in many cases, have been
attenuated to nothing but a myth, for the Goa that is
romanticised and hankered after is specifically the
colony of Portugal that existed before 1961.[40] But
the myth is still a charter for action, in this case
preparedness to leave Karachi for some surrogate Goa
in the West. In 1958 some 5,000 Karachi Goans joined
forces to send an emissary to their fellows in Bombay
urging them not to back the Indian 'Quit Goa' campaign
against the Portuguese. With the Portuguese gone and
Goa absorbed in India, they said, 'their future would
be as ambiguous as that of the Anglo-Indians'.[41] Now
Goans see themselves as a 'homeless people ... like
the wandering Jews'. Whereas, formerly, it was
possession of land in Goa which gave prestige to a
family, now it is the ability to leave Pakistan.
This means having both the money and the relatives
abroad who will sponsor migration - those who have are
very ready to say so.

Religious behaviour in a multi-religious society
has a quality both expressive of communal piety and
instrumental in strengthening group boundaries.
Religious practice is not just an expression of
devoutness but is structurally relevant. This is
because the smaller the community, the clearer is the
threat of assimilation and the clearer it is that its
future depends upon the desire of each individual to
affiliate and thereby affirm the survival of the
group. To the individual community ties have both

practical and psychological utility: a middle-aged
spinster said that she was a member both of the
Women's Sodality and the Catholic Women's Guild because
otherwise 'Who would look after me if I fell ill?'
A couple reported that they had joined the Karachi Goan
Association when their daughter was unmarried so that
she could meet the 'right sort of young men'. Among
the Goans the nuclear family has become the norm and
the ties of parish, neighbourhood and association have
replaced the extended kin-circle and acquired the
immediacy of kinship. The ties of godparenthood and
the disappearance of caste endogamy have also induced a
vertical tightening, so that the entire community is
cross-cut with affinial and fictive kin ties. Kinship
and religion Cohen[42] sees as two major media for
informal political organization - as groups migrate to
towns the extensiveness of their original rural kinship ties declines, and religious ties become a more
viable and practical alternative. Religion and religious associations, however, also unite the community
for dealing with the outside world. Each parish has a
church for its nucleus but also a whole range of
satellite institutions - a school, hospital or
dispensary, catechistic centre, Scouts' meeting centre
and a parish hall maintained and managed jointly by
the clergy and parishioners. The visibility of the
church buildings and their unmistakably western origin
provide a physical basis for the community as well as
a feeling of being separate and different. This
psychological locus is further reinforced by the
facilities such as education, medical aid, advice,
financial help and leisure activities which radiate
from this centre, and by the accessibility and close
involvement of the parish clergy in the individual and
corporate lives of their parishioners.

The Goans receive a great deal of satisfaction
from being and coming together as Christians. Within
the family they meet for the daily rosary at the family
altar or dining table. As members of a congregation
they gather on Sundays or during the Perpetual
Novenas on Wednesdays - their year is filled with
feast days and Days of Obligation, anniversaries and
pageants, Nativity and Passion plays, retreats and
sodality outings. Life in St Patrick's parish is
almost lived to the ringing of the cathedral bell from
morning to evening angelus. Apart from the sanctions
and rewards which operate to keep the Goan a 'good

Catholic' and thereby nourish the group's cohesion, the
norms of Christianity are held to be the basis of his
proverbial honesty which makes employers say, 'Give me
a de Souza and I'll give him the keys of my safe'.
    Religion both separates and enfolds. The obser-
vance of Christian life-crisis rituals, for example,
distinguishes the Goans from the host society. But
the style of their observance also distinguishes them
as a cultural isolate within the larger Christian
population of Karachi. Thus while the Goans have
expensive western-style christenings, first communions,
weddings and funerals, Panjabi Roman Catholics in
Karachi do not observe many of these occasions at all.
(Panjabis at their funerals would not have a cortege, a
polished coffin, pallbearers and wreaths, and at
weddings the union would be quietly blessed in church
the day before, while the actual celebrations are
riotously indigenous.) Yet the Goan feels himself
included in the great tradition of Catholicism. Though
on the little tradition level there is a tendency to
hagiolatry characteristic of Catholics all over the
world, many Goans have been on pilgrimage to Rome,
Fatima and Lourdes, and many others are saving up for
this ultimate trip to the fountainhead. In invoking
St Anthony on the one hand and Father Agnelo of Pilar
in Goa on the other, the Goan is confirming his dual
heritage of the West and the Venerable Church in India.

The Adaptive Capacity of the Community

Since formal political power is outside the grasp of
the Goans in Karachi, they have concentrated on acquiring an effective bargaining position. To this end
they have streamlined the institutions through which
they control communal assets and have also strengthened
the community network with a number of associations
which run through all levels of society and draw in
all the different ages, sexes, and socio-economic
classes. Nearly every Goan is a member of at least
one. These organizations counter external pressure,
secure the cooperation of members in the common
cause and ultimately mobilize the support of the whole
community.
    As has been seen the Goans in the British period
came to occupy a special niche in Karachi society. It
was a relatively comfortable niche, minority status
caused little painful tension, there may have been some

advantage in being Christian and there is a suggestion
that the British favoured the smaller minorities. At
partition this position was threatened by large scale
social and demographic upheavals. However, despite new
institutionalized constraints, on the whole the community continued to maximize its assets. To this end some
Goan organizations acquired new functions. Originally
they had acted as antennae externally and as supervisors of community welfare and intercommunicators
internally. Now they took on the role of players of
the 'politics of respect'[43] with the host community.
In the first year after independence representatives
of the Karachi Goan Association (KGA) personally
waited on Pakistan's new leaders and presented them
with assurances of loyalty. Politicians were invited
to fetes and foundation-laying ceremonies as guests of
honour. Whereas previously the KGA had been an
exclusively Goan club, a guest night was instituted to
which Muslim bureaucrats and politicians were invited.
(How important it is not to be too exclusive is
evidenced by the closing of Lodge Zoroaster in Pakistan. This Masonic Lodge was almost exclusively
composed of Parsis, with whom Pakistani Muslim society
had friendly relations. But Masonic secrecy was
rumoured to be a cover for Zionist activities and over-
night the organization was declared illegal.) Goans
also made play with the fact that the Muslims were
themselves a liberated minority and keen to further
communal harmony. The KGA collected census and other
information for the policy makers and submitted
memoranda outlining the rights of minorities. At the
same time the more vociferous Karachi Goan Union (KGU)
appealed to the government against enforced flat-
sharing in the overcrowded city and the imposition of
the Quran upon Christian schools.

The status of the Goans is in part the product of
the highly-valued resources controlled by them,
namely schools and hospitals. As far as the majority
community is concerned the most valuable asset the
Goans control and administer is the schools. In
Karachi, schools are divided into high-status and low-
status, depending on their size, their primary language
(Urdu medium or English), the area they are in and the
scale of fees charged. Graphically, the division is
between those that have a board outside announcing
them, and those that are known landmarks. Of the
latter some of the oldest are Goan. As far back as

1890 St Patrick's Roman Catholic High School stood out
- and had done since 1870: 'It has an extremely fine
appearance, with a well-to-do, solid and substantial
look.' St Joseph's Convent School, with boarding and
day sections and an English-teaching Madrasa poor
school, was scarcely less well known. Two of the most
prestigious schools are still controlled by the Archdiocese of Karachi, and there is heavy demand for
admission to these. The principals of these two are
inundated with requests from Ministers to accept this
applicant or that. Many of these Ministers and government officials may themselves be old boys of the
schools. There is thus an old-boy network, or rather
a built-in respect among the powers-that-be for their
old teachers. This gives the priests a certain amount
of influence that they can activate in favour or their
community. The fact that in the first decade after
partition five new religious organizations came into
existence under the aegis of different missionaries,
manifestly for the purpose of providing social services
and education for the increased population of Karachi,
also created much goodwill with the outside community.
One of the features of the changed economic and
political situation since partition has been a shift
in the Goan elite away from the Westernized, cosmopo-
litan 'upper classes', towards the clergy as leaders
and brokers.

There are also Catholic associations which are not
exclusive to the Goans, though, because they operate
in English, Goans predominate. Sixteen such organizations exist in Karachi, ten in the old Goan stronghold
of St Patrick's parish. Examples are the League of
Mary, the Society of St Vincent de Paul, Mite Box
Action and the Apostleship of Prayer. The overt purpose of these is spiritual regeneration, but since
this entails regular meetings and inter-parish visiting
this builds up a network of communication valuable to
the individual but available, too, for collective
action. But there are other wider organizations which
undertake large, long-term projects for the whole
Christian community. One of these is the Pakistan
Christian Industrial Services intended to promote a
Christian attitude towards 'the social, economic an
spiritual dimensions of urbanisation and industrialisation in Pakistan' by carrying out surveys, initiating pilot projects, representing Christian groups
before civic authorities and bringing together laity

and clergy, labour and management, urban residents and
municipal authorities. Others are the Catholic
Social Services and the Christian Research Centre which
in 1975 formulated an ambitious Socio-Economic Development Plan.

Lastly there are the Goan clubs proper: the Karachi
Goan Association and the Karachi Goan Union. These
clubs give the Goans a sense of continuity by their
long histories, their old buildings and the sequence of
portraits of past presidents. In the past, when unity
was less important, caste had been an important factor
in Goan society. Stratification was reflected in the
social structure of these institutions: the KGA was
exclusively for Brahmans and the KGU for other castes.
But since partition there has been a change in the
ideology of the community so that disparities in
wealth, learning and lineage are played down and the
equality of all individuals in the collectivity
emphasized. The point was made by a leading woman
journalist, member of a patrician Goan family, in an
article 'How Goans Think' in *Dawn*, July 1953:

> The Goan community because of the smallness of its
> numbers and the difference of its culture will
> always dwell in a state of siege .... The power of
> the community does not lie in the few who have
> scaled the ladder of success. It lies in the rank
> and file. It is there that the communal heart
> beats loudest .... Hence the strength of the Goan
> community does not lie in its doctors, its
> lawyers or educationists. It comes from the lives
> of those whose names will never appear in print;
> whose days are spent in the small unexciting
> triangle made by home, office and their parish
> church.

At times the KGA is almost moribund now, a place for
seasonal dances, drinking or billiards, but at others
it is a forum for recognition where Goans pick each
other out by their clothes or manners as being Chardos
or Brahmans. However, since caste has been discounted
for practical purposes such as marriage such comment
is as merely another sign of Goanness, without any
deeper significance. Indeed the presence of such
idosyncrasies in a regulated setting also provides the
community with a sense of continuity, reinforcing
rather than endangering communal solidarity.

This study has been concerned with the adaptation

of a minority to a situation of long-term change and
externally-imposed constraints. That minority was a
marginal one in the past and is so today, but it has
contrived to maximize its assets and retain its control
of them by preserving a collective ideal of its own
identity. This has been achieved in an urban setting,
the skills and assets involved have been those of city
dwellers, and it may be asked indeed whether one reason
for Goan success - and of Parsi success, too - may not
be found in the actual urban settlement pattern: in
the multi-apartment chauls used for the Coors, in
Cinninnatus Town, and in the close-knit parishes. St
Patrick's, for example, apart from being the site of
the Cathedral and the nucleus from which directives
and trends emanate through such satellite organizations
as the Christian Research Centre, welfare services and
the newspaper *Christian Voice,* defines very clearly the
Goan social ambit. This is the constellation formed by
church, neighbourhood, school, club, bazar, cemetery
and sometimes place of work too. In the commercial
heart of the city, this parish is a microcosm of what
Furnival calls a 'plural society',[44] where different
ethnic groups meet but do not merge. It contains
within a circle of a mile or so all the manifestations
of the Goan collectivity - church, convent, school and
college, association and union and gymkhana.
   Panjabi Christians also share the parish, 416
Panjabi to 843 Goan Catholic households. But whereas
the upwardly mobile Panjabi Christian may drop his
traditional ethnicity and attempt to pass into the
dominant cultural group, this strategy is totally
inapplicable to the Goan. To use the cultural attributes of the host population as a reference model
would require prevarication about religious affiliations, fluency in Urdu and the adoption of the norms
of an Islamic life-style. All these transformations
would be anathema to Goans, conflicting with their
self-definition, and would in practice be very difficult to achieve. In fact the Goans, like the 'tribals'
in India, are outside the system of emulating the
dominant society. The Goans seem always to have been
structurally and culturally marginal to the various
groups with whom they have had to interact. This is a
historical modus vivendi under which the Goans have
been linked to the surrounding society by contracts
based on mutual interest. Externally there is
collaboration based on complementary assets, and the

requisite for this is differential control of these
assets and the maintenance of a boundary. Internally
there are sanctions to reinforce the boundary and
rewards to sustain member support, externally a
relinquishment of too competitive an approach or any
fight for political power. This is why the Goans,
though they have elite status in terms of economic
prosperity, cultural and social sophistication, and a
highly developed organization and authority structure,
have shown little wish to convert these assets into
political power in the wider arena.

In the British period there was some imitation of
an upper-class western life style - an overlay of
British cultural properties on Portuguese ones. But
ties with the ruling power never became emotionally
charged. Unlike the Anglo-Indians, who on the basis
of kinship tried constantly to penetrate the barrier
and so set up a syndrome of dependence and rejection,
the Goans never claimed special favours or depended
on the British for their self-esteem. In Barth's
explanation of minority situations 'prized goals are
outside the field organized by the minority's culture
and categories' - but for Goans, an elite in Karachi
society, this is just not so, they are virtually
autonomous in internal affairs and the status and
influence they seek lies within this internal
hierarchy. Structural and psychological marginality
has thus become functional to the well-being of the
community. Goan marginality is not imposed; it is a
self-generated accommodation. This has become
embedded in the group consciousness, so that the Goans,
among the oldest residents of Karachi, still fit
Simmel's category of the stranger: 'the wanderer who
came today and stayed tomorrow'.[45]

Field work was carried out over a period of one year, from July 1975 to July 1976. The method was mainly participant observation and most of it was carried out in St Patrick's parish, which is the oldest of the fifteen parishes in the Archdiocese of Karachi and one which has the greatest concentration of Goans. Qualitative observation was enriched with specific quantitative data derived from interviews, church archives, i.e. the baptismal and marriage records dating from the 1850s in St Patrick's Parish registers, Chamber of Commerce records and old issues of the *Christian Voice*. Out of a total of 833 households in St Patrick's, I extrapolated a sample of 150, i.e. about 21 per cent, who were systematically interviewed. Though this was not random, it was representative, because present-day Goan society is fairly homogeneous in terms of culture and in St Patrick's in terms of socio-economic characteristics as well. Of those interviewed 98 per cent were adults, and the sexes were present in nearly equal proportions. There seems to be a weighting of the sample in favour of middle age, i.e. above 30, and 52 of the respondents were in fact fifty or older. This gave me a diachronic perspective which I could contrast with present-day trends, e.g. work experiences in British days contrasted with work experiences now. The questionnaires were divided into sections covering the various aspects of Goan life, e.g. apart from socio-economic data and personal data I had a section on religious life, caste, ties with Goa, emigration plans, and I also included the Bogardus social distance and attitude test. From my own observation and sometimes member-participation in the various religious, social and welfare organizations, I got a fair idea of the infrastructure of the community. Finally since urban anthropology necessitates an understanding of the complex, contextual structures which surround and impinge on the group studied, I had to take into account my subjects' relationship with the total city environment. In pursuance of this, I had to cultivate an awareness of those other groups which lie adjacent to the Goans, for example the other religious minorities, the Hindus, Parsis, Ahmadiyas, who are all in a definitionally similar situation but who insist on very different cultural identities and organize themselves differently as regards their relation to

the dominant group. The affinities and disparities
between the Panjabi Catholics and the Goans were
studied in slightly greater depth.

Haward, 'An Urban Minority: The Goan Christian
Community in Karachi'

1. This section draws upon Mohammad Zafar Ahman
Khan, *The Development of a Pre-industrial City, an
Economic Geography of Karachi* (Ph.D. thesis, London
University 1968), and upon the centenary history of
the Karachi Chamber of Commerce and Industry, Herbert
Feldman, *Karachi Through A Hundred Years* (Karachi 1960).
 2. A.F. Baillie, *Kurachee: Past, Present and
Future* (Calcutta 1890), p.28. He writes of 1839:
'access to the town from the port was most difficult
... the town itself was a small, closely built, dirty
place and ... the number of inhabitants was about
14,000.'
 3. E. Thornton, *A Gazetteer of the countries
adjacent to India on the North West ...*, 2 vols.
(London 1844).
 4. Khan, op.cit., pp.49-55.
 5. Feldman, op.cit., pp.10-11, 27-28.
 6. J.W. Smyth, *Gazetteer of the Province of Sind*,
B.vol.i., *Karachi District* (Bombay 1919), pp.84-85.
 7. Khan, op.cit., p.68.
 8. Baillie, op.cit., p.118.
 9. Ibid., p.98.
 10. Smyth, op.cit., pp.77-78.
 11. *Souvenir of the Golden Jubilee of the Karachi
Goan Association, 1886-1936* (Karachi 1936). Smyth
comments upon the substantial nature of the club
building on Frere Street.
 12. H. Calvert, *The Wealth and Welfare of the
Punjab* (Lahore 1922).
 13. Feldman, op.cit., p.57.
 14. B. Temple, *The Karachi Hand-book and Directory*
(Karachi 1914).
 15. O.E. Baptista, *The Coor System - A Study of
Goan Club Life in Bombay* (M.Phil. thesis, Bombay
University 1958).
 16. J.M.L. Montemayor, *A Sociological Analysis of
a Goan Village Community* (Ph.D. thesis, Delhi University 1970). *Gaunkars*: descendants of the founders of
the village; *Bhatkars*: landholders.
 17. A.W. Hughes, *Gazetteer of the Province of Sind*
(London 1876), pp.360-361, and Smyth, op.cit., pp.37-39,

both comment on the handsome stone-built Catholic
schools. Baillie, after recording Protestant activity
in Karachi, proceeds: 'The Roman Catholic Mission is a
more important body. Belonging to it are the St.
Patrick's High School and the St. Joseph's Convent
School, both situated in Camp. The latter is conducted
by the Daughters of the Cross, and comprises a boarding
school, a day school, and an English teaching *Madrasa*
poor school.' (p.98). On the High School he adds,
'The Military Chaplain and Superior of the Roman
Catholic Mission presides over a considerable staff of
teachers, amongst whom are Professors of the Portuguese,
Persian and Sindee languages.' (p.162). It is interesting to note that in 1890 Portuguese was still taught
formally in this leading Goan school.

18. Montagu de P. Webb, *The Karachi Handbook and
Directory, 1921* (Karachi 1922).

19. See Khan, op.cit., p.89 for the figures for
trade from 1913-14 to 1943-44.

20. Ibid., p.93.

21. Feldman, op.cit., pp.195-196.

22. Khan, op.cit., p.165.

23. D.N. Patel, *Karachi Guide and Directory for
1915* (Karachi 1915); A.E. Mirams, *Report on the
Development of Karachi* (Bombay 1923), and Khan, op.cit.,
pp.177-190.

24. Ibid., pp.155-156. A more recent example of
such housing is found in the parish of Our Lady of
Fatima in the vast, distinct block of flats called
Misquita Gardens.

25. Cp. p.305.

26. *Souvenir Volume of the Karachi Goan Association,
1886-1956* (Karachi 1956).

27. See the Franciscan publication, *In the Land of
the Sindhi and the Baluchi. A Report on Catholic
Activities in Sind and Baluchistan, 1935-1947.*
(Karachi 1947).

28. Ibid.

29. Ibid.

30. Agha M. Ghaus, *The Economy of Pakistan, a
Review* (Karachi 1961); Khan, op.cit., p.106.

31. *Census of Pakistan*, 1951; 1961.

32. *Report of the Christian Research Centre*
(Karachi 1973).

33. T. Parsons and E. Shils (eds.), *Towards a
General Theory of Action* (New York 1965).

34. The prestige of the elite had several sources,

internal and external. The same Goans who were judges, lawyers, engineers and doctors were also chairmen or directors of Goan firms. They also became presidents and executive members of Goan social clubs and religious and welfare organizations. But additionally they were members of elite clubs like the Sind Club and the Gymkhana, which had been exclusively British. Status was further validated by their having relatives in positions of authority in the Church. In British India ultimate validation of eminence was the award of a knighthood; for Goans who were not British subjects the alternative accolade was the award of a Papal Order.

35. See P. Hardy, *The Muslims of British India* (Cambridge 1972), p.283: 'Zimmi: in Islamic law, one whom, as a non-Muslim, the Muslim state undertakes to protect in the practice of his religion on certain conditions.'

36. Ibid., p.275: 'Ahl al kitab: people of a revealed book or scripture; in Islamic law such non-Muslim peoples are to be publicly tolerated in the dar al Islam on their acceptance of the status of zimmi.'

37. See the correspondence colums of the *Goan World*.

38. F. Barth, *Ethnic Groups and Boundaries; The Social Organization of Culture Difference* (London 1969).

39. N.P. Gist and R.D. Wright, *Marginality and Identity: Anglo-Indians as a Racially Mixed Minority in India* (Leiden 1973).

40. B.G. D'Souza, *Goan Society in Transition* (Bombay 1975).

41. *Goan World*, July 1958.

42. Abner Cohen, 'The Lesson of Ethnicity' in Abner Cohen (ed.), *Urban Ethnicity* (London 1974).

43. R. Holloman, 'Ethnic Boundary Maintenance and Re-adaptation in the San Blas Islands of Panama', in H. Hoetinck (ed.), *Ethnicity and Resource Competition in Plural Societies* (The Hague 1975).

44. J.S. Furnival, *Colonial Policy and Practice* (Cambridge 1948).

45. G. Simmel, *Conflict and the Web of Group Affiliations* (New York).

CITY, TOWN AND VILLAGE: THE CONTINUUM RECONSIDERED

Christine Cottam

Over the last few decades economic development and social change in the Third World have been the focus of intense interest. There has been an implicit assumption that urban areas will 'modernize' or 'westernize' more rapidly than the rural areas and that the cities will be the source of the changes taking place in the villages. With regard to South Asian studies, two approaches have characterized research proceeding from this basic assumption. On the one hand, the unit of study has been the village, around which an imaginary boundary is delineated. Here social change is considered as it occurs, without taking into account influences from the city, or their formation in the city itself. On the other hand, the unit of study has been the city (or large town) and the changes taking place within it are tabulated, then assumed to diffuse downwards through the different levels in the settlement hierarchy, without actually specifying how this works in practice. In very many village studies, in particular, it is argued that the rural/urban dichotomy is not just an analytical oversight or heuristic device but reflects a very real separation between city or town on the one hand, and village on the other. To take just one example, D.N. Majumdar has argued: 'There are two distinct constellations of values and there are sharp dividing lines between levels of living and experience.'[1] That is, an ideological barrier prevents, or at least inhibits, urban influences from operating in the villages; yet one of the most comprehensive analyses of rural-urban linkages is to be found in this study of a particular village only eight miles from Lucknow. Majumdar concludes, rather confusingly: 'It is not an absolutely communicating village, it is not urbanized, as could be expected, but it lies on the periphery of an urban area - it communicates through the many individuals who have contacts with the town, and who go out and return to the village regularly and occasionally.'[2] Leaving aside the intriguing question of what constitutes 'an absolutely communicating village' two questions spring to mind. Firstly, can there be rigid

324

ideological differences if there is so much contact?
And secondly, how is change possible if ideological
differences are so rigid?

These problems derive from the concept of the
peasant which presently prevails, that is, that
peasantries are part-societies and part-cultures,
functionally inter-related with a pre-industrial urban
centre, as seen by Foster, or, more recently, functionally integrated into the larger state society, as seen
by Wolf.[3] Although the peasant is regarded as part of
the larger society, he is the bearer of the 'little' or
'folk' tradition whereas the townsman is the formulator,
custodian and beneficiary of the 'great' tradition.[4]
'The pace-setters are the urban elite; by the time the
fashions of this elite trickle down and out to the
peasant, new fashions are in vogue in the urban environment. So the peasant is the perpetual old-fashioned
rustic.'[5] The peasant is portrayed as simultaneously
ignored and exploited. Peasant surplus production is
siphoned off to capitalize national projects which
have little or no significance for peasants themselves.
They are directed from above and without. Unsurpri-
singly, the peasant is suspicious of the great
tradition and prefers the security of the little
tradition as a means of avoiding exploitation.[6] In a
word, the peasant is *afraid* of the city and all that it
stands for.

Since the peasant is, by definition, limited to the
confines of his village and has a world view conditioned by its traditions how does this concept of the
peasantry cope with economic development and social
change? It is supposed that the peasant cannot resist
the bright lights of the big city. He is hypnotized by
the glitter of the great tradition, which he instinc-
tively recognizes as more prestigious. Realizing the
inadequacy of the peasant economy to provide the bene-
fits of twentieth century civilization he simply
'reacts' by salvaging what he can - innovation - or
cutting his losses - migration.[7] He is a thoroughly
confused individual, making hasty and economically
inexplicable decisions.[8]

In fact, the divergencies between peasant and
urban society may not be as great as some writers
describe them and this is especially the case in the
South Asian material. In a largely forgotten article,
Opler discusses a number of 'extensions' linking one
village with the outside world.[9] These are: common

origin and descent shared with surrounding villages;
village exogamy creating kinship ties with other
villages; caste assemblies cutting across village
lines; customary work obligations consisting of
practical and ritual services in other village communities; participation in religious movements such as
the Arya Samaj and political movements such as the
nationalist struggle; pilgrimages to distant shrines
and religious centres and visits from itinerant
priests; connections with market towns and the courts,
land record offices and government operated seed and
implement stores; and temporary out-migration for
education.

Of course, Opler's focus is a single village and
conceptually he envisages the world as composed of
this village and its hinterland. Again, many of the
extensions which he lists are with other rural areas
and the urban contacts are merely a special case.
However, most importantly he mentions: 'Another point
that seems worth noting is that the basic articulation
of Senapur and Senapur people with other communities
and far-flung places is not a recent development or a
consequence of modern systems of communication and
transportation. They rest upon ancient practices and
traditions.'[10]

In the same vein, though without the single village
outlook, Cohn and Marriott discuss supralocal rural
networks of social relationships such as trade, marriage, politics and contacts formed by religious
travellers. Like Opler they remark that these are not
new:

> But trading networks beyond the village have been
> well-developed in India since at least Muslim
> times. Cash was in use for taxation and trans-
> actions in agricultural produce. Trade routes were
> extensive and protected over large areas. Itiner-
> ant traders and in some areas itinerant markets
> still do a large share of all business. Networks
> of marriage ties are extensive, especially in North
> India, where as many as 100,000 persons, spread
> over thousands of square miles, are often linked
> directly or indirectly. Political networks consist
> primarily of ties of clan and kinship among rulers
> and the dominant landlord groups of the country-
> side.[11]

These linkages, particularly market networks and

the use of cash transactions in northern India, reveal
that the isolation of the village is not as longstand-
ing or complete as some retrospective accounts would
lead us to believe. Furthermore, they suggest
villagers were used to conducting their affairs through
specialized middlemen , the greater part of whose
talents lay in their knowledge of and connections with
other places, and specifically urban markets. Surprisingly, this whole area of middle ground between the
two broad streams of research has been relatively
unexplored. There are few studies both of merchants,
who are in the ideal position to act as patrons and
brokers, and of small towns which, being neither truly
rural nor truly urban, articulate the less urbanized
areas with the more urbanized.[12] It is here that the
key to the problem of how change happens may lie,
although it is not possible to achieve more than a
bare indication of this in such a preliminary study.
I shall start by sketching the contours of a small
bazar which is fairly representative of its kind in
northern and western India in order to demonstrate the
importance of traders and trading to these settlements.
I shall then turn to the traditional merchant castes
of Rajasthan, better known perhaps as Marwaris, and
attempt to show their crucial function as a nexus in
the rural urban flow of information. In particular I
shall deal with the links of marriage and kinship
between merchant families.[13] Lastly I shall offer a
few tentative conclusions and suggestions for future
research.

'Mandi': small-town India

Mandi is a fairly typical desert settlement.[14] It lies
on one of the historic trade routes of India. The
surrounding countryside is a flat dusty plain, feature-
less except for the odd sand dune, and the mountain
under which the town nestles is a major land mark.
The region supports one of the lowest population
densities in Rajasthan, about 75 per square mile,
distributed in hamlets about four or five miles apart.[15]
On land use maps the plain is classified as semi-arid
steppe, but the local word for it is *jangal*. Apart
from a limited area of irrigated land to the south,
sand dunes come up to the municipal boundary and
occasionally encroach on the town itself. Tradition
has it that Mandi was once situated on the other side

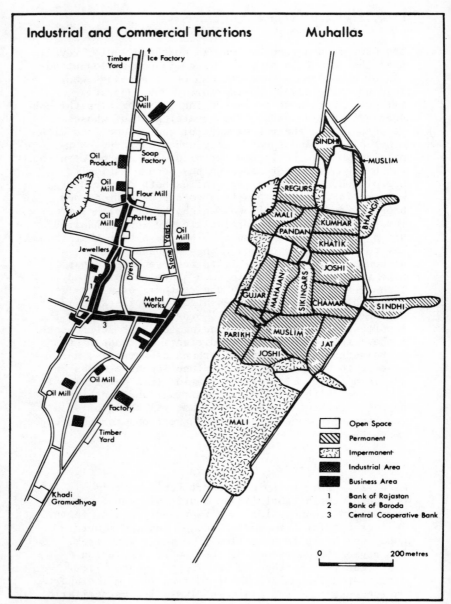

Industrial and Commercial Functions

Timber Yard
Ice Factory
Oil Mill
Oil Products
Soap Factory
Oil Mill
Flour Mill
Oil Mill
Potters
Oil Mill
Jewellers
Stone Yards
Dyers
1
2
3
Metal Works
Oil Mill
Oil Mill
Factory
Timber Yard
Khadi Gramudhyog

Muhallas

SINDHI
MUSLIM
REGURS
BHANGI
MALI
KUMHAR
PANDAN
KHATIK
JOSHI
GUJAR
MAHAJAN
SIKINGARS
CHAMAR
SINDHI
PARIKH
MUSLIM
JAT
JOSHI
MALI

Open Space
Permanent
Impermanent
Industrial Area
Business Area
1 Bank of Rajastan
2 Bank of Baroda
3 Central Cooperative Bank

0   200 metres

MANDI

of the mountain but was destroyed for its iniquities
by a sand storm, and was reputedly built on the present
site by the semi-mythical raja Naruka who constructed
the reservoirs which ensure a permanent water supply.
Naruka is one of the clan names of the Rajputs and it
is tempting to speculate that Mandi was rebuilt when
the Rajputs were subjugating the previous inhabitants
of Rajasthan, the Minas, a tribal people. Naruka is
also the clan name of the present *thakur* of Mandi.
The old palace is clearly a military conception, though
less so than the fort on top of the mountain, a Mughal
contribution. Mandi, though small and remote, was
incorporated into Akbar's design for subduing the
Rajputs in their turn on account of the excellence of
the sheer-sided mountain for defensive purposes.

Because of its permanent water supply at the
reservoirs, Mandi has long been a caravanserai for
traders. The importance of water to a settlement
cannot be overestimated, particularly a permanent
water supply in a desert area. The nearest water
supplies are strung out along the highway, 16 miles
away in one direction and 20 miles away in the other,
both a convenient day's walking distance. When
travellers stopped at Mandi, they needed to be fed,
housed and entertained. For these services they had
to pay, either in cash or by barter, and so it all
began. Even today caravans stop at Mandi on their
journeys from Afghanistan to Central India, and so do
their twentieth-century counterparts, the long-distance
truck drivers.

The importance of Mandi as a trading centre is
substantiated by the distribution of the various castes
in the *muhallas* (wards) of the town. The oldest and
previously most prestigious part of the town is that
adjacent to Naruka's palace, a closely-developed
labyrinth of lanes connecting the oldest and principal
temples. The main activity is the pursuit of
religion, though there is a concentration of small
businesses near the temples dealing in incense and
dried flowers. It is still a high-caste area, with a
concentration of both the religiously inclined and
the homes of the rich; and the religious status of the
area has led to vertical expansion for residential use.
Thence the business community has spread outwards
along the two main bazars, and the whole of the
adjacent muhallas are now collectively called the Mahajan muhalla, while the religious area is increeasingly

being called the Parik (Pariks are the hereditary
Brahman priests of Naruka Rajputs). As the Majahans,
or merchants, move outwards in search of bigger
building plots on which to construct larger and more
prestigious houses, the prestige of the Parik muhalla
and its inhabitants is declining accordingly. The main
activity of the Mahajan muhalla is business and the
large rambling *havelis* of the merchant community with
their massive wooden doors and strongly barred
windows testify that this is a very wealthy area.
Unlike Western towns and cities, the separation of the
prestigious residential areas from commerce or industry does not exist and yet the social factor in the
distribution of status groups is crucial. The inner
zone of Indian cities is characterized by high density
of population and high income and high-ranking castes,
whereas Western cities exhibit a low density of
population and low income and low status groups
resident in the core area.[16]

Next to this inner zone is a transitional zone, a
curious mixture of tenement slums and the spacious
homes of those rich families unable to find space for
a house near the centre. These hug the boundaries of
the Mahajan muhalla as closely as possible in order
to minimize their loss of prestige. This zone
includes the homes of the castes who give their names
to the muhallas, such as potters, carpenters and
masons, and scattered clumps of mud houses belonging
to the poorer, Muslim castes such as weavers and
woolcarders.

The outer zone is not permanently built over and
for large tracts is not even named. The Maliyan
muhalla contains Minas and Bhils (tribal people),
Muslims and some Sindhi refugees as well as the
gardener caste for whom it is named. This is the abode
of the lowest castes and poorest people, some of whom
are untouchable, such as sweepers and leatherworkers.
It consists of formless masses of one- or two-room
mud huts. There are no paths or roads, no standpipes
or street lights, merely spaces between the houses
where pigs and dogs wallow in stagnant water, rotting
vegetation and refuse. The price of land here, if
anyone wanted to buy it, would be about Rs.10 per
square metre compared with about Rs.300 per square
metre along the two main bazars and Rs.150 in the
Mahajan muhalla, away from the bazars.

Perhaps enough data has been given to suggest a

general idea of the economic and social outlines of
Mandi. It should be fairly clear that, from its
inception as a settlement, trade and traders have
dominated its existence. The population at present
stands at about 7,000 inhabitants, of whom about one-
third belong to the merchant castes. In fact,
together they comprise the largest, most influential
and wealthiest segment of the population. Their
traditional calling is trade, but not only do they
dominate business generally, they predominate in the
most profitable businesses. It is to this immensely
influential section of the town which we must now turn.

The merchant castes of Mandi

In keeping with the desert environment, the merchant
castes are rather like a mirage, from the distance
easily perceived but apt to disappear when approached.
Almost everyone in India can tell you that merchants
are called Banias and those who have classical
scriptural knowledge will say that Bania derives from
the Sanskrit *Vanij*, meaning a merchant or trader.
They may add that Banias originate from the *Vaisyas*,
the trader and merchant category of the four *Varnas*
and hence are often called *Vaishnu* as a diminutive.
Even more literate persons, often amateur historians,
will argue that it is because the Vaishnavite sect
(arising in Orissa during the fourteenth century AD)
made many converts amongst the Banias that they are
called Vaishnu.

In other words, a Bania is a trader, a merchant or
a businessman. Nonetheless, buying and selling in
Mandi increasingly involves large numbers of people
whose traditional caste calling in no way involves
trade. Are these also Banias? Generally, the feeling
is that they are not and that whereas in 'such places'
as Delhi and Bombay all shopkeepers and traders would
be called Banias, in Mandi everyone would know their
origins. Somewhat ironically, having pruned away the
non-Banias, we find that the 'real' Banias say that
they are something else. Whilst Banias are not ashamed
of their occupation in the way that an untouchable
would be, they prefer to use a different term of
reference for themselves. This is because 'Bania'
is popularly used as a term of abuse meaning thief,
cheat, or miser.

Basically, Banias in Mandi consist of those who

call themselves and are called in turn Mahajan, synon-
ymous locally with Maharaj and meaning 'Lord'. The
Mahajans can be divided into Jains and Vaishnavas by
sect, further divided into two major subcastes and a
number of minor ones: Agarwal, Khandelwal, and Oswal,
Maheshwari, Srimal, Jaiswal, Porwal and Paliwal.

These subcastes are of great antiquity in India;
however until the famous migrations of the Marwaris
began in the last century they seem always to have been
restricted in their distribution to the formerly
princely states of Rajasthan, Gujarat and the southern
districts of the Panjab. The principal division
between them appears not to be by sect, as might have
anticipated, but into endogamous units or jati. The
rules of marriage are very different, for example
Khandelwals must avoid four gotras (or descent lines)
- their father's, their mother's, their father's
father's and mother's mother's - whereas Agrawals need
avoid only one - their father's. Not surprisingly,
the number of Khandelwal gotras is prolific - 86
whereas the number of Agrawal gotras is confined to
17½.[17] This means that Khandelwals have wider marriage
networks than Agrawals, but both are very much more
mobile in their choice of marriage partners for sons
and daughters than other castes. There are further
differences which do not concern us here for, principally, it is the similarities which are most apparent
and religious differences particularly are rather
blurred. Indeed, Agrawal Vaishnavas and Agrawal Jains
may intermarry (there are examples of such marriages)
though Khandelwal Vaishnavas and Khandewal Jains may
not. The other jatis are not sub-divided into sects:
therefore the issue does not arise. All are vegetarian,
teetotal and lay enormous stress on avoiding injury to
living creatures - straining water through little
muslin bags to avoid ingesting insects and avoiding
root vegetables and leafy plants because they may
harbour tiny grubs. The stress upon non-injury
(*ahimsa*) extends as far as avoiding onions and garlic
and similar plants which germinate if left in dark
places, and plants containing many seeds, such as
aubergines, tomatoes and guavas. These foods contain
the added danger of exciting the passions.

Although sectarian differences are not acute, this
is not to say that religion is unimportant; indeed to
the outsider the prominence of religious ritual in the
conduct of business is striking. Most merchants begin

begin the day with *Lakshmipuja*, or worship of the Hindu goddess of wealth, even the Jains. All offices have pictures or images of Lakshmi or Ganesh for prosperity and good luck, and also their owners' favourite gods or goddesses, such as Mahavir for Jains or Krishna for Vaishnavas. The Mahajans say that if a man has faith his business will prosper; the images are there to inspire the faith from which all else follows. Hence Jains do well in business 'because the Jain religion is simple and easy to follow' and the Vaishnavas 'because they follow the rules of dharma'.

In fact, both inside and outside Rajasthan, the merchant castes of Marwar have a reputation for conservatism in outlook deriving from their religiosity, which amounts to eccentricity in the eyes of other castes.[18] Mahajan women, for example, keep strict purdah and are rarely seen outside the house, in striking contrast to the relatively free and easy lives of other Rajasthani women. Mahajans are commonly nicknamed *dhalbattis*, for rice and lentils are more or less the substance when their dietary restrictions are kept. This is often attributed to meanness, and they are also called *kanjus* (misers) and *makkijus* (fly-suckers) because they are alleged to suck the *ghi* from flies which have fallen into their soup so that nothing will be wasted. In Mandi, Mahajans were reported to prefer Hindi newspapers to English language newspapers because they cost less, though this was patently untrue.

And yet conservatism in lifestyle is not connected with economic conservatism. Since independence, the economy of India has changed greatly and Marwaris have played a highly significant role in this.[19] In Mandi itself the simple wholesaling and retailing of commodities has been replaced by the growth of commission agencies and more recently the development of small-scale industries. There are now 13 oil mills, four flour mills, a soap and candle factory and an ice factory, all run by local merchant families. Mandi is rightly regarded by the state administration of Rajasthan as a progressive place, fruitful soil for their 'bring the Marwaris back to Marwar' campaign. By injecting large sums of capital into an industrial development programme, the administration hopes to stimulate the growth of industry on a large scale.

Various explanations of Marwari business success have been proferred. There is the negative evaluation

of business by other castes, which they consider to be
degrading, anti-social and parasitic. They are not
being polite when they say that Banias have the knack
of making money. Equally important are their famous or
infamous business skills.[20] Another, possibly more
important factor arises from their traditional slot in
the social hierarchy, centuries of dedication to
business during which time they have been working hard
at establishing, maintaining and consolidating good
budiness connections and linkages of all sorts with
important or influential people.

The manipulation of connections

The first and most obviously well-oiled network of
contacts is that between the shopkeeper and his
clients, largely from the plethora of small hamlets
mentioned above. Clients of this sort fall into two
broad divisions: other Mahajans, who run very small
general stores in other villages, some of them carrying
out an itinerant trade by bullock cart from a central
base; and the farmer castes, who come to town from
time to time to stock up on non-subsistence commodities, sometimes buying goods on commission for their
neighbours. Shopkeepers vie with one another to
build up a steady stream of regular customers,
offering credit terms at rock bottom prices to clients
whose custom they particularly value, especially the
village Mahajans and commission purchasers. The
latter are, incidentally, often village headmen who
are believed to be more capable in dealing with the
wiles of cunning Banias than other mortals. Shopkeepers also endeavour to personalize business
relations as much as possible, asking clients how many
children they have, whether their buffalo has calved
this year and so on. One Mahajan in Mandi claims to
know the personal circumstances of 200 customers:
whether their parents are still alive, how many children, acres of land and cattle they possess, if and
when their sons and daughters are getting married.
This wins the confidence of the customer and offers a
rough and ready cross check on the viability of credit,
both with that particular individual and the village
from which he originates. If his cow died in
mysterious circumstances, for example, it is unlikely
that this is an isolated incident and may presage an
epidemic.

Thus the shopkeeper is constantly washed by a flow
of information of varying kinds. It permits him to
perform an ongoing policy review. If economic circumstances in the villages turn upwards, he may decide
that the market can stand the innovation of new
consumer durables - a more elaborate type of trans-
istor radio, or synthetic fibre saris. Furthermore,
it enables him to predict with a fair degree of
precision which sorts of innovation will 'take' and
which will not. He will know that pale pink for
women's or mustard for men's clothing is out of the
question, and that brushed nylon will be more popular
in the winter months than georgette. Conversely, his
contacts in the bigger towns and cities are constantly
offering new products for his evaluation and approval.
From nasal inhalant to pre-packed chilli powder and
sheepdip, the small town shopkeeper acts as a mini-
computer matching consumers and suppliers. This is
why the shopkeepers' own best customers are also
middlemen.

A second and equally well-oiled set of contacts
is that between merchants and other merchants, both
within Mandi itself and merchants in the big cities.
Such contacts would be those between a shopkeeper and
his suppliers and commission agents with commodity
brokers in the cities. The latter are particularly
concerned with maintaining useful contacts outside
Mandi, for in order to bid effectively in the daily
food grain, oil seed or spice auctions, in their own
bazars they must be attuned to price and commodity
flows on Dalal Street. Information in their business
and lack of knowledge can cause not only smaller
profits but actual losses. If a commission agent made
too high a bid for an already overstocked commodity
which a client in Bombay refused to accept, he would
be left to bear the loss, paying substantial warehous-
ing charges and taking the risk that prices might rise
in the near future, whilst in the meantime his capital
would be tied up completely.

It is no accident therefore that the first non-
traditional activities, the oil mills, which have
paved the way for subsequent industrial development,
are owned and operated by commission agent families,
not always in the oil seed business. One informant
explained how his family decided to start an oil mill:
in much the same way as the first millowners in Mandi,
this family got the names of businessmen in Jaipur who

could handle the processed vegetable oils, supply
metal containers and provide transport, by tanker if
necessary. They also visited oil mills in Jaipur run
by a family firm belonging to the same jati as
themselves and thus obtained the necessary technical
knowledge of machinery and factory organization. They
now process about 35,000 barrels of vegetable oil per
year at an estimated profit of Rs.6 per barrel. The
waste is sent to a daughter's husband's cattle cake
factory in Gujarat from whence, reprocessed, it is
exported to the U.K., U.S.A. and Japan.

In a state-directed economy, such as that of India,
there is a constant need for commodity licences of
various sorts and the more complicated technologically
an enterprise becomes the more licences are involved.
This requires repeated trips to the state capital,
Jaipur, or even to Delhi. One commission agent complained that he had had to visit Jaipur forty times
before he obtained a licence to deal in wheat. Much
is left to the discretion of officials and even when
permission is semi-automatic it may require the
co-ordination of several government departments. Two
major consequences arise: people either bypass the
system by means of *bakshish*, that is, they give
bribes, or they manipulate the system via 'friends of
friends'. Thus, connections with political figures in
high places become themselves a valued commodity.
Involvement in politics is a sort of by-product of
entrepreneurial activity and again it is not merely
co-incidental that all the big entrepreneurs in Mandi
have served on the Municipal Board at some time: it is
because favours are not traded for nothing; they are
exchanged for 'guaranteed' votes for seats in the State
Legislative Assembly, or support in a more 'general'
way. Having invested time and energy in vote-collect-
ing for others, to stand for elections and thus bypass
the lowest rung in the hierarchy of string-pullers
requires little effort. Disagreeable and dangerous
though most Mahajans find these political connections,
they become an offer which entrepreneurs cannot refuse.
Almost against their will, it seems, some Mahajans are
forced into public office, thus occasioning the
opprobrium of other Mahajans because of particular
Mahajani ideas about prestige and status. Access to
public office can only be achieved by wealthy individuals, but not all wealthy individuals wish to become
public figures. Indeed, most avoid the public status

which their wealth could confer, by giving them a ticket to public life, because of a horror of making
themselves conspicuous and attracting too much
attention. To advertise one's wealth is to invite
others to take it away and, given the choice between
honour and money, they prefer the money. However,
preference for private obscurity does not mean that
Mahajans are loathe to use the services of those in the
public eye. To give a historical example, before
independence Gandhi, himself a Gujarati Mahajan though
belonging to the Lohana jati and from an eminent
family of East African commission agents, frequently
was given hospitality in the Marwari *dharmshalla*
(religious hostel) in Delhi to which prominent members
of the merchant community in Mandi subscribed.

Perhaps enough has been said about the connections
which the merchant castes seek to establish and maintain with both the city, on the one hand, and the
village, on the other, for them to appear real and
substantial. We now need to think about the ways in
which connections and linkages are consolidated. This
is principally via the mechanisms of kinship and
marriage. For as Barth has pointed out, there is
often a close correspondence between the way in which
marriages are arranged and the convergence of interests
at the time of marriage, and whilst most marriages have
nothing to do with politics, people do tend not to
marry their enemies.[21] We may add by way of a rider
that affines may become enemies and merchant and
politician alike cannot afford to be bound by kinship
in the choice of allies and formulation of strategy.
Nonetheless, the kinship bond is more permanent than
most, and, even when it forms the extrinsic pretext
for interaction of a rather different order, it still
permits the speedy activation of dormant relations
should necessity occasion it.

The way in which marriages are made symbolizes the
supra-local and even supra-regional orientation of the
merchant castes. Every entrepreneurial family has
married its sons and daughters further and further
away as its fortunes have progressed; in Indore and
Gwalior (Madhya Pradesh), Jamnagar and Porbander
(Gujarat), and Delhi. It reveals their need for wider
and wider linkages. Non-entrepreneurial families
marry their children within Mandi itself, or in the
neighbouring villages or in Jaipur, filling in rather
than extending the boundaries of their regional

network. Let us take an example from one of the entrepreneurial families, the origins and destinations of marriage connections and their change through time being summarized in tabular form:

Successive Marriage Alliances in an Entrepreneurial Family

Daughters-in-law		Daughters	
Origins	Distance (miles)	Destinations	Distance (miles)
1. Lalset	4	1. Sanganer	35
2. Vatika	8	2. Jaipur	40
3. Dausa	40	3. Jamnagar	400
4. Sanganer	35		
5. Tonk	20		
6. Ahmedabad	200		

Note: Tonk is a large town, population 25,000, and therefore more prestigious than Dausa and Sanganer. These two towns are the same size, population 5,000, but Sanganer is more prosperous.

Successive Marriage Alliances in a non-Entrepreneurial Family

Daughters-in-law		Daughters	
Origins	Distance (miles)	Destinations	Distance (miles)
1. Jaipur	40	1. Jaipur	40
2. Todaraisingh	20	2. Jaipur	40
3. Malpura	15		
4. Mandi	-		

Both these examples could be repeated many times, but space precludes a thorough analysis of all the marriages made by merchant families, even in the last generation. The usefulness of affines in Jamnagar for one such family was cited earlier and needs little further amplification here as an example of the way in which marriage alliances can be mobilized. Alliances between cloth merchants and textile factory owners in Indore and Gwalior, thus ensuring a steady supply of a government-regulated commodity on the one hand and a steady outlet for goods on the other, follow the same principles. So do marriage alliances in the opposite direction with the village Mahajans. Here, a typical transaction would be, say, the exchange of rural debt collection favours for 'influence' with the Tax Inspectorate.

A whole and quite complex theory has been built up in Mandi to explain marriage choices. Those who have made supra-regional marriage connections feel that they are snubbing local Mahajans, by implying that their children are not up to scratch in some way. In the case of girls, this would probably mean that their dowry was considered rather insufficient. In return, those who have made local or intra-regional marriage ties believe that the former are forced to look outside the familiar network, because they cannot find a local family prepared to intermarry with them, because of their involvement in politics. Thus marriage choices and family alliances are political in both the formal and informal senses of the word, as people seek to make their own definitions of what is an acceptable justification for their choices prevail over the definitions of others.

Marriage is not all there is to kinship. Agnates do have some part to play, though in view of the strong normative ideal of the joint family and the powerful bond which this exerts in practice by keeping brothers together in their family business, contacts in the cities or villages who are not affines are necessarily rather few. Nonetheless, there are several examples. Thus Gujar Mal Tongya has a son, Narender, who runs a transport business in Jaipur; Madan Gopal Mehta has an elder brother in Jaipur, into whose diamond brokers' business he hopes his eldest son will enter when he comes of age, as well as a paternal cousin in Iran who, though a doctor, has proved very useful in effecting introductions to Irani companies.

Such extensions from the joint family are largely the perogative of very wealthy Mahajan families, contrary to public opinion in Mandi. It is the very wealthy families who have the surplus capital and subsequent risk-taking orientation which enables them to set up subsidiary 'agencies' in the cities. They are also in greater need of absolutely trustworthy agents to act on their own behalf, than other families, because of their superior volume of business. If the extensions need to be retracred, they can safely retreat back to Mandi where credit is good and contacts tried and tested. In the meantime, they perform a very useful function in establishing more contacts, gathering more information, and being on the spot to iron out difficulties, be they problems in repayment or a consignment of goods which had mysteriously disappeared.

Agnatic linkages, just like marriage alliances, are what one wants to make of them. Quarrels can and do occur and relationships become moribund as social interaction, or the *need* for social interaction, diminishes. Brothers and cousins may hate each other as much as 'in-laws', and with greater intensity some- times, due to greater emotional involvement. Equally, chances of reconciliation between agnates and affines are very much greater than between persons who have quarrelled and are not linked by kinship, should the occasion arise. The point is that, both as an extrin- sic pretext for and intrinsic part of interactions, kinship exerts not only a normative but an affective swing, invoking a whole complex of rights, duties and obligations, backed up by an appeal to the emotions. This is, no doubt, the reason why marriage dominates the conversation of the Mahajans of Mandi - when they are not talking about making money. To a very great extent, the one process is dependent upon the other relationship.

Conclusions

The first point is that the village community is not and was never as isolated as many writers would have us believe. Some sort of continuum between city, town and village has to be conceded, no matter how tenuous and tortuous the connections may be at times. The second point is that mere proximity to the city is not sufficient for there to be change (or to explain change). Spatial contiguity and the degree of modern- ization, or Westernization, are not necessarily coterminous. In endeavouring to understand the nature of economic and social change the focus must be on hinge groups, middlemen of all sorts, if any sense is to be made of the complexity, and on the middle ground of small towns and merchants in particular, for these are in the ideal position to articulate the rural with the urban.

Cottam, 'City, Town and Village: The Continuum
Reconsidered'

1. *Caste and Communication in an Indian Village*
(Bombay 1958), p.329.
2. Ibid.
3. George M. Foster, 'What is Folk Culture?',
American Anthropologist, vol. lv (1953), p.163; Eric
Wolf, *Peasants* (Englewood Cliffs 1966), p.11.
4. Robert Redfield and Milton B. Singer, 'City and
Countryside: the Cultural Independence', in T. Shanin
(ed.), *Peasants and Peasant Societies* (Harmondsworth
1971).
5. George M. Foster, 'Introduction: What is a
Peasant', in Jack M. Potter, May N. Diaz and George M.
Foster (eds.), *Peasant Society* (Boston 1967), p.23.
6. F.G. Bailey, 'The Peasant View of the Bad Life',
in Shanin, op.cit.
7. William Douglas, 'Peasant Emigrants: Reactors or
Actors?', in *Proceedings of the 1970 Annual Spring
Meeting*, American Ethnological Society, pp.21-36.
8. Julian Wolpert, 'Migration as an Adjustment to
Environmental Stress', *Journal of Social Issues*, vol.
xxii (1966), pp.92-102.
9. Morris Opler, 'The Extension of an Indian
Village', *Journal of Asian Studies*, vol.xvi (1956),
pp.5-10.
10. Ibid., p.8.
11. Bernard S. Cohn and McKim Marriott, 'Networks
and Centres in the Integration of Indian Civilisation',
Journal of Social Research, vol.i (1958), p.14.
12. Except Richard Fox, *From Zamindar to Ballot
Box: Community Change in a North Indian Market Town*
(Ithaca 1969); Leighton W. Hazlehurst, *Entrepreneurship
and the Merchant Castes in a Panjab City* (Durham, N.C.
1966), Helen Lamb, 'The Indian Merchant', in Milton B.
Singer (ed.), *Traditional India: Structure and Indian
Change* (Philadelphia 1959).   There have been more
forays by historians than by anthropologists: C.A.
Bayly, 'The Urban Merchant Family in North India during
the Nineteenth Century' (Kaplan Memorial Lecture,
University of Pennsylvania 1972); D.R. Gadgil, *Origins
of the Modern Indian Business Class: and Interim
Report* (New York 1959); Blair B. Kling, 'Entrepreneur-

ship and Regional Identity in Bengal', in David Kopf
(ed.), *Bengal: Regional Identity* (East Lansing,
Michigan 1969); Thomas A. Timberg, 'A North Indian Firm
as Seen Through its Business Records, 1860-1914',
Indian Economic and Social History Review, 8 (1971),
pp.264-283; Timberg, 'Three Types of the Marwari Firm',
Indian Economic and Social History Review, 10 (1973),
pp.1-36; Timberg, *The Marwaris: from Traders to
Industrialists* (New Delhi 1978).

13. The data which form the basis of this discussion were collected in Rajasthan during fourteen
months' fieldwork over 1974-5, financed by the Social
Science Research Council. My supervisor was
Professor A.C. Mayer, whose support and encouragement
have been inestimable.

14. Mandi is not its real name. My informants, for
many excellent reasons, therefore remain anonymous and,
I hope, unidentifiable.

15. Nitya Nand, 'Distribution and Spacial Arrangement of Rural Population in East Rajasthan', *Geographical Review* (1966), pp.205-219.

16. R.L. Singh, *Benares: a Study in Urban Geography*
(Benares 1955), p.19.

17. Badlu Ram Gupta, *The Aggarwals* (New Delhi 1976);
H.A. Hilman, *The Marwaris: a Study of a Group of Trading
Castes* (M.A. Thesis, University of California,
Berkeley 1954).

18. Alan R. Coren, *Tradition, Values and Inter-Role
Conflict in Indian Family Businesses* (Ph.D. Thesis,
Harvard Business School 1967).

19. Vinod K. Agarwal, *Initiative, Enterprise and
Economic Choices in India: a Study of the Patterns of
Entrepreneurship* (New Delhi 1975).

20. Hazlehurst, op.cit., pp.44-48.

21. Frederick Barth, *Political Leadership among
the Swat Pathans* (London 1959), p.93.